TRENT VALLEY LANDSCAPES

The Archaeology of 500,000 Years of Change

TRENT VALLEY LANDSCAPES

The Archaeology of 500,000 Years of Change

By David Knight and Andy J. Howard

With contributions by
Lee Elliott, Howard Jones, Ruth Leary and Peter Marshall

Trent Valley Geoarchaeology

ISBN 0-9544456-4-3

Front Cover:
Romano-British settlement at Moor Pool Close, Rampton, Nottinghamshire (photograph: D. Knight)

Back cover:
Top left: late prehistoric palaeochannel of the Trent near Collingham, Nottinghamshire (photograph: D. Knight)
Top right: Iron Age pit alignment at Fleak Close, Barrow-upon-Trent, Derbyshire (photograph: D. Knight)
Bottom left: late prehistoric burnt mound at Gonalston, Nottinghamshire, showing spread of heat-shattered
stones and trough filled with alluvium in the centre foreground (photograph: L.Elliott)

Typeset and published by:

eritage

Heritage Marketing and Publications Ltd
Hill Farm – Unit F
Castle Acre Road
Great Dunham
King's Lynn
Norfolk PE32 2LP
Tel: 01760 755645
Fax: 01760 755316
Email: publishing@heritagemp.com
Website: www.heritagemp.com

CONTENTS

LIST OF ILLUSTRATIONS

ACKNOWLEDGEMENTS

This volume, which represents the culmination of over two decades of archaeological research by the authors in the Trent Valley, was funded by the Aggregates Levy Sustainability Fund through Defra and English Heritage. The project formed part of a much wider research programme, Trent Valley 2002, which was co-ordinated by Trent Valley GeoArchaeology. This organisation was established in 2001 as a co-operative of stake-holders, including researchers, heritage managers and industrial representatives, and provides a mutually supportive framework for multidisciplinary geoarchaeological research within the region. All members of this group must be thanked for their contributions to furthering our understanding of the landscape history of the region. Mike Bishop and Ursilla Spence of Nottinghamshire County Council and Jon Humble, Jonathan Last and Jim Williams of English Heritage have been integral to developing and maintaining momentum within this group, and deserve our special thanks. Acknowledgement must also be extended to the wide range of commercial organisations and other bodies that have funded archaeological research in the Valley, and to the many individuals and organisations, too numerous to mention, whose investigations in the region have provided such a rich body of archaeological data.

Thanks are due to the many staff of Trent & Peak Archaeological Unit who have assisted in the preparation of this book, including Eileen Appleton (preparation of the index, proof-reading, editing of lists of references accompanying each chapter and administrative assistance), Steve Baker (preparation of Figs 1.2–5 and site distribution maps, scanning of most text figures and technical advice) Richard Sheppard (drawing of Fig.3.9 and scanning of selected figures) and Doug Gilbert (preparation of Fig.5.16). Jane Goddard drew Figs 5.10, 5.11, 5.12, 5.13, 5.17 and 6.17. Thanks are also extended to the many individuals and organisations, credited in the figure captions, who kindly gave their permission to reproduce original maps, diagrams, other illustrations and photographs.

We are indebted to the following individuals for access to unpublished data: Matt Beamish, Paul Buckland, Patrick Clay, Peter Connolly, Lynden Cooper, Neil Finn, Daryl Garton, Malcolm Greenwood, Graeme Guilbert, Roger Jacobi, Gavin Kinsley, Lloyd Laing, James Rackham, Rob Scaife, Chris Salisbury, David Smith, Blaise Vyner and Dave Yates. Stuart Brookes provided information on Trent Valley archaeological sites prior to completion of his bibliographic database of archaeology in the Trent Valley (prepared as part of the ALSF-funded Trent Valley 2002 project). Glyn Davies, Paul Pettitt and Chris Stringer provided access to imagery.

Gratitude must be expressed to Richard Bradley for refereeing the volume and to the following for refereeing individual chapters: David Bridgland and John McNabb (Pleistocene), Roger Jacobi (Pleistocene and Mesolithic), Andy Myers (Mesolithic), Mark Pearce (Neolithic and Early Bronze Age), Steve Willis (Late Bronze Age and Iron Age), Michael Jones and John Walker (Romano-British) and Mike Bishop (Medieval). Jen Heathcote, Jonathan Last and Jim Williams of English Heritage kindly read through the entire volume and provided valuable comments. Comments on the medieval chapter were kindly provided by Kirsten Jarrett, Gavin Kinsley, Kevin Leahy and Nick Stoodley. Peter Marshall of English Heritage provided advice on radiocarbon dating and calibrated the radiocarbon dates included in this volume. All mistakes and opinions expressed within this volume, however, remain our own.

Finally, the authors would like to thank their families, who have lived with this volume for the past year, and Michael de Bootman of Heritage Marketing and Publications Ltd for his assistance during the publication of this monograph.

GLOSSARY

Agger: cambered embankment carrying a Roman road.

Aggradation: the process of building up a surface with sediment by water or wind.

Alluvium: geologically, this term can apply to any sediment transported and deposited by rivers, but in the archaeological community, its use is usually restricted to fine-grained (silt and clay) sediment deposited on the floodplain.

Anastomosing: applied to a river whose planform comprises multiple, low sinuosity channels within a stable floodplain. These rivers usually transport finer grained sediments, have cohesive banks and are surrounded by wetlands.

Assart: creation of farmland by the colonisation or clearance of waste or woodland.

Avulsion: a sudden change in a river's course.

Braided: applied to a river whose planform comprises multiple, low sinuosity shallow channels within an unstable floodplain. These rivers usually transport coarse material such as sand and gravel.

Breck: two field system of infield-outfield; the infield was in permanent occupation as an open field, while the outfield acted as a common, intermittently used for cropping.

Chute: a minor channel eroded into the surface of a channel bar, which carries water during times of high river flow. Where formed on the inside of a point bar, curving parallel to the river bank, they may later form part of 'ridge and swale' topography.

Chute bar: a small accumulation of sediment usually developed at the downstream end of a chute on a channel bar.

Clast: an individual rock fragment or eroded organic material.

Colluvium: collective term for soil and other sediment transported downslope by a combination of processes including the forces of gravity and hillwash.

Disafforestation: the removal of land from forest law.

Discharge: the rate of river flow, usually measured in cubic metres per second, at a particular moment in time.

Entomology: the scientific study of insects.

Interfluve: the area of high ground between two river valleys.

Meandering: applied to a river whose planform comprises highly sinuous channels within a relatively stable floodplain. These rivers usually transport fine sediments and have cohesive banks.

Meander core: the central growth point of a meander.

Palynology: the study of pollen and spores.

Pedogenesis: the process of soil formation depending on the interplay between parent material, climate, organisms and time.

Point bar: a depositional feature composed of sand and gravel that accumulates on the inside of a meander bend.

Saproxylic: referring to insects which feed off dead wood

Scroll bar: a low curving ridge on a floodplain running essentially parallel with the loop of a meander. Multiple scroll bars form 'ridge and swale' topography.

Sinuosity: the degree to which a river channel meanders.

Thermophilous: requiring or thriving best in a high temperature.

RADIOCARBON CONVENTIONS

PETER MARSHALL

All dates quoted in the text are conventional radiocarbon ages (Stuiver and Polach 1977), and are quoted in accordance with the international standard known as the Trondheim convention (Stuiver and Kra 1986). The radiocarbon determinations have been calibrated with data from Stuiver *et al*. (1998), using OxCal (v3.5) (Bronk Ramsey 1995; 1998). The date ranges have been calculated according to the maximum intercept method (Stuiver and Reimer 1986), and are cited at two sigma (95% confidence). They are quoted in the form recommended by Mook (1986), with the end points rounded outwards to ten years if the error term is greater than or equal to 25 radiocarbon years, or to five years if it is less.

REFERENCES

Bronk Ramsey, C. 1995. Radiocarbon calibration and analysis of stratigraphy: the OxCal program, *Radiocarbon* **37**, 425-430.

Bronk Ramsey, C. 1998. Probability and dating, *Radiocarbon* **40**, 461–474.

Mook, W.G. 1986. Business meeting: recommendations/resolutions adopted by the Twelfth International Radiocarbon Conference, *Radiocarbon* **28**, 799.

Stuiver, M. and Kra, R.S. 1986. Editorial comment, *Radiocarbon* **28** (2B), ii.

Stuiver, M. and Polach, H.A. 1977. Reporting of ^{14}C data, *Radiocarbon* **19**, 355-363.

Stuiver, M. and Reimer, P.J. 1986. A computer program for radiocarbon age calculation, *Radiocarbon* **28**, 1022-1030.

Stuiver, M., Reimer, P.J., Bard, E., Beck, J.W., Burr, G.S., Hughen, K.A., Kromer, B., McCormac, G., van der Plicht, J. and Spurk, M. 1998. INTCAL98 Radiocarbon age calibration, 24,000-0 cal BP, *Radiocarbon* **40**, 1041-1083.

1   INTRODUCTION

DAVID KNIGHT AND ANDY J. HOWARD

The River Trent is one of the major arterial rivers of Britain, forming a natural physiographic divide between the uplands of the north and west and the lowlands of the south and east (Fig.1.2). Its location at the interface between the highland and lowland zones of Britain renders it unique among major English rivers, giving it the characteristics of both an upland and a lowland river system. This has significant implications for interpretation not only of its fluvial geomorphology but also of spatial patterning in the archaeological record. From the latter viewpoint, contrasts between lowland and upland communities either side of the Trent may be postulated from prehistoric times, but are perhaps best exemplified during the later Iron Age and Roman periods when the Trent may have emerged as a significant social boundary.

The Trent rises on Biddulph Moor near the south-western margin of the Staffordshire Moorlands, at an altitude of approximately 250m OD, and flows a distance of some 210km through the counties of Staffordshire, Derbyshire, Leicestershire, Nottinghamshire and Lincolnshire to its confluence with the Humber Estuary at Trent Falls. Geologically, the catchment comprises a mixture of rock types (Fig.1.4). In its headwaters, the Trent and its northern tributaries drain sandstones, limestones, shales and coal-rich lithologies of Carboniferous age, but for most of its length the Trent flows across Triassic mudstones. It is joined in its middle reaches by tributaries from the south and east, draining Jurassic limestones and mudstones, and farther downstream by rivers draining Permian and Triassic mudstones, limestones and sandstones to the west.

Fig.1.1 *The Trent Valley: main physiographic features (source: A.J. Howard)*

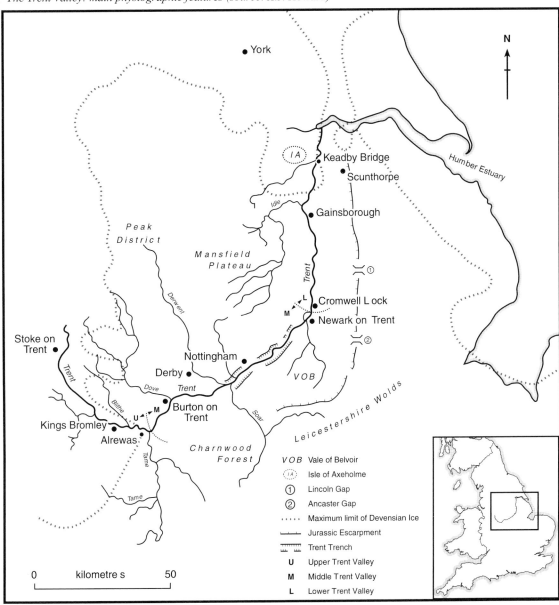

The valley through which the river now flows was formed before the beginning of the last glacial stage, the Devensian, over one hundred thousand years ago. The anomalous course of the river through the 'Trent Trench' between Nottingham and Newark-on-Trent, Nottinghamshire (Fig.1.1) and the sinuous spreads of gravels between Newark and Lincoln (Fig.1.5) demonstrate the impact of drainage diversion upon the landscape, most probably associated with glaciation during a pre-Devensian cold stage (Brandon and Sumbler 1988; 1991; Howard 1992; Posnansky 1960; Straw 1963). Natural processes have moulded the present Valley into three distinct zones, defined on the basis of variations in valley width, gradient and channel morphology. These comprise the Upper Trent Valley upstream of the Trent's confluence with the River Tame near Alrewas, Staffordshire, the Middle Trent Valley between Alrewas and Newark, and the Lower Trent Valley downstream of Newark. The contrasts in geology, valley width, river activity, soil fertility and even climate between each zone would undoubtedly have influenced the way in which human communities used the landscape through time, as will be demonstrated in later chapters of this volume.

Although only the fifth longest river in Britain (Ward 1981, 8), the Trent has the second highest drainage area (7490 square kilometres). The river is joined in its upper reaches by the Tame, which drains a large part of the Birmingham conurbation, and in its lower reaches by the Idle and its tributaries, which drain eastwards from the Mansfield Plateau. In the Middle Trent, between Burton-on-Trent in Staffordshire and Nottingham, the river is joined by three important tributaries. The Rivers Dove and Derwent between them drain the uplands of the Peak District south of Bleaklow Hill, whilst the River Soar drains a catchment including part of the Leicestershire Wolds and Charnwood Forest. The Trent has the second highest mean annual discharge in Britain (Ward 1981, 8), and the significant contribution of these tributaries to this discharge demonstrates clearly the influence of the uplands on the river system. The River Derwent, for example, provides on average 35% of the Trent's total discharge and up to 60% during the biggest flood events (Brown and Quine 1999, 11). Until the construction of substantial revetments and flood banks in the post-medieval period, this abundance of energy caused the Trent to migrate back and forth across its valley floor, particularly in its middle reaches, leading to both the destruction and preservation of major archaeological remains. These include mill dams, bridges, fish weirs and log boats, stratified within thick sequences of reworked sands and gravels, most notably around the Trent-Derwent-Soar confluence (Clay 1992; Cooper 2003; Salisbury 1992).

For most of its length, the contemporary river comprises a single thread and a relatively stable channel, inset below river terraces dating mainly from the late Pleistocene. In a few places, including Kings Bromley, Alrewas and Burton-on-Trent in Staffordshire and farther downstream at Newark in Nottinghamshire, the channel divides into two. Documentary evidence demonstrates that some of these bifurcating courses, such as the Kelham channel at

Newark, are artificial cuts (Salisbury 1984, 55), but the plan-form morphology of these cuts and of the wider valley floor suggests that river engineers may often have utilised pre-existing natural channels. Downstream of Alrewas, where the narrow valley floor of the Upper Trent widens, the sinuosity of the channel increases. Well-developed meanders are an important characteristic of the river system, particularly in the wide valley downstream of Newark, with isolated pools, oxbow lakes, sinuous hedge lines and parish boundaries all providing evidence for abandoned courses of the river (Baker 2003). In the Lower Trent Valley, the influence of marine processes has always been important. Today, the upstream influence of saline waters is restricted to Keadby Bridge, west of Scunthorpe, Lincolnshire (Van de Noort and Ellis 1998, 33), while the building of Cromwell Lock in Nottinghamshire, downstream of Newark, has restricted the tidal limit of the river (Fig.1.1).

Attention is focused in this study upon a 10km-wide corridor centred on the River Trent from its source on Biddulph Moor to Trent Falls (Fig.1.3), with particular emphasis upon the rich archaeological and environmental resource of the Pleistocene river-terraces and Holocene floodplain. It builds upon the foundations of *Archaeology and Alluvium in the Trent Valley*, which provided a geoarchaeological review of the Valley in Derbyshire and Nottinghamshire for the respective County Councils and English Heritage (Knight and Howard 1995), and presents a synthesis of changes in the natural and cultural landscape of the Valley from the Lower Palaeolithic to the end of the medieval period. Six period-based reviews are presented, dealing respectively with the Palaeolithic, Mesolithic, Neolithic to Early Bronze Age, Middle Bronze Age to Iron Age, Romano-British and medieval periods. Each chapter provides a synthesis of environmental and cultural knowledge and explores key issues and research themes, some of regional significance and others of national and international importance. The study forms part of a much wider research programme, Trent Valley 2002, which was funded by the Aggregates Levy Sustainability Fund through Defra and English Heritage and co-ordinated by Trent Valley GeoArchaeology (http://www.tvg. org). This organisation was established in 2001 as a co-operative of stake-holders, including researchers, heritage managers and industrial representatives, and provides a mutually supportive framework for multidisciplinary geoarchaeological research within the region of benefit to the entire community.

Since the implementation of Planning Policy Guidance note 16 (PPG16), issued by the Department of the Environment in November 1990, the number of developer-funded archaeological interventions undertaken in the Trent Valley has increased dramatically. Much of this work has been carried out on behalf of the aggregates industry, which has funded extensive archaeological investigations throughout the Valley. This has created a massive body of largely undigested data relating to the cultural and natural environment, much of which forms the focus of long-term post-excavation programmes or is buried in unpublished 'grey' reports archived by County-based Sites and Monuments Records and archaeological units spread widely across the country. All readily accessible unpublished literature from these sources has been reviewed as part of this study, in addition to work published in archaeological and landscape-orientated journals and monographs (Brookes 2003), but the limited timescale of this review has prevented a full analysis of information held by County Sites and Monuments Records. These latter sources provide a rich database for further research on the issues discussed in this study, which it is hoped will serve as a foundation for further geoarchaeological research within the region. Ongoing and future archaeological interventions, combined with analysis and publication of key unpublished sites within the region, will undoubtedly change and refine our interpretations of the natural development and human history of the Trent Valley, and should contribute to wider recognition of the nationally important alluvial archaeological landscape of this major European river.

Fig.1.2 *Relief and drainage of the Trent basin and adjoining regions. Reproduced by permission of the Ordnance Survey on behalf of The Controller of Her Majesty's Stationery Office. © Crown Copyright 100020618*

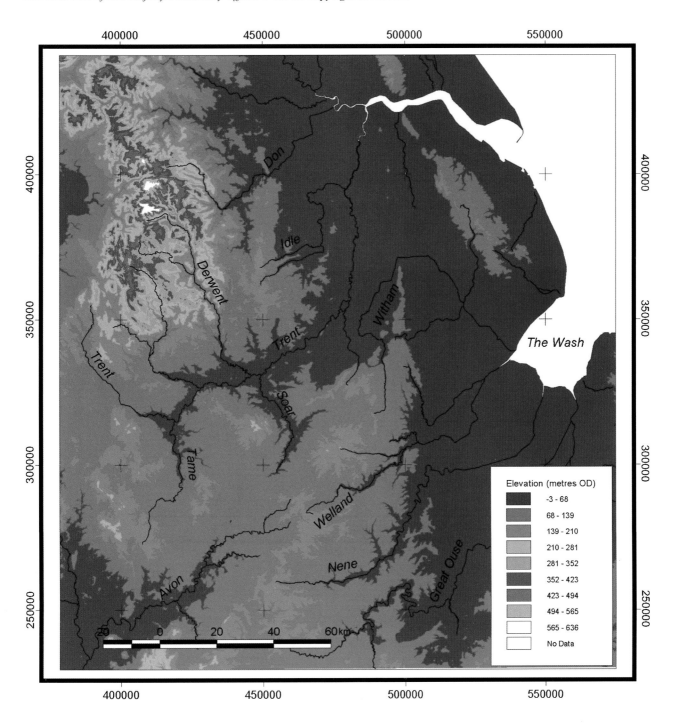

Fig.1.3 *Alluvial and terrace deposits within the project area. Geological data reproduced by permission of the British Geological Survey. © NERC. All rights reserved. IPR/54-50. Topographic data reproduced by permission of the Ordnance Survey on behalf of The Controller of Her Majesty's Stationery Office. © Crown Copyright 100020618*

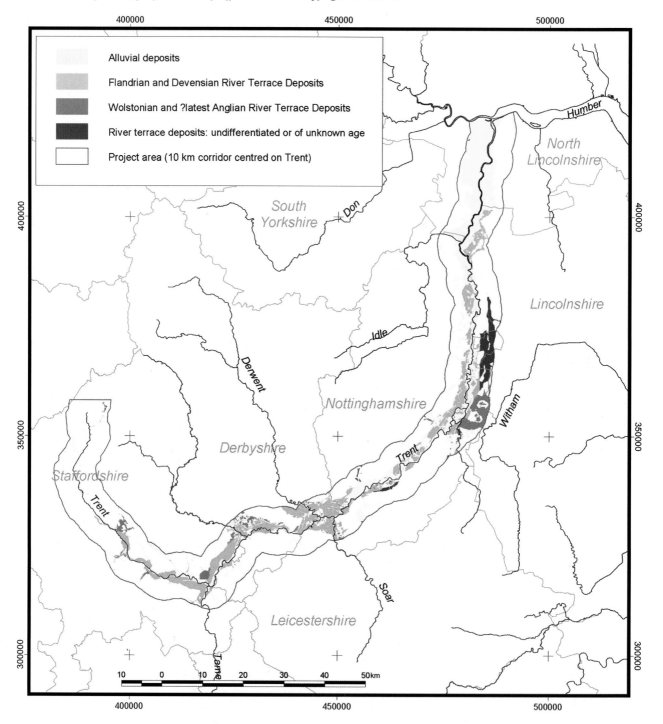

Fig.1.4   *Solid geology of the Trent Valley. Geological data reproduced by permission of the British Geological Survey. © NERC. All rights reserved.   IPR/54-50. Topographic data reproduced by permission of the Ordnance Survey on behalf of The Controller of Her Majesty's Stationery Office. © Crown Copyright 100020618*

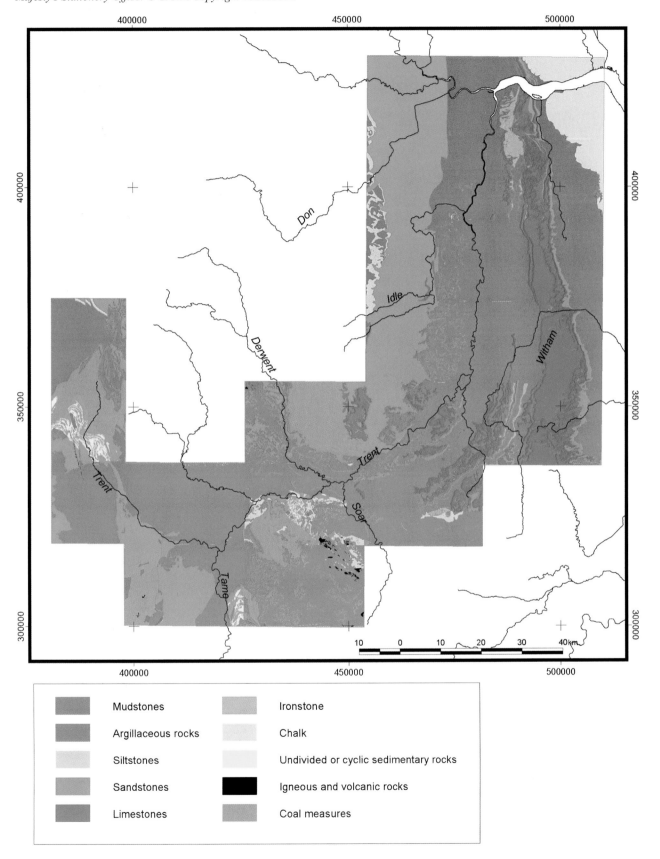

	Mudstones		Ironstone
	Argillaceous rocks		Chalk
	Siltstones		Undivided or cyclic sedimentary rocks
	Sandstones		Igneous and volcanic rocks
	Limestones		Coal measures

Fig.1.5 *Drift geology of the Trent Valley. Geological data reproduced by permission of the British Geological Survey. © NERC. All rights reserved. IPR/54-50. Topographic data reproduced by permission of the Ordnance Survey on behalf of The Controller of Her Majesty's Stationery Office. © Crown Copyright 100020618*

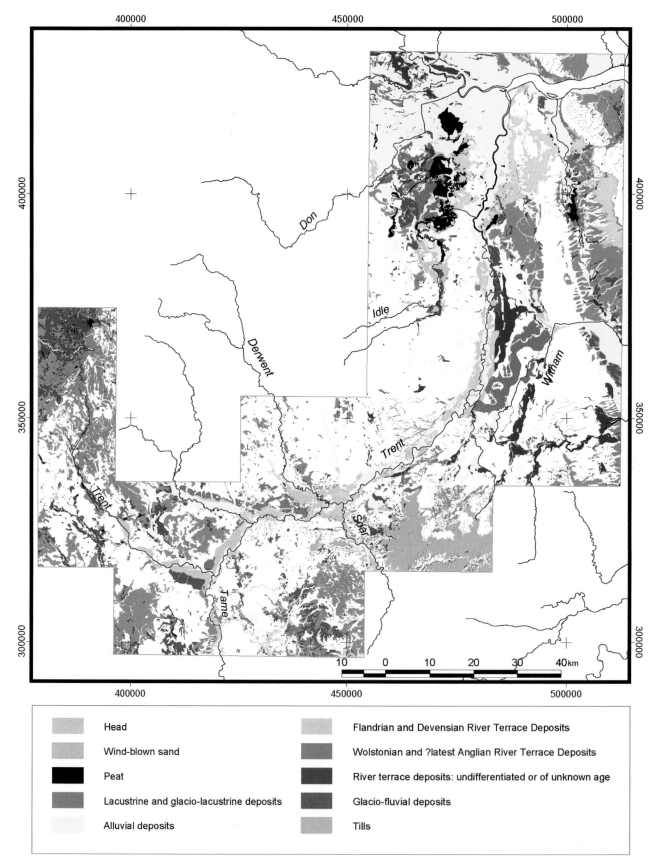

Head

Wind-blown sand

Peat

Lacustrine and glacio-lacustrine deposits

Alluvial deposits

Flandrian and Devensian River Terrace Deposits

Wolstonian and ?latest Anglian River Terrace Deposits

River terrace deposits: undifferentiated or of unknown age

Glacio-fluvial deposits

Tills

REFERENCES

Baker, S. 2003. The Trent Valley: Palaeochannel Mapping from Aerial Photographs, Trent Valley 2002: Advancing the Agenda in Archaeology and Alluvium (Component 2a). Trent & Peak Archaeological Unit, University Park, Nottingham. http://www.tvg.org.uk/palaeochannels.pdf

Brandon, A. and Sumbler, M.G. 1988. An Ipswichian fluvial deposit at Fulbeck, Lincolnshire and the chronology of the Trent terraces, *J. Quat. Sci.* **3** (2), 127-133.

Brandon, A. and Sumbler, M.G. 1991. The Balderton Sand and Gravel: pre-Ipswichian cold stage fluvial deposits near Lincoln, England, *J. Quat. Sci.* **6** (2), 117-138.

Brookes, S. 2003. Bibliographic Database of Archaeology in the Trent Valley, Trent Valley 2002: Advancing the Agenda in Archaeology and Alluvium (Component 5). Department of Archaeology, University of Nottingham. http://www.tvg.org.uk/references.pdf

Brown, A.G. and Quine, T. 1999. Fluvial processes and environmental change: an overview, in A.G. Brown and T.A. Quine (eds), *Fluvial Processes and Environmental Change*, 1-27.

Brown, A.G. and Quine, T.A. (eds) 1999. *Fluvial Processes and Environmental Change.* Chichester: Wiley.

Clay, P. 1992. A Norman mill dam at Hemington Fields, Castle Donington, Leicestershire, in S. Needham and M.G. Macklin (eds), *Alluvial Archaeology in Britain*, 163-168.

Cooper, L.P. 2003. Hemington Quarry, Castle Donington, Leicestershire, UK: a decade beneath the alluvium in the confluence zone, in A.J. Howard, M.G. Macklin and D.G. Passmore (eds), *Alluvial Archaeology in Europe,* 27-41.

Department of the Environment. 1990. *Planning Policy Guidance: Archaeology and Planning.* PPG 16. London: Department of the Environment.

Howard, A.J. 1992. The Quaternary Geology and Geomorphology of the Area Between Newark and Lincoln. Unpublished PhD thesis, University of Derby.

Howard, A.J., Macklin, M.G. and Passmore, D.G. (eds) 2003. *Alluvial Archaeology in Europe.* Netherlands: Swets & Zeitlinger.

Knight, D. and Howard, A.J. 1995. *Archaeology and Alluvium in the Trent Valley.* Trent & Peak Archaeological Unit, University Park, Nottingham.

Lewin, J. (ed) 1981. *British Rivers.* London: Allen & Unwin.

Needham, S. and Macklin, M.G. (eds) 1992. *Alluvial Archaeology in Britain.* Oxbow Monogr. **27**. Oxford: Oxbow.

Posnansky, M. 1960. The Pleistocene succession in the Middle Trent Basin, *Proc. Geol. Ass.* **71**, 285-311.

Salisbury, C.R. 1984. An early Tudor map of the River Trent in Nottinghamshire, *Trans. Thoroton Soc. Nottinghamshire* **87**, 54-59.

Salisbury, C.R. 1992. The archaeological evidence for palaeochannels in the Trent Valley, in S. Needham and M.G. Macklin (eds), *Alluvial Archaeology in Britain*, 155-162.

Straw, A. 1963. The Quaternary evolution of the Lower and Middle Trent, *E. Midland Geogr.* **3**, 171-189.

Van de Noort, R. and Ellis, S. (eds) 1998. *Wetland Heritage of the Ancholme and Lower Trent Valleys: an Archaeological Survey.* Humber Wetlands Project, University of Hull.

Ward, R.C. 1981. River systems and river regimes, in J. Lewin (ed), *British Rivers*, 1-33.

2   THE PLEISTOCENE BACKGROUND

ANDY J. HOWARD AND DAVID KNIGHT

2.1   Introduction

The first major review of the Palaeolithic in the Trent Valley was published by Posnansky (1963), who brought together the limited evidence for Lower and Middle Palaeolithic activity within the region. More recent syntheses of parts of the study area have been compiled by May (1966, 177–180), O'Brien (1978, 2–3), Richer (1991), Toms (1995) and Graf (2002), while the evidence for the earliest phases of human activity in the Trent Valley was reviewed by Wymer (1999, 114–20, map 32) as part of his survey of the Lower Palaeolithic occupation of Britain. The Pleistocene archaeology of the middle and lower reaches of the Trent Valley was reviewed by McNabb (2001) as part of the East Midlands Research Frameworks Project, drawing upon County assessments by Bishop (2001), Knox (2001), Membury (2001) and Myers (2001), while papers on the Palaeolithic of the Staffordshire Trent Valley have recently been prepared by Buteux and Lang (2003) and Myers (2003) as part of the West Midlands Research Frameworks Project.

The chronological framework employed in this chapter follows broadly that proposed for the East Midlands area by McNabb, thus facilitating integration of the results of this synthesis with the most recent overview of the Lower to Upper Palaeolithic of most of the Trent basin (McNabb 2001, 3–4, figs 4–5). McNabb's scheme, which identifies five archaeological periods within the traditional framework of Lower, Middle and Upper Palaeolithic, is summarised in Fig.2.1. This may be compared with the chronological scheme prepared as part of the Ancient Human Occupation of Britain project (AHOB), which provides a succinct summary of the key climatic, palaeogeographical and archaeological changes of this long and complex period (Fig.2.2). For that part of the Pleistocene falling within the limits of radiocarbon dating, time is expressed in uncalibrated years before present (BP). For earlier periods, where radiocarbon cannot be applied and where dating is more fluid, the simple convention of 'years ago' is employed (*cf.* Graf 2002, 1; McNabb 2001, 3).

For much of the Palaeolithic, low sea levels ensured that Britain remained a peninsula of Continental Europe, extending across the southern North Sea basin to Scandinavia. This extensive plain formed part of an area defined recently as 'Doggerland', drained by a network of rivers whose configuration was constantly changing (Coles 1998). Attention is focused below upon the origins and development of the Trent drainage system, with consideration of the impact of climatic fluctuation upon fluvial geomorphology, fauna and vegetation. A synthesis is also provided of the sparse and often ambiguous evidence for human activity, which in this region cannot yet be identified with certainty prior to the Levallois Lower Palaeolithic.

The oldest recorded terrace sands and gravels in the Trent Valley are probably of late Anglian age (OIS 12) in view of their degree of weathering and their stratigraphic position within the terrace staircase. The terrace sequence was first identified by Geological Survey fieldworkers in the late nineteenth century (Bemrose and Deeley 1898; Ussher 1888) and this work formed the basis for a number of subsequent studies (Pocock 1929; Swinnerton 1937; Clayton 1953; Posnansky 1960; Straw 1963; 1970). By the beginning of the 1970s, three broad units were recognised within the stratigraphic framework, though it should be noted that Pocock (1929) had recognised six terrace units. In descending order of height, these were named the Hilton, Beeston and Floodplain Terraces (Clayton 1953; Posnansky 1960; Straw 1963), although Clayton recognised an Upper and Lower division of the Hilton Terrace. This tripartite sequence was delimited in the Middle Trent around Derby and was correlated with sand and gravel deposits extending from Newark to Lincoln along former courses of the Trent draining via the Lincoln Gap.

In more recent years, renewed research has taken place on the terrace sediments, firstly in the Newark to Lincoln area (Brandon and Sumbler 1988; 1991; Howard 1992; Lister and Brandon 1991) and latterly in the Middle Trent Valley around Derby and Nottingham (Brandon 1996; 1997; Brandon and Cooper 1997). Together with further work on Quaternary stratigraphy through advances in dating and analyses of climatic signals from deep ocean sediments and ice cores (e.g. Lowe and Walker 1997), this has allowed the construction of a revised stratigraphic framework for the Trent terraces (Bowen ed. 1999). This new framework implies much greater complexity to the terrace history than previously suggested (Fig. 2.3). It also indicates that former correlations between terrace deposits along the Trent cannot be substantiated for two key reasons. Firstly, it was assumed by earlier workers that terrace surfaces and their underlying sediments were of the same age and hence downstream terrace correlation could be achieved by extrapolating terrace gradients (i.e. reconstructing terrace long profiles). Subsequent work on a number of terrace sequences (e.g. Bridgland 1994) indicates that this cannot be assumed, as has been demonstrated in south Derbyshire (Jones and Charsley 1985). Secondly, between the deposits of the Middle Trent and those of the Lower Trent (including the area between Newark and Lincoln) the river flows through a major, anomalous physiographic feature called the 'Trent Trench', which cuts across the dipslope of the Mercia Mudstone Group. This feature is poorly understood, although Posnansky (1960) suggested it was cut during the diversion of the Trent around a stagnant ice lobe occupying the Vale of Belvoir during a pre-Devensian glacial period. The creation of this feature altered fluvial gradients along the Trent and, because the Trench contains no fluvial deposits other than sands and gravels of late Devensian age, correlations of deposits through this zone have proved problematic. Elsewhere in Britain, recent research has demonstrated that uplift associated with isostatic rebound during deglaciation can also affect fluvial terrace gradients (Maddy 1997) and, although not investigated, the influence of isostatic processes on the Trent should not be underestimated.

Fig.2.1 *Archaeological periods of the British Palaeolithic. Reproduced by permission of Dr J. McNabb*

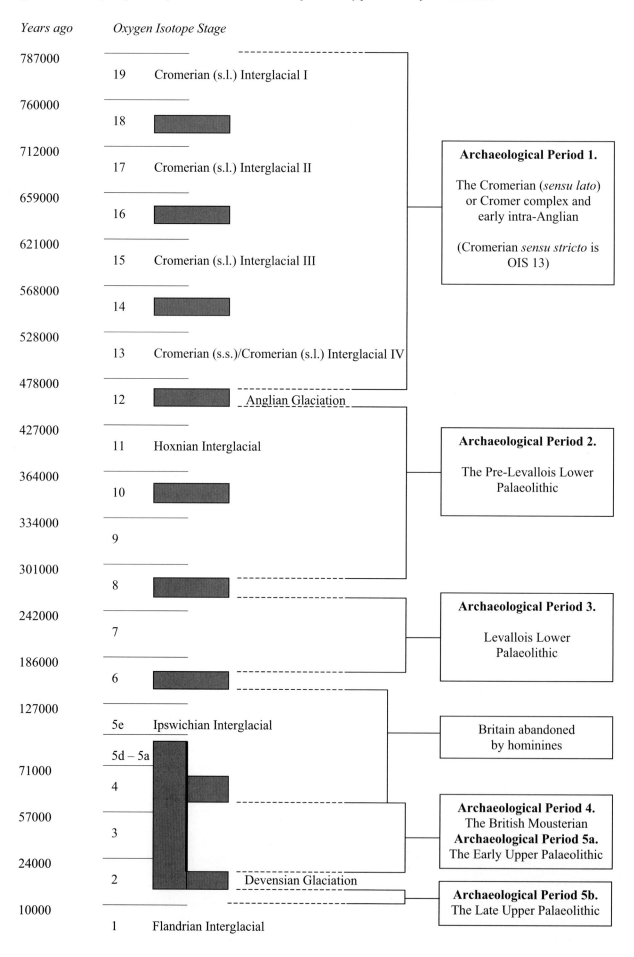

Fig. 2.2 *Pleistocene chronological framework, including additional information derived from the geological and archaeological record. Reproduced with permission from the Ancient Human Occupation of Britain project, funded by the Leverhulme Trust*

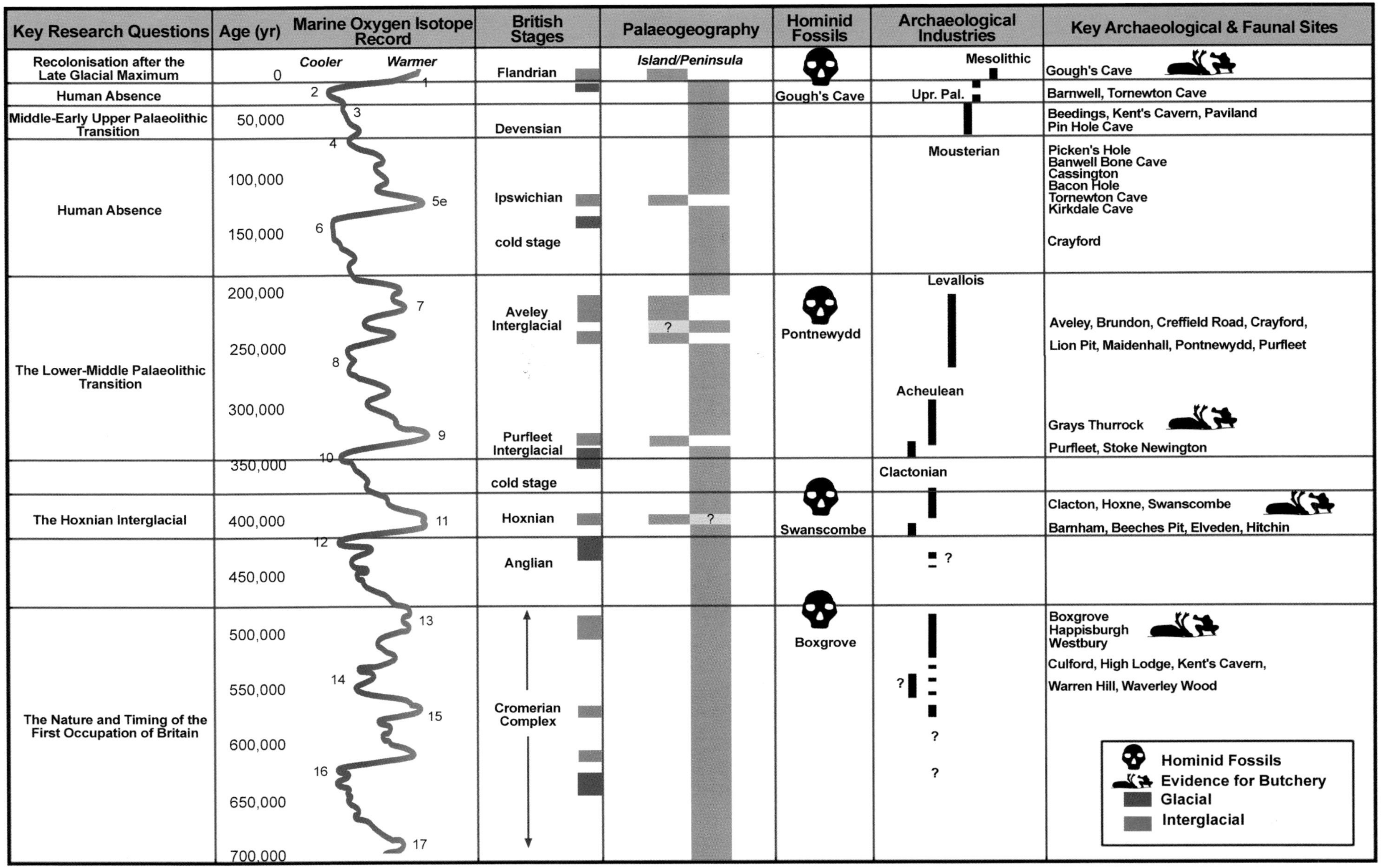

Fig.2.3 *Revised correlations of terrace deposits in the Trent Valley, modified from work by Brandon and Sumbler (1988, 1991), Howard (1992) and Brandon and Cooper (1997)*

Conventional Quaternary Stage	OIS	Trent (above Nottingham) and lower Dove and Derwent	Trent (Newark to Lincoln)	Approx. age Ky
Holocene	1	Floodplain deposits Hemington Terrace deposits * Ambaston Terrace deposits *	Floodplain deposits	10
Devensian	2	Holme Pierrepont Sand and Gravel *	Holme Pierrepont Sand and Gravel *	26
	3			65
	4	Allenton Sand and Gravel Beeston Sand and Gravel	Scarle Sand and Gravel *	80
	5d-a			115
Ipswichian	5e	Crown Hill Beds *	Fulbeck Sand and Gravel *	128
	6	Borrowash Sand and Gravel Egginton Common Sand and Gravel	Balderton Sand and Gravel *	195
	7		Thorpe on the Hill Beds *	240
	8	Ockbrook Sand and Gravel Etwall Sand and Gravel	Whisby Farm Sand and Gravel	297
Hoxnian	9-11			330
Anglian	12	Eagle Moor Sand and Gravel Findern Clay Oadby Till Thrussington Till	Eagle Moor Sand and Gravel Skellingthorpe Clay	400

* signifies that the deposit is assigned to an oxygen isotope stage on the basis of biostratigraphy, absolute age determination , detailed stratigraphy, sedimentology or palaeosols. Other deposits are ascribed on the basis of altimetry.

2.2 Archaeological Period 1: The Pre-Anglian and Intra-Anglian Lower Palaeolithic (OIS 19-12)

This period embraces the complex sequence of pre-Anglian interglacial and glacial phases of OIS 19-13, which together form 'The Cromerian' (*sensu lato*), and the Anglian glacial of OIS 12. These overlap the period of earliest hominin activity in Britain, from around 700,000 to 400,000 years ago, although unequivocal evidence for hunter-gatherer penetration along the precursors of the Trent and its tributaries has yet to be recovered. This may reflect a genuine absence of human occupation in this region, but it is worth recalling Wymer's suggestion that settlement in this era of fluctuating climate may have been significantly more extensive than can at present be demonstrated (Wymer 1999, 323).

2.2.1 Geomorphology

The pre-Anglian drainage of the Midlands, including that of the Trent basin, remains poorly understood by comparison with other major river systems in the UK, such as the Thames (Bridgland 1994). The existence of drainage gaps in the Jurassic escarpment at Lincoln and Ancaster led early workers to propose that the Tertiary and early Pleistocene drainage of eastern England was dominated by two major eastward-flowing rivers termed by Swinnerton (1937) the Lincoln and Ancaster Rivers. Subsequently, Linton (1951) suggested that an early proto-Trent flowed through the Ancaster Gap. More recently, the term Ancaster River has been reused by both Clayton (2000) and Rose *et al.* (2001) to describe a major pre-Anglian river draining the Carboniferous uplands via the Ancaster Gap and flowing along the edge of present day

north Norfolk into the North Sea basin, although the precise position of the coastline at this time is unknown. These fluvial sediments extend back in time to at least OIS 65 and work is ongoing to place them within a secure stratigraphic framework (Rose *et al.* 2001).

Whether this Ancaster River was a forerunner of the present Trent is unclear. Part of the problem revolves around the lack of early Pleistocene fluvial deposits in the Middle Trent Valley and Ancaster area. The drainage of the region is further complicated by the recognition of a major buried valley, infilled by pre-Anglian and Anglian fluvial sands and gravels (Maddy's [1999a] Baginton Formation and Shotton's [1953] Baginton-Lillington Gravel and Baginton Sand) and by glacial sediments, extending from Snitterfield near Stratford upon Avon, Warwickshire, to Thurmaston, near Leicester. Drainage of this river from south-west to north-east is confirmed by palaeocurrent measurements from the deposits (Maddy *et al.* 1994). Some workers, notably Rose (1987; 1994), have argued on lithological grounds for an extension of this fluvial system north-eastwards beneath the present-day Wreake Valley and across East Anglia, where it is correlated with deposits of a pre-Anglian River Thames (the Kesgrave Sands and Gravels). This major midland drainage route has been termed the Bytham River, while the associated sediments are referred to as the Bytham Sands and Gravels (Rose 1994). However, the precise course of this river north of Leicester is not undisputed. Rice (1991) urged caution in interpretation, suggesting that the direction of former drainage along the Wreake Valley was not necessarily towards the east, while Shotton (1953) preferred drainage northwards from Leicester along the present Soar Valley towards the Trent Valley (although no continuation of the Baginton Formation

Fig.2.4 *The Trent as it may have appeared during the cold stages of the Pleistocene: a large braided river outwash plain (Photograph: I. Sutton)*

has ever been found in the lower Soar Valley). It should also be noted that several large, pre-Anglian buried palaeovalleys, the most notable being the 'Elvaston Channel', have been recorded beneath the Middle Trent in the area of Derby (Derbyshire and Jones 1980; Brandon and Cooper 1997). These are possibly sub-glacial in origin and, although their precise age is unclear, add further complexity to the regional drainage pattern.

Whatever the precise configuration of the regional drainage network, these major valley systems would potentially have provided important ecological corridors for the movement of humans and animals in Archaeological Period 1 (McNabb 2001). Furthermore, the palaeogeographic reconstructions of both Maddy (1999a) and Rose (1994) imply that the Bytham River extended from the Leicester region northwards into the Carboniferous uplands of the Peak District. Rose *et al.* (2001) also suggest that there is lithological evidence for a northern tributary entering the Bytham River system just west of Melton Mowbray, Leicestershire, suggesting further possibilities of migration routes through to the Trent basin and farther north.

2.2.2 Vegetation and Fauna

Palaeobotanical and faunal data have been obtained from several deposits attributable to the pre-Anglian period, including organic sediments within the basal gravels of the Baginton Formation (the Waverley Wood Beds) and the Brooksby sand and gravel, from beneath the Bytham River deposits. Amino acid geochronologies derived from

molluscan remains collected from the Waverley Wood Beds suggest correlation of the unit with OIS 15 (Bowen *et al.* 1989), thus confirming its pre-Anglian status, while Maddy *et al.* (1994) suggest that the Baginton Formation spans the period between OIS 15 and OIS 12. The Bytham Sands and Gravels and Baginton Formation are interpreted as cold-climate braided river deposits (Fig.2.4) accumulated within a tundra vegetational environment, although pollen, plant macrofossils, Mollusca and Coleoptera from the Waverley Wood Beds suggest that this included at least one period of temperate climatic conditions (Shotton *et al.* 1993; Maddy *et al.* 1994).

In the Wreake Valley near Rearsby, Leicestershire, organic deposits with possible temperate affinities have been recorded beneath the Bytham River deposits, in a unit termed the Brooksby sand and gravel (Rice 1991). Although no detailed work has been undertaken on this organic unit within the Brooksby deposit, it has been identified and evaluated in subsequent geoarchaeological work in the Brooksby area of Leicestershire (Challis and Howard 1999). The only floral material that could be identified was a single achene of the buttercup family (*Ranunculus*, subgenus *Batrachium*). This is a damp ground or waterside species and suggests the presence of marsh or shallow water in the area. There were also abundant sclerotia of soil fungus and several pre-Pleistocene megaspores. There are few concrete conclusions to be drawn from this small assemblage, but the soil fungus and pre-Pleistocene material suggest active erosion of soil profiles and/or pre-Pleistocene deposits. Molluscan material was similarly sparse. Only two identifiable shells were retrieved from the sample, one of *Pupilla muscorum bigranata*, the other of *Gyraulus laevis*. The former is a species of dry grassland and is common throughout much of the Pleistocene. It *may* indicate cool or cold stage deposition. The sub-species "*bigranata*" is only known in modern assemblages of *Pupilla muscorum* as a small (<2%) proportion of the total of the species. It is more numerous in the Middle Pleistocene, occurring abundantly at Waverley Wood, Warwickshire (Shotton *et al.* 1993) and at Snitterfield, near Stratford-upon-Avon, Warwickshire (Lister *et al.* 1990), in a similar stratigraphic context to Brooksby, within or below the Baginton Formation. The other shell, a specimen of *Gyraulus laevis*, is an aquatic gastropod which lives in slow-flowing or still water. It likes some weed growth, but is also able to colonise new pools in deglaciated terrain.

2.2.3 Human Activity

Unequivocal evidence for a human presence in the Trent drainage basin during the pre-Anglian (OIS 19-13) or Anglian (OIS 12) periods has not yet been obtained, although discoveries to the south and east of activity foci dating not only from pre-Anglian warm phases but also from the Early and Late Anglian suggest that this may reflect a dearth of evidence rather than a genuine absence of activity. This is especially likely during the Pre-Anglian phase, when these neighbouring areas may have been linked via the Bytham River system (Graf 2002, 12; Wymer 1999, 129–32, fig.46).

Pre-Anglian (Cromerian Complex) Human Activity

This phase embraced at least four interglacials with climatic conditions suitable for human activity. The potential of these warm phases for attracting human settlement is emphasised by discoveries of Lower Palaeolithic artefacts at more southerly sites within a wide range of ecological zones – notably at the coastal sites of Boxgrove, Sussex (Pitts and Roberts 1997) and Kent's Cavern, Devon (Cook and Jacobi 1998), in each case in association with deposits attributable to pre-Anglian phases of climatic amelioration. The most significant discoveries from a Trent Valley perspective include finds of Lower Palaeolithic handaxes and other lithic artefacts from sites such as High Lodge in Suffolk (Ashton *et al.* 1992) and Waverley Wood in Warwickshire (Shotton *et al.* 1993; Graf 2002, 18), in each case associated with sediments attributed to the Bytham River. These discoveries suggest that archaeological remains of this period may well survive if deposits of this age can be found within the Trent Valley (Graf 2002, 14–16). The archaeological deposits at Waverley Wood were closely associated with organic remains yielding important proxy records of climate and landscape for Archaeological Period 1 (Shotton *et al.* 1993). For this reason, every opportunity should be taken to investigate Period 1 deposits prior to development – as exemplified by recent work in advance of potential sand and gravel extraction at Brooksby (Challis and Howard 1999).

Human Activity during the Anglian Glaciation

The Anglian glaciation was the most extensive in Britain for which terrestrial evidence has survived. Its ice-sheets extended as far south as north and north-east London, and caused the southerly diversion of the River Thames into its present channel (Bridgland 1994). This glaciation obliterated the Midlands drainage network, burying the Bytham Valley beneath glacial sediments, and would have erased totally any surface archaeological remains (Graf 2002, fig.7d).

There were undoubtedly times during the Anglian glaciation, particularly either side of the glacial maximum, when climate would have been more favourable to occupation. Traces of occupation have been recorded at several sites to the south and east of the study area, notably within Bytham River deposits at Warren Hill, Suffolk, where a range of artefacts, mainly handaxes, has been recovered from presumed early Anglian (pre-glacial) sediments (Lewis 1998). Whilst some of these artefacts were abraded and may be derived from Cromerian land surfaces, others were fresher and could signify activity broadly contemporary with the deposition of the fluvial deposits. Similarly, scattered sites in the Thames Valley might indicate periodic visitations by hunter-gatherer groups during the Anglian. This may be indicated by the retrieval of large numbers of handaxes, scrapers, waste cores and flakes from the gravels of the Anglian-age Caversham Loop near Henley, Oxfordshire (Wymer 1999, 50), although all of these artefacts could have been redeposited from earlier phases of activity. In the East Midlands, it has been suggested that occasional finds of Lower Palaeolithic handaxes and other lithic artefacts in Anglian outwash deposits could signify redeposition from unknown sites of intra-Anglian or earlier activity – notably around Hinckley, Leicestershire, and Nuneaton, Warwickshire, where quartzite and flint Palaeolithic surface finds have been recovered, possibly derived from early Anglian Wigston Sand and Gravel deposits (Graf 2002, 20–1; R. Jacobi: pers. comm.). The possibility must also be entertained, however, of redeposition from post-Anglian sites by later erosion of overlying sediments (McNabb 2001, 9). None of the possible OIS 12 (Anglian) deposits in the Trent Valley, which comprise sediments deposited directly by glaciers and by outwash processes (the Eagle Moor Sand and Gravel, Findern Clay, and Oadby and Thrussington Tills; Fig.2.3), has yielded artefacts. The case for intra-Anglian or pre-Anglian human activity within the region must for the present, therefore, be regarded as unproven.

2.3 Archaeological Period 2: The Pre-Levallois Lower Palaeolithic (OIS 12-8)

Archaeological Period 2 spans the time from the late Anglian (OIS 12) to the OIS 8 cold stage, from around 450,000 to 250,000 years ago, thus embracing the OIS 11 and OIS 9 interglacials recorded within a number of fluvial terrace sequences (Bridgland 1994; Bridgland *et al.* 2001; Keen *et al.* 1997; Schreve 2001; Schreve *et al.* 2002). It also includes the intervening OIS 10 cold stage, which Sumbler (1995) suggested included a period of glaciation (cf. Maddy *et al.* 1995). Climatic conditions would have been unfavourable for settlement during much of this period, but some of the most famous sites of the British Lower Palaeolithic may be dated to temperate interludes, most notably at Swanscombe, Kent (OIS 11). From investigations in the Thames Valley and East Anglia, we may postulate the movement of hunter-gatherers along river corridors to a variety of ecological zones during these temperate phases, but on present evidence there are no indications of activity north of the Nene Valley (McNabb 2001, 11–12).

2.3.1 Geomorphology, Vegetation and Fauna

With the exception of till and sand and gravel deposits associated directly with the Anglian glaciation (the Eagle Moor Sand and Gravel, Findern Clay and Oadby and Thrussington Tills; Fig. 2.3), no deposits spanning the time from OIS 12 to OIS 9 are known from the Trent Valley. The Anglian glacial and outwash deposits form isolated and heavily dissected patches at varying altitudes on the north-bank hilltops and interfluves of the Middle Trent Valley and on the Graffoe Hills between Newark and Lincoln (Brandon and Cooper 1997; Brandon and Sumbler 1988; Howard 1992); these suggest drainage of outwash towards the Lincoln Gap. In the Middle Trent, these deposits form part of the 'High Level Valley Gravel' of Fox-Strangways (1905), corresponding to the 'Fluvio-Glacial Gravels' of later Geological Survey workers (Stevenson and Mitchell 1955). Despite significant research, no organic-rich sediments or mammalian remains have been recovered from these deposits along the Trent. This contrasts with other major river systems such as the Thames, where temperate fluvial sediments relating to OIS 11 have been recognised at Swanscombe and Clacton-on-Sea, Essex (Bridgland 1994; Bridgland *et al.* 1999; Schreve 2001), and where OIS 9 deposits have been identified elsewhere in Essex at Barling (Bridgland 2000; Bridgland *et al.* 2001) and Purfleet (Schreve *et al.* 2002). At Barling, the reconstruction of palaeotemperatures from Coleoptera remains suggests a thermal maximum of 17–26°C and a minimum of –11 to –13°C.

In the Trent Valley, such temperate deposits may have eluded discovery, although this seems unlikely as many of the older deposits were worked by less mechanised approaches and hence are likely to have been recorded if exposed. Alternatively, some deposits may have been reworked by subsequent geomorphic processes, including glacial erosion (see below). The identification of OIS 11 and OIS 9 temperate deposits in the Trent Valley is of paramount importance, for such deposits are often closely associated with evidence of human activity in river valleys (Bridgland, 1994; Schreve *et al.* 2002).

Cold climate outwash sands and gravels deposited in the Middle Trent, most probably during OIS 8, are known as the Etwall Sand and Gravel, formerly the Upper Hilton Terrace of Clayton (1953). In the Lower Trent Valley beyond Newark, the Whisby Farm Sand and Gravel was deposited during this time, possibly as a solifluction unit derived from the Eagle Moor Sand and Gravel (Brandon and Sumbler 1991). However, no faunal or floral remains are known from either of these deposits.

2.3.2 Human Activity

The West and East Midlands have yielded virtually no evidence for activity in this period, in sharp contrast to the Thames Valley and East Anglia where a rich sequence of Clactonian and Acheulian industries developing from the Hoxnian Interglacial demonstrates exploitation of a wide range of open and forested environments (including river valleys, lake margins and higher ground). No archaeological remains of this period have been recovered from sites within the Trent drainage system, despite long phases of congenial climatic conditions during the OIS 11 and OIS 9 interglacials. This curious absence of evidence may reflect its obliteration by ice during subsequent glacial episodes, as suggested for the pre-Anglian period, but we should not rule out the possibility of abandonment. One possibility, ventured by McNabb (2001, 12), is that for some of the period the deep fjord-like feature into which the Nene had flowed near Peterborough might, along with the river, have posed too great an obstacle to cross, hence restricting the movements of hunter-gatherers to areas farther south.

2.4 Archaeological Period 3: The Levallois Lower Palaeolithic (OIS 8-6)

This period, which sees the appearance from near the end of the OIS 8 cold stage of Levallois (prepared core) technology, may be interpreted either as the beginning of the British Middle Palaeolithic sequence (following Wymer 1999) or a late technological phase of the Lower Palaeolithic during which established Acheulian traditions were enriched by the addition of Levallois technology (McNabb 2001, 12). The latter interpretation is preferred here, as stated in the introduction to this chapter. In chronological terms, the Levallois Lower Palaeolithic spans broadly the period from around 250,000 to 150,000 years ago, embracing the OIS 8 and early OIS 6 cold stages and the intervening OIS 7 interglacial; this has now been recognised at a number of localities including Marsworth, Buckinghamshire, in the Chilterns (Murton *et al.* 2001), and Stanton Harcourt, Oxfordshire (Buckingham *et al.* 1996) and Aveley, Essex (Bowen *et al.* 1989; Bridgland 1994; Schreve 2001) in the Thames terrace sequence. Closer to the Trent Valley, a probable Stage 7 mammalian fauna has been recorded from an organic channel at Bielsbeck in the Foulness Valley, East Yorkshire (Schreve 1999). East of the Lincoln Gap, possible Stage 7 organic channels have been identified at the Lincolnshire sites of Coronation Farm in the Witham Valley and Tattershall Thorpe in the Bain Valley (Brandon and Sumbler 1991), although Holyoak and Preece (1985) have assigned this latter site to the Ipswichian (OIS 5e).

There may have been a genuine hiatus in occupation following the OIS 7 interglacial, correlating broadly with the period from late OIS 6 to OIS 4 (see below). The western part of Doggerland that shrank with rising sea levels to form eventually the British Isles may not have been recolonised until early OIS 3. We see then the appearance of Mousterian industries and Neanderthal communities very different from the early Neanderthal or late *Homo heidelbergensis* groups that may have been responsible for the lithic industries of OIS 8-6.

2.4.1 Geomorphology

Between Newark and Lincoln, a continuous, sinuous tract of sand and gravel, previously referred to as a downstream extension of the Beeston Terrace deposits (Straw 1963), provides evidence for a course of the Trent through the Lincoln Gap during the Levallois Lower Palaeolithic. This sinuous

Fig.2.5 *Mammoth tusk recovered from the Balderton Sand and Gravel at Whisby Quarry, Lincolnshire (photograph: A.J. Howard)*

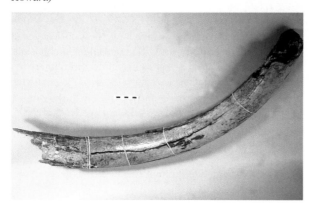

deposit has now been split on stratigraphic grounds into the Whisby Farm Sand and Gravel (OIS 8) and the Balderton Sand and Gravel (OIS 6), separated by a rock-step (Brandon and Sumbler 1991). In the Middle Trent Valley, deposits of sands and gravels previously referred to collectively as the Hilton Terrace (Clayton 1953) form isolated and dissected patches at varying altitudes on the north-bank hilltops and interfluves. Recent work by Brandon and Cooper (1997) has revised this classification, dividing the deposit into the Etwall Sand and Gravel (equivalent to Clayton's Upper Hilton Terrace) and the Egginton Common Sand and Gravel (equivalent to Clayton's Lower Hilton Terrace); these correlate respectively with the Whisby Farm Sand and Gravel and the Balderton Sand and Gravel of the lower Trent Valley (Fig.2.3).

Electron Spin Resonance age determinations on fossil elephant teeth and amino acid analyses on molluscs from the Balderton Sand and Gravel have been used to argue that the deposit was aggraded during OIS 6, although the whole complex could span the period from OIS 8 to OIS 6 (Brandon and Sumbler 1991). The evidence from absolute dating has been reinforced by geomorphological arguments, including the position of the Balderton Sand and Gravel in the terrace staircase above the 'Ipswichian' Fulbeck Sand and Gravel (OIS 5e) and the development of an Ipswichian palaeosol across its surface (Fig.2.6; Brandon and Sumbler 1988; 1991). However, neither the absolute dating nor the geomorphological evidence is without controversy (Howard *et al.* 1999a; Miller and Hollin 1991).

Assuming that the Balderton Sand and Gravel was partially deposited during OIS 6, interesting palaeogeographic questions are raised regarding the mechanism of drainage diversion. This could signify the presence of post-Anglian, pre-Devensian ice within the Lower Trent Valley during OIS 6. Terrace sediments mapped in both the Severn Valley (Maddy *et al.* 1995) and Nar Valley of East Anglia (Gibbard *et al.* 1992; Lewis 1999) have been argued to provide evidence for glaciation across midland Britain during OIS 6, and such erosive processes operating in the Trent Valley during this stage would explain the absence regionally of post-Anglian (OIS 11 and 9) temperate sediments.

2.4.2 Vegetation and Fauna

Organic sediments preserved within a channel incised into bedrock below the Balderton Sand and Gravel (Thorpe on

the Hill Bed) have yielded large mammal remains (Fig.2.5), molluscs (including *Corbicula Fluminalis*), pollen, plant macrofossils and beetles, all indicative of temperate conditions attributable probably to OIS 7 (Brandon *et al.* unpublished, see Maddy 1999b, 42). The Balderton Sand and Gravel itself, however, appears to have accumulated during cold-climate conditions. Recent work on this deposit by Brandon and Sumbler (1991) and Howard (1992) has demonstrated that these deposits were laid down by a braided river system with intraformational ice wedge casts indicating regional permafrost – and hence tundra vegetational conditions (Fig.2.5). Further evidence for cold-climate conditions is provided by discoveries of pollen, molluscan, ostracod and Coleopteran assemblages within small organic channels at a number of localities within the Balderton Sand and Gravel; the insect remains suggest mean July temperatures of around 10°C and mean January temperatures at or below –20°C (Brandon and Sumbler 1991). The Balderton Sand and Gravel has also yielded an abundant large vertebrate fauna (Fig.2.5 and Fig.2.7) dominated by mammoth and woolly rhinoceros; although mixed, it is argued to represent a generally cold assemblage, probably including interstadial elements (Lister and Brandon 1991).

Fig.2.6 *Braided river deposits of the Balderton Sand and Gravel with cryoturbated organic silts indicating severe freeze thaw processes. The reddened upper horizon reflects the effects of pedogenic processes during the Ipswichian interglacial (photograph: A.J. Howard)*

2.4.3 Human Activity

Classic Levallois Lower Palaeolithic sites, such as Baker's Hole, Kent, in the Thames Valley (Wenban-Smith 1995) and Caddington, Bedfordshire, in the Chilterns (White 1997), are easily diagnosed by merit of the combination of Acheulian and Levallois technology. There are, however, many problems in distinguishing Period 3 from Period 2 or Period 4 sites – especially in the East or West Midlands, which lack the rich artefact record of areas such as the Thames Valley or East Anglia. In particular, not all Period 3 sites preserve evidence of Levallois technique in association with Acheulian handaxes, flakes and flake tools, while the sporadic use of this prepared core technology in the succeeding Mousterian (Period 4) can lead to confusion between Periods 3 and 4. Hence, without typologically diagnostic artefacts and the stratigraphic control provided by secure associations with river terrace sequences that can be correlated with OIS stages, dating remains extremely problematic.

Fig.2.7. *The mammalian fauna recovered from the Balderton Sand and Gravel, modified from Lister and Brandon (1991)*

Taxon	Total number of identifiable specimens	% of the total number of identifiable specimens
Mammuthus primigenius (Blum.), mammoth	163	61.0
Coelodonta antiquitatis (Blum.), woolly rhinoceros	50	19.0
Equus caballus L., horse	15	6.0
Cervus elephus L., red deer	10	4.0
Paleoloxodon antiquus (Falc. & Caut.), st-t elephant	9	3.0
Bison/Bos, bison or aurochs	8	3.0
Rangifer tarandus (L.), reindeer	5	2.0
Ovibos moschatus Zimmerman, musk ox	4	1.5
Canis lupus L., wolf	1	0.4
Panthera leo (L.) lion	1	0.4
Ursus arctos L., brown bear	1	0.4
Dicerorhinus cf. *hemitoechus* (Falc.), narrow-nosed rhino	1	0.4
Total	**268**	**100.0**

In the Trent Valley, significant discoveries of Palaeolithic artefacts, in rare instances indicating Levallois technique, have been made within late OIS 8 and OIS 6 terrace deposits, most particularly the Etwall Sand and Gravel of OIS 8 and the Egginton Common and Balderton Sands and Gravels of OIS 6 (Posnansky 1963; Wymer 1999, 114–20, map 32). The greatest concentration of finds has been retrieved during quarrying of the gravel terraces on the northern side of the Trent and Dove rivers in Derbyshire. These have been obtained mainly from the Etwall Sands and Gravels (Clayton's Upper Hilton Terrace), but small quantities have also been recovered from the Egginton Common deposits (Clayton's Lower Hilton Terrace; Wymer 1999, map 32; Myers 2001, 4–6, Table 1). The most important lithic collections were recovered by Armstrong (1942) from quarries in the Etwall Sand and Gravel at Hilton and Willington in Derbyshire (Fig.2.8; see also Posnansky 1963, 364–5, 376–8, figs 2–10). These incorporated artefacts which were mainly of the Acheulian tradition, with an emphasis upon pointed and ovate handaxes (reflecting probably recovery biases: *ibid.*, 365), together with a range of retouched and unretouched flakes, occasional cores and one comparatively unrolled flake preserving evidence of Levallois technique (Armstrong 1942, 37; R. Jacobi: pers. comm.). Rare Palaeolithic finds have also been recovered during excavations of later sites on the gravel terraces – notably at Swarkestone Lowes, Derbyshire, where archaeological excavations recovered three rolled struck flakes from the surface of the Etwall Sand and Gravel (Jacobi and Garton 1999, 115). This site also yielded two quartzite cobble-tools, perhaps of Middle Palaeolithic origin but possibly much later in date (*ibid.* fig.12).

Considerably fewer Palaeolithic artefacts have been recovered from OIS 8-6 terrace contexts in the Lower Trent Valley. Smaller numbers of flint handaxes of Acheulian tradition have been recovered during the past hundred years from deposits which probably form part of the Balderton Sand and Gravel, although their precise provenance is far from clear (Wymer 1999, 115). Examples include three heavily rolled Acheulian split pebble handaxes, two made of quartzite and one from dacite or andesite (from the Borrowdale Volcanic Group),

which were recovered from the Balderton Sand and Gravel at the Lincolnshire sites of North Hykeham and Norton Bottoms, near Norton Disney (Brandon and Sumbler 1991, 126). Most of the artefacts linked with these sands and gravels, however, are heavily worn, leading Brandon and Sumbler (1991) to suggest that many may be reworked from the Eagle Moor Sand and Gravel or upstream correlatives (*cf.* Wymer 1999, 115). An exception to this may be a handaxe described by Armstrong (1939, 98) as 'highly lustrous of reddish brown patina and practically unrolled', which was collected by Swinnerton (1937) from Whisby, Lincolnshire. Brandon and Sumbler (1991) have suggested that this artefact might be contemporary with the deposition of the Balderton Sand and Gravel, but the context of this surface find remains in doubt (R. Jacobi: pers. comm.).

The above artefact concentrations provide possible evidence for the manufacture and use of lithic artefacts within the valley during OIS 8 and OIS 6, although much of this material could have been redeposited and hence may predate significantly the deposition of the drift deposits. The same problem applies to discoveries of artefacts in the Beeston Sands and Gravels near Nottingham, quarrying of which has yielded significant quantities of flint handaxes and other artefacts, mostly heavily rolled (notably at Stoney Street and Tottle Brook, Beeston: Fig.2.9; Posnansky 1963, 379, figs 11-12). This terrace may be attributed to OIS 4 (Fig.2.3), which may be correlated with a period of human abandonment of Britain (Chapter 2.5), and it has been suggested that these often very heavily rolled artefacts had derived from deposits predating OIS 4 (McNabb 2001, 17–18; *cf.* Wymer 1999, 115).

2.5   The Late OIS6 – OIS4 Abandonment

There are strong grounds to suggest that Britain was abandoned by hominines from OIS 6, through the Ipswichian Interglacial (OIS 5e) and into the early cooling stages of the final (Devensian) glaciation (OIS 5a-5d and 4; Currant and Jacobi 1997). The reasons cited for abandonment include the harsh climate of Stage 6, the breaching of the Strait of Dover, hence severing the land bridge, and changes in both climate

Fig. 2.8 *Palaeolithic flint handaxes from the Etwall Sand and Gravel, Hilton, Derbyshire (scale 1:2; source: Posnansky 1963; reproduced by permission of The Prehistoric Society)*

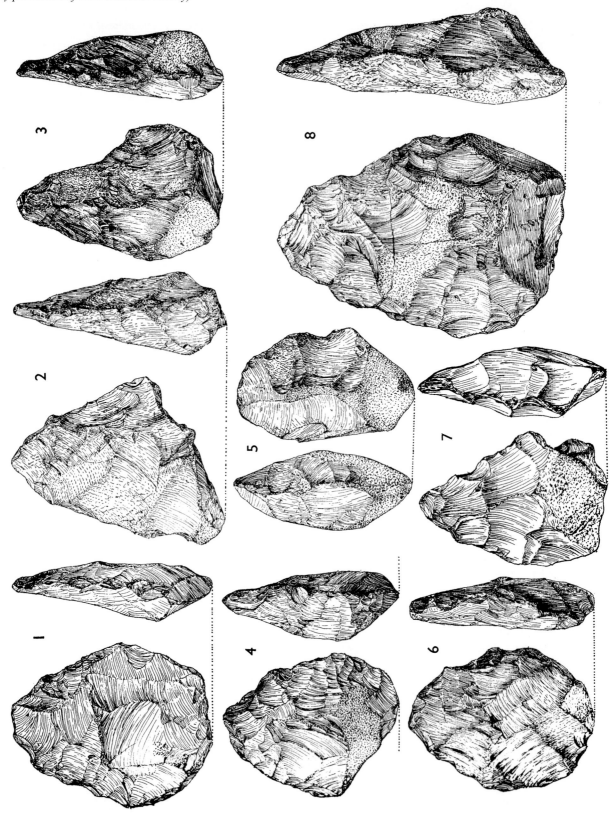

and habitat preferences by human groups (Ashton and Lewis 2002). Certainly there is no evidence of activity in the Trent basin, which on current evidence may have been abandoned until recolonisation in OIS 3 by Neanderthal communities characterised in the archaeological record by Mousterian artefact assemblages.

2.5.1   Geomorphology

Across southern Britain, a number of organic-rich channels of Ipswichian age have been studied in detail and suggest the development of mixed oak forests and summer temperatures at least 4°C higher than those of the present day (Keen *et al.* 1999

Fig.2.9 *Palaeolithic flint handaxes from the Beeston Sand and Gravel, Tottle Brook Pit, Beeston, Nottinghamshire (scale 1:2; source: Posnansky 1963; reproduced by permission of The Prehistoric Society)*

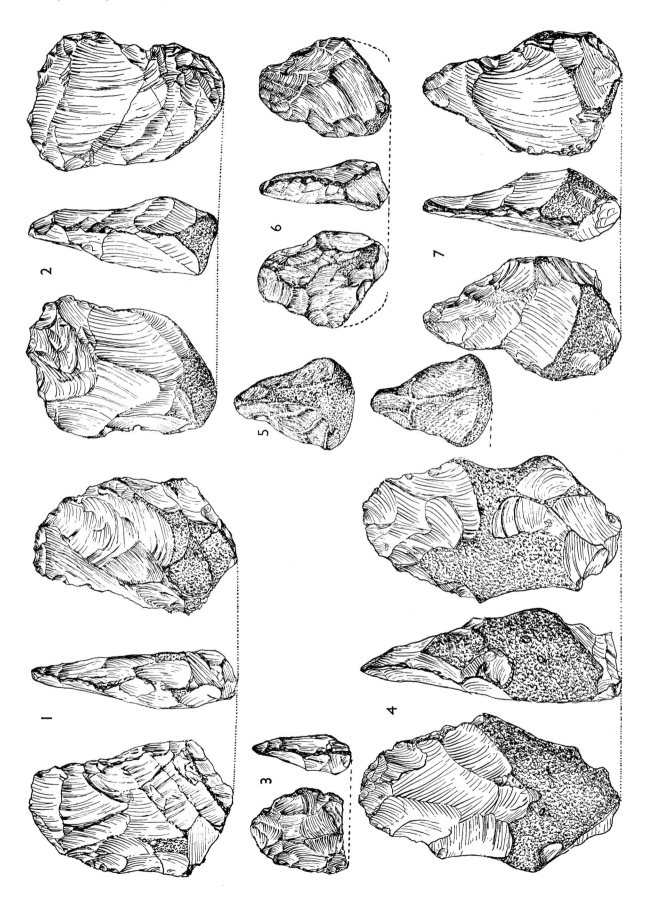

Fig.2.10 *The mammalian fauna recovered from the Allenton Terrace at Boulton Moor near Derby (after Jones and Stanley 1974)*

Taxon	
Hippopotamus amphibius L.	Hippopotamus
?*Palaeoloxodon antiquus* Falc.	
& Caut. St-t elephant	Elephant
?*Dicerorhinus hemitoechus* Falc.	
narrow nosed rhino	Rhinoceros
Ursus cf. *arctos* L.	Brown bear
Crocuta crocuta Erxleben	Hyaena
Cervus elephus L.	Red deer
Bos sp. or *Bison* sp.	Auroch or bison

and Gao *et al.* 2000). Discoveries of characteristic Ipswichian faunas within some valley gravels provide valuable evidence for terrace aggradations in the middle and lower Trent during OIS5e. In the middle Trent, Ipswichian faunal associations have been recorded in the Crown Hill Beds, beneath the Allenton Terrace of the Derwent (Fig.2.10), and in the Allenton Terrace itself (considered a correlative of the Beeston Terrace by Clayton [1953] and Straw [1963]) – although much of the Allenton Terrace may have been aggraded in the early Devensian. Between Newark and Lincoln, an Ipswichian fauna has been attributed to the Fulbeck Sand and Gravel (Brandon and Sumbler 1988), suggesting drainage of the River Brant via the Lincoln Gap. Brandon and Sumbler (1991) have argued that the Scarle Sand and Gravel, mapped on the east bank of the Trent north of Newark, provides evidence that the river (Trent) was flowing at this time to the Humber Estuary. However, reindeer remains from the Scarle Sand and Gravel suggest that the majority of this deposit was probably laid down more recently than the Ipswichian (OIS 5e). This argument may also apply to the Fulbeck Sand and Gravel (Howard *et al.* 1999a), the Allenton Sand and Gravel and the Beeston Sand and Gravel (Brandon and Cooper 1997).

2.5.2 Vegetation and Fauna

In 1895, the Crown Hill Beds beneath the Allenton Terrace yielded plant material and large vertebrate remains, mostly hippopotamus from a channel fill. Nearly a century later, in 1973, these finds were augmented by the recovery approximately 1 km to the south-east of hippopotamus and other mammalian remains from a sewer trench excavated through the Allenton Terrace at Boulton Moor, Derby (Fig.2.10; Jones and Stanley 1974). Hippopotamus is recognised as a characteristic feature of Ipswichian interglacial faunal assemblages (Currant and Jacobi 2001). Between Newark and Lincoln, an Ipswichian fauna has been attributed to the Fulbeck Sand and Gravel (Brandon and Sumbler 1988), while east of the Lincoln Gap Holyoak and Preece (1985) assigned organic deposits at Tattershall, Lincolnshire, to the Ipswichian (*cf.* Brandon and Sumbler 1991).

In the Lower Trent catchment, interglacial sediments assigned to OIS 5e have been recorded in Older River Sand and Gravel in the Idle Valley at Austerfield, Nottinghamshire. Associated pollen and insect remains provide evidence for a marsh-bound lake surrounded by temperate woodland attributable to Pollen Zone II (Gaunt *et al.* 1972). More regionally, within the Humber system at Langham, East Yorkshire, pollen, plant

debris and dinoflagellate cysts recovered from a borehole close to the M18-M62 interchange revealed evidence of brackish water conditions and possible salt-marsh environments, surrounded by pine, oak and local alder woodland (Gaunt *et al.* 1974). A second borehole at Westfield Farm, East Yorkshire, encountered silty clay within Older River Sand and Gravel and yielded a similar dinoflagellate cyst assemblage as at Langham; in this case, however, the arboreal pollen assemblage was dominated by pine with hornbeam present in appreciable amounts (Gaunt *et al.* 1974).

2.6 Archaeological Period 4: The Mousterian (OIS 3)

The warmer conditions of early OIS 3 witnessed renewed colonisation of Britain by Neanderthal groups employing Mousterian technology. Occupation may have been sporadic, in view of the evidence from OIS 3 for frequent alternations of cooler and warmer conditions within what appears generally to have been a cool, dry environment. Study of the Mousterian is complicated by the general scarcity of diagnostic artefactual remains (most notably triangular handaxes); the latter problem is compounded by the difficulties of distinguishing Period 4 from Period 3 artefacts at sites lacking an extended stratigraphic sequence. Despite recent efforts by researchers such as Currant and Jacobi (1997), our knowledge of this period therefore remains extremely limited, although significant advances have been made recently on the subject of Mousterian chronology. Particular attention may be drawn to optically stimulated luminescence dates from Lynford Quarry, Norfolk (Boismier 2003) and, immediately north of the Trent, Uranium-series, electron spin resonance and recent unpublished radiocarbon determinations from Creswell Crags, Derbyshire (Jacobi *et al.* 1998; Jacobi and Grun 2003; R. Jacobi: pers. comm.). The latter dates would suggest Mousterian activity within the gorge no earlier than 50,000 years ago.

2.6.1 Geomorphology

In the Trent Valley, no fluvial sediments relating to OIS 4 have been recorded, and until recently no fluvial sediments relating to OIS 3 were known. However, in 2002, the remains of at least four woolly rhinoceros were discovered at Whitemoor Haye, Staffordshire, in terrace sands and gravels close to the contemporary floodplain of the River Tame (Fig.2.11). Woolly rhinoceros is a major component of OIS 3 faunal assemblages (Currant and Jacobi 2001) while the position of the sediments within the valley floor would also suggest a late Pleistocene context. Interpretation of the deposits at Whitemoor Haye is still in progress, but it appears that the faunal assemblage was confined to a lower sandy gravel unit infilling a braided river channel incised into the Mercia Mudstone bedrock (Buteux *et al.* 2003). Periglacial structures in the upper part of the sequence suggest the presence of localised ground ice after deposition of the faunal remains.

2.6.2 Vegetation and Fauna

Evidence from Britain generally suggests that for much of this time, certainly during OIS 3, the West and East Midlands would have been linked to eastern Russia by a zone of dry

Fig.2.11 *Woolly rhinoceros remains recovered from probable OIS 3 sand and gravel deposits at Whitemoor Haye Quarry, Staffordshire (© Birmingham Archaeology)*

open grassland with plentiful game, termed 'mammoth steppe' (McNabb 2001, 22, fig.7), thus facilitating the westwards expansion of Neanderthal populations. Regionally, the faunal assemblage recovered from the Lower Cave Earth at Pin Hole, Creswell Crags, which includes mountain hare, wolf, red fox, brown bear, spotted hyaena, lion, wild horse, giant deer, bison, woolly mammoth and woolly rhinoceros, is considered to be characteristic of OIS 3 (Currant and Jacobi 1997).

In the Trent Valley, organic sediments at Whitemoor Haye, exposed in a channel incised into the bedrock and preserved in eroded clasts within the sandy gravel, have yielded preliminary Coleopteran, plant macrofossil and pollen information indicative of cool climatic conditions similar to those prevailing in present-day northern Norway (Buteux *et al.* 2003). The environmental context of Whitemoor Haye provides broadly comparable data to organic sediments recovered from three other localities within the Tame catchment dated to around 32,160 BP (Coope and Sands 1966). Insect remains from these three localities suggest a mean annual air temperature of about –2°C, with a mean July temperature of 4°C.

2.6.3 Human Activity

Although the West and East Midlands would have provided favourable environments for early hominines for much of this period, with extensive dry open grasslands suitable for grazing by large mammals, the case for Mousterian re-occupation of the region rests at present upon a thin scatter of open-air and cave sites yielding diagnostic lithic artefacts – most notably Mousterian triangular handaxes (McNabb 2001, 22; Roe 1981). The most significant concentration of

sites is focused at Creswell Crags, within a deep limestone gorge immediately north of the Trent Valley. Small numbers of handaxes and flake tools in the deposits of Pin Hole and Robin Hood's Cave, Mother Grundy's Parlour and Church Hole suggest repeated visits by hunter-gatherer groups, none of which may have stayed for any length of time (Jenkinson 1984). This would accord with current interpretations of Neanderthal occupation elsewhere in western Doggerland, which it has been suggested may have been settled by small numbers of widely ranging hunter-gatherer bands, occupying cave or open-air sites on a seasonal basis. Examination of the Creswell collections and Mousterian artefacts from nearby sites such as Ash Tree Cave, Whitwell, Derbyshire, suggest utilisation of local stone resources such as quartzite and clay ironstone, the latter from the nearby Coal Measures, and non-local flint, as implied by two heavily re-sharpened flint handaxes from Robin Hood's Cave (Jenkinson 1984). We should not imagine, therefore, long-term occupation on any of these sites, but rather repeated visits to preferred locations such as the Creswell gorge, which on topographic grounds would have provided a prime hunting site.

2.7 Archaeological Period 5: The Upper Palaeolithic (OIS 2)

Upper Palaeolithic activity has been identified in Britain either side of the Dimlington Stadial of *c.*25000 to *c.*13000 BP (Rose 1985). During this time full glacial conditions and ice-sheets returned to western Doggerland, accompanied by a regression in mean sea level, with the ice sheets reaching their maximum extent between *c.*22000 and *c.*18000 BP (Eyles *et al.* 1994). This archaeological period coincides, most importantly, with the appearance in Europe of the earliest anatomically modern humans (*Homo sapiens sapiens*), broadly between *c*.40000 and *c*.35000 BP – although much debate has focused upon the dating of the earliest specimens (McNabb 2001, 23).

The earlier phase of human activity, prior to the Dimlington Stadial, is conventionally referred to as the Early Upper Palaeolithic, and dates broadly from *c*.40000 to *c*.25000 BP. The post-Dimlington Stadial period, from around *c*.13000 BP, is referred to as the Late Devensian Lateglacial, and is divided into two climatic episodes prior to the commencement of the final phase of climatic warming which marks the transition from the late Pleistocene to the Holocene (although the record from mainland Europe suggests that there may be more complexity to this broad subdivision). The earlier and warmer of these two episodes is known as the Windermere Interstadial (*c*.13000–11000 BP) and the later colder phase as the Loch Lomond Stadial (*c*.11000–10000 BP). The latter saw the development of extensive ice-caps over the Western Highlands of Scotland and corrie glaciers across other upland regions of England. Dating of the resumption of human activity after the Dimlington Stadial is problematic, but current evidence would suggest renewed settlement of Britain by at least *c*.13000 BP (Housley *et al.* 1997). This final phase of Late Upper Palaeolithic activity sees a progression in lithic technology from Creswellian assemblages characterised by Creswell and Cheddar points (*c*.13000–11800 BP) to a toolkit of penknife points, well represented at Mother Grundy's Parlour (R. Jacobi: pers. comm.), and straight-backed blades and bladelets comparable to those occurring at Hengistbury Head, Dorset, and Brockhill, Surrey (*c*.11800–10800 BP). These later industries preceded another likely break in occupation, coinciding with the coldest phase of the Loch Lomond Stadial, from *c*.10800 to *c*.10300 BP. Climatic amelioration after *c*.10300 BP heralded a phase of quite rapid recolonisation, distinguished in the archaeological record by 'long-blade' industries dating from *c*.10300–9700 BP (*cf*. Laude, Leicestershire: Cooper 1997), and marks the transition from the Pleistocene to the current Holocene Interglacial.

2.7.1 Geomorphology

During OIS 2, ice skirted the Peak District and probably penetrated the Upper Trent Valley as far as the Trent-Tame confluence and the Dove Valley as far as Uttoxeter, Staffordshire, leading to the deposition of braided outwash sands and gravels across the valley floor. Incision through these sand and gravel deposits towards the end of and after the Dimlington Stadial and during the early Holocene led to the creation of terraces within the valley floor (Brandon and Sumbler 1988; Straw 1963) which have remained important foci for human occupation throughout the Holocene. These terrace deposits, formerly known as the Floodplain Terrace (e.g. Straw 1963) have recently been renamed the Holme Pierrepont Sands and Gravels by the British Geological Survey (Brandon and Cooper 1997). Ice also entered the Lower Trent Valley during the Dimlington Stadial, and may have surged as far south as Wroot, South Yorkshire, before retreating back to a more stable position marked by the York and Escrick Moraines (Gaunt 1976; 1981; but *cf.* Straw 2002). Blockage of drainage via the Humber led to the development of a large glacial lake (Humber) across the southern part of

the Vale of York. It seems likely that this lake extended up the Lower Trent Valley, although little evidence can be found for its extent and it seems unlikely to have been as extensive as envisaged by Straw (1979). During this time, therefore, most of the Trent Valley was within the periglacial zone and was subjected to a range of periglacial processes including the development of discontinuous permafrost, as recorded by large ice wedge pseudomorphs truncating the Balderton Sand and Gravel in the Lower Trent Valley (Fig. 2.12; Howard 1995). Within the sparsely vegetated landscape of the Dimlington Stadial and the subsequent Lateglacial period, fine-grained fluvioglacial deposits were subject to processes of wind erosion, depositing extensive sheets of coversand across eastern England (Bateman 1995; Bateman *et al.* 1999; Bateman *et al.* 2000). In the Lower Trent Valley, extensive sand sheets are mapped on the terraces of Holme Pierrepont Sand and Gravel on the eastern side of the valley floor (Brandon and Sumbler 1988) and in the Idle Valley around Tiln, Nottinghamshire (Howard *et al.* 1999b).

2.7.2 Vegetation and Fauna

The intense climatic cooling preceding the onset of the full glacial conditions associated with the Dimlington Stadial of *c*.25000 to *c*.13000 BP caused a dramatic decline in the tundra vegetation prevailing in the earlier part of this period. This is exemplified at Four Ashes, Staffordshire, which is the type locality for the Devensian (OIS 4-2), where the

Fig.2.12 *Large ice-wedge pseudomorph of probable Dimlington Stadial age (OIS 2) truncating deposits of the Balderton Sand and Gravel at Whisby Quarry, Lincolnshire (photograph: A.J. Howard)*

youngest organic material was radiocarbon-dated to around *c*.30000 BP; the absence of organic material later than this date is explained by the onset of polar-desert conditions (Morgan 1973).

Following maximum glaciation, the most striking evidence for climatic change around *c*.13000 BP is provided by fossil Coleoptera. These show a rapid transition from arctic to thermophilous species, indicating increases in temperature of the order of 1°C per decade and 7°C per century (Coope and Brophy 1972). The thermal maximum of the Windermere Interstadial appears to have occurred between *c*.13000 and *c*.12500 BP with mean July temperatures of 16–18°C. Vegetational records show a lag, particularly for the first thousand years of the interstadial (Pennington 1986), but then catch up with the expansion from sedges and grasses through secondary colonisers such as juniper, willow and crowberry to boreal woodland dominated by birch (Pennington and Bonny 1970). Between *c*.11000 and *c*.10000 BP, during the Loch Lomond Stadial, the return to cold, probably more arid climatic conditions saw the replacement of this vegetation assemblage by scrub and tundra communities, particularly those indicative of unstable soils. Coleopteran assemblages from this cold episode suggest a decrease of 7–8°C in the mean July air temperature from the climatic maximum of the preceding Windermere Interstadial (Coope and Lemdahl 1995).

The faunal assemblage from the cave earth and breccia at Gough's Cave, Cheddar, Somerset, is considered to be characteristic of the Windermere Interstadial and much of the Loch Lomond Stadial, and includes mammoth, mountain hare, wolf, red fox, brown bear and wild horse (Currant and Jacobi 1997). Analyses of faunal assemblages from this period suggest variations in faunal composition in response to changes in climatic conditions and vegetation. A radiocarbon date of 12460±160 BP (OxA-1204; 13640–12140 cal BC) on the right calcaneum of a mammoth from Pin Hole, Creswell Crags, provides important evidence for the local survival of this species in the dry open environment that would have prevailed in the early part of the Windermere Interstadial (Archaeometry 30 (1) 1988, 158). A richer fauna is indicated in the increasingly wooded environment which characterised the later part of the Windermere Interstadial, with a more diverse range of animals including wild cattle, red deer and reindeer (R. Jacobi: pers. comm.).

In the Trent Valley, palaeoenvironmental records from the Lateglacial period are rare; organic rich channels have been identified recently at Holme Pierrepont, Nottinghamshire, but await further investigation (Fig. 2.13). An eroded clast of organic material from near the base of the sand and gravel sequence at Hemington Quarry dated to 13180 ± 250 BP (Beta 93855, 14640–12530 cal BC) provides the only palaeobiological record from the main valley (Greenwood and Smith, in press). The accuracy of this radiocarbon date may be questioned because of the possible impact of 'hardwater effects' (M. Greenwood: pers. comm.). Nevertheless, the recorded species list includes Coleoptera that are today restricted to sub-arctic environments and those now limited to montane areas. The insect assemblage suggests that the deposit probably accumulated in a still, stagnant, non-acidic pool of water, which was surrounded by dwarf willow and sedges. Palaeotemperature reconstruction from the insect remains at Hemington, Leicestershire, suggests that the mean annual temperature was between –6°C and –10°C with July temperatures as low as 10°C and winter temperatures as low as –20°C (Greenwood and Smith, in press). The discovery in the Idle Valley at Tiln of an organic deposit infilling a scour hollow in the upper surface of braided river sands and gravels dated to 11250 ± 80 BP (Beta-100931, 11820–11050 cal BC) indicates a slow, moving or static water body (Howard *et al.* 1999b). This was fringed with reeds, sedges and wet moss in a grassland landscape largely devoid of trees, providing thereby an ideal environment for the reindeer which are represented in faunal records of this period from northern Britain (R. Jacobi: pers. comm.).

2.7.3 Human Activity

Evidence for Early Upper Palaeolithic activity in the West and East Midlands derives largely from stray finds of diagnostic lithic artefacts, recovered mainly during fieldwalking, plus rare finds of EUP artefacts in cave sites, particularly at Creswell Crags, where finds have been made of leaf-points and Gravettian Font-Robert points (McNabb 2001, 26). The remarkable discovery during recent work at Glaston, Rutland, of an open-air hyaena den associated with an EUP leaf point, a blade core and a waste blade which it has been suggested might represent a leaf point blank (Thomas and Jacobi 2001, 182–3) raises the possibility of surviving EUP open sites within the region, although the circumstances of deposition of these artefacts remain unclear. In the Trent Valley, by contrast, no material which may certainly be attributed to this early phase has been recovered, and the nature and extent of activity in the Valley during this period remains uncertain.

Evidence for Late Upper Palaeolithic activity, from *c*.13000 to *c*.10000 BP, is far more extensive, including several terrace locations within the Trent Valley which could signify open-air settlements or specialised activity foci. The most significant of these was located during fieldwalking of the Floodplain Terrace adjacent to the Fosse Way at Farndon Fields, Newark (Garton 1993; Kinsley and Knight 1992, 105). A scatter of retouched Creswellian flintwork and debitage, together with similarly corticated material of undiagnostic form that it was suggested could also derive from LUP activity, was recovered from an area of at least 8ha in extent (Fig. 2.14). This scatter incorporated a tight cluster of flint tools and knapping waste, only 10m in diameter, including a Creswell point, a long-end scraper and the tip of a backed piece, all typical of Creswellian assemblages. Close typological parallels may be drawn between material from this site and Creswellian artefacts from Creswell Crags, some 50km to the north-west, and we might speculate whether this represents a temporary settlement of hunter-gatherer bands ranging between the Trent Valley and the cave sites of the Magnesian limestone escarpment.

Scattered surface finds from sites in or close to the Trent Valley may also be attributed to the Late Upper Palaeolithic, including Cheddar Points from near Lound and East Stoke, Nottinghamshire (Jacobi *et al.* 2001, 18–20; fig.1a, b), penknife points from Cotgrave, Nottinghamshire (*ibid.* 20, fig.1c) and from the Beeston Terrace at Potlock, Derbyshire (*ibid.* 20) and single flint artefacts from Castle Donington, Lockington and Hemington in Leicestershire (Cooper and Jacobi 2001). In addition to surface finds, LUP flintwork

Fig.2.13 *Organic channels exposed within late Devensian braided river sands and gravels at Holme Pierrepont Quarry, Nottinghamshire (photograph: A.J. Howard)*

Fig.2.14 *Creswellian flintwork from Farndon Fields, Nottinghamshire (© R. Jacobi; photograph by G. Owen)*

has occasionally been retrieved from later features, notably at Gonalston, Nottinghamshire, where a Creswell point and a burin made on a long blade had been redeposited in later prehistoric contexts (Jacobi *et al.* 2001, 17). Interpretation of this finds distribution is difficult, but the prevailing model of widely ranging hunter-gatherer bands (e.g. O'Brien 1978, 3) would provide an appropriate interpretative framework.

Farther afield, we may note the accumulating evidence for open-air sites elsewhere in the East and West Midlands, including a recently discovered Creswellian site in Bradgate Park, Leicestershire (McNabb 2001, 31) and a dense

distribution of flintwork indicative of a *c.*10300–9700 BP 'long blade' site at Launde, Leicestershire (Cooper 1997). In addition to open-air sites, activity had resumed inside or adjacent to caves, as at Creswell Crags, where extensive evidence of human activity during the Lateglacial Interstadial has been recovered from Pin Hole, Robin Hood's Cave, Mother Grundy's Parlour and Church Hole (including bone, antler and ivory artefacts in addition to lithic finds such as Creswell, Cheddar and Penknife Points; Jenkinson 1984). Analysis of the Creswell material has emphasised the mobility of these later Upper Palaeolithic groups, implied by the procurement of flint and perhaps amber from distant sources. Robin Hood's Cave has revealed evidence in the form of numerous bones with cut marks that could signify usage of the cave for the trapping and processing of arctic hares (Charles and Jacobi 1994). In addition, evidence has been obtained from Mother Grundy's Parlour for the hunting of wild horses, while a single cut bone from a wild cow was obtained from Church Hole (R.Jacobi: pers. comm.). A recent discovery of international significance is the identification in Church Hole of figurative rock carvings interpreted as an ibex and two anthropomorphs, which on stylistic grounds have been dated to around *c.*12500–12000 BP (Bahn *et al.* 2003). The depiction of an ibex (Fig.2.15) is significant since no bones of this animal have been unequivocally identified at Creswell or elsewhere in Britain. The drawing may indicate the presence of ibex in Britain, but Bahn *et al.* (2003) favour a sighting in continental Europe. As with other information derived from Creswell Crags, this would reinforce the evidence for highly mobile groups during the Late Upper Palaeolithic.

Fig.2.15 *Engraving of ibex in Church Hole, Creswell Crags (copyright S. Ripoll and courtesy of P. Bahn, P. Pettitt and S. Ripoll)*

Fig.2.16 *Palaeolithic sites referred to in the text, compiled by S. Baker*
(1.Ash Tree Cave; 2.Austerfield; 3.Beeston; 4.Bradgate Park; 5.Brooksby; 6.Castle Donington; 7.Coronation Farm; 8.Cotgrave; 9.Creswell Crags; 10.Derby; 11.East Stoke; 12.Farndon Fields; 13.Four Ashes; 14.Glaston; 15.Gonalston; 16.Hemington; 17.Hilton; 18.Hinckley; 19.Holme Pierrepont; 20.Launde; 21.Leicester; 22.Lincoln; 23.Lockington; 24.Lound; 25.Melton Mowbray; 26.Newark; 27.North Hykeham, 28.Norton Bottoms; 29.Nottingham; 30.Nuneaton; 31.Peterborough; 32.Potlock; 33.Rearsby; 34.Snitterfield; 35.Swarkestone Lowes; 36.Tattershall Thorpe; 37.Thurmaston; 38.Tiln; 39.Uttoxeter; 40.Waverley Wood; 41.Whisby; 42.Whitemoor Haye; 43.Willington; 44.Wroot)

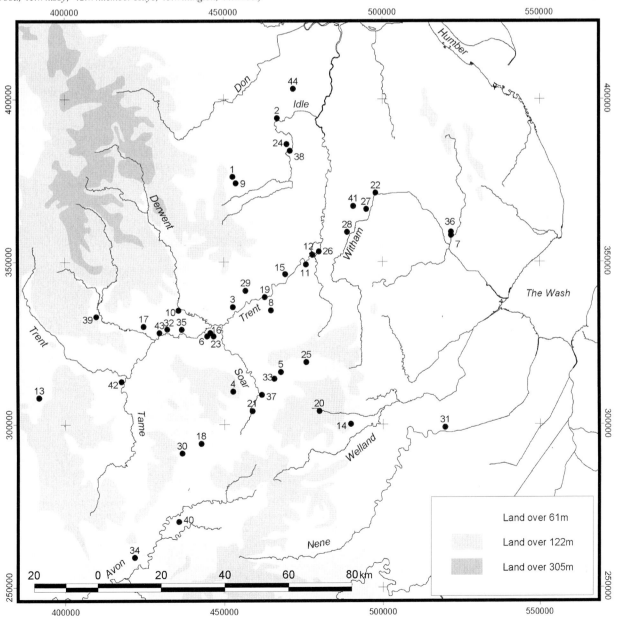

REFERENCES

Andrews, P. and Banham, R. (eds) 1999. *Late Cenozoic Environments and Hominid Evolution: a Tribute to Bill Bishop.* London: Geological Society.

Armstrong, L. 1942. Palaeolithic man in the north Midlands, *J. Derbyshire Archaeol. Nat. Hist. Soc.* **63**, 28–60.

Ashton, N. and Lewis, S.G. 2002. Deserted Britain: declining populations in the British Late Middle Pleistocene, *Antiquity* **76**, 388–396.

Ashton, N.M., Cook, J., Lewis, S.G. and Rose, J. (eds) 1992. *High Lodge: excavations by G. de G. Sieveking 1962–68 and J. Cook 1998.* London: British Museum.

Ashton, N., Healy, F. and Pettitt, P. (eds) 1998. *Stone Age Archaeology: Essays in Honour of John Wymer.* Lithic Studies Society Occ. Pub. **6**; Oxbow Monogr. **102**. Oxford: Oxbow Books.

Bahn, P., Pettitt, P. and Ripoll, S. 2003. Discovery of Palaeolithic cave art in Britain, *Antiquity* **77**, 227–231.

Bateman, M.D. 1995. Thermoluminescence dating of the British coversand deposits, *Quat. Sci. Rev.* **14**, 791–798.

Bateman, M.D., Hannam, J. and Livingstone, I. 1999. Late Quaternary dunes at Twigmoor Woods, Lincolnshire, UK: a preliminary investigation, *Zeitschrift für Geomorphologie Neue Folge* **116**, 131–146.

Bateman, M.D., Murton, J.B. and Crowe, W. 2000. Late Devensian and Holocene depositional environments associated with the coversand around Caistor, north Lincolnshire, UK, *Boreas* **29**, 1–15.

Bemrose, H.H.A. and Deeley, R.M. 1898. Discovery of mammalian remains in the old river gravels of the Derwent near Derby, *Quart. J. Geol. Soc. Lond.* **52**, 497–510.

Bishop, M. 2001. An archaeological resource assessment of the Palaeolithic and Mesolithic in Nottinghamshire. *East Midlands Archaeological Research Framework.* http://www.le.ac.uk/a/pdf-files/emidpal.pdf.

Boismier, W.A. 2003. A Middle Palaeolithic site at Lynford Quarry, Mundford, Norfolk: interim statement, *Proc. Prehist. Soc.* **69**, 315–324.

Bowen, D.Q. (ed) 1999. *A Revised Correlation of Quaternary Deposits in the British Isles.* Geol. Soc. Spec.Rep. **23**. Bath: Geological Society.

Bowen, D.Q., Huges, S., Sykes, G.A. and Miller, G.H. 1989. Land-sea correlations in the Pleistocene based on isoleucine empirimization in non-marine mollusks, *Nature* **340**, 49–51.

Brandon, A. 1996. Geology of the Lower Derwent Valley: 1:10 000 sheets SK 33SE, 43SW & 43SE. British Geological Survey Technical Report **WA/96/07**.

Brandon, A. 1997. Geology of the Stretton and Repton areas: 1:10 000 sheets SK 22NE & 32NW. British Geological Survey Technical Report **WA/97/02**.

Brandon, A. and Cooper, A.H. 1997. Geology of the Etwall area: 1:10 000 sheet SK 23SE. British Geological Survey Technical Report **WA/97/03**.

Brandon, A. and Sumbler, M.G. 1988. An Ipswichian fluvial deposit at Fulbeck, Lincolnshire and the chronology of the Trent terraces, *J. Quat. Sci.* **3**, 127–133.

Brandon, A. and Sumbler, M.G. 1991. The Balderton Sand and Gravel: pre-Ipswichian cold stage fluvial deposits near Lincoln, England, *J. Quat. Sci.* **6** (2), 117–138.

Bridgland, D.R. 1994. *Quaternary of the Thames.* Geological Conservation Review Series **7**. London: Chapman & Hall.

Bridgland, D.R. 2000. River terrace systems in north-west Europe: an archive of environmental change, uplift and early human occupation, *Quat. Sci. Rev.* **19**, 1293–1303.

Bridgland, D.R., Allen, P. and Haggart, B.A. 1995. *The Quaternary of the Lower Thames: Field Guide.* London: Quaternary Research Association.

Bridgland, D.R., Field, M.H., Holmes, J.A., McNabb, J., Preece, R.C., Selby, I., Wymer, J.J., Boreham, S., Irving, B., Parfitt, S.A. and Stuart, A.J. 1999. Middle Pleistocene interglacial Thames-Medway deposits at Clacton-on-Sea, England: reconsideration of the biostratigraphical and environmental context of the type Clactonian Palaeolithic industry, *Quat. Sci. Rev.* **18**, 109–146.

Bridgland, D.R., Horton, B.P. and Innes, J.B. 1999. *The Quaternary of North East England: Field Guide.* London: Quaternary Research Association.

Bridgland, D.R., Preece, R.C., Roe, H.M., Tipping, R.M., Coope, G.R., Field, M.H., Robinson, J.E., Schreve, D.C. and Crowe, K. 2001. Middle Pleistocene interglacial deposits at Barling, Essex, England: evidence for a longer chronology for the Thames terrace sequence, *J. Quat. Sci.* **16** (8), 813–840.

Buckingham, C.M., Roe, D.A. and Scott, K. 1996. Preliminary report on the Stanton Harcourt channel deposits (Oxfordshire, England); geological context, vertebrate remains and Palaeolithic stone artifacts, *J. Quat. Sci.* **11** (5), 397–415.

Buteux, S. and Lang, A.T.O. 2003. Lost but not forgotten: the Lower and Middle Palaeolithic occupation of the West Midlands, *West Midlands Regional Research Framework for Archaeology Seminar 1.* http//www.arch-ant.bham.ac.uk/wmrrfa/sem1.htm.

Buteux, S., Brooks, S., Candy, I., Coates, G., Coope, R., Currant, A., Field, M., Greenwood, M., Greig, J., Howard, A., Limbrey, S., Paddock, E., Schreve, D., Smith, D. and Toms, P. 2003. The Whitemoor Haye Woolly Rhino Site, Whitemoor Haye Quarry, Staffordshire (SK 173127). Assessment report on scientific investigations funded by the ALSF through a grant administered by English Nature. Unpublished report, University of Birmingham Field Archaeology Unit.

Challis, K. and Howard, A.J. 1999. Brooksby Agricultural College: Archaeological Evaluation of a Potential Quarry for LaFarge Redland Ltd. Unpublished report, Trent & Peak Archaeological Unit, University Park, Nottingham.

Charles, R. and Jacobi, R.M. 1994. The Lateglacial fauna from the Robin Hood Cave, Creswell Crags: a reassessment, *Oxford J. Archaeol.* **13**, 1–32.

Clayton, K.M. 1953. The glacial chronology of part of the middle Trent Basin, *Proc. Geol. Assoc.* **64**, 198–207.

Clayton, K.M. 2000. Glacial erosion of the Wash and Fen basin and the deposition of the chalky till in eastern England, *Quat. Sci. Rev.* **19**, 811–822.

Coles, B.J. 1998. Doggerland: a speculative survey, *Proc. Prehist. Soc.* **64**, 45–81.

Cook, J. and Jacobi, R. 1998. Observations on the artifacts from the breccia at Kent's Cavern, in N. Ashton, F. Healy and P. Pettitt (eds), *Stone Age Archaeology. Essays in Honour of John Wymer*, 77–89.

Coope, G.R. and Brophy, J.A. 1972. Late glacial environmental changes indicated by a coleopteran succession from North Wales, *Boreas* **1**, 97–142.

Coope, G.R. and Lemdahl, G. 1995. Regional differences in the Lateglacial climate of northern Europe based on coleopteran analysis, *J. Quat. Sci.* **10**, 391–395.

Coope, G.R. and Sands, C.H.S. 1966. Insect faunas of the last glaciation from the Tame Valley, Warwickshire, *Proc. Roy. Soc.* **B165**, 389–412.

Cooper, L. 1997. Launde, *Trans. Leicestershire Archaeol. Hist. Soc.* **71**, 91–93.

Cooper, L. and Jacobi, R. 2001. Two late glacial finds from north-west Leicestershire, *Trans. Leicestershire Archaeol. Hist. Soc.* **75**, 118–121.

Currant, A. and Jacobi, R. 1997. Vertebrate faunas of the British Late Pleistocene and the chronology of human settlement, *Quat. Newslett.* **82**, 1–9.

Currant, A. and Jacobi, R. 2001. A formal mammalian biostratigraphy for the Late Pleistocene of Britain, *Quat. Sci. Rev.* **20**, 1707–1716.

Derbyshire, E. and Jones, P.F. 1980. Systematic fissuring of a matrix dominated lodgement till at Church Wilne, Derbyshire, England. *Geol. Mag.* **117**, 243–254.

Edwards, K.C. (ed) 1966. *Nottingham and its Region.* Nottingham: British Association for the Advancement of Science.

Elliott, L. and Knight, D. 1999. An early Mesolithic site and first millennium BC settlement and pit alignments at Swarkstone Lowes, Derbyshire, *Derbyshire Archaeol. J.* **119**, 79–153.

Eyles, N., McCabe, A.M. and Bowen, D.Q. 1994. The stratigraphic and sedimentological significance of Late Devensian ice sheet surging in Holderness, Yorkshire, UK, *Quat. Sci. Rev.* **13**, 727-759.

Fox-Strangways, C. 1905. *The Geology of the Country between Derby, Burton-on-Trent, Ashby-de-la-Zouch and Loughborough.* Mem. Geol. Surv. GB. London: HMSO.

Gao, C., Keen, D.H., Boreham, S., Coope, G.R., Pettit, M.E., Stuart, A.J. and Gibbard, P.L. 2000. Last interglacial and Devensian deposits of the River Great Ouse at Woolpack Farm, Fenstanton, Cambridgeshire, UK. *Quat. Sci. Rev.* **19**, 787–810.

Garton, D. 1993. A Late Upper Paleolithic site near Newark, Nottinghamshire, *Trans. Thoroton Soc. Nottinghamshire* **97**, 144.

Gaunt, G.D. 1976. The Devensian maximum ice limit in the Vale of York, *Proc. Yorkshire Geol. Soc.* **40**, 631–637.

Gaunt, G.D. 1981. Quaternary history of the southern part of the Vale of York, in J. Neale and D. Flenley (eds), *The Quaternary in Britain: Essays, Reviews and Original Work on the Quaternary*, 82–97.

Gaunt, G.D., Bartley, D.D. and Harland, R. 1974. Two interglacial deposits proved in boreholes in the southern part of the Vale of York and their bearing on contemporaneous sea levels, *Bull. Geol. Surv. GB.* **48**, 1–23.

Gaunt, G.D., Coope, G.R., Osborne, P.J. and Franks, J.W. 1972. *An Interglacial Deposit near Austerfield, Southern Yorkshire.* NERC (IGS) report **72/4**. London: HMSO.

Gibbard, P.L., Andrew, R. and Pettit, M. 1992. The margin of a Middle Pleistocene ice advance at Tottenhill, Norfolk, England, *Geol. Mag.* **129**, 59–76.

Graf, A. 2002. Lower and Middle Palaeolithic Leicestershire and Rutland: progress and potential, *Trans. Leicestershire Archaeol. Hist. Soc.* **76**, 1–46.

Greenwood, M., and Smith, D.N. in press. Changing fluvial conditions and landscapes in the Trent Valley: a review of palaeoentomological evidence, in D.N. Smith, M.B. Brickley and K.M. Smith, *The Fertile Ground: Papers in Honour of Professor Susan Limbrey*.

Hedges, R.E.M., Housley, R.A., Law, I.A. and Perry, C. 1988. Radiocarbon dates from the Oxford AMS system: Archaeometry datelist 7, *Archaeometry* **30** (1), 155–164.

Holyoak, D.T. and Preece, R.C. 1985. Late Pleistocene interglacial deposits at Tattershall, Lincolnshire, *Phil. Trans. Roy. Soc. London* **B331**, 193–236.

Housley, R.A., Gamble, C.S., Street, M. and Pettitt, P. 1997. Radiocarbon evidence for the Lateglacial human recolonisation of Northern Europe, *Proc. Prehist. Soc.* **63**, 25–54.

Howard, A.J. 1992. The Quaternary Geology and Geomorphology of the area between Newark and Lincoln. Unpublished PhD thesis, University of Derby.

Howard, A.J. 1995. Patterned ground in the Lower Trent Valley, near Brough, between Newark and Lincoln, *Mercian Geol.* **13**, 183–186.

Howard, A.J., Bateman, M.D., Garton, D., Green, F.M.L., Wagner, P. and Priest, V. 1999b. Evidence of Late Devensian and early Flandrian processes and environments in the Idle Valley at Tiln, North Nottinghamshire, *Proc. Yorkshire Geol. Soc.* **52**, 383–393.

Howard, A.J., Keen, D.H. and Hollin, J.T. 1999a. Amino acid dating of a molluscan fauna from Bassingham Fen, Lincolnshire: implications for the chronology of the Trent Terraces, *Proc. Geol. Assoc.* **110**, 233–239.

Jacobi, R. and Garton, D. 1999. Palaeolithic artifacts, in L. Elliott and D. Knight, An early Mesolithic site and first millennium BC settlement and pit alignments at Swarkstone Lowes, Derbyshire, 115–116.

Jacobi, R. and Grün, R. 2003. ESR dates from Robin Hood Cave, Creswell Crags, Derbyshire, UK and the age of its Neanderthal occupation, *Quat. Newslett.* **100**, 1–12.

Jacobi, R., Garton, D. and Brown, J. 2001. Field-walking and the late Upper Palaeolithic of Nottinghamshire, *Trans. Thoroton Soc. Nottinghamshire*, **105**, 17–22.

Jacobi, R., Rowe, P.J., Gilmour, M.A., Grun, R. and Atkinson, T.C. 1998. Radiometric dating of the Middle Plaeolithic tool industry and associated fauna of Pin Hole Cave, Creswell Crags, England, *J. Quat. Sci.* **13** (1), 29–42.

Jenkinson, R.D.S. 1984. *Creswell Crags: Late Pleistocene Sites in the East Midlands.* BAR Brit. Ser. **122**.

Jones, P.F. and Charsley, T.J. 1985. A re-appraisal of the denudation chronology of south Derbyshire, England, *Proc. Geol. Assoc.* **96** (1), 73–86.

Jones, P.F. and Stanley, M.F. 1974. Ipswichian mammalian fauna from the Beeston Terrace at Boulton Moor, near Derby, *Geol. Mag.* **111**, 515–520.

Keen, D.H., Bateman, M.D., Coope, G.R., Field, M.H., Langford, H.E., Merry, J.S. and Mighall, T.M. 1999. Sedimentology, palaeoecology and geochronology of Last Interglacial deposits from Deeping St James, Lincolnshire, England, *J. Quat. Sci.* **14**, 411–436.

Keen, D.H., Coope, G.R., Jones, R.L., Field, M.H., Griffiths, H.I., Lewis, S.G. and Bowen, D.Q. 1997. Middle Pleistocene deposits at Froghall Pit, Stretton on Dunsmore, Warwickshire, England, and their implications for the age of the type Wolstonian, *J. Quat. Sci.* **12**, 183–208.

Kinsley, G. and Knight, D. 1992. Archaeology of the Fosse Way. Vol. 2: Newark to Widmerpool. Unpublished report, Trent & Peak Archaeological Trust, University Park, Nottingham.

Knox, R. 2001. An archaeological resource assessment of Palaeolithic Leicestershire and Rutland, *East Midlands Archaeological Research Framework*. http://www.le.ac.uk/a/pdf-files/emidpal.pdf.

Lewis, S.G. 1998. Quaternary stratigraphy and Lower Palaeolithic archaeology of the Lark Valley, Suffolk, in N. Ashton, F. Healy and P. Pettitt (eds), *Stone Age Archaeology: Essays in Honour of John Wymer*, 43–51.

Lewis, S.G. 1999. Eastern England, in D.Q. Bowen (ed), *A Revised Correlation of Quaternary Deposits in the British Isles,* 10–27.

Linton, D.L. 1951. Midland drainage: some considerations bearing on its origin, *Brit. Ass. Advancement Sci.* **11** (28), 449–456.

Lister, A.M. and Brandon, A. 1991. A pre-Ipswichian cold stage mammalian fauna from the Balderton Sand and Gravel, Lincolnshire, England, *J. Quat. Sci.* **6** (2), 139–157.

Lister, A.M., Keen, D.H. and Crossling, J. 1990. Elephant and molluscan remains from the basal levels of the Bagington-Lillington gravels at Snitterfield, Warwickshire, *Proc. Geol. Assoc.* **101** (3), 203–212.

Lowe, J.J. and Walker, M.J.C. 1997. *Reconstructing Quaternary Environments*. Harlow: Longman.

McNabb, J. 2001. An archaeological resource assessment and research agenda for the Palaeolithic of the East Midlands (part of Western Doggerland), *East Midlands Archaeological Research Framework*. http://www.le.ac.uk/a/pdf-files/emidpal.pdf.

Maddy, D. 1997. Uplift-driven valley incision and river terrace formation in southern England, *J. Quat. Sci.* **12**, 539–545.

Maddy, D. 1999a. Middle Pleistocene reconstruction of the Baginton River Basin: implications for the Thames drainage basin, in P. Andrews and R. Banham (eds), *Late Cenozoic Environments and Hominid Evolution: a Tribute to Bill Bishop*, 169–182.

Maddy, D. 1999b. English Midlands, in D.Q. Bowen (ed), *A Revised Correlation of Quaternary Deposits in the British Isles*, 28–44.

Maddy, D., Coope, G.R., Gibbard, P.L., Green, C.P. and Lewis, S.G. 1994. Reappraisal of Middle Pleistocene fluvial deposits near Brandon, Warwickshire and their significance for the Wolston glacial sequence, *J. Geol. Soc. London* **151**, 221–233.

Maddy, D., Green, C.P., Lewis, S.G. and Bowen, D.Q. 1995. Pleistocene geology of the Lower Severn Valley, UK, *Quat. Sci. Rev.* **14**, 209–222.

May, J. 1966. Prehistory, in K.C. Edwards (ed), *Nottingham and its Region*, 177–190.

Membury, S. 2001. An archaeological resource assessment of the Palaeolithic in Lincolnshire, *East Midlands Archaeological Research Framework*. http://www.le.ac.uk/a/pdf-files/emidpal.pdf.

Miller, G.H. and Hollin, J.T. 1991. Amino acid epimerization dates from the Balderton Sand and Gravel, Appendix 6 in A. Brandon and M.G. Sumbler, The Balderton Sand and Gravel: pre-Ipswichian cold stage fluvial deposits near Lincoln, England, 136–137.

Morgan, A. 1973. Late Pleistocene environmental changes indicated by fossil insect faunas of the English Midlands, *Boreas* **2**, 173–212.

Murton, J.B., Baker, A., Bowen, D.Q., Caseldine, C.J., Coope, G.R., Currant, A.P., Evans, J.G., Field, M.H., Green, C.P., Hatton, J., Ito, M., Jones, R.L., Keen, D.H., Kerney, M.P., McEwan, R., McGregor, D.F.M., Parish, D., Robinson, J.E., Schreve D.C. and Smart, P.L. 2001. A Middle Pleistocene temperate-periglacial-temperate sequence (Oxygen Isotope Stages 7-5e) near Marsworth, Buckinghamshire, UK, *Quat. Sci. Rev.* **20**, 1787–1825.

Myers, A. 2001. An archaeological resource assessment of the Palaeolithic in Derbyshire, *East Midlands Archaeological Research Framework*. http://www.le.ac.uk/a/pdf-files/emidpal.pdf.

Myers, A. 2003. The Upper Palaeolithic and Mesolithic archaeology of the West Midlands region, *West Midlands Regional Research Framework for Archaeology Seminar 1*. http://www.arch-ant.bham.ac.uk/wmrrfa/sem1.htm.

Neale, J. and Flenley, D. (eds) 1981. *The Quaternary in Britain: Essays, Reviews and Original Work on the Quaternary*. Oxford: Pergamon Press.

O'Brien, C. 1978. Land and settlement in Nottinghamshire and lowland Derbyshire, *E. Midlands Archaeol. Bull.* **12**.

Pennington, W. 1986. Lags in adjustment of vegetation to climate caused by the pace of soil developments: evidence from Britain, *Vegetatio* **67**, 105–118.

Pennington, W. and Bonny, A.P. 1970. Absolute pollen diagram from the British Late-glacial, *Nature* **226**, 871–873.

Pitts, M. and Roberts, M.B. 1997. *Fairweather Eden: Life in Britain Half a Million Years Ago as Revealed by Excavations at Boxgrove*. London: Century.

Pocock, T.I. 1929. The Trent Valley in the glacial period. *Zeitschrift für Gletscherkunde* **17**, 302–318.

Posnansky, M. 1960. The Pleistocene succession in the Middle Trent Basin, *Proc. Geol. Assoc.* **71**, 285–311.

Posnansky, M. 1963.   The Lower and Middle Palaeolithic industries of the English East Midlands, *Proc. Prehist. Soc.* **29**, 357–394.

Rice, J. 1991.   Distribution and provenance of the Baginton Sand and Gravel in the Wreake Valley, northern Leicestershire, England: implications for inter-regional correlation, *J. Quat. Sci.* **6** (1), 39–54.

Richer, P. 1991.   A Reappraisal of the Significance of L.A. Armstrong's Researches in the Trent Valley Gravels. Unpublished BA dissertation, Department of Archaeology, University of Nottingham.

Roe, D. 1981.   *The Lower and Middle Palaeolithic Periods in Britain.* London: Routledge and Kegan Paul.

Rose, J. 1985.   The Dimlington Stadial/Chronozone: a proposal for renaming the main glacial episode of the Late Devensian in Britain, *Boreas* **14**, 225–230.

Rose, J. 1987.   The status of the Wolstonian glaciation in the British Quaternary, *Quat. Newslett.* **53**, 1–9.

Rose, J. 1994.   Major river systems of central and southern Britain during the Early and Midddle Pleistocene, *Terra Nova* **6** (5), 435–443.

Rose, J., Moorlock, B.S.P. and Hamblin, R.J.O. 2001.   Pre-Anglian fluvial and coastal deposits in Eastern England: lithostratigraphy and palaeoenvironments, *Quat. International* **79**, 5–22.

Schreve, D.C. 1999.   Bielsbeck Farm, East Yorkshire (SE 861378), in D.R. Bridgland, B.P. Horton and J.B. Innes, *The Quaternary of North East England: Field Guide,* 176–179.

Schreve, D.C. 2001.   Mammalian evidence from Middle Pleistocene fluvial sequences for complex environmental change at the Oxygen Isotope Substage level, *Quat. International* **79**, 65–74.

Schreve, D.C., Bridgland, D.R., Allen, P., Blackford, J.J., Gleed-Owen, C.P., Griffiths, H.I., Keen, D.H. and White, M.J. 2002.   Sedimentology, palaeontology and archaeology of late Middle Pleistocene River Thames terrace deposits at Purfleet, Essex, UK, *Quat. Sci. Rev.* **21**, 1423–1464.

Shotton, F.W. 1953.   The Pleistocene deposits of the area between Coventry, Rugby and Leamington, and their bearing upon the topographic development of the Midlands, *Phil. Trans. Roy. Soc. London,* **B254**, 387–400.

Shotton, F.W., Keen, D.H., Coope, G.R., Current, A.P., Gibbard, P.L., Aalto, M., Peglar, S.M. and Robinson, J.E. 1993.   The middle Pleistocene deposits at Waverley Wood Pit, Warwickshire, England, *J. Quat. Sci.* **8**, 293–325.

Smith, D.N., Brickley, M.B. and Smith, K.M. in press.   *The Fertile Ground: Papers in Honour of Professor Susan Limbrey.* Oxford: Oxbow Books.

Stevenson, I.P. and Mitchell, G.H. 1955.   *Geology of the country between Burton on Trent, Rugeley and Uttoxeter.* Mem. Geol. Surv. GB. London: HMSO.

Straw, A. 1963.   The Quaternary evolution of the Lower and Middle Trent, *E. Midlands Geogr.* **3**, 171–189.

Straw, A. 1970.   Wind-gaps and water-gaps in eastern England, *E. Midlands Geogr.* **5** (1,2), 97–106.

Straw, A. 1979.   Eastern England, in A. Straw and K.M. Clayton, *Eastern and Central England. Geomorphology of the British Isles,* 1–139.

Straw, A. 2002.   The Late Devensian ice limit in the Humberhead area – a reappraisal, *Quat. Newslett.* **97**, 1–10.

Straw, A. and Clayton, K.M. 1979.   *Eastern and Central England. Geomorphology of the British Isles.* London and New York: Methuen.

Sumbler, M.G. 1995.   The terraces of the River Thames and their bearing on the chronology of glaciation in central and eastern England, *Proc. Geol. Ass.* **106**, 93–106.

Swinnerton, H.H. 1937.   The problem of the Lincoln Gap, *Trans. Lincolnshire Naturalists' Union* **9**, 145–158.

Thomas, J. and Jacobi, R. 2001.   Glaston, *Curr. Archaeol.* **173**, 180–184.

Toms, E. 1995.   The Lower and Middle Palaeolithic of Lincolnshire and Nottinghamshire, with Special Reference to Beeston. Unpublished BA dissertation, Department of Archaeology, University of Nottingham.

Ussher, W.A.E. 1888.   *The Geology of the Country around Lincoln.* Mem. Geol. Surv. GB. London: HMSO.

Wenban-Smith, F.F. 1995.   The Ebbsfleet Valley, Northfleet (Baker's Hole) TQ 615735, in D.R. Bridgland, P. Allen and B.A. Haggart, *The Quaternary of the Lower Thames: Field Guide,* 147–174.

White, M. 1997.   The earlier Palaeolithic occupation of the Chilterns (southern England): reassessing the sites of Worthington G. Smith, *Antiquity* **71**, 912–931.

White, M.J. and Jacobi, R.M. 2002.   Two sides to every story: *bout coupé* handaxes revisited, *Oxford J. Archaeol.* **21** (2), 109–133.

Wymer, J.J. 1999.   *The Lower Palaeolithic Occupation of Britain.* Salisbury: Wessex Archaeology and English Heritage.

3   MESOLITHIC HUNTER-GATHERERS

ANDY J. HOWARD AND DAVID KNIGHT

3.1   Introduction

Attention is focused in this chapter upon the period from after the disappearance of the 'long blade' industries, dated currently from between *c*.10300 and *c*.9700 BP, to the beginning of the Neolithic, from *c*.5200 BP. The period may be divided on the basis of changes in lithic tool technology into an earlier and later Mesolithic, the transition between which may be placed within the mid-ninth millennium BP (*c*.8650 BP according to Myers 2001b, 5). In technological terms, earlier Mesolithic industries within the region may be distinguished by their emphasis upon large non-geometric microliths made by the micro-burin technique, and include a range of obliquely blunted points, isosceles triangles and elongated trapezes, also end-scrapers on flakes and blades, burins and tranchet adzes (e.g. Swarkestone Lowes, Derbyshire: Figs 3.6–7; Garton and Brown 1999; Misterton Carr, Nottinghamshire: Buckland and Dolby 1973). The later Mesolithic, by contrast, is characterised by a wide range of smaller microliths, including scalene and isosceles triangles, straight-backed bladelets, oblique points, rhomboids and lunates (e.g. Newton Cliffs, near Newton-on-Trent, Lincolnshire: Fig. 3.9; Garton *et al.* 1989, 114–9, 127–41). Full details of these technological changes and the problematic relationship between 'long blade' and earlier Mesolithic lithic industries are considered at length elsewhere (e.g. Barton 1998; Jacobi 1973; 1976; 1978; Mellars 1974) and here discussion will concentrate upon the evidence for landscape change between the earlier and later Mesolithic and developments in the social and economic structure of the hunter-gatherer groups who exploited the rich valley environment of the Early Holocene. As in previous periods, human groups were both small and highly mobile, and discussion must extend beyond the confines of the Trent Valley to neighbouring regions.

Little work has been carried out in the Trent Valley by comparison with nearby areas such as the gritstone uplands of the southern Pennines (e.g. Jacobi 1978; Jacobi *et al.* 1976; Radley and Marshall 1965; Radley and Mellars 1964; Spikens 1999), the Magnesian limestone escarpment of north-eastern Derbyshire (e.g. Armstrong 1925; 1929; 1937; 1956; Jenkinson 1984), the Carboniferous limestone of the White Peak (e.g. Bramwell 1959; 1971; Chadwick and Evans 2000; Kelly 1976) and the coversands of north Lincolnshire (e.g. Armstrong 1932; Dudley 1949). Indeed, the Mesolithic of this region escaped serious scrutiny well into the 1960's, until Manby (1963) brought together the limited lithic evidence from sites in the middle and upper reaches of the Trent Valley. Another milestone in the history of Mesolithic studies in the Valley was the discovery at Misterton Carr in the late 1960's of a major earlier Mesolithic finds scatter (Buckland and Dolby 1973). This artefact collection was of a scale hitherto unimagined in the Valley and, despite the absence of associated structural and environmental remains, provided some indication of the

appeal which the well-wooded and wetland environments of the Lower Trent and Idle Valleys may have exerted for early post-glacial communities in search of faunal and plant resources. Since then, the expansion of developer-funded excavations and field surveys has added significantly to the available evidence – most notably at excavated sites such as Staythorpe, Nottinghamshire (Davies 2001) and Swarkestone Lowes (Elliott and Knight 1999), and during systematic field walking surveys at sites such as Collingham, Nottinghamshire (Knight and Kennett 1994) and along the Fosse Way from Newark in Nottinghamshire to Widmerpool in Leicestershire (Kinsley and Knight 1992). The region has also benefited from several recent syntheses of the Mesolithic of northern England, notably by Jacobi (1978) and Spikens (1999). Most recently, syntheses of the Trent Valley have been prepared by Myers (2001b; 2003) as part of the East and West Midlands Archaeological Research Framework projects (see also Bishop 2001; Knox 2001; Membury 2001; Myers 2001a).

3.2   The Environmental Background

The onset of the Holocene was marked by a rapid climatic amelioration throughout Britain. Botanical and Coleopteran records indicate that temperatures broadly comparable to those of today were reached within several hundred years, between *c*.9800 and *c*.9500 BP (Atkinson *et al.* 1987; Coope and Lemdahl 1995). The retreat of the ice sheets led to eustatic (global) sea level rise, from around –55m OD at the onset of the Holocene to present day levels by *c*.6000 BP (*c*.4900 cal BC: Tooley and Shennan 1987), although local factors such as subsidence led to some regional variation (*cf.* Chapter 4.2).

3.2.1   Geomorphology

In the lowest parts of the Trent Valley, the plug of glacial material blocking the Humber Estuary was breached (Chapter 2.7.1). This permitted the newly established rivers of the region to incise their courses locally down to –20m OD, in response to continuing low sea levels. Through time, marine transgression, associated with climatic amelioration, resulted in sedimentation and infilling of these incised courses (Gaunt 1981; 1994; Kirby 2001; Long *et al.* 1998; Metcalfe *et al.* 2000). By around 6100 BP (*c*.5000 cal BC), the mean high water of spring tides was at about –10m OD, and there are indications that saline waters were encroaching into the lower Yorkshire Ouse system (and most probably the lower Trent). The intercalation of freshwater peats and marine clays dating to around 5300 BP (*c*.4100 cal BC) which has been recorded in the Lower Trent north of Gainsborough, Lincolnshire, indicates the delicate balance between marine and freshwater processes. In the lower Trent, peat beds have been recorded within and beneath the alluvium flanking the deeply incised river

Fig.3.1 *Holocene pollen and climatic zones. Reproduced by permission of Pearson Education Ltd from M. Bell and M. J. C. Walker 1992, Late Quaternary Environmental Change*

Period	Climate	Evidence
Sub-Atlantic	cold and wet	poorly-humidified *Sphagnum* peat
Sub-Boreal	warm and dry	pine stumps in humidified peat
Atlantic	warm and wet	poorly-humidified *Sphagnum* peat
Boreal	warm and dry	pine stumps in humidified peat
Pre-Boreal	subarctic	macrofossils of subarctic plants in peat

(a)

Years before present	Pollen zone		Blytt-Sernander period	Climate
—1000 —2000	VIII	F1-III	Sub-Atlantic	Deterioration
—3000 —4000 —5000	VIIb		Sub-Boreal	Climatic optimum
—6000 —7000	VIIa	F1-II	Atlantic	
—8000 —9000	VI	F1-I	Boreal	Rapid amelioration
	V			
—10000	IV		Pre-Boreal	
	III		Younger Dryas	Cold
—11000	II		Alleröd	Rapid amelioration

Fig. 3.2 *The River Trent as it may have appeared during the early Holocene: a multi-channelled (anastomosed) river system with extensive areas of wetland, flowing through a heavily forested landscape (photograph: A.J. Howard)*

to 9130 ± 70 BP (Beta-70228, 8540–8230 cal BC), the pollen spectrum suggests a wooded landscape dominated by scots pine and birch with high frequencies of fern spores (Brayshay 1994). The limited spatial extent of the deposit provides little information on fluvial environments, other than the observation that the density of vegetation on the floodplain was sufficient to provide a supply of material for organic accumulation and that floodplain processes allowed sediment preservation. Despite its limitations, the pollen data-set recorded by Brayshay (1994) provides a useful snapshot of early post-glacial riverine landscapes and processes in the Middle Trent Valley.

In the tributary valley of the River Dove at Dove Bridge, Derbyshire, organic silt sampled from scour hollows within the top of a sand and gravel unit and dated to 9370 ± 60 BP (Beta-100929, 8800–8450 cal BC) yielded a small but diverse insect fauna providing valuable environmental evidence (Smith 1996). The majority comprised water beetles that are often associated with fast-flowing water running over sand and gravel substrates, including *Hydraena riparia* and Elmids (commonly known as Riffle beetles) such as *Helichus substriatus, Elmis aenea, Esolus parallelepipedus, Oulimnius* spp. and *Limnius volckmari* (Friday 1988). Some of these invertebrates are clearly indicative of woodland, including *Haplocnemus nigricornis* and *Phloeotrya rufipes*, which are associated with decaying and fallen timbers on the woodland floor. The scolytids *Ptelobius vittatus* and *Scolytus scolytus* are associated with elm trees. *Curculio* species of the size recorded are often associated with oak, while *Dryocoetes alni* are commonly associated with alder (Koch 1992). In combination, therefore, these species suggest a mature and stable woodland environment.

Although increasing vegetation cover may have reduced the impact of geomorphological processes, there is still evidence for some landscape instability around this time. At the north Nottinghamshire site of Tiln in the Idle Valley, for example, thermoluminescence dating has shown that coversands were being reworked on the valley floor from around 8500 BP (Fig.3.3; Howard *et al.* 1999). Whether this was a result of natural environmental change such as

course, and may have been initiated during the wetter climate and changing groundwater conditions of the Atlantic, around 7000 BP; most of these peat beds, however, are probably a few thousand years younger (Gaunt 1994; Lillie 1998).

In lowland river landscapes, particularly those of midland and southern Britain, several studies indicate that the combination of low channel gradients and the predominance of fine-grained sediment and vegetated channel banks resulted in the development of stable, possibly multi-channelled (anastomosed) river systems (Smith 1983) from the early Holocene (Fig.3.2; Brown 1987; Brown *et al.* 1994; Rose *et al.* 1980). In the Trent Valley, the earliest record of post-glacial fluvial environments is derived from the palynological assessment of a thin bed of peat infilling a small channel at Shardlow Quarry in the Middle Trent Valley to the south of Derby. Dated by a fragment of wood

Fig.3.3 *Tiln, Nottinghamshire: late Devensian organic sediments overlain by a palaeosol buried beneath coversand deposits containing a dense Mesolithic flintwork assemblage. Thermoluminescence dating has demonstrated that the coversands were reworked around 8500 BP, possibly due to human interference of vegetation (photograph: A.J. Howard)*

increased aridity or due to human activity remains unclear. Associated lithic artefacts suggest extensive Mesolithic activity, but it is doubtful whether this would have impacted significantly upon the environment. Extensive sheets of coversand have been observed blanketing terrace deposits elsewhere in the Lower Trent Valley, notably around Girton and Collingham in Nottinghamshire, and it is possible that similar reworking occurred there also.

3.2.2   Vegetational and Faunal Change

Climatic amelioration during the early Holocene caused tree species to migrate north from their southern refuges, with initial colonisation by birch and pine woodland. This was replaced over time by mixed deciduous forest comprising hazel and elm, followed by oak, lime, alder and ash (Bennett 1983). The broad characteristics of the early Holocene vegetational history of the Midlands are provided by a number of published sequences. At Crosby Mere, Shropshire, Beales (1980) has noted that birch woodland had developed by c.10300 BP, replacing juniper. Mixed deciduous forest developed, initially with the expansion of hazel accompanied by oak and elm. Pine expanded about 8500 BP and was well established by c.7900 BP (c.6700 cal

BC). At Kings Pool, Stafford, Bartley and Morgan (1990) recorded an early Holocene vegetational record dominated by open woodland, scrub and heath vegetation whose major components included birch, juniper, crowberry and heather. From around 7000 BP (c.5800 cal BC), alder and lime increased at the expense of pine. These vegetational changes would have been accompanied by some dramatic changes in the range of fauna, including the appearance of red and roe deer, aurochs, boar and elk, thus providing a rich source of meat for hunter-gatherer populations – as recorded in the isotopic composition of human bone recovered from excavations at Staythorpe (Davies 2001; Chapter 3.3.4).

At present, long palaeoenvironmental sequences dating to the early Holocene are only known from the Lower Trent Valley, where the wide floodplain has provided suitable conditions for these relatively old records to be preserved. Pollen and Coleopteran remains have been studied in detail at Bole Ings, Girton and Staythorpe in Nottinghamshire, and demonstrate that by at least 7500 cal BC large channels were being abandoned, infilled by organic material and preserved on the valley floor of the Lower Trent. At Rampton, Nottinghamshire, a single radiocarbon age estimate on peat of 8450 ± 90 BP (Beta-159220, 7610–7200 cal BC) confirms this organic sedimentation, although no palaeoenvironmental analyses were undertaken on this deposit (Howard and Knight 2001).

Bole Ings

At Bole Ings, close to Gainsborough, analysis of a c.8m thickness of organic-rich sediment from one borehole has provided the most complete record of palaeoenvironments for the Trent Valley, for a period of about 6500 years between c.8200 and c.2200 BP (Fig.3.4; Dinnin 1997; Dinnin and Brayshay 1999). The palaeobiological data illustrate that the early to mid-Holocene landscape of c.8200–6300 BP was characterised by a wooded floodplain with scots pine on gravel islands and ridges, willow and poplar along the riverbank, and wetland margins and deciduous hardwoods of oak, lime and elm at some distance on drier areas of the floodplain. The low frequencies of plants and Coleoptera associated with disturbed ground and grassland suggest that such open habitats were a relatively minor but persistent component of the vegetation mosaic. The sediments of four additional boreholes were dominated by coarse sands and gravels, which have been interpreted as high energy braided river deposits laid down in a series of unstable channels shifting across the valley floor. The Coleopteran remains corroborate the assemblage of tree species identified from pollen, while the increasingly diverse saproxylic component of the Coleopteran assemblage indicates the increasing abundance of dead wood within the forest of the floodplain. Overall the environment probably comprised relatively fast-flowing, clear, well-oxygenated waters, but with areas of stagnant, weed-choked water, fringed by reedswamp. The braided channel system at Bole Ings was replaced progressively by a stabilised, anastomosed or single channel river regime, probably as rising sea levels altered floodplain hydrology and vegetation stabilised unconsolidated bank-side sediments. Elsewhere in the Midlands, there is evidence for the progressive abandonment of secondary

Fig. 3.4 *Bole Ings, Nottinghamshire: pollen percentage diagram for selected taxa, Borehole C; depth in cm. Reproduced with the permission of the Geological Society of London and Drs M. Dinnin and B. Brayshay*

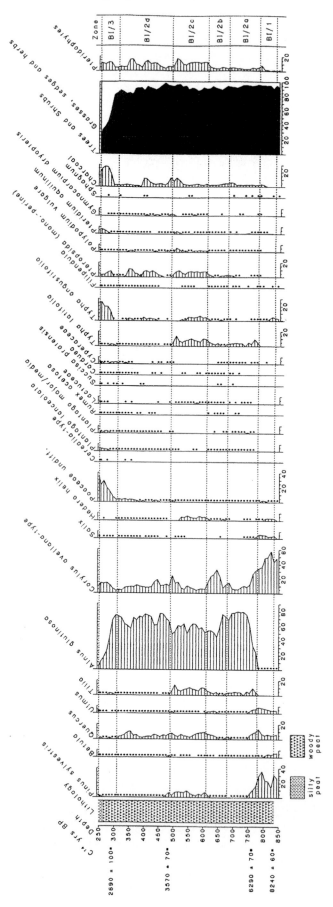

braid channels as part of this development towards a more stable floodplain system (Brown *et al.* 1994).

Around 6300 BP, alder carr woodland developed on the floodplain at Bole Ings. This may have been a response to continuing changes in catchment hydrology associated with sea level change and rising groundwater tables leading to waterlogging. In the understorey of the fen carr, ground cover included ferns, and woody climbing plants such as common ivy. However, despite this change in the riparian corridor, the continued expansion of oak, elm and lime suggests that overall there was less overbank flooding and increased stabilisation of the floodplain landscape.

Girton

At Girton, approximately 25 km upstream of Bole Ings, a *c.*2.5m thickness of sediment from a peat-infilled palaeochannel has provided a palaeoenvironmental record from a broadly similar time period ranging from *c.*8000–2800 BP (Grattan 1990; Green 1991; Dinnin 1992; Lillie and Gearey 1992; D. Garton: pers. comm., unpublished radiocarbon dates). Ten samples were taken from the peaty material within the palaeochannel described by Grattan (1990) for palynological analysis (Green 1991). The lowest part of the sequence (Samples 10–9) was dominated by non-tree pollen, principally herbaceous grasses and sedges. Other herbaceous species typical of wet environments were present, including bulrush. The limited tree pollen comprised birch, pine and shrubs such as hazel. Tree pollen increased from Sample 8 upwards, notably from oak, alder and elm, while pine and birch decreased in abundance. Hazel declined slightly from Sample 6 upwards, but nonetheless remained a prominent feature of the flora. Sedge pollen also decreased over time, but grasses increased in abundance (peaking around Sample 4). The pollen indicates a mixed woodland environment, with increasing oak, alder and elm and decreasing birch, pine and (to a lesser extent) hazel, presumably in response to the onset of warmer, wetter, more oceanic climatic conditions. The basal layers were correlated by Green (1991) with the Early Boreal period and the upper samples with the Boreal/Atlantic transition. The composition of the assemblage suggests that woodland may have existed quite close to the channel, although the pine pollen is more durable and could have been derived from a considerable distance. The earliest radiocarbon date on the basal part of the sequence is 8170 ± 60 BP (AA-29318, 7450–7050 cal BC) with an upper age limit of 2890 ± 60 BP (AA-29321, 1290–900 cal BC).

Staythorpe

The excavation of two borrow pits at the site of Staythorpe Power Station, Nottinghamshire, led to the identification of three palaeochannels, two of which were dated by radiocarbon to the later Mesolithic. Palaeochannel B yielded age estimates of 6180 ± 60 BP (Beta-142214, 5300–4860 cal BC) and 6070 ± 60 BP (Beta-142215, 5210–4790 cal BC) on reeds and wood respectively. Palaeochannel C yielded age estimates of 6040 ± 70 BP (Beta-142218, 5210–4730 cal BC) on wood, 6790 ± 40 BP on human bone (Beta-144016, 5740–5620 cal BC) and 6640 ± 60 BP on wood adjacent to the bone (Beta-142217, 5670–5470 cal BC) and suggests that this channel was infilled over a period of a thousand years. The human remains were recovered from the palaeochannel, together with animal bone showing evidence of butchery (Fig.3.10–11). As described in Chapter 3.3.4, the recovery of Mesolithic human remains, evidence of butchery and the associated stable isotope analyses of the human bone make this research at Staythorpe nationally important.

The analyses of pollen and Coleopteran remains provide a detailed picture of the environmental setting of later Mesolithic human activity within the area (Davies 2001). Pollen evidence suggests that the floodplain was a mixed alder and willow carr with aspen also present. Away from the floodplain, oak, hazel, sloe, red berried elder, dogwood and birch grew on the higher, drier terraces, with lime at the floodplain margins and damp grassland within the understorey. Water-abraded, macroscopic charcoal and charred wood was also recovered, suggesting fire within the landscape (see Chapter 3.3.6).

The list of Coleoptera remains recovered from the later Mesolithic context corroborates the palynological evidence and provides additional information about vegetation type. Species usually associated with aquatic grasses, nettles and deadly nightshade were found, together with species associated with orchards, other rosaceous trees and small-leaved and common lime. Pollen evidence suggested that the floodplain soils were unstable, with tree-throws a common occurrence. This may also be deduced from the Coleoptera assemblage by the recognition of species commonly associated with decaying timber and associated fungi. Despite the recovery of over fifty elminthids of at least six species associated with clean, fast-flowing water, most species suggest little in the way of open water and several indicate wet mud. It is suggested the elminthids were incorporated into the channel during a flood (Davies 2001).

3.3 Hunter-Gatherer Activity

3.3.1 Density of Activity

One of the main results of recent fieldwork has been to demonstrate a significantly higher density of Mesolithic activity within the Valley than was hitherto imagined. This is in stark contrast to the scant distribution of finds recorded by Manby (1963) and later by Wymer (1977), but is in keeping with the accumulating evidence from other areas of the Midlands (e.g. Clay 2002, 109–11; Garton and Brown 1999, 122, Table 6; Myers 2001b, 7–8, 15–17, table 1; 2003, 9). This has resulted mainly from the expansion since 1990 of developer-funded excavation and field survey, which together have revealed a significant number of hitherto unknown activity foci and background artefact scatters in the Valley and neighbouring areas.

The major contribution of large-scale field survey may be illustrated by the results of fieldwalking carried out

in advance of dualling a *c.*28km stretch of the A46 between Newark in Nottinghamshire and Widmerpool in Leicestershire (Kinsley and Knight 1992; Garton and Brown 1999, 123–4). The A46 follows closely the Roman Fosse Way, but from the Mesolithic viewpoint may be viewed as a randomly located transect traversing a wide range of landscape zones, including to the south-west of Newark alluvial and terrace deposits between the Rivers Trent and Devon (Kinsley and Knight 1992, fig.2). Virtually no material of this period had been recorded along the route prior to the survey, but a systematically walked corridor of 100m width either side of the Fosse Way revealed a thin background scatter of Mesolithic material in many fields plus three artefact scatters with slightly higher densities of typologically diagnostic material which could signify later Mesolithic activity foci. The latter were spread over several fields on the Mercia Mudstone escarpment in the vicinity of Cropwell Bishop, Nottinghamshire (*ibid.* fig.38: site B) and the Roman town of *Margidunum,* East Bridgford, Nottinghamshire (*ibid.* fig.38: site D) and on river-terrace deposits to the south of the Roman town of *Ad Pontem*, Thorpe, Nottinghamshire (*ibid.* fig.38: site G, fields 337–347). Interpretation of these artefact scatters is complicated by the very small numbers of finds which may be dated securely to the Mesolithic period (generally one or two per field), the problem of distinguishing typologically later Mesolithic from earlier Neolithic artefacts and the presence on the field surface of other flintwork ranging in date from the Neolithic to Bronze Age periods (*ibid.,* 72, 85, 97; *cf.* Appleton *et al.* 2004, 8–9). Additional evaluation work would be required to investigate further the spatial extent, date range and character of these sites, but at the very least the recorded distribution of surface finds implies a much wider spread of activity than was previously anticipated.

Similar conclusions may be drawn from other locations in the Trent Valley where systematic fieldwalking has been carried out, as at the Nottinghamshire sites of South Muskham (Garton 2002), Collingham (Knight and Kennett 1994; Knight 1994) and Tiln (Garton *et al.* 2003, 7, 12). Intensive fieldwalking of thirty fields around South Muskham revealed a thin background scatter of Mesolithic debitage, diagnosed from the presence of small blades and cores, plus a single microburin on a wide blade (Fig.3.5; Garton 2002, 26, fig.5). At Collingham, fieldwalking of part of the Trent floodplain and a low-lying gravel island in advance of a quarrying application revealed a remarkably high density of prehistoric flintwork on the gravel island (40–62 flints per hectare, comparing with a maximum of 7.7 per hectare at South Muskham: Garton 2002, fig.5). Assessment of this material suggested a later Mesolithic focus along the western margin of the gravel island and a predominance of Neolithic and Bronze Age activity over the remainder of the terrace (Garton 1994). The latter area also preserved one or possibly two clusters of earlier Neolithic/Mesolithic flintwork, raising the possibility of additional early activity areas away from the terrace-edge. The alluvial zone yielded virtually no surface finds of flintwork, the distribution of which could continue beneath later riverine deposits – thus raising the option of well-preserved sub-alluvial Mesolithic levels. Subsequent

Fig. 3.5 *South Muskham, Nottinghamshire: distribution of Mesolithic and later flintwork recovered by fieldwalking (source: Garton 2002; reproduced by permission of D. Garton and the Thoroton Society of Nottinghamshire)*

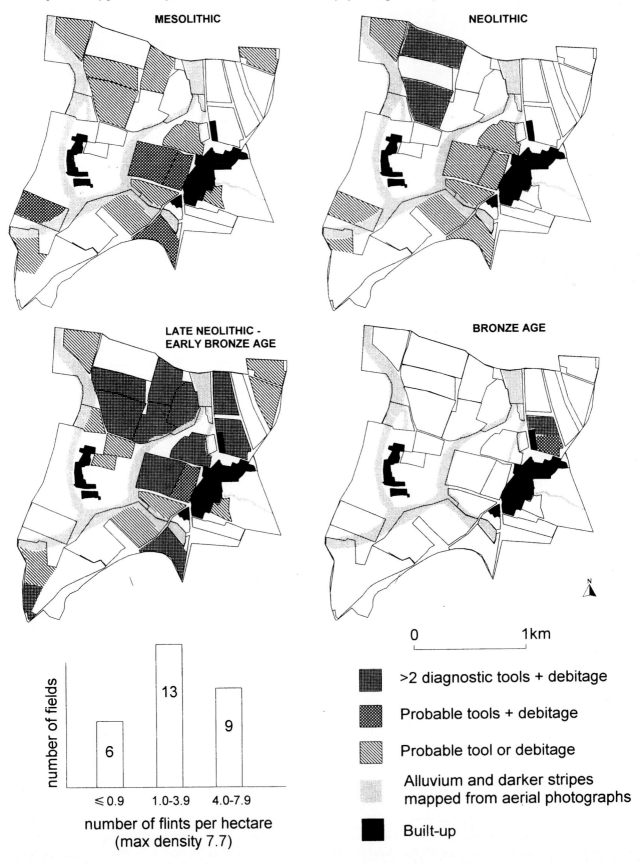

test-pitting of the flint scatter suggested that a substantial proportion of this material could relate to *in situ* activity, but trial excavations yielded no evidence of associated features (Knight 1994).

Farther upstream into Derbyshire, a notable spread of earlier Mesolithic flintwork was recorded at Swarkestone Lowes during fieldwalking and excavations along the crest and upper slopes of a prominent gravel-capped ridge of

Fig. 3.6 *Probable earlier Mesolithic flint cores (1–4) and core rejuvenation flakes from Swarkestone Lowes, Derbyshire (source: Garton and Brown 1999; reproduced by courtesy of D. Garton, J. Brown and the Derbyshire Archaeological Society)*

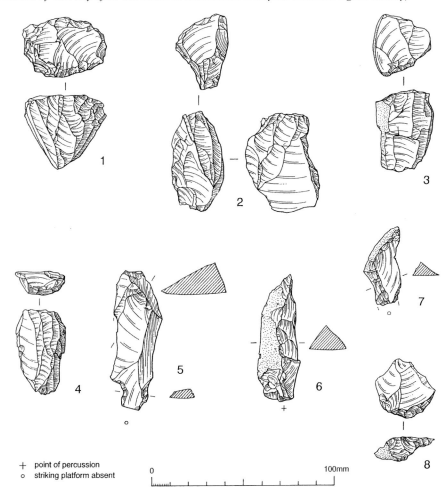

+ point of percussion
o striking platform absent

0   100mm

Fig. 3.7 *Probable earlier Mesolithic flint tools from Swarkestone Lowes, Derbyshire (source: Garton and Brown 1999; reproduced by courtesy of D. Garton, J. Brown and the Derbyshire Archaeological Society)*

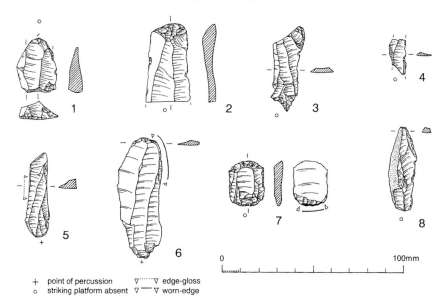

+ point of percussion   ▽┈┈┈▽ edge-gloss
o striking platform absent ▽───▽ worn-edge

0   100mm

Mercia Mudstone (Figs 3.6–7; Garton and Brown 1999). Earlier Mesolithic material was spread widely along the ridge (*ibid.* figs 13–15) but variations in the density of flintwork suggested to the lithic analysts several activity foci, notably around trenches 10, 11 and 19/20 and close

to two Early Bronze Age Barrows (II & IV; *ibid.* 117–8, fig.15).

Although the density of known Mesolithic sites has increased significantly in recent years, problems remain in establishing the character of these sites (Chapter 3.3.3) and changes in their density over time. Too few lithic collections have been analysed in detail for contrasts between the density of earlier and later Mesolithic sites to be established with confidence. However, the impression from surveys such as that carried out along the Fosse Way and around South Muskham, or beyond the Valley on the Magnesian limestone escarpment at Elmton, Derbyshire (Knight *et al.* 1998), is of an increased representation of later Mesolithic sites (*cf.* Manby 1963, 11). This cannot be explained by reference to problems of identification, for earlier Mesolithic material is generally easier to spot as the blades are larger (as at Swarkestone Lowes: Garton and Brown 1999; Figs 3.6–3.7; contrast Fig.3.9). In addition, artefacts of this period were commonly produced from a highly distinctive Wolds-type flint which it is argued below was characteristic mainly of the earlier Mesolithic period throughout the Valley (Chapter 3.3.5). The disparity between the frequencies of earlier and later Mesolithic artefacts is perhaps most simply explained by reference to the significantly greater length of the later Mesolithic period (Chapter 3.1), and although some have raised the possibility of increases in population levels (e.g. Spikens 1999) this argument is at present difficult to sustain. More speculatively, it is worth pondering whether the increased density of finds scatters in the later Mesolithic might equate in part with increased levels of group mobility, which in turn may have impacted upon the density of contemporary activity foci liable to generate significant concentrations of finds (R. Jacobi: pers. comm.).

3.3.2 Spatial Distribution of Activity

Recent survey and excavation work has broadened significantly the distribution of Mesolithic material within the Trent Valley and neighbouring regions (e.g. Myers 2001b, 2003), and would support the view that hunter-gatherers had ranged widely across the Valley terraces and floodplain and into neighbouring ecological zones. Several researchers have drawn attention to an apparent preference for elevated locations which, depending upon woodland cover, would have provided extensive views (Myers 2001b, 21) – as exemplified by the earlier Mesolithic ridge-top site at Swarkestone Lowes (Elliott and Knight 1999). Biases of lithic data towards more elevated ground could also reflect the difficulties of penetrating some of the dense woodlands which would have grown up on the valley bottoms during the Mesolithic as the climate ameliorated. Alternatively, and much more likely, the known distribution of sites could be skewed by natural geomorphological processes, particularly the burial of valley floor sites beneath later alluvial and colluvial material. This process of 'geological filtering' (Bettis and Mandel 2002) has been postulated above with reference to the lithic remains at Collingham and may be illustrated further by the results of excavations at Gonalston, Nottinghamshire (Elliott and Knight in prep.). No surface traces of Mesolithic activity were recorded at the latter site within the area to be quarried, despite prior fieldwalking and evaluation trenching. However, large-scale area stripping of areas sealed beneath thin layers of alluvium revealed a significant concentration of Mesolithic flintwork in one area and a large pit of irregular shape incorporating within its fill a collection of Mesolithic

blades and charcoal. The lithic artefacts could have been redeposited, given that scattered early to late Neolithic pits were recorded close to this feature, or the feature could perhaps relate to a late Mesolithic activity focus preserved beneath later alluvial sediments.

The potential of the valley bottom for the preservation of Mesolithic material is emphasised by occasional discoveries during gravel quarrying on the floodplain and the Holme Pierrepont Terrace of organic artefacts dating from this period. The most notable of these is a small and at present unique bilaterally barbed later Mesolithic antler harpoon with a circular drilled hole at the base for securing the line, obtained from the bank of the Trent in Thrumpton, Nottinghamshire, or Long Eaton, Derbyshire (Fig.3.8; Nottingham City Museums and Galleries: NCMB 1977–770; R. Jacobi and A. Inscker: pers. comm.). Other important finds include the lower end of a later Mesolithic red deer antler beam axe, from the 'Attenborough gravels' near Nottingham (Nottingham University Museum: ATT 66.80 R. Jacobi: pers. comm.) and a shed red deer antler from Holme Pierrepont preserving groove and splinter work comparable to that employed at Star Carr (in Nottingham City Museums and Galleries; R. Jacobi: pers. comm.).

Fig. 3.8 *Bilaterally barbed later Mesolithic antler harpoon from the Trent riverbank at Long Eaton, Derbyshire or Thrumpton, Nottinghamshire; length 98 mm (photograph: A. Inscker)*

3.3.3 Site Morphology and Size

Rare examples have been recorded on sites in the East Midlands of pits, gullies and other features yielding lithic artefacts of Mesolithic type, notably at Lismore Fields, Buxton, Derbyshire (Garton 1987; 1991, 12–13), Croft Quarry, Leicestershire (Hughes and Roseff 1995), Chalk Lane, Northampton (Williams and Shaw 1981) and possibly Unstone, Derbyshire (Ataman 1978; Courtney 1977). In the Trent Valley, rare examples of pits which could conceivably relate to Mesolithic activity have been recorded at Gonalston (Elliott and Knight, in prep.) and during excavations of a flint scatter at Newton Cliffs, Lincolnshire (Fig.3.9; Garton *et al* 1989). At all of these sites, however, interpretation is complicated by the possibility of redeposition of Mesolithic artefacts in features of later date, and on certain sites by the difficulty of distinguishing deliberately dug features from tree-throws – as, for example, at Croft Quarry (Hughes and Roseff 1995) and Lordsmill Street, Chesterfield, Derbyshire (Foundations Archaeology 1999).

With the above exceptions, sites of this period are represented in the Trent Valley solely by unstratified scatters of lithic tools and debitage or by finds, including bone and

Fig.3.9 *Later Mesolithic flint microliths from Newton Cliffs, Lincolnshire (drawing by R. Sheppard)*

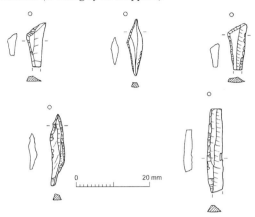

other organic remains, retrieved from palaeochannel fills (e.g. Staythorpe: Davies 2001). Some of these lithic spreads extend over quite extensive areas – notably at Swarkestone Lowes, where it has been suggested that several foci of Mesolithic activity may be identified within a wider scatter extending at least 0.8km along the ridge-top (Garton and Brown 1999, fig.13). Similarly, at Collingham Mesolithic flintwork was observed to extend along the terrace-edge for at least 400m (Knight and Kennett 1994, fig.7), while at Misterton Carr several activity foci extended over an area *c.*700m wide (Buckland and Dolby 1973, fig.2). These scatters, although extensive, may represent many repeat visits to preferred locations, and hence need imply only small hunter-gatherer bands. Detailed analyses of lithic concentrations in the south Pennines and some other areas of the Midlands have suggested a general reduction in site size in the later Mesolithic, as measured by their spatial extent and the size of the lithic collection (Myers 2001b, 8). In the Trent Valley, however, there is currently insufficient detailed evidence to establish significant chronological variations in the spatial extent of sites or by implication the size of the group, and further research on this issue is required.

Attention should be drawn finally to the firm emphasis in the Valley upon open-air sites, in sharp contrast to the neighbouring uplands of the White Peak and the Magnesian limestone escarpment of north-eastern Derbyshire. In those regions evidence for Mesolithic activity has quite commonly been retrieved from caves and rock shelters – notably at the Derbyshire sites of Ash Tree Cave, Whitwell (Armstrong 1956), Whaley, Elmton (Radley 1967) and Mother Grundy's Parlour, Creswell Crags (Armstrong 1925; Jenkinson 1984, 20–35) and in the Manifold Valley on the border of Derbyshire and Staffordshire (Kelly 1976).

3.3.4 Food Procurement Strategies

Detailed quantitative analyses of selected lithic assemblages, including examples from the Trent Valley, have shown a progression towards increasingly complex projectile points – culminating in the later Mesolithic with assemblages dominated by a variety of specialised microlith types (Mellars 1976; Myers 1987). These assemblages contrast strongly with the less specialised assemblages of the

earlier Mesolithic, and have been cited as evidence for the development in the later Mesolithic of more sophisticated hunting strategies (e.g. Myers 2001b, 6–9). Detailed discussion of these strategies is thwarted in many areas by the dearth of associated faunal remains, with the crucial exception of sites such as Star Carr (Clark 1954), and details of the range of game that may have been exploited by communities moving through the Trent Valley remain elusive. One of the most significant finds in this respect is the discovery at Staythorpe of a human female femur, analysis of which has demonstrated a diet with an unexpectedly high emphasis upon animal protein (Fig.3.10; Davies 2001, 83). This rare discovery, radiocarbon dated to 6790 ± 40 BP (Beta-144016, 5740–5620 cal BC), was retrieved from the fill of one of two later Mesolithic palaeochannels, and currently provides the only example of Mesolithic human remains from the Trent Valley. Stable isotope analysis of the femur has revealed a reliance upon animal protein, implying a wholly terrestrial range for the last ten years of life, a dearth of plant foods and no influence of coastal dietary resources (Davies 2001). Red deer and auroch bones, two with cut marks (Fig.3.11), provide clues to some of the hunted species. Too much emphasis should obviously not be placed upon a single specimen, but the Staythorpe find clearly has major implications for our current understanding of the balance between plant and animal foods and the contribution of freshwater and marine resources to Mesolithic food procurement strategies. It also emphasises the potentially crucial role of palaeochannel sequences for furthering our understanding of the Mesolithic, and provides an important vindication of the current emphasis in planning procedures upon the identification and targeted investigation of these landforms prior to development.

Fig. 3.10 *Human female femur from Staythorpe, Nottinghamshire (© ARCUS, University of Sheffield)*

Fig. 3.11 *Red deer antler with cut mark from Staythorpe, Nottinghamshire (© ARCUS, University of Sheffield)*

3.3.5 Patterns of Mobility

Analyses of earlier Mesolithic lithic assemblages from the Trent Valley have provided crucial evidence for the movements of early Holocene hunter-gatherer bands around the increasingly wooded landscapes of the Valley and neighbouring regions (Myers 1989; 2001b, 4). These early hunter-gatherer communities may be shown to have operated over extremely large territories, involving regular annual movements between the southern Pennines and the Trent Valley in pursuit of food and raw material sources (Jacobi 1978, 304). Important evidence in support of this hypothesis has been obtained from analyses of earlier Mesolithic flint collections such as that at Misterton Carr, which in view of the large quantity and wide spatial spread of finds obtained from fieldwalking and excavation may represent a long-established residential base, located in a rich wetland environment (Buckland and Dolby 1973, 6–7), from which task groups had set out on hunting or other missions. The lithic collection from Misterton Carr and from other assemblages such as Swarkestone Lowes includes large blade-cores of Wolds-type flint, which is an opaque mottled grey-cream flint typical of that occurring in the Wolds of Lincolnshire and Yorkshire (Henson 1985, 2–5). Preformed blade-cores of this type may be shown to have been transported to south Pennine sites such as Deepcar (Radley and Mellars 1964), the debitage from which implies knapping on site of imported Wolds-type flint cores. Knapping of these would have created a variety of artefacts which could then have been used to enhance the hunting kits of small groups moving within a complex network of established base camps, temporary encampments and specialised activity foci.

The Wolds-type flint which was recovered from Misterton Carr preserves a highly contused skin indicative of derivation from a high-energy gravel rather than the primary chalk outcrops of the Lincolnshire or Yorkshire Wolds, and could derive from a local valley source such as one of the river terraces (R. Jacobi: pers. comm.). Drift sources may be postulated on other earlier Mesolithic sites within the Valley, although the raw material source cannot always be closely provenanced. At Swarkestone Lowes, for example, approximately one third of the raw material compares with Wolds-type flint, but again had derived from rolled nodules rather than being fresh flint. The locally occurring tills incorporate shattered flint which would have been unsuitable for knapping large flakes and blades, and no other nearby source of suitable flint was located (Garton and Brown 1999, 108). A more distant source may therefore be postulated, probably within a river-gravel context, from which nodules would have been collected and transported – probably without modification in view of the large numbers of flints preserving cortex (*ibid.* 108).

Wolds-type flint apparently occurs in significant quantities only in earlier Mesolithic assemblages in the Trent Valley (*cf.* Jacobi 1978, 302–4). In the later Mesolithic, there is a significant shift of emphasis amongst Valley communities towards a dark grey or brown translucent flint, derived from rolled nodules, which is readily obtainable from the river-gravels (Henson 1989b, 11; e.g. Newton Cliffs: Garton *et al.* 1989, 127–45; *cf.* Garton and Brown 1999, 118–24). Raw material of this type may also be identified in earlier Mesolithic collections in the Valley, notably at Swarkestone Lowes, where significant proportions of a translucent or semi-translucent dark grey or brown flint, sometimes with speckles and mottles, were utilised in the earlier Mesolithic alongside Wolds-type flint. Translucent flint, possibly derived from river-gravel or till sources, is also recorded on earlier Mesolithic sites in the south Pennines, while some later Mesolithic flint industries in the uplands can include significant quantities of translucent and speckled flint (R. Jacobi: pers. comm.). In contrast to the Trent Valley, Wolds flint remained an important component of some later Mesolithic lithic collections from the Pennines, although later assemblages from this area often show a pronounced emphasis upon Carboniferous chert obtained from a range of Pennine limestones (Myers 2001b, 6–7). Chert is also known on earlier Mesolithic sites in the Pennines, but in significantly smaller quantities (R. Jacobi: pers. comm.), suggesting perhaps that in this area an increasing emphasis may have been placed in the later Mesolithic upon easily obtainable local raw materials (Myers 2001b, 6–7).

Mention should also be made of rare discoveries in earlier and later Mesolithic collections from the Trent Valley of pieces of Carboniferous chert derived ultimately from limestone sources in the Pennines – notably from Collingham (Garton 1994), Castle Pit Hill, Melbourne, Derbyshire (Manby 1963, 13–16; A. Myers: pers. comm.), Swarkestone Lowes (Garton and Brown 1999, 108, 116–7) and Newton Cliffs (Henson 1989a, 173). Such artefacts are invariably very few and include small blades (e.g. Swarkestone Lowes: Garton and Brown 1999, 116) and cores (e.g. Collingham, findcode ATV: Garton 1994). Some of this material could have been obtained from Peak District outcrops such as the Eyam or Monsal Dale limestones (Garton and Brown 1999, 108), thus providing additional evidence for links between the Trent Valley and the south Pennines, continuing into the later Mesolithic. This argument may be supported by the discovery of small amounts of chert in flint collections fringing the Peak District (*ibid.* 108), although the issue of sourcing is complicated by the presence of chert in Carboniferous outliers to the south of the Trent (J. Carney: pers. comm.). The argument is complicated further by the presence of small quantities of rolled chert in the gravels of the Trent, which makes a local source possible – as argued at Newton Cliffs, for example, where several chert nodules preserving rolled and battered external surfaces and four river-rolled chert pebbles were recorded (Henson 1989a, 173). The paucity of chert highlights some interesting contrasts with the Magnesian limestone escarpment near Creswell Crags, where black chert artefacts and debitage occur in comparative abundance – implying perhaps that chert had been transported in largely unmodified form some distance from its source (e.g. Elmton: Knight *et al.* 1998).

3.3.6 Human Environmental Impact

Unequivocal evidence that Mesolithic hunter-gatherers had precipitated landscape change within the Trent Valley has yet to be obtained, although it has been noted above that

Fig. 3.12 *Mesolithic sites referred to in the text, compiled by S. Baker*
(1.Ash Tree Cave; 2.Attenborough; 3.Bole Ings; 4.Chesterfield; 5.Collingham; 6.Creswell Crags; 7.Croft; 8.Cropwell Bishop; 9.Deepcar; 10.Dove Bridge; 11.East Bridgford; 12.Elmton; 13.Girton; 14.Gonalston; 15.Holme Pierrepont; 16.Lismore Fields; 17.Long Eaton; 18.Melbourne; 19.Misterton Carr; 20.Newton Cliffs; 21.Northampton; 22.Rampton; 23.Shardlow; 24.South Muskham; 25.Stafford; 26.Staythorpe; 27.Swarkestone Lowes; 28.Tattershall Thorpe; 29.Thorpe; 30.Thorpe Common; 31.Thrumpton; 32.Tiln; 33.Unstone; 34.Whaley)

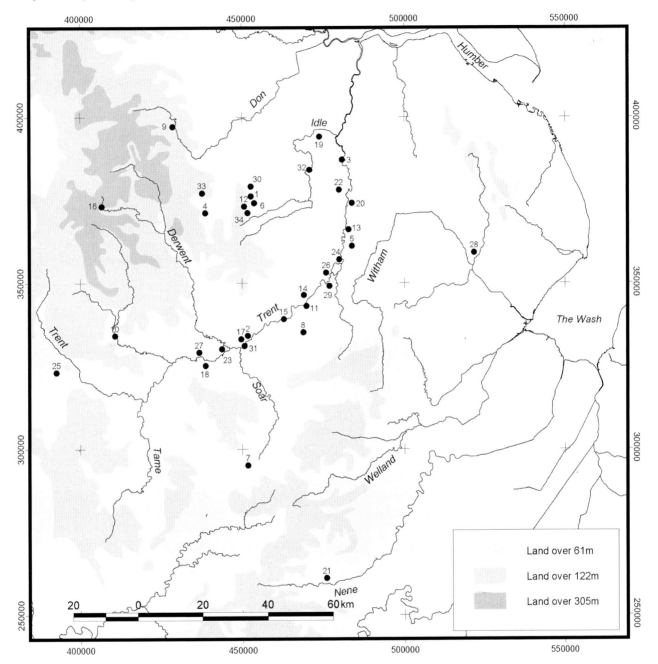

the reworking of coversands at Tiln from *c.*8500 BP could have been due partly to human activity (Chapter 3.2.1; Fig.3.3). Discoveries elsewhere in the Midlands would support the hypothesis that hunter-gatherer communities, particular in the later Mesolithic, may have sought further control over their environment by selective burning and clearance (Jacobi 1978, 325). Regeneration of these cleared areas would have created botanically more diverse and productive woodland clearings, thereby enhancing the browse resource for red deer and other large herbivores (Mellars 1976) and beginning the process of environmental change that accelerated with the agricultural clearances of the Neolithic and later periods. These animals may

have been controlled in part by herding, thus laying the foundations for the more controlled animal husbandry of the Neolithic. Burning may also have been undertaken to encourage the growth of plants for human consumption, while several scholars have raised the possibility of some tending and cultivation of plants (Zvelebil 1994). The possibility of some limited experimentation with cereal cultivation has also been suggested, although this has yet to be demonstrated convincingly by reference to the palaeobotanical or artefact data (Mithen 1999, 54).

Key sites include Lismore Fields, Buxton, where charcoal within pollen samples from the site suggested limited clearance by burning (Wiltshire and Edwards 1993), and various locations on the gritstone East Moors of Derbyshire, where charcoal in organic-rich columns extracted from peat bogs has been argued to imply selective Mesolithic burning of the native woodlands (Hicks 1972; Long, Chambers and Barnatt 1998; Williams 1985). In the Trent Valley, water-abraded macroscopic charcoal and charred wood remains have been recovered from late Mesolithic organic

sediments within a palaeochannel at Staythorpe (Davies 2001), but it is uncertain whether this was the product of human activity. Other data which might signify clearance by burning have yet to be obtained from the Valley, and the identification of such evidence should be regarded as a key research priority in the analysis of palaeochannel fills and other organic deposits from the region.

REFERENCES

Appleton, E., Brown, J., Kinsley, G., Knight, D., Leary, R. and Johnson, T. 2004. A46 Newark to Widmerpool Improvement. Geophysical Survey, Fieldwalking and Landscape Interpretation at Margidunum, Nottinghamshire. Unpublished report, Trent & Peak Archaeological Unit, University Park, Nottingham.

Armstrong, A.L. 1925. Excavations at Mother Grundy's Parlour, Creswell Crags, Derbyshire 1924, *J. Roy. Anthropol. Inst.* **55**.

Armstrong, A.L. 1929. Excavations at Creswell Crags 1924–26, Pin Hole Cave, *Trans. Hunter Archaeol. Soc.* **3**, 116–122.

Armstrong A.L. 1932. Upper Palaeolithic and Mesolithic stations in N. Lincs, *Proc. Prehist. Soc. East Anglia* 7, 130–131.

Armstrong, A.L. 1937. Excavations at Creswell Crags, the Pin Hole Cave 1928–32, *Trans. Hunter Archaeol. Soc.* **4**, 178–184.

Armstrong A.L. 1956. Report on the excavation of Ash Tree Cave, near Whitwell, Derbyshire, 1949 to 1957, *J. Derbyshire Archaeol. Nat. Hist. Soc.* **76**, 57–64.

Ashton, N.M., Healey, F. and Pettit, P.B. (eds) 1998. *Stone Age Archaeology: Essays in Honour of John Wymer.* Lithic Studies Occ. Pap. **6**; Oxbow Monogr. **102**. Oxford: Oxbow Books.

Ashworth, A.C., Buckland, P.C. and Sadler, J.P. (eds) 1997. *Studies in Quaternary Entomology. An Inordinate Fondness for Insects.* Quaternary Proceedings **5**. London: Quaternary Research Association.

Ataman, K. 1978. Excavations at Unstone, Derbyshire, 1978. Unpublished report, North Derbyshire Archaeological Committee.

Atkinson, T.C., Briffa, K.R. and Coope, G.R. 1987. Seasonal temperatures in Britain during the last 22,000 years, reconstructed using beetle remains, *Nature* **325**, 587–592.

Bartley, D.D. and Morgan, A.V. 1990. The palynological record from King's Pool, Stafford, England, *New Phytologist* **116**, 177–194.

Barton, R.N.E. 1998. Long blade technology and the question of the British late Palaeolithic/early Holocene lithic assemblage, in N.M. Ashton, F. Healey and P.B. Pettit (eds), *Stone Age Archaeology: Essays in Honour of John Wymer,* 158–164.

Bateman, M.D., Buckland, P.C., Frederick, C.D. and Whitehouse, N.J. (eds) 2001. *The Quaternary of East Yorkshire and North Lincolnshire: Field Guide.* London: Quaternary Research Association.

Beales, P.W. 1980. The Late Devensian and Flandrian vegetational history of Cross Mere, Shropshire, *New Phytologist* **85**, 520–523.

Bennett, K.D. 1983. Postglacial population expansion of forest trees in Norfolk, UK, *Nature* **303**, 164–167.

Bettis, E.A. and Mandel, R.D. 2002. The effects of temporal and spatial patterns of Holocene erosion and alluviation on the archaeological record of the Central and Eastern Great Plains, USA, *Geoarchaeology* **17**, 141–154.

Bishop, M. 2001. Resource assessment: Palaeolithic and Mesolithic in Nottinghamshire, *East Midlands Archaeological Research Framework Project Stage 1: an Archaeological Resource Assessment.* Draft. University of Leicester Archaeological Services. http://www.le.ac.uk/archaeology/east_midlands_research_framework.htm

Bramwell, D. 1959. Excavation of Dowel Cave, Earl Sterndale, 1958-9, *Derbyshire Archaeol. J.* **79**, 97–109.

Bramwell, D. 1971. Excavations at Foxhole Cave, High Wheeldon, 1961-1970, *Derbyshire Archaeol. J.* **91**, 1–19.

Brayshay, B. 1994. Palynological Assessment of Sediment Sample SLS/02/0011 from Shardlow, Derbyshire. Unpublished Report 175, ARCUS, University of Sheffield.

Brooks, I and Phillips, P. (eds) 1989. *Breaking the Stony Silence: Papers from the Sheffield Lithics Conference 1988.* BAR Brit. Ser. **213**.

Brown, A.G. 1987. Holocene floodplain sedimentation and channel response of the lower Severn, United Kingdom, *Zeitschrift für Geomorphologie* **31**, 293–310.

Brown, A.G. and Edmonds, M. (eds) 1987. *Lithic Analysis and Later British Prehistory.* BAR Brit. Ser. **162.**

Brown, A.G., Keough, M. and Rice, R.J. 1994. Floodplain evolution in the East Midlands, United Kingdom: the Lateglacial and Flandrian alluvial record from the Soar and Nene valleys, *Phil. Trans. Roy. Soc. London* **A348**, 261–293.

Buckland, P.C. and Dolby, M.J. 1973. Mesolithic and later material from Misterton Carr, Notts. – an interim report, *Trans. Thoroton Soc. Nottinghamshire* **77**, 5–33.

Chadwick, A.M. and Evans, H. 2000. Reading Roystone's rocks: landscape survey and lithic analysis from test-pitting at Roystone Grange, Ballidon, Derbyshire, and its implications for previous interpretations of the region, *Derbyshire Archaeol. J.* **120**, 101–122.

Chambers, F.M. (ed) 1993. *Climate Change and Human Impact on the Landscape.* London: Chapman & Hall.

Clark, J.D.G. 1954. *Excavations at Star Carr.* Cambridge University Press.

Clay, P. 2002. *The Prehistory of the East Midlands Claylands.* Leicester Archaeol. Monogr. **9**. School of Archaeological Studies, University of Leicester.

Collingson, J.D. and Lewin, J. (eds) 1983. *International Association of Sedimentologists Special Publication* **6**. Oxford: Blackwell Scientific.

Coope, G.R. and Lemdahl, G. 1995. Regional differences in the lateglacial climate of northern Europe based on Coleopteran analysis, *J. Quat. Sci.* **10**, 391–395.

Courtney, T. 1977. A Stone Age Site: Unstone, Derbyshire. Unpublished report, North Derbyshire Archaeological Committee.

Cullingford, R.A., Davidson, D.A. and Lewin, J. (eds) 1980. *Timescales in Geomorphology*. Chichester: Wiley.

Davies, G. 2001. Interim Statement on the Archaeological Works at Staythorpe Power Station. Unpublished report 438f, ARCUS, University of Sheffield.

Dinnin, M.H. 1992. Islands within Islands: the Development of the British Entomofauna during the Holocene and the Implications for Conservation. Unpublished PhD thesis, University of Sheffield.

Dinnin, M. 1997. Holocene beetle assemblages from the Lower Trent floodplain at Bole Ings, Nottinghamshire, UK, in A.C. Ashworth, P.C. Buckland and J.P. Sadler (eds), *Studies in Quaternary Entomology. An Inordinate Fondness for Insects,* 83–104.

Dinnin, M.H. and Brayshay, B. 1999. The contribution of a multiproxy approach in reconstructing floodplain development, in S.B. Marriott and J. Alexander (eds), *Floodplains: Interdisciplinary Approaches*, 179–195.

Dudley, H. 1949. *Early Days in North-West Lincolnshire. A Regional Archaeology*. Scunthorpe.

Elliott, L. and Knight, D.K. 1999. An early Mesolithic and first millennium BC settlement and pit alignments at Swarkestone Lowes, Derbyshire, *Derbyshire Archaeol. J.* **119**, 79–153.

Elliott, L. and Knight, D. in prep. Prehistoric and Romano-British settlement at Gonalston, Nottinghamshire.

Foundations Archaeology. 1999. Lordsmill Street, Chesterfield, Derbyshire: Post Excavation Assessment. Unpublished report, Foundations Archaeology.

Friday, L.E. 1988. A key to the adults of the British water beetles, *Field. Stud.* **7**, 1–152.

Garton, D. 1987. Buxton, *Curr. Archaeol.* **103**, 250–253.

Garton, D. 1991. Neolithic settlement in the Peak District: perspective and prospects, in R. Hodges and K. Smith (eds), *Recent Developments in the Archaeology of the Peak District*, 3–21.

Garton, D. 1994. Flint assessment, Appendix 2 in D. Knight and A. Kennett, Proposed Gravel Quarry at Collingham, Notts: Fieldwalking Survey. Summary Report and Recommendations for Further Work.

Garton, D. 2002. Walking fields in South Muskham and its implications for Romano-British cropmark landscapes in Nottinghamshire, *Trans. Thoroton Soc. Nottinghamshire* **106**, 17–39.

Garton, D. and Brown, J. 1999. Flint, quartzite and polished stone artifacts, in L. Elliott and D. Knight, An early Mesolithic and first millennium BC settlement and pit alignments at Swarkestone Lowes, Derbyshire, 106–124.

Garton, D., Leary, R. and Richards, G. 2003. A Report on the Fieldwalking 2003 at Tiln North, Nottinghamshire. Unpublished report, Trent & Peak Archaeological Unit, University Park, Nottingham.

Garton, D., Phillips, P. and Henson, D. 1989. Newton Cliffs: a flintworking and settlement site in the Trent Valley, in P. Phillips (ed), *Archaeology and Landscape Studies in North Lincolnshire. Part ii: Aerial and Surface Survey on the Lincolnshire Wolds and Excavation at Newton Cliffs, North Lincolnshire*. BAR Brit. Ser. **208**, 81–180.

Gaunt, G.D. 1981. Quaternary history of the southern part of the Vale of York, in J. Neale and J. Flenley (eds), *The Quaternary in Britain: Essays, Reviews and Original Work on the Quaternary*. 82–97.

Gaunt, G.D. (ed) 1994. *Geology of the Country around Goole, Doncaster and the Isle of Axholme. Memoir for one-inch sheets 79 and 88 (England and Wales)*. London: HMSO.

Grattan, J.P. 1990. An Investigation of the Origins and Development of a Palaeochannel located in Girton Quarry on the Floodplain of the River Trent. Unpublished MSc thesis, University of Sheffield.

Green, F. 1991. Girton Gravel Pit SK825670. Preliminary Report of Palaeobotany. Unpublished report, Trent & Peak Archaeological Trust, University Park, Nottingham.

Henson, D. 1985. The flint resources of Yorkshire and the East Midlands, *Lithics* **6**, 2–9.

Henson, D. 1989a. The raw materials, in D. Garton, P. Phillips and D. Henson, Newton Cliffs: a flintworking and settlement site in the Trent Valley, 173.

Henson, D. 1989b. Away from the core? A northerner's view of flint exploitation, in I. Brooks and P. Phillips (eds), *Breaking the Stony Silence*, 5–31.

Hicks, S.P. 1972. The impact of Man on the East Moor of Derbyshire from Mesolithic times, *Archaeol. J.* **129**, 1–21.

Hodges, R. and Smith, K. (eds) 1991. *Recent Developments in the Archaeology of the Peak District*. Department of Archaeology and Prehistory, University of Sheffield.

Howard, A.J. and Knight, D. 2001. South Ings Close, Rampton, Nottinghamshire. Auger Survey of the Floodplain Deposits. Unpublished report, Trent & Peak Archaeological Unit, University Park, Nottingham.

Howard, A.J., Bateman, M.D., Garton, D., Green, F.M.L., Wagner, P. and Priest, V. 1999. Evidence of late Devensian and early Flandrian processes and environments in the Idle Valley at Tiln, North Nottinghamshire, *Proc. Yorkshire Geol. Soc.* **52** (4), 383–393.

Hughes, G. and Roseff, R. 1995. Excavations at Croft Quarry (SP517968), *Trans. Leicestershire Archaeol. Hist. Soc.* **69**, 100–108.

Hunter, J. and Ralston, I. (eds) 1999. *The Archaeology of Britain*. London: Routledge.

Jacobi, R.M. 1973. Aspects of the Mesolithic Age in Great Britain, in S.K. Koslowski (ed), *The Mesolithic in Europe*, 237–265.

Jacobi, R.M. 1976. Britain inside and outside Mesolithic Europe, *Proc. Prehist. Soc.* **42**, 67–84.

Jacobi, R.M. 1978. Northern England in the eighth millennium b.c.: an essay, in P. Mellars (ed), *The Early Postglacial Settlement of Northern Europe*, 295–332.

Jacobi, R.M., Tallis, J.H. and Mellars, P.A. 1976. The Southern Pennine Mesolithic and the ecological record, *J. Archaeol. Sci.* **3**, 307–320.

Jenkinson, R.D.S. 1984. *Creswell Crags: Late Pleistocene Sites in the East Midlands*. BAR Brit. Ser. **122**.

Kelly, J.H. 1976. *The Excavation of Wetton Mill Rock Shelter, Manifold Valley, Staffordshire*. Stoke-on-Trent Museum Archaeological Society.

Kinsley, G. and Knight, D. 1992. Archaeology of the Fosse Way. Vol. 2: Newark to Widmerpool. Unpublished report, Trent & Peak Archaeological Trust, University Park, Nottingham.

Kirby, J. R. 2001. Regional late Quaternary marine and perimarine records, in M.D. Bateman, P.C. Buckland, C.D. Frederick and N.J. Whitehouse (eds), *The Quaternary of East Yorkshire and North Lincolnshire*, 25–34.

Knight, D. 1994. Cromwell Quarry Extension, Notts: Summary Report on Trial Trenching and Test-pitting. Unpublished report, Trent & Peak Archaeological Unit, University Park, Nottingham.

Knight, D. and Kennett, A. 1994. Proposed Gravel Quarry at Collingham, Notts: Fieldwalking Survey. Summary Report and Recommendations for Further Work. Unpublished report, Trent & Peak Archaeological Unit, University Park, Nottingham.

Knight, D., Garton, D. and Leary, R. 1998. The Elmton fieldwalking survey: prehistoric and Romano-British artefact scatters, *Derbyshire Archaeol. J.* **118**, 69–85.

Knox, R. 2001. An archaeological resource assessment of the Mesolithic in Leicestershire and Rutland, *East Midlands Archaeological Resource Framework Project Stage 1: an Archaeological Resource Assessment*. Draft. University of Leicester Archaeological Services. http://www.le.ac.uk/archaeology/east_midlands_research_framework.htm

Koch, K. 1992. *Die Käfe, Miteleuropas*. Okologie Band **3**. Krefeld: Goecke und Evers.

Koslowski, S.K. (ed) 1973. *The Mesolithic in Europe*. Warsaw.

Lillie, M. 1998. The palaeoenvironmental survey of the lower Trent valley and Winterton Beck, in R. Van de Noort and S. Ellis (eds), *Wetland Heritage of the Ancholme and Lower Trent Valleys: an Archaeological Survey*, 33–72.

Lillie, M.C. and Gearey, B. 1992. Girton Quarry: Analysis of a Palaeochannel of the River Trent. Unpublished report, Trent & Peak Archaeological Trust, University Park, Nottingham.

Long, A.J., Innes, J.B., Kirby, J.R., Lloyd, J.M., Rutherford, M.M., Shennan, I. and Tooley, M.J. 1998. Holocene sea-level change and coastal evolution in the Humber estuary, eastern England: an assessment of rapid coastal change, *The Holocene* **8**, 229–247.

Long, D.J., Chambers, F.M. and Barnatt, J. 1998. The palaeoenvironment and the vegetation history of a later prehistoric field system at Stoke Flat on the gritstone uplands of the Peak District, *J. Archaeol. Sci.* **25**, 505–519.

Manby, T.G. 1963. Some Mesolithic sites in the Peak District and Trent basin, *Derbyshire Archaeol. J.* **83**, 10–23.

Marriott, S.B. and Alexander, J. (eds) 1999. *Floodplains: Interdisciplinary Approaches*. Geological Society of London Special Publication **163**.

Mellars, P.A. 1974. The Palaeolithic and the Mesolithic, in C. Renfrew, *British Prehistory: a New Outline*, 41–99.

Mellars, P. 1976. Fire ecology, animal populations and man: a study of some ecological relationships in prehistory, *Proc. Prehist. Soc.* **42**, 15–45.

Mellars P. (ed) 1978. *The Early Postglacial Settlement of Northern Europe*. London: Duckworth.

Membury, S. 2001. An archaeological resource assessment of the Palaeolithic and Mesolithic periods in Lincolnshire, *East Midlands Archaeological Research Framework Project Stage 1: an Archaeological Resource Assessment*. Draft. University of Leicester Archaeological Services. http://www.le.ac.uk/archaeology/east_midlands_research_framework.htm

Metcalfe, S.E., Ellis, S., Horton, B.P., Innes, J.B., McArthur, J., Mitlehner, A., Parkes, A., Pethick, J.S., Rees, J., Ridgway, J., Rutherford, M.M., Shennan, I. and Tooley, M.J. 2000. The Holocene evolution of the Humber Estuary: reconstructing change in a dynamic environment, in I. Shennan and J. Andrews (eds), *Holocene Land-Ocean Interaction and Environmental Change around the North Sea*, 97–118.

Mithen, S. 1999. Hunter-gatherers of the Mesolithic, in J. Hunter and I. Ralston (eds), *The Archaeology of Britain*, 35–57.

Myers, A.M. 1987. All shot to pieces? Inter-assemblage variability, lithic analysis and Mesolithic assemblage 'types': some preliminary observations, in A.G. Brown and M. Edmonds (eds), *Lithic Analysis and Later British Prehistory*, 137–153.

Myers, A.M. 1989. Lithics, risk and change in the Mesolithic, in I. Brooks and P. Phillips (eds), *Breaking the Stony Silence: Papers from the Sheffield Lithics Conference 1988*, 131–160.

Myers, A.M. 2001a. The Mesolithic in Derbyshire: a resource assessment, *East Midlands Archaeological Research Framework Project Stage 1: an Archaeological Resource Assessment*. Draft. University of Leicester Archaeological Services. http://www.le.ac.uk/archaeology/east_midlands_research_framework.htm

Myers, A.M. 2001b. An archaeological resource assessment and research agenda for the Mesolithic in the East Midlands, *East Midlands Archaeological Research Framework*. Draft. University of Leicester Archaeological Services. http://www.le.ac.uk/archaeology/east_midlands_research_framework.htm

Myers, A.M. 2003. The upper Palaeolithic and Mesolithic archaeology of the West Midlands region, *West Midlands Regional Research Framework for Archaeology*. http://www.arch-ant.bham.ac.uk/wmrrfa/sem1.htm

Neale, J. and Flenley, J. (eds) 1981. *The Quaternary in Britain: Essays, Reviews and Original Work on the Quaternary*. Oxford: Pergamon Press.

Radley, J. 1967. Excavations at a rock shelter at Whaley, Derbyshire, *Derbyshire Archaeol. J.* **87**, 1–17.

Radley, J. and Marshall, G. 1965. Maglemosian sites in the Pennines, *Yorkshire Archaeol. J.* **41**, 394–402.

Radley, J. and Mellars, P.A. 1964. A Mesolithic structure at Deepcar, Yorkshire, England, and the affinities of its associated flint industry, *Proc. Prehist. Soc.* **30**, 1–24.

Renfrew, C. (ed) 1974. *British Prehistory: a New Outline*. London: Duckworth.

Reynier, M.J. 1998. Early Mesolithic settlement in England and Wales: some preliminary observations, in N. Ashton, F. Healy and P. Pettitt (eds), *Stone Age Archaeology: Essays in Honour of John Wymer*, 174–184.

Rose, J., Turner, C., Coope, G.R. and Bryan, M.D. 1980. Channel changes in a lowland river catchment over the last 13,000 years, in R.A. Cullingford, D.A. Davidson and J. Lewin (eds), *Timescales in Geomorphology*, 159–176.

Shennan, I. and Andrews, J. (eds) 2000. *Holocene Land-Ocean Interaction and Environmental Change around the North Sea*. Geological Society, London, Special Publications **166**.

Smith, D.G. 1983. Anastomosed fluvial deposits: modern examples from western Canada, in J.D. Collingson and J. Lewin (eds), *International Association of Sedimentologists Special Publication* **6**, 155–168.

Smith, D.N. 1996. Dove Villa: the Insect Remains. Unpublished report, Trent & Peak Archaeological Trust, University Park, Nottingham.

Spikens, P. 1999. *Mesolithic Northern England: Environment, Population and Settlement*. BAR Brit. Ser. **283**.

Tooley, M.J. and Shennan, I. (eds) 1987. *Sea Level Changes*. Oxford: Blackwell.

Van de Noort, R. and Ellis, S. (eds), 1998. *Wetland Heritage of the Ancholme and Lower Trent Valleys: an Archaeological Survey*. Humber Wetlands Project, University of Hull.

Williams, C.T. 1985. *Mesolithic Exploitation Patterns in the Central Pennines: a Palynological Study of Soyland Moor*. BAR Brit. Ser. **139**.

Williams, J.H. and Shaw, M. 1981. Excavations in Chalk Lane, Northampton 1975–1978, *Northamptonshire Archaeol.* **16**, 87–136.

Wiltshire, P.E.J. and Edwards, K.J. 1993. Mesolithic, early Neolithic and later prehistoric impacts on vegetation at a riverine site in Derbyshire, England, in F.M. Chambers (ed), *Climate Change and Human Impact on the Landscape*, 157–168.

Wymer, J. J. 1977. *Gazetteer of Mesolithic Sites in England and Wales with a Gazetteer of Upper Palaeolithic Sites in England and Wales*. CBA Res. Rep. **20**.

Zvelebil, M. 1994. Plant use in the Mesolithic and its role in the transition to farming, *Proc. Prehist. Soc.* **60**, 35–74.

4 FROM NEOLITHIC TO EARLY BRONZE AGE: THE FIRST AGRICULTURAL LANDSCAPES

DAVID KNIGHT AND ANDY J. HOWARD

4.1 Introduction

This chapter deals with the period from *c*.4000 to *c*.1500 cal BC, straddling the conventional divide between the Neolithic and the Early Bronze Age at around 2050 cal BC (Needham 1996, fig.1). In terms of the accepted metalwork sequence, this encompasses the metal-using phases of the later Neolithic (*c*.2500 to *c*.2050 cal BC), during which period we see also the development of Beaker ceramic and funerary traditions, and the sequence of Early Bronze Age metalwork assemblages preceding the introduction of Acton Park metalwork at the transition to the Middle Bronze Age (Needham 1996; 1997). The Neolithic is divided for the purposes of discussion into an earlier and a later phase, separated at around 3000 cal BC, as this provides a reasonable correlation with changes in the ceramic and lithic record and developments in monument typology (*cf.* Whittle 1999, 59). Most of the limited metalwork of this period has been recovered from the River Trent and other unstratified contexts, and dating for the majority of sites relies upon associations with poorly dated ceramic and lithic artefacts. This evidence is supplemented by a growing number of radiocarbon dates, which have transformed our understanding of changes in the Valley environment.

This period of over two millennia witnessed some fundamental changes in the landscape of the Trent Valley, associated in large part with the gradual transition from a hunter-gatherer to a predominantly agricultural economy. Many questions remain regarding the mobility of early agricultural groups, the permanence of their settlements and cultivation plots, and the balance between traditional hunter-gatherer and agricultural activities. There is, however, compelling evidence for progressive clearance in some parts of the Valley of the dense mixed oak woodland that would have cloaked the valley floor in the fifth millennium BC, and for a gradual expansion of both pasture and cereal cultivation. The period also witnessed the development of the first funerary and ceremonial enclosures, heralding a significant shift in the relationship between human communities and their landscape. Some of these monuments continued in use well into the second millennium BC, but this tradition of monumental architecture waned significantly during the Middle Bronze Age at the same time as Deverel-Rimbury funerary and ceramic traditions rose to prominence. This movement away from monumental ceremonial and funerary enclosures marks a significant watershed in the archaeological sequence, both in this region and elsewhere in Britain (*cf.* Champion 1999, 95) and underpins the division in this volume between the Early and Middle/Late Bronze Ages. In other Midlands river valleys and along the western margins of the Fens, there is persuasive evidence for the emergence during the Middle Bronze Age of the region's first field systems and settlement enclosures, emphasising further the pivotal position of the later second millennium BC in

the development of the landscape (Yates forthcoming). The Trent Valley, by contrast, appears at present to have remained an essentially unenclosed environment well into the first millennium BC. This dichotomy has puzzled many students of the period (e.g. Pryor 1998, 144–5) and is highlighted as a key issue for further investigation in both this chapter and the next.

Early workers within the Trent Valley postulated a densely wooded and sparsely populated environment during the Neolithic and Early Bronze Age (*cf.* Smith 1978, 91), in contrast to neighbouring upland areas such as the White Peak where extensive earthworks of these periods had long attracted the interest of eighteenth and nineteenth century antiquarians such as Hayman Rooke and Thomas Bateman (Barnatt and Smith 1991; Garton 1991). This model reflected in part the rarity of upstanding Neolithic and earlier Bronze Age monuments, which with the exception of occasional earthworks such as the ridge-top barrow cemetery at Swarkestone Lowes, Derbyshire (Greenfield 1960; Posnansky 1955a; 1956b), the massive mound set within a hengiform ditch at Round Hill, Twyford, Derbyshire (Harding with Lee 1987, 116–7, 119) and a possible henge close to the Trent at Gunthorpe, Nottinghamshire (Bishop 2001; Nottinghamshire Sites and Monuments Record 01820a) had long been ploughed away. More recent work has shown this paucity of remains to be more apparent than real, particularly in the later Neolithic and Early Bronze Age, and has necessitated a fundamental reappraisal of the impact of these early communities upon the Valley landscape. Air photographic research, following on from the publication in 1960 of the pioneering RCHME volume *A Matter of Time*, has revealed in some areas a high density of crop-marks indicative of Neolithic and Bronze Age activity. The most ubiquitous of these are ring-ditches, represented by an annular ditch enclosing areas averaging between 10 and 25m in diameter, many of which may originally have demarcated the areas occupied by funerary barrows. Traces have also survived of more elaborate multiple ring-ditches, pit circles, cursuses, causewayed enclosures and henges, implying a regionally varied tradition of monumental architecture developing between the fourth and second millennia BC. These sites are unevenly distributed along the Valley, and may be observed to cluster within a zone between the Rivers Dove and Derwent and around the Trent-Tame confluence, within monument complexes rivalling those of other lowland river valleys such as the Nene, around Rauds, Northamptonshire (Chapman 2001, 5–8, 11–12; Healy and Harding 2003; Windell 1989) and the Thames around Dorchester, Oxfordshire (Atkinson *et al.* 1951; Loveday 2001; Whittle *et al.* 1992).

Extensive fieldwalking surveys and excavations, many carried out since the shift to developer-funding from 1990, have enhanced significantly the crop-mark evidence and have strengthened the impression of a hitherto unexpected density of activity, particularly during the later Neolithic and Early Bronze Age. Systematic fieldwalking surveys have been carried out in some stretches of the Valley, including an area of the Lower Trent around South Muskham, Nottinghamshire (Garton 2002), a broad zone along the Nottinghamshire Fosse Way where it follows the eastern edge of the Trent Valley from East Stoke northwards to Newark and Brough-on-Fosse (Kinsley and Knight 1992), the Middle Trent Valley to the south of Derby (Myers 2001a, 5) and the Lower Trent north of Gainsborough, Lincolnshire (Van de Noort and Ellis eds 1998). Many fields on the gravel terraces have yielded extensive surface scatters of Neolithic and Bronze Age lithic artefacts, including localised concentrations indicative of activity foci, although it should be stressed that even after excavation the character of this activity may remain unclear (e.g. Garton et al. 1989; Garton and Beswick 1983). The expansion of large-scale archaeological excavations and watching briefs in advance of quarrying and highway construction has permitted extensive stripping of terrace and floodplain zones, and has revealed an unexpected density of earlier prehistoric sites, many preserved beneath alluvium. This has widened significantly the distribution of known sites and has changed fundamentally our understanding of certain classes of monument. Chief amongst these are burnt mounds, which prior to recent investigations in advance of gravel quarrying at Waycar Pasture, Girton, Nottinghamshire (Garton 1993) were unknown in the Trent Valley. Such large-scale work has also partly redressed the historic bias towards the later Neolithic and Early Bronze Age periods. Discoveries in large-scale quarry excavations of more ephemeral earlier Neolithic features, as at Gonalston in Nottinghamshire, have provided useful additional information on a period that has always been comparatively poorly represented archaeologically (Chapter 4.8.1). In addition, monitoring of large-scale quarrying at sites such as Colwick, Holme Pierrepont, Girton and Langford Lowfields in Nottinghamshire has revealed palaeochannels, preserved land surfaces and other environmental deposits, which together have provided organic data of major significance for the study of landscape change in this period (see Garton et al. 1996; 1997; Salisbury et al. 1984).

A considerable body of evidence is now available for study of the Neolithic and Bronze Age periods in the Trent Valley, but despite the potential for analysis few general syntheses have been attempted. The earliest general study was provided by Merrick Posnansky (1956a), who brought together the evidence for Lower Palaeolithic to Bronze Age activity in the Middle Trent as part of his doctoral thesis. More recent surveys of the Neolithic and Bronze Age in parts of the Trent Valley have been published by O'Brien (1978), Vine (1982), Van de Noort and Davies (1993, 53–64) and Van de Noort and Ellis (1998, 289–96), while the precursor of this volume sought to provide a general review of the Valley on the basis of selected case studies (Knight and Howard 1995). Several useful reviews have also been published recently of neighbouring regions, which together carry important implications for our understanding of the Neolithic and Bronze Age in the Trent Valley. These include Clay's study of the East Midlands claylands (Clay 2002), reviews

by Barnatt and others of contemporary communities in the Peak District (e.g. Barnatt 2000; Barnatt and Smith 1991; Garton 1991) and a recent review of Bronze Age activity in the Cheshire Basin (Mullin 2003). Attention should also be drawn to several studies of specific artefact and monument types from the region, particularly the studies by Scurfield (1997) and Davis (1999; 2003) of Bronze Age metalwork from the Trent and the survey by Allen et al. (1987) of Deverel-Rimbury funerary and ceramic traditions within the region. Most recently, the Trent Valley has featured prominently in contributions to the East and West Midlands Archaeological Research Framework project. Data from the Trent Valley downstream of Staffordshire have been incorporated in a general review of the East Midlands by Clay (2001b), building upon assessments of Derbyshire (Myers 2001a), Leicestershire (Clay 2001a), Lincolnshire (Membery 2001) and Nottinghamshire (Bishop 2001). Reviews of the Neolithic and Bronze Ages in the uppermost reaches of the Trent are incorporated in assessments of the West Midlands data by Barber (2003), Garwood (2003), Ray (2003) and Woodward (2003).

4.2   Climatic Change

The Neolithic overlaps the Climatic Optimum of the current interglacial, dated in Britain to between c.8000 BP and c.4500 BP (Bell and Walker 1992, 70–1). Precipitation levels varied within this period (ibid. 71), but average annual temperatures approximately 1–2°C higher than today may be postulated from consideration of the spatial distribution of key botanical and faunal indicator species. This period of maximum warmth was followed by a phase of gradual climatic deterioration, characterised by irregularly falling temperatures and rising precipitation levels (ibid. 71–2). Records of bog surface wetness, deduced from the analysis of cores recovered from ombrotrophic mires, provide high resolution climatic signals which reflect synchronous subcontinental scale variations in climate (Barber et al. 1994; 2000). Records have been obtained from the uplands of northern Britain which provide evidence for periods of wetter and/or cooler climate during the later Neolithic and Early Bronze Age. At Walton Moss, Cumbria, Hughes et al. (2000) identified wet shifts around 3350 cal BC, 2460–2040 cal BC and 1550 cal BC. Farther north at Talla Moss in the Scottish borders, Chambers et al. (1997) have identified climatic deterioration between c.1950 and c.1550 cal BC at five sites in the north-west Scottish Highlands. However, although these records accurately reflect climatic trends in the uplands of northern Britain, caution must be urged in their use as climatic indicators at lower altitudes. Despite these reservations, Barber et al. (2000) have argued that regional palaeoclimatic teleconnections can be demonstrated between the signals recorded in the uplands and raised mires in lowland contexts. Further, Macklin (1999) has argued that periods of enhanced fluvial activity across Britain can be linked with periods of climatic deterioration identified from the record at Bolton Fell Moss, particularly around 3000 cal BC and c.2100–1700 cal BC. In the floodplain of the River Thames, archaeological investigations at Runnymede Bridge, Surrey, have identified a major flood event dated to around *c.* 2050 cal BC (Needham 1992, 257, fig. 23.5) which Macklin (1999) has argued coincides with a major climatic deterioration at Bolton Fell Moss (Barber *et al.* 1994). In the Trent Valley, some of the environmental changes discussed in this chapter could relate partly to the impact of increased precipitation upon surface run-off, river and stream silt loads and groundwater levels. In addition, reductions in the length of the growing season might have affected cropping strategies and the balance between land managed for pastoral and arable activities (particularly in floodplain areas vulnerable to rising groundwater levels), although little detailed information on crop and animal husbandry is currently available (Chapter 4.5).

Another factor to bear in mind when considering changes in ground wetness is the possibility of sea level rises. By around 4100 cal BC sea level had all but ceased to rise in the Lower Trent Valley, although the intercalation of marine clays and freshwater peats to the north of Gainsborough, noted in Chapter 3.2.1, indicates a continuing delicate balance between marine and freshwater processes of sedimentation (Lillie 1998). Observed changes in groundwater levels in the lowest reaches of the Trent, discussed in greater detail in the following section, may reflect sea level as well as climatic fluctuations. It is also likely that surface run-off rates and soil erosion had increased during this period as a result of progressive woodland clearance (Chapter 4.4).

4.3   Fluvial Geomorphology

The geomorphological data provide evidence for a phase of significant lateral reworking of river channels in the Middle and Lower Trent from around 4000 cal BC, resulting in an increasingly unstable floodplain environment characterised by extensive tree-throw and higher river silt loads. There are also indications of increasing ground wetness in the lowermost reaches of the Trent, which it is suggested below may reflect hydrological changes in the upper reaches of the catchment, due in part to increasing human impact upon the valley ecosystem and localised sea level change.

4.3.1   Lateral Reworking of River Channels

The geomorphological evidence suggests that the character of the valley-floor landscape changed during the fourth millennium BC as floodplain zones close to contemporary channels were reworked vigorously by a laterally unstable river. This period of instability may be identified in a number of quarries between Derby in the Middle Trent and Langford Lowfields in the Lower Trent on the basis of dendrochronologically and radiometrically-dated oak tree trunks stratified within the valley-floor sands and gravels. These trees, many with intact root boles, were first noted by Salisbury *et al.* (1984) in the complex of gravel quarries around Colwick and Holme Pierrepont near Nottingham, with one group of 27 trunks dating to between *c.*4200–3900 cal BC and another group of eleven trunks to *c.*2000–1600 cal BC; a number of other trunks spanned a range of time-scales. Despite careful examination, no evidence was recorded for felling by either humans or animals such as beaver (Coles 1992; 2001). Salisbury's pioneering work

also recognised trunks in quarries at Barrow-upon-Trent, Derbyshire and in the Meadows in Nottingham. In recent years, large tree remains stratified within river sands and gravels have been identified at a number of other quarries along the Trent Valley, including examples at Attenborough, Nottinghamshire (A.J. Howard: unpublished information; C. Salisbury: pers. comm.) and Besthorpe, Nottinghamshire (Howard 1992).

From an environmental and cultural perspective, one of the key later Neolithic-Early Bronze Age sites identified and excavated in the region in recent years was found at Langford Lowfields Quarry, some 8 km downstream of Newark. Within the quarry, a *c.*4m depth of sand and gravel was exposed, with large inter-bedded tree trunks, many with intact root boles, recorded throughout the sequence (Fig.4.1). The locations of all trunks were recorded, demonstrating that they occurred both in isolation and as part of a log-jam structure within a sand-filled palaeochannel (Garton *et al.* 1996; 1997). The results of dendrochronological analysis suggested that the deposition of tree remains within the channel log-jam dated to *c.*2300–2000 cal BC, while samples of wood elsewhere in the quarry were dated to *c.*2900 cal BC and *c.*4200–4100 cal BC (Hillam 1998; Howard *et al.* 1999b). The date ranges of the trunks from Langford Lowfields compare well with the data collected from Colwick, but in contrast to that site many of the tree remains in the log-jam preserved evidence of working prior to deposition. Coleopteran remains extracted from sediments within a tree bole and from sands and silts deposited within the log-jam provided important evidence for contemporary fluvial environments around Langford Lowfields (Howard *et al.* 1999b). The invertebrate fauna, which was dated by its association with a radiometrically-dated human rib found stratified within the log-jam (3780 ± 50 BP, Beta-87093, 2400–2030 cal BC), includes a significant proportion of Elmids (commonly known as riffle beetles), which are indicative of fast-flowing water conditions. In addition, between 20% and 30% of the terrestrial invertebrate fauna were associated with closed canopy woodland, including oak, elm, beech, lime, ash, hazel and alder, although some evidence of grazed clearings was provided by species associated with grassland and animal dung. The recognition of cut timbers within the log-jam provides important direct evidence for human manipulation of the woodland canopy.

No tree remains earlier than *c.*4500 cal BC have been identified in the sands and gravels of the floodplain. Their occurrence at approximately the same time period (*c.*4000 cal BC) and in similar stratigraphic contexts at Colwick and Langford Lowfields, about 25km apart, may indicate some synchronicity of floodplain processes. The size range of the trees suggests that they were part of a dense floodplain woodland canopy, which supports the palynological and entomological findings of a generally well-vegetated, anastomosed channel system during this period (Howard *et al.* 1999b). The preservation of intact root boles on many of these trees suggests that they were uprooted by the undercutting of river-banks during periods of enhanced fluvial activity, probably during flood events. The direct association of human activity and environmental remains

Fig.4.1 *One of many Neolithic and Bronze Age oak trunks preserved in the gravels at Langford Lowfields, Nottinghamshire (photograph: L. Elliott)*

at Langford Lowfields, including the evidence for worked wood, makes this arguably the most important site known from this time period within the Trent Valley and a site of major national importance. Unfortunately, although the environmental context has been published (Howard *et al.* 1999b) the archaeological evidence, including a sizeable collection of human remains and animal bone, has yet to be analysed fully and published (see summaries in Garton *et al.* 1996; 1997).

The mechanisms underlying the deposition of vast quantities of mainly unworked mature tree trunks in channels of the Trent remain uncertain. There appears no obvious link with climate, given that the period of deposition falls mainly within the Climatic Optimum of *c.*8000 – 4500 BP, and outside the windows of climatic deterioration identified from records of bog surface wetness (Chapter 4.2). Increased surface run-off arising from removal of the protective woodland canopy would provide a plausible explanation for increased bank erosion and tree-throw along the middle and lower reaches of the river. If correct, however, this would raise the question of why similar phenomena have not been observed more widely in other river valleys of southern Britain. The explanation for this contrast may lie in the position of the Trent at the interface between the highland and lowland zones. The river receives exceptionally high discharges from its tributaries draining the southern Pennines, and has been shown to have been particularly sensitive to changing hydrological conditions within the catchment prior to the extensive flood alleviation works of the post-medieval period (Brown 1998).

4.3.2 Changing Groundwater Levels

Evidence for increases in ground wetness in the topographically lowest reaches of the Trent is provided by the development in some areas of the lower Trent of alder carr woodland, replacing the closed canopy forest that had developed during the Mesolithic. The origins of this process may in fact reach back to the later Mesolithic, as suggested by a site at Bole Ings, Nottinghamshire, some 25km downstream of Langford Lowfields (Chapter 3.2.2). An observed progression to alder carr woodland at that site was interpreted as a response to rising ground waters associated with sea level change around 5200 cal BC. This change was marked by a reduction in woodland and scrub taxa, a corresponding increase in grassland and reedswamp, and a transition from woody silty peat to organic silty clay deposition (Brayshay and Dinnin 1999). No corresponding rise in beetle faunas indicative of grassland, disturbed or open ground taxa could be identified. Brayshay and Dinnin concluded that the sedimentological and palaeoecological changes supported the hypothesis of increased wetness, possibly associated with sea level change in the Humber Estuary (Long *et al.* 1998), rather than the expansion of grassland or agricultural activity.

Evidence for the expansion of alder carr wetland during the Bronze Age was obtained during archaeological investigations at Newington Quarry, just outside the study area near Misson, Nottinghamshire, in the lower Idle Valley. This revealed a thin peat layer (< 1m thick) with inter-bedded tree remains, overlying sands and gravels

(Northern Archaeological Associates 2002). Charcoal fragments collected from fluvial silts, which may represent a pedogenically-altered land surface beneath the peat, have been dated to 4050 ± 50 BP (Beta-168361, 2860–2460 cal BC) and provide evidence for localised burning, possibly of an earlier dry phase of woodland. No evidence for anthropogenic activity has been observed in association with the charcoal-rich sediments (Gearey and Lillie 2002; Rackham 2002), although this must remain a possibility. Radiocarbon dating of the overlying peat sequence demonstrates that it had accumulated as an alder carr wetland from the end of the Early Bronze Age (Gearey and Lillie 2002). Dendrochronological dating of 43 sampled timbers inter-bedded within the peats at Newington has provided a continuous sequence spanning 627 years from 1580 to 954 BC (Tyers 2003). The sequence almost certainly extends back as far as 1660 BC and forward as late as 900 BC, although suitable samples of timber need to be identified and analysed to confirm this hypothesis (Tyers 2003, 6). The development of peat indicates that the valley floor was becoming progressively wetter. The decline in oak woodland probably also reflects the effects of waterlogging. Whilst this increasing wetness may be a response to changing climate and possibly sea level change in this part of the lower Trent basin, a minerogenic silt horizon in the upper part of the peat deposited by flooding coincided with a reduction in the woodland component of the pollen spectra (Gearey and Lillie 2002; Rackham 2002). This may indicate changing hydrological conditions within the catchment associated with woodland clearance, which as argued in the following section appears to have accelerated significantly during this period.

4.4 Woodland Clearance

A dense forest cover over the entire Valley should not be assumed at the beginning of the fourth millennium BC, although undoubtedly much of the area would have been characterised at that time by closed canopy mixed oak 'wildwood'. We have discussed above the evidence for the expansion of alder carr wetlands in some floodplain environments from the later Mesolithic, and their continued expansion during the Neolithic and Bronze Age. Reference was also made in Chapter 3.3.6 to the likelihood that some areas of woodland had been deliberately burnt to enhance the browse resource for large herbivores, particularly red deer, or to encourage plant growth for human consumption, although at present evidence of such activity is mainly focused upon moorland and heathland environments such as the south Pennines (e.g. Bleaklow; see Bell and Walker 1992, 157). In general, however, the earliest Neolithic communities would have operated within a confined 'wildwood' environment, contrasting with the significantly more open landscapes that may be argued to have developed in some stretches of the Trent Valley by the end of the Early Bronze Age. The palaeoenvironmental evidence for increasing woodland clearance and the expansion of pasture and arable is reviewed below, with a more detailed consideration of the crop and animal husbandry regimes in the following section (Chapter 4.5).

It has been suggested above that the remarkable buried landscapes of redeposited tree trunks that have been recognised in the middle and lower reaches of the Valley at Colwick, Langford Lowfields and elsewhere reflect the clearance from the earlier Neolithic of closed canopy valley woodland, the removal of which would have exposed previously protected forest soils to the effects of rainwash and soil erosion. Support for the hypothesis of progressive woodland clearance is provided by an increasing body of palaeoenvironmental data, obtained largely from palaeochannel fills, preserved soils and a wide variety of archaeological features recorded during the excavation of settlements, burial and ceremonial monuments (*cf.* Monckton 2003, Appendix E2).

4.4.1 Palaeochannel Fills

Considerable efforts have been expended over the last decade on the collection of organic samples from datable palaeochannel fills, with the aim of elucidating the vegetational history of the Valley and, in particular, the impact of anthropogenic activity upon the environment. The more significant of these sites are discussed below, commencing with examples from the lower reaches of the Valley and progressing to a consideration of the Middle Trent. This should facilitate assessment of intra-regional variability in the environmental record, as well as emphasising the requirement for sustained research into the uppermost reaches of the Valley.

Valuable insights into the environment of the Lower Trent in the broad floodplain zone extending between Newark and Gainsborough are provided by organic samples from the Nottinghamshire sites of Cottam and Collingham. At Cottam, pollen recovered from organic sediments sampled during augering of the floodplain showed a clear succession of vegetation between two local pollen assemblage zones (Scaife and Allen 1999). The earlier pollen assemblage zone was dominated by trees and shrubs, including alder, hazel, oak, pine, ash and lime. Small percentages of elm were also present (*ibid.* fig.3), suggesting to the pollen analyst a post-elm decline (c.5300–5000 BP) date for the assemblage. In contrast, although the later pollen assemblage zone incorporated similar types and percentages of tree and shrub pollen, including a small proportion of elm, there was a noticeable increase in herbaceous pollen (up to 30%) and a representation of cereal type pollen and taxa associated with bare and disturbed ground; these taxa included pollen of ribwort plantain, cabbage family, fathen/goosefoot type and dock/sorrel. Although the sequence is not securely dated by radiocarbon analysis, this may indicate farming activities developing in the later Neolithic and Early Bronze Age (*ibid.* 20).

Similar evidence for early woodland clearance and pre-elm decline cereal cultivation was provided by organic samples obtained from a palaeochannel near Collingham (Fig. 4.2; Knight 1994). Assessment of pollen preserved within this major palaeochannel of the Trent provided evidence for a progression from relatively high to low proportions of elm pollen, possibly implying that this vegetation sequence had spanned the elm decline (Hunt 1994). In addition to a mixed deciduous forest comprising oak, hazel, elm, lime, pine and ash, alder was probably an important component of the wetter parts of the floodplain, together with plants typical of

Fig.4.2 *Late prehistoric palaeochannel of the Trent near Collingham, Nottinghamshire (photograph: D. Knight)*

marsh and wet grasslands such as plantain and dock/sorrel. Evidence for human activity in the immediate vicinity of the channel, both before and after the elm decline, was provided by associated cereal pollen, fragments of charcoal and burnt bone. It remains uncertain, however, whether the elm decline in the local area was a direct result of human manipulation of the woodland canopy or whether it reflected the operation of other factors such as disease.

Farther upstream, at Staythorpe, Nottinghamshire, a Coleopteran assemblage dated from associated wood and reeds from 1750–1430 cal BC provides a picture of a largely cleared environment by the end of the Early Bronze Age (3320 ± 50 BP, Beta-142211, 1740–1460 cal BC; 3380 ± 40 BP, Beta-142212, 1750–1520 cal BC; 3290 ± 50 BP, Beta-142213, 1690–1430 cal BC). A diverse dung beetle fauna indicates that pasture had extended down to the riverbank, with only a few trees fringing the channel (Davies 2001, 73–6). Furthermore, the presence of weevil species, typically found on young pine trees and heather, has led to the suggestion that some of the gravel terraces may have become podsolised, possibly through intensive agricultural use. Probably as a result of clearance, the river near Staythorpe appears to have carried a significant silt load with abandoned channels infilled rapidly and overgrown with reedswamp.

A similar picture to that of the Lower Trent may be suggested for the Middle Trent Valley, most notably from several organically rich palaeochannels dating from the

Fig.4.3 *Late prehistoric palaeochannel of the Trent at Hicken's Bridge, Derbyshire (photograph: A.J. Howard)*

Neolithic and Early Bronze Age upstream of the Trent-Derwent confluence at Hicken's Bridge, Shardlow Quarry and Chapel Farm, Shardlow, Derbyshire and Croft Quarry, Leicestershire (Fig. 4.3). Two of the channel fills, on adjacent parts of the floodplain at Hicken's Bridge and Shardlow Quarry, have yielded macroscopic plants and Coleoptera remains indicating sediment accumulation in a series of abandoned channel wetlands (Howard *et al.*, submitted). Differences in the vegetational sequences recorded from pollen at these sites can be explained by reference to taphonomic processes, and together these sequences provide a detailed picture of local and regional valley floor environments. The pollen data indicate that the regional woodland was dominated by oak, with smaller proportions of alder and hazel, although the virtual absence of Coleopteran species or macroscopic plant remains associated with this type of woodland suggests that it was some distance away, probably at the floodplain edge. A cleared landscape may be postulated around the riparian zone, with Coleoptera providing evidence for pastoral activity and both pollen and macroscopic plant remains implying cultivation. The abandoned channels formed areas of shallow, slow-flowing or standing water, although diatoms indicative of nutrient-rich conditions suggest that the channels were recharged occasionally with fresh water, probably during flood events. The water surface was covered in places with duckweeds and water milfoils and may occasionally have dried out to form areas of marshy grassland. The channels were surrounded by dense marshy vegetation, including stands of alder carr and reedbed, colonising mud and silt substrates.

A similar environmental picture to that described for Hicken's Bridge and Shardlow Quarry was revealed during augering of two channels incorporating organic sediments on a site just upstream of the Trent-Derwent confluence at Chapel Farm, Shardlow (Knight and Malone 1997). The first channel (P) was dated to 4150 ± 60 BP (Beta-099237, 2890–2490 cal BC) and the second (V) to 3540 ± 70 BP (Beta-099239; 2120–1680 cal BC). Pollen analysis of deposits in the latter channel provided evidence for short, heavily trampled grassland, possibly around water holes, and areas of longer grass and hay meadow (Greig 1997). These latter sediments also included significant amounts of heather pollen (*ibid.*, 35). Heather may have been growing close enough to the area to contribute this amount of pollen, or alternatively could have been imported for another purpose, possibly as bedding.

A channel dated by associated peat and ash wood at Croft Quarry on the River Soar in Leicestershire has provided valuable evidence for wider catchment conditions in the Neolithic (4670 ± 160 BP, Beta-74199, 3780–2910 cal BC; 3470 ± 80 BP, Beta-78006, 2020–1530 cal BC; Smith *et al.* 2005). As in the vicinity of the Trent-Derwent-Soar confluence, associated Coleoptera indicate a mixture of fluvial environments, including both fast-flowing and slow-flowing or stagnant waters. Pollen analysis indicates that the earliest organic sediments were formed in a wooded environment comprising hazel, bog myrtle, birch and some willow. Over time, alder carr became dominant across the floodplain, with lime, oak and hazel restricted to the surrounding valley sides. Both pollen and Coleoptera demonstrate some limited areas of open ground, with dung beetles indicating limited pastoral activity.

4.4.2 Preserved Soils and Archaeological Features

Some of the earliest work on woodland clearance was based upon palaeoenvironmental analyses of ancient soils preserved beneath barrows or in other archaeological contexts, enabling rare glimpses of landscape conditions prior to construction of these monuments. At Swarkestone Lowes, for example, excavations in 1955 by Posnansky (1955a; 1956b) of Barrow II revealed a pre-barrow soil incorporating, in the uppermost horizon, a poorly preserved pollen assemblage which it was suggested could imply an environment of 'open mixed woodland with hazel thickets and large grassy areas' (Pearson 1956, 25). The arboreal pollen implied a mixed oak woodland, with good representation of lime, alder and hazel, while the significant non-arboreal element included a high proportion of grasses with few cereal species and some typical weeds of cultivated or disturbed ground (*ibid.*, 26). Pollen associated with turves used in the construction of the primary and secondary mounds of Barrow IV at Swarkestone Lowes (Greenfield 1960) was argued by Dimbleby (1960) to imply a less wooded environment than suggested above, although the exact source of the turves is a matter for debate. High values of plantain (*Plantago*) and grasses (*Graminae*) were noted, in addition to woodland species such as oak, alder, lime and hazel, but none of the samples yielded cereal pollen. As a final illustration of this theme, soil samples recovered from beneath two barrows at Lockington, Leicestershire, may be noted. The first of these derived from a buried soil revealed during excavations of a low barrow mound by Posnansky (1955b), charcoal from which was interpreted as evidence of 'burning and tillage' (Cornwall 1955, 27). The second sample was obtained during recent excavations of a severely denuded barrow threatened by construction of the Derby Southern Bypass (Hughes 2000). Micromorphological studies of a soil preserved beneath the barrow yielded indirect evidence of pasture, in the form of calcite spherulites of the kind produced in the gut of grazing animals (Limbrey 2000; *cf.* Canti 1999). This supported Greig's (2000) palynological work at Lockington, which suggested an open agricultural landscape, and corroborates the accumulating evidence for the progressive clearance for agricultural purposes of the region's native woodland.

Attention should also be drawn to the gradually growing corpus of pollen and charred or waterlogged plant remains recovered from Neolithic and Early Bronze Age features recorded during the excavation of settlement, burial and ceremonial sites in the region (Monckton 2003, Table E1). These have provided further evidence for the gradual expansion of pasture and arable at the expense of native woodland and, despite doubts concerning the extent of clearance and the character of the agricultural economy, have added usefully to our limited knowledge of crop husbandry practices during this period. This evidence is particularly relevant to interpretations of the agricultural economy and issues such as mobility versus sedentism, and further discussion is reserved until a later section (Chapter 4.5).

4.4.3 Summary: Spatial and Chronological Variations of Clearance

The examples from sites on the Lower Trent, such as Bole Ings (Chapter 4.3.2), Cottam, Collingham and Staythorpe (Chapter 4.4.1), indicate that even within a relatively small geographical area the extent of clearance and the intensity of farming activity may have varied significantly. Proximity to the Humber Estuary and exposure in the lowermost reaches of the Trent to the effects of sea level change and tidal fluctuations may have been especially crucial in this respect. This would have influenced significantly the nature of the geomorphological processes, vegetational development and human activity at sites such as Bole Ings on the River Trent and Newington on the River Idle. Behind this local variability, the general picture to emerge in the Middle and Lower Trent Valley towards the end of the Early Bronze Age is one of an anastomosing river flowing through a mosaic of intensively cleared farmland near the contemporary channel, with mixed oak woodland on the more distant gravel terraces. Close to the main channel, the river would have been laterally mobile and bank erosion and tree-throw would have been pronounced features of the environment. In the more minor and abandoned channels fringed by reedswamp, minerogenic and organic sediments would have accumulated under lower energy conditions. The continued intensification of agriculture resulted in the first evidence for significant quantities of silt being carried and deposited by the region's rivers, as suggested at Staythorpe, and reflects the delivery of fine-grained sediment to the channel as a result of catchment soil erosion. The environmental history of the Upper Trent is poorly documented by comparison. However, the evidence discussed later in this chapter for significant monument concentrations, particularly around Alrewas and Mavesyn Ridware in Staffordshire, would imply that some stretches of the Valley upstream of the Trent-Tame confluence had also been affected by significant clearance of floodplain and terrace woodland.

4.5 The Agricultural Economy

Many questions remain regarding the animal and crop husbandry regimes of the Trent Valley, and in particular the vexed issue of the relationship between hunter-gatherer and agricultural modes of subsistence. We have noted in the previous chapter the possibility that Mesolithic hunter-gatherers ranging across areas such as the southern Pennines may have begun the process of woodland clearance by selective burning to enhance the browse resource for red deer and other large herbivores, which may have been controlled in part by herding (Chapter 3.3.6). Burning may also have been undertaken to encourage the growth of plants for human consumption, while several scholars have raised the possibility of some tending and cultivation of plants (Zvelebil 1994). Some limited experimentation with cereal cultivation has also been postulated, although the evidence remains inconclusive (Mithen 1999, 54). Further significant changes in the relationship between human communities and their environment may be demonstrated during the fourth and third millennia BC, with the gradual addition to the subsistence base of cultivated crops such as emmer wheat and domesticated livestock such as cattle and sheep. These should be viewed as supplements to the food procurement strategy, which throughout the period would have incorporated variable proportions of products obtained by hunting and gathering (*cf.* Jones 2000). This would explain, for example, the presence of hazelnuts in later Neolithic/Early Bronze Age pits at Langford, Nottinghamshire (Snelling and Rackham 2001, 22), the discovery of a pit containing a 'cache' of crab apples, nutshells and some cereal grains at Willow Farm, Castle Donington, Leicestershire (Monckton 2003, 9) and the retrieval of mainly wild resources such as hazelnuts and sloe stones but only limited cereal remains at Willington, Derbyshire (Beamish 2001, 9–10).

4.5.1   Crop Husbandry

A small number of Neolithic and Early Bronze Age sites in the Trent Valley have yielded charred plant remains indicative of cereal cultivation or processing (*cf.* Monckton 2003, Appendix E1), but generally little may be deduced from these beyond assessment of the range of crop types which may have been cultivated. These undoubtedly included emmer wheat and barley, to judge by rare discoveries at sites such as Aston-upon-Trent, Derbyshire, where emmer wheat seeds were found with sherds of Neolithic Grimston Ware pottery in a hearth sealed beneath a barrow (Alvey 1964; Loveday 2000; Reaney 1968, 71, 77: Aston 1), and the Potlock cursus, Derbyshire (Guilbert 1996) where undifferentiated wheat and barley grains were recovered from low in the fill of the southern cursus ditch alongside hazelnuts, plants indicative of grassy and disturbed ground and seeds of blackberry, sloe, elder and hawthorn; some of the latter seeds could conceivably have derived from an associated hedge. In addition, excavations of an Early Bronze Age barrow at Lockington revealed a small quantity of cereal grains in the mound make-up (derived from the adjacent land surface and hence probably residual) and various other contexts, including an encircling ring-ditch, a central pit and a charcoal spread beneath the mound (Moffett and Monckton 2000). Cereals included emmer wheat, glume wheat and hulled barley. Other plants included hazel nutshells and either sloe or hawthorn. Spelt wheat grains have been recovered from some later Neolithic and Early Bronze Age contexts – notably from Langford, together with undifferentiated barley grains in features incorporating Peterborough Ware and Beaker sherds and sealed beneath the Roman Fosse Way (Snelling and Rackham 2001, 22), and just beyond the end of our period from a pit at Lockington dated by associated hazel and buckthorn charcoal to 3039 ± 80 BP (Beta-83722, 1500–1010 cal BC; Moffett and Monckton 2000, 79; *cf.* Chapter 5.6). It is uncertain, however, how widely this crop was cultivated before the period of its major expansion in the first millennium BC (Chapter 5.6).

4.5.2   Animal Husbandry

Plentiful evidence has been recovered from palaeochannel fills and other contexts for an expansion of pasture, particularly on the floodplain (Chapter 4.4), but the balance between arable and pasture and the extent to which this may have varied regionally or have changed over time remain

far from clear. Detailed discussion of the specific animal husbandry regime is complicated by the extreme paucity of faunal remains. The acidic soils of the terrace gravels are extremely unfavourable for bone preservation, and little may be deduced from the small quantities of animal bone retrieved from most sites of this period beyond the range of domesticated and other species that may have been exploited (*cf.* Monckton 2003, 10). The most spectacular site from the faunal perspective is Langford Lowfields, where excavations revealed an accumulation of several hundred animal and human bones associated with timbers and brushwood in what was interpreted as a log-jam besides a gravel bar in an abandoned channel of the Trent (Garton *et al.* 1996; 1997). An initial 2 x 2m evaluation trench revealed almost 200 well-preserved human and animal bones, including the remains of wild (aurochs) and domestic cattle, pig and possibly wild boar, red and roe deer, horse, dog and sheep; these were mostly single bones, but some groups of semi-articulated bone were noted (including part of a human rib-cage and pelvis). Further excavations uncovered, in addition to at least thirteen human skulls, the skulls of three sheep, one aurochs, four domesticated cattle, one deer and two dogs, together with five large antlers. A fragment of bone was dated to 3780 ± 50 BP (Beta-87093, 2400–2030 cal BC), placing this 'event' in the very late Neolithic (although the calibrated date range actually just overlaps the proposed threshold between the Neolithic and Early Bronze Age at *c.* 2050 cal BC: Chapter 4.1). The excavators suggested that this association should be viewed within a funerary or ritual rather than domestic context (Chapter 4.6.2), but it provides nonetheless an excellent snapshot of the variety of domesticated and wild fauna present in the Trent Valley during the closing centuries of the third millennium BC.

4.6   The Role of the River

The wetland environments of the valley floor would have provided a rich resource base for communities within the region, permitting exploitation of a wide range of subsistence and other products such as fish, wildfowl and building materials (e.g. reeds), while the river itself may have assumed a variety of social and economic roles. The anastomosing channels of the Trent are likely to have provided convenient routes of communication between dispersed Valley communities, facilitating the exchange of commodities such as stone axes derived from sources in Great Langdale, Charnwood Forest and elsewhere, although at present the first direct evidence for river transport dates from no earlier than the Middle Bronze Age (Chapter 5.4.1). In addition to its obvious significance as a communication route, the river appears to have developed increasingly as a focus for funerary rituals and ceremonial acts of deposition, particularly of metalwork. As part of this development, certain confluence zones may have emerged as areas of special significance. These include the Trent-Derwent-Soar confluence, downstream of the monument complex incorporating the Aston and Potlock cursuses, and the Trent-Tame confluence, near to which were located the causewayed enclosures at Mavesyn Ridware and Alrewas and the Fisherwick monument complex of the Lower Tame Valley. Evidence has also survived for a variety of specialised riverine structures, including burnt mounds and one example of a possible fish-weir, which together provide useful evidence for the role of the river within the subsistence economy. Some of these specialised structures may also have been linked to ritual and ceremonial activities, supporting current views of the key role of ritual in all aspects of everyday life during this period.

4.6.1 Metalwork Deposition

Substantial quantities of Bronze Age metalwork have been recovered from the Trent Valley, much of this from contemporary riverine contexts and other wet or marshy locations (Davis 1999; Scurfield 1997). The great majority of this may be ascribed on typological grounds to the Middle and Late Bronze Ages (Chapter 5.4.2), but a small proportion of the typologically diagnostic material may be dated to the Early Bronze Age. These early finds are very thinly scattered along the valley, with some minor concentrations correlating with areas of extensive quarrying and urban development, particularly in the vicinity of Attenborough and between Colwick and Holme Pierrepont (Scurfield 1997, fig.4). This spatial distribution almost certainly reflects the accident of survival rather than contemporary variability in the density of activity, but the marked variations in the density of artefacts by period may well signify genuine temporal differences in the frequency of deposition. This riverine concentration invites comparison with other lowland rivers such as the Thames (*cf.* Bradley 1984, 96–127), although for this early period the quantities involved are significantly smaller.

Some of the comparatively small numbers of Early Bronze Age artefacts which have been recovered were retrieved from the river during fishing or dredging, but most were obtained during quarrying of sub-alluvial gravel deposits or organic deposits correlating with palaeochannels of the Trent. The original circumstances of deposition of this material can no longer be ascertained, but these objects may have been deposited singly or together with other finds in contemporary river channels and other wet or marshy locations, possibly as ceremonial or ritual offerings, as goods accompanying burial, or as a result of processes such as casual loss, erosion from bankside settlements or river battles (*ibid.* 100). Some of these might even correlate with timber trackways (Chapter 4.6.4), bearing in mind the long-lived tradition of deliberate deposition of metalwork and other artefacts alongside such structures in other parts of the country (Field and Parker-Pearson 2003, 184–7; Pryor 2001, 295–8, 421–36; *cf.* Clifton, Nottinghamshire: Chapter 5.4.2).

4.6.2 Human Burials

Attention has been drawn above to the exceptional finds of human and animal remains which it has been suggested had accumulated at a log-jam in a former channel of the Trent at Langford Lowfields (Chapter 4.5.2; Fig.4.4). This site is unparalleled in the Trent Valley, and provides a unique insight into the kinds of riverside funerary or ritual practices which may provide the background to some of the metalwork deposits discussed above. Two explanations have been proposed for the combination

Fig.4.4 *Langford Lowfields, Nottinghamshire: later Neolithic human skulls preserved within a log-jam in a former channel of the Trent (photograph: D.Garton)*

Fig.4.5 *Willington, Derbyshire: Neolithic and Bronze Age palaeochannels, burnt mounds and other archaeological remains (source: Beamish 2001; reproduced by courtesy of M. Beamish and the Derbyshire Archaeological Society)*

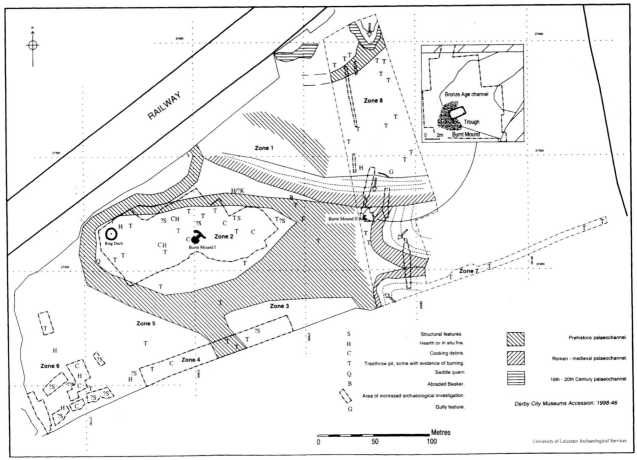

of human and animal remains recorded in the log-jam. The first proposes a catastrophic event such as a flood, causing people and animals to be swept downstream until encountering the tangle of tree-trunks and brushwood blocking the river course. The second envisages a link with riverside mortuary rituals which, on the basis of the preserved human remains, may have embraced both sexes and a range of ages from child to adult (Garton *et al.* 1996; 1997). The latter interpretation was favoured by the excavators, who suggested that the skeletal material might imply excarnation with a ritual emphasis upon human and animal skulls, and speculated on the disturbance by flood of the focus of ritual activity (*ibid.* 9). Excarnation, which has been claimed on other Neolithic and Bronze Age sites in the East Midlands, such as Wigber Low in Derbyshire (Collis 1983), would provide a convenient explanation for the disposal of members of the community who were not buried in barrows. This practice could also explain also the comparative dearth of first millennium BC burials from the region (Chapter 5.4.2).

Elsewhere within the region, rare discoveries of skulls and other human remains have been recorded near riverine finds of Bronze Age metalwork, notably at Clifton, Nottinghamshire (Phillips 1941,134) and Elvaston, Derbyshire (Davis 2003), recalling the evidence for possible associations between Bronze Age metalwork deposits and human skulls in the Thames Valley (Bradley and Gordon 1988). Unequivocal evidence for an association between the deposition of metalwork and riverine burials

has yet to be obtained, however, while at present all of the closely dated examples from the Trent Valley may be attributed to the Middle or Late Bronze Ages.

4.6.3 Burnt Mounds

In the past few years, a number of burnt mounds of Neolithic and Bronze Age date have been identified close to former channels and tributaries of the Trent, expanding further the distribution of a class of monument which until recent work in areas such as Staffordshire, Hampshire and East Anglia had been regarded as principally a feature of the Highland Zone (Barfield and Hodder 1989; Leah and Crowson 1994; Martin 1988; Pasmore and Pallister 1967; Welch 1994). Excavations of Valley sites such as Waycar Pasture, Girton (Garton 1993), Holme Dyke, Gonalston (Elliott and Knight 1998) and Willington (Fig. 4.5; Beamish and Ripper 2000) suggest mounds of heat-shattered stones, accompanied originally by hearths for heating stones and receptacles for water – perhaps a pit with a wooden or stone trough – into which heated stones would have been thrown.

The many possible functions of these burnt mounds have been intensely debated (e.g. Buckley ed. 1990; Hodder and Barfield eds 1991). The available ethnographic and folk evidence, combined with experimental work and assessments of documentary records from areas such as Ireland and the Northern Isles, suggest an association of many monuments with the preparation and consumption

Fig.4.6 *View during excavation of a burnt mound at Waycar Pasture, Girton, Nottinghamshire (photograph: L. Elliott)*

of food for domestic or other purposes (e.g. Hedges 1975; O'Kelly 1954). Alternative functions such as saunas (Barfield 1991; Barfield and Hodder 1987) or links with specialised craft or industrial activities such as textile production (Jeffery 1991) should also be considered, although it seems likely that many sites had in fact performed multiple functions.

Few of the burnt mounds in the Trent Valley have been closely dated, but several examples have yielded evidence which could imply an origin in the later Neolithic or earlier Bronze Age (see Chapter 5.7.1 for later examples). The most impressive of these was recorded during excavations at Willington, in a rather atypical location near the crest of a gravel island bordered by palaeochannels (Beamish 2001, 10: Burnt Mound I; Beamish and Ripper 2000). The monument comprised a low crescentic mound of heat-affected stones, approximately seven by five metres in diameter, incorporating Peterborough Ware sherds and flintwork. A hearth, trough and pit were set in a line at the centre of the mound, while another possible hearth and a pit were recorded on the south and south-east edges of the mound. Charred hazelnuts and sloe stones were recorded in the mound and trough deposits, while the latter also yielded a calcined cattle tooth. The presence of a cattle tooth recalls the discovery of faunal remains at several other burnt mounds within the region, and as argued by the excavator may support the case for an association with food preparation and possibly feasting (Beamish 2001, 10).

Another potentially early burnt mound was recorded at Holme Dyke, Gonalston, on the edge of the Holme Pierrepont Terrace adjacent to a wide alluvial zone preserving several shallow linear depressions interpreted as palaeochannels (Elliott and Knight 1998). The remains were exposed in the side of a drainage ditch, and comprised a compacted layer of small heat-affected stones interpreted as the truncated remains of a burnt mound. This sealed two pits and was cut by a third pit, all yielding large quantities of small heat-affected stones. No direct evidence for the function of this mound was obtained. However, thermoluminescence dates of 1940 ± 350 BC (QTLS-THM22) and 2720 ± 420 BC (QTLS-THM35) at one sigma for burnt stones obtained from pits sealed by the layer of heat-affected stones, together with an infra-red stimulated luminescence date of 2590 ± 460 BC at one sigma obtained

from this overlying layer, would support a Neolithic or Early Bronze Age date (*ibid.* 19–20).

One other example which might date from this early period was recorded beneath alluvium, adjacent to a peat-filled palaeochannel at Waycar Pasture, Girton (Fig. 4.6; Garton 1993). This site, which at the time of excavation was the first burnt mound to have been recorded in the Trent Valley, comprised a low approximately oval mound of burnt stone and black soil, some 10–12m in diameter and up to 0.4m high. Redeposited mound material was observed at a low level in the palaeochannel, suggesting that the mound had flanked a contemporary water course. Two tree trunks, one with cut marks, were observed on top of this layer of redeposited mound material, and were interpreted as possibly evidence of an area of hard standing between the mound and the river channel. No hearths survived, but a large boat-shaped pit on the eastern edge of the mound, backfilled with burnt stones beneath clean sand, may represent the remains of a trough; another smaller pit was sealed by mound deposits. Samples were taken for radiocarbon and dendrochronological dating, but at present the only dating evidence comprises a grog-tempered body sherd typical of Early and Middle Bronze Age ceramic vessels from the Middle and Lower Trent Valley (*cf.* Allen *et al.* 1987, 213–5). This was obtained from the mound make-up, together with burnt clay, a burnt whetstone and some flintwork, and hence could have been redeposited from an earlier phase of activity.

A thin scatter of Neolithic and Bronze Age pits and post-holes was recorded in the vicinity of the mounds at Gonalston (Elliott and Knight 1998, 15–16) and Willington (Beamish and Ripper 2000, 37), suggesting that both might have formed components of more elaborate settlements. At Girton, a ditch, probable post-holes and other features were recorded in a quarry face on the opposite side of the palaeochannel, sealed beneath the peaty upper fill of the channel (Garton 1993). The similar stratigraphic position of the burnt mound and these features, several of which also yielded burnt pebbles, prompted the excavator to suggest that they might have been broadly contemporary. Whether or not this or other burnt mounds had stood in splendid isolation or had formed components of more extensive sites, there are grounds to postulate more permanent structures than are suggested by the feeble structural remains which characterise most settlements of this period in the Trent Valley (Chapter 4.8). Such monuments would have provided highly visible landmarks which could, therefore, have acted as important social foci for the mobile communities which dominate recent models of Neolithic society in southern England (e.g. Whittle 1999), although the issue of permanent versus mobile settlement has yet to be satisfactorily resolved for this period (Chapter 4.8.3).

4.6.4 Fishweirs

Although the river remained a fundamentally untamed resource during this period, the discovery at Castle Donington of a possible Neolithic fishweir provides interesting evidence for the beginnings of human manipulation of this important environmental resource. A

Fig.4.7 *Bronze Age log boat at Argosy Washolme, Aston-upon-Trent, Derbyshire, with possible cargo of sandstone blocks in situ (photograph: D.Garton)*

palaeochannel recorded during quarrying at this site yielded nine posts of purging buckthorn, willow, holly and elder, associated with a fragment of a wattlework panel (Clay and Salisbury 1990, 290, fig.14: Channel II). A sample from a post of purging buckthorn yielded a radiocarbon date of 4720 ± 70 BP (Har-8508; 3650–3350 cal BC; Clay 2001b, 9; C.Salisbury: pers. comm.). Comparisons with other timber structures from the region suggested to the excavators that the structure might represent part of a fishweir (Clay and Salisbury 1990, 290). If so, its discovery would have major implications for our understanding of the management of river resources during this period.

4.6.5   Causeways and Boats

Movements of people and stock across wet and boggy areas within the floodplain may have been facilitated by wooden trackways linking higher sand and gravel islands, comparable to those recorded in the Somerset Levels (Coles and Coles 1986) or, within later Bronze Age and Iron Age contexts, at Flag Fen, Cambridgeshire (Pryor 1992) and Fiskerton, Lincolnshire (Field and Parker-Pearson 2003). Fragmentary remains of two linear structures, possibly forming part of a single wooden trackway which may have been built and repaired over a protracted time period, were recorded during quarry watching briefs at Argosy Washolme, Aston-upon-Trent (Garton *et al.* 2001; C.Salisbury and D.Garton: pers. comm.). The structural remains and other finds from this site straddle the time periods considered in this and the following chapter, but for convenience are discussed together here.

The first of the linear structures was recorded by Salisbury in 1997, and comprised a layer of brushwood pierced by sharpened posts penetrating a foundation layer of sandstone blocks and driven into the underlying gravel. Samples from brushwood and the outer rings of a post yielded dates of 3060 ± 50 BP (Beta-118363, 1430–1130 cal BC) and 3070 ± 60 BP (Beta-115407, 1490–1120 cal BC) respectively. Later investigations close to this site revealed a deposit of oak logs, some with cut marks and preserving tool-marks and perforations, overlying a layer of brushwood infilling a silty depression. No stone foundations were recorded. Radiocarbon measurements were obtained from the brushwood of 3160 ± 60 BP (GU-5811, 1530–1310 cal BC) and 3000 ± 150 BP (GU-5812, 1600–830 cal BC), and from ash stakes of 3140 ± 50 BP (GU-5809, 1520–1260 cal BC) and 3190 ± 50 BP (Gu-5810, 1600–1320 cal BC). These are not statistically different from those obtained from the other linear structure and, as both structures followed approximately the same alignment, it is possible to postulate a single causeway across the floodplain which may have varied in the method of construction.

The most spectacular find at Argosy Washolme was a largely intact log boat, jammed against several oak logs, some 22m away from one of the linear timber structures (Fig. 4.7). Both the bow and the stern had been broken accidentally during quarrying, but sufficient fragments of the bow remained to permit reconstruction (Garton *et al.* 2001, fig.2). The boat contained several blocks of Bromsgrove Sandstone, some of considerable size, the nearest source of which would have been some 3km upstream. The stone could represent a contemporary cargo, conceivably for use in the construction of the stone foundation of part of the trackway. Two radiocarbon measurements from the outer rings of the boat provided dates of 3117 ± 35 BP (OxA-9536, 1490–1260 cal BC) and 3113 ± 34 BP (OxA-9537, 149–1260 cal BC), which when combined provide a weighted mean age of 3115 ± 24 BP, calibrated to 1440–1310 cal BC at 2 sigma (C. Salisbury: pers. comm.). Yet more recently, another well preserved log boat has been recorded in the quarry, less than 1km to the south-west of the initial discovery (C. Salisbury: pers. comm.). Radiocarbon samples were taken from this boat during the course of writing this chapter, and the results are awaited with interest. Further investigations have also shown the boats and causeways to be located within a wide floodplain zone which in the Bronze Age may have incorporated extensive areas of open water and marshland. A total of twelve Middle to Late Bronze Age metal artefacts has been recovered so far from this area, mainly from areas which it has been suggested may at the time of deposition have lain at the interface between dry and wet land (C. Salisbury: pers. comm.; Chapter 5.4.2), and the site provides an excellent example of the depositional practices discussed in an earlier section of this chapter (Chapter 4.6.1; also Chapter 5.4.2).

4.7   Ordering the Landscape

Significant changes may be observed in the human impact upon the Valley landscape during the fourth and third millennia BC, with the construction of a varied range of ditched and embanked enclosures and timber settings demarcating funerary and ceremonial foci and defining corridors of movement. These developed alongside the first funerary barrows, many of which were placed within clearly defined enclosures whose purpose may have been to separate physically the living from the dead, and imply a growing preoccupation with the demarcation of ritual zones within the landscape. Few of these monuments have been the focus of intrusive archaeological excavations, with the notable exception of round barrows and ring-ditches (Chapter 4.7.1). Hence assessment of their chronology and functions must rest in large part upon comparisons with excavated monuments of related form elsewhere in Britain, with the key proviso that typology and functions are likely to have varied significantly regionally. Such comparisons have permitted recognition of a wide range of enclosure types spanning the period from the earlier Neolithic to the Early Bronze Age, including causewayed enclosures, henges, timber circles, ring-ditches and cursus monuments. Classification is complicated by the morphological overlap between monument classes – as exemplified by Round Hill, Twyford, which combines a hengiform enclosure with a substantial mound reminiscent of the 'great barrows' of the White Peak (Harding with Lee 1987, 116–7, 119) – and too much emphasis should not be placed upon the finer typological distinctions between monument types (cf. Last 1999, 86–7). Caution should also be urged in applying too uncritically hypotheses devised for regions such as Wessex, which during this period may have differed significantly in environmental, social and economic terms.

One of the key themes of this section is the role of enclosure as a means by which early communities sought to bound and order their environment, and in order to elucidate this theme enclosures have been grouped for the purposes of discussion into those which may have performed a primarily sepulchral role, those which appear to have been connected with a broader range of ceremonial, exchange and other activities (which may in some cases have included burial) and those whose principal purpose might have been to focus and channel movement. The one prevailing theme, which distances these sites from the enclosures discussed in the following chapter, is the emphasis upon ceremony rather than settlement, although it should be emphasised that analyses of the abundant enclosed settlements of the first millennium BC also demand that the symbolism of enclosure be considered (Chapter 5.7.2). Barrows, since they were commonly demarcated in this region by ring-ditches, are grouped in the following section with funerary enclosures.

4.7.1   Funerary Enclosures and Barrows

Several categories of monument may have functioned primarily as funerary enclosures, both for the burial of the dead and, perhaps, as foci for ceremonies celebrating ancestral links. Such monuments may have symbolised enduring associations with real or imagined ancestors, perhaps binding dispersed communities more closely together and emphasising their historic ties with particular localities. These communities may have operated within the framework of a mobile or sedentary lifestyle (Chapter 4.8.3) and hence assessments of their role within the landscape must take account of a variety of scenarios ranging from close associations between permanent settlements and burial monuments within well-defined territories to periodic revisitations of monuments by widely ranging mobile communities.

The most ubiquitous of these monuments is the 'ring-ditch', examples of which are widely but unevenly distributed throughout the length of the Valley. The recorded distribution is based largely upon crop-mark data, and not surprisingly is biased mainly towards the well-drained soils of the river terraces. Serious distributional biases arise from the variable impact of quarrying and urban expansion, the burial of valley-bottom sites beneath alluvial and colluvial deposits and intra-regional variations in agricultural practices, but despite these problems there are clear implications of significant spatial variations in the overall densities of ring-ditches. Particularly high densities of ring-ditches, which may reflect genuine variations in the level of activity, have been recorded along the Middle Trent around the Tame-Trent confluence and upstream of the Trent-Derwent-Soar confluence (cf. Garwood 2003, 1–3; Loveday 2004; Woodward 2003, 3), recalling the distribution patterns for cursus monuments and larger ceremonial enclosures which are discussed below (cf. Vine 1982, maps AC, AE, AF). In addition, several clusters of ring-ditches, some associated with denuded barrows and indicative of major cemetery complexes, have been identified within the region – as at Swarkestone Lowes (Elliott and Knight 1999, fig.2:

Fig.4.8 *View of Barrow VI at Lockington, Leicestershire, during excavation (source: Hughes 2000; photograph by Gwilym Hughes, reproduced with the permission of Birmingham Archaeology)*

Barrows I–VI) and Lockington (Hughes 2000, fig.2: Barrows I–VI; Fig. 4.8). In general, however, ring-ditches are more evenly scattered along the terraces.

Ring-ditches are defined by the presence of an annular ditch enclosing an area with an average internal diameter of *c*.10–25m or by more complex arrangements of multiple concentric ditches extending over significantly larger areas (e.g. Aston-upon-Trent: Garton *et al.* 1994; Knight 1998; Whitemoor Haye, Alrewas, Staffordshire: Coates 2002, 9–13). Excavations have demonstrated complex sequences of ditch recuts on a number of sites (e.g. Great Briggs, Holme Pierrepont: Guilbert, undated; Aston 1: Reaney 1968), creating in some cases a spurious impression of multiple concentric ditches (e.g. Fatholme, Staffordshire: Losco-Bradley 1984), but a small proportion of monuments seem genuinely to have been defined by several annular ditches (e.g. Aston-upon-Trent: Garton *et al.* 1994; Knight 1998). Some ditches may be shown to have demarcated the area occupied by a contemporary funerary barrow, in which case the ditch could have provided a convenient source of constructional material as well as a symbolic barrier between the living and the dead (e.g. Swarkestone Barrow II: Posnansky 1955a). Not all barrows, however, have preserved traces of an associated ditched boundary (e.g. earliest phase of Swarkestone Barrow IV: Greenfield 1960, 4) while an unknown proportion of graves may have lacked any form of surface demarcation. Notable examples of ring-ditches demarcating barrows have been recorded in cemeteries at Swarkestone Lowes (Elliott and Knight 1999, 82, fig.2: Barrows I–VI) and Lockington (Hughes 2000; Posnansky 1955b), inside the Aston cursus (Loveday 2000; 2004; Reaney 1968: Aston 1)

and at Cromwell, Nottinghamshire (Dauncey and Hurrell 1951). The former presence of barrows has also been postulated from ditch silting patterns (e.g. Weston 1, Derbyshire: Reaney 1968, 75), although interpretations of differential ditch silting are complicated by the possibility that material had weathered from an internal or external bank rather than a barrow. In most cases, however, insufficient evidence has survived to demonstrate the presence of an associated barrow (e.g. Tucklesholme Farm, Barton-under-Needwood, Staffordshire: Martin and Allen 2002; Clifton, Nottinghamshire: Allen *et al.* 1994; Fiskerton, Nottinghamshire: O'Brien 1979a; Shelford, Nottinghamshire: Revill 1974). Interpretations of these sites must embrace a range of options from the truncation of a former mound by ploughing (e.g. Hughes 2000, 100) to the construction of embanked and/or ditched arenas for funerary or ceremonial purposes, recalling in this latter respect the well-preserved ring-cairns of the Peak District (*cf.* Barnatt 1990; e.g. Fernello Sitch, Barrow-upon-Trent: Knight 1996; Willington: Beamish 2001, 10, fig.2: 'ring-ditch'). Further problems of interpretation arise in intensively farmed areas from the serious denudation of features cut into subsoil, and the consequent loss of structural, artefactual and bone evidence indicative of an association with burial. Such difficulties are exemplified by truncated ring-ditches at Tucklesholme Farm (Martin and Allen 2002), Great Briggs (Guilbert, undated) and Holme Dyke, Gonalston (Elliott and Knight 1998, 15, fig.2: A), where extensive open-area excavations of plough-denuded ring-ditches yielded no evidence of associated burials. This may reflect only the accident of survival, but such cases should urge a cautious approach to the equation of ring-ditches with funerary monuments (*cf.* Hughes 2002, 2).

Despite the above problems, current evidence would support the contention that ring-ditches had commonly demarcated burial areas, and that the majority of sites of this type were constructed during the Neolithic and Early Bronze Age. Most of the excavated examples appear to date from no earlier than the later Neolithic, but their origins may be traced with reasonable confidence to the fourth millennium BC. The earliest recorded monument of this type from the Valley is a multi-phased ring-ditch at Great Briggs, although as noted above the site had been severely truncated by later ploughing and positive evidence for burial was not obtained (Guilbert, undated; Knight and Howard 1995, 34–5, fig.3.13). Five or possibly six intercutting concentric ditches were recorded during excavation. These enclosed an area *c.*12m in diameter containing five shallow pits and a hollow, and had apparently been recut consistently outwards – suggesting progressive enlargement of the monument to a maximum eventual diameter of *c.*15m internally. This complex sequence of recuts is difficult to explain in purely practical terms, and it is possible that the process of ditch excavation was itself a symbolic activity, the process of digging serving to draw together the members of the social group. These ditches may have enclosed a central mound, which could in turn have been associated with burials, although no traces of these had survived. Artefacts from the ring-ditch sections included earlier Neolithic (Grimston Ware) pottery, flintwork of earlier Neolithic character and two polished stone axe fragments. The internal pits and the hollow also incorporated Grimston Ware sherds and flintwork. Four small pits away from the ring-ditch yielded later Neolithic and Bronze Age pottery, raising the possibility that the monument had acted as a focus for later domestic activity.

Most other excavated ring-ditches within the region would appear to date from the later Neolithic and Early Bronze Age periods, including single ring-ditches at Swarkestone Lowes (Elliott and Knight 1999), Lockington (Hughes 2000; Posnansky 1955b), Fernello Sitch (Knight 1996) and Tucklesholme Farm (Martin and Allen 2002) and an impressive multiple ring-ditch at Aston-upon-Trent (Garton *et al.* 1994; Knight 1998). Many of these monuments have yielded positive evidence for single or multiple burials (invariably of small numbers of individuals), study of which suggests a wide variety of funerary rituals which are likely to have varied significantly regionally and over time. Full discussion of these developing sepulchral rituals is beyond the scope of the present work, but attention may be drawn to the presence of both inhumations, which in the absence of preserved human remains may be deduced from the inclusion of pots, stone wrist-guards and other diagnostic artefacts of the Beaker tradition (e.g. Knight and Beswick 2000; Reaney 1968), and single or multiple cremation burials inside urns, coffins or other containers, laid directly on the ground surface or placed in small pits (e.g. Swarkestone Lowes Barrows I–IV: Greenfield 1960; Posnansky 1955a). Associated non-ceramic finds have rarely been recorded, especially by contrast with the rich graves of areas such as Wessex (Piggott 1938), but occasional discoveries of prestige metalwork and other goods suggest access by some communities to high-value commodities (e.g. Lockington I: Posnansky 1955b). The comparative rarity of rich grave finds may carry important implications for the wealth and status of Valley

communities during this period, although caution should obviously be exercised in equating surviving grave goods with the status of either individuals or communities.

Excavations at several sites in the region have revealed stratigraphic evidence for enclosures preceding the construction of ring-ditches, suggesting that the latter may on some sites represent the final stage in a protracted process of enclosure and funerary ritual. The sequence is best exemplified at Lockington, where recent excavations of a ring-ditch and denuded barrow revealed a narrow, discontinuous ring-gully, shown on stratigraphic grounds to have preceded construction of the ring-ditch and associated barrow; this was interpreted as possibly the foundation trench for a palisade defining an earlier roughly circular mortuary enclosure (Hughes 2000, 95–102). A link with funerary activities may be provided by a small pit on the line of this 'palisade' gully, yielding an unusual combination of objects which individually are well-known components of grave deposits, and marked apparently by a carved stone of the kind commonly associated with burials. These comprise two incomplete inverted Beakers, one inside the other, a copper dagger with an organic scabbard dated to *c.*2200–1900 BC (Fig. 4.9; Needham 2000, 46) and two gold armlets dated to *c.* 2100–1700 BC (Fig. 4.10), but no traces of inhumation or cremation remains were recovered (Hughes 2000, 9–10, fig.9, plates 14–17: Lockington VI;

Fig.4.9 *Copper dagger with remnants of organic scabbard from a pit at Lockington, Leicestershire (source: Hughes 2000; photograph by Graeme Norrie, reproduced with the permission of Birmingham Archaeology)*

Fig.4.10 *Gold armlets from a pit at Lockington, Leicestershire (source: Hughes 2000; photograph by Graeme Norrie, reproduced with the permission of Birmingham Archaeology)*

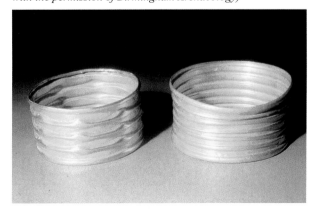

Needham 2000; Woodward 2000). At a later stage, pyre material was redeposited within an area demarcated by the ring-ditch and a central mound was constructed. These phases may signify unrelated events separated widely in time, or alternatively could imply a protracted ritual process following directly on from the construction of a mortuary enclosure and culminating in the physical separation of the cremated remains of the corpses and the grave goods. This has important implications for other ring-ditches in the region which have yielded evidence of similar stratigraphically early ring-gullies, as at Tucklesholme Farm (Martin and Allen 2002), and could imply on some sites a complex process of enclosure from initial mortuary compound to the final demarcation of the monument from the outside world by the construction of the ring-ditch.

It is worth noting finally the evidence for elongated quadrilateral single-ditched enclosures, discussed some time ago by Loveday and Petchey (1982). These authors drew attention to the air photographic evidence from the Trent Valley for this category of enclosure, some of which they suggested could represent ploughed-out versions of the Neolithic long barrows which are conspicuously absent from the Valley. The argument for an association with burial has been developed by later researchers such as Whimster (1989, 68, fig.39: E, F), who noted two examples at Cromwell of elongated quadrilateral enclosures with rounded corners which he suggested compared typologically with Neolithic funerary or ceremonial enclosures from southern England. Subsequent air photographic research has extended significantly the distribution of this crop-mark type (Clay 2001b, 8). We may note also the suggestion by Loveday that a long narrow enclosure at Mavesyn Ridware could represent a ploughed-out 'bank barrow' (ibid. 8; 2004, 1), comparable perhaps to the elongated earthwork at Long Low, Derbyshire (Barnatt 1996, fig. 2; Barnatt and Collis 1996). No excavations have yet been carried out on these long subrectangular enclosures within the Trent Valley, but work outside the region suggests that the option of a Neolithic origin for at least some monuments should be accorded serious consideration. At Eye Kettleby, Leicestershire, for example, excavations revealed two subrectangular elongated earlier Neolithic enclosures (Finn 1998), while in the Nene Valley excavations at the Northamptonshire sites of Aldwincle (Jackson 1976), Grendon (Gibson and McCormick 1985) and Stanwick (Keevill 1992) have revealed a complex pattern of both long enclosures and long barrows of earlier Neolithic date.

4.7.2 Major Ceremonial Enclosures: Causewayed Enclosures, Henges and Pit Circles

A small number of crop-mark and earthwork enclosures within the region may be compared on typological grounds with causewayed enclosures (Darvill and Thomas eds 2001; Oswald et al. 2001), henges (Harding with Lee 1987; Harding 2003) and timber circles (e.g. East Stoke, Nottinghamshire: Harding with Lee 1987, 28–9), thus raising the possibility of a range of major ceremonial enclosures within the Trent Valley. Few of these, unfortunately, have been examined by excavation, and

hence considerable doubts must be expressed regarding their dating, morphology and functions.

The largest enclosures are represented by a pair of Staffordshire sites upstream of the Trent-Tame confluence at Alrewas (Mercer 1990, 10–11, Fig.2.1; Oswald et al. 2001, 155: Site 76, fig.4.9; Palmer 1976, 164, 173, 175,184) and Mavesyn Ridware (Fig.4.11; Mercer 1990, 10–11; Oswald et al. 2001, 155: Site 75, fig. 4.18; Palmer 1976, 164, 173, 184). Aerial photographs have revealed crop-marks indicative of two egg-shaped enclosures defined by up to three concentric interrupted ditches enclosing areas ranging from c.3.0–4.15ha at Alrewas (Palmer 1976, 184, Plate 17, fig.13.2) and c.3.14–4.15ha at Mavesyn Ridware (ibid, 184, fig.13.1; Riley 1987, fig.67). The concentric interrupted ditches invite close comparison with well-known causewayed enclosures such as Knap Hill or Windmill Hill in Wiltshire (e.g. Mercer 1990; Oswald et al. 2001), in which case an origin in the earlier Neolithic would be possible. Parallels with such sites would also imply discontinuous internal banks and possibly also associated timber structures (ibid. 2–3, fig.1.2), although any traces of ditches have long since been obliterated by ploughing.

Both sites are located significantly farther north than the main focus of causewayed enclosures in southern England, and were long regarded as the most northerly outliers of this monument class (Palmer 1976, 164, fig.1). More recent discoveries, however, in northern England, Wales, the Isle of Man, Northern Ireland and southern Scotland, have suggested a far wider distribution than was originally imagined (Oswald et al. 2001, fig.5.1). Although falling well within the distribution zone of such monuments, they are otherwise unparalleled in the Trent Valley. The close spacing of the Staffordshire enclosures, only a few kilometres apart, is therefore even more remarkable, recalling the close proximity of the cursus monuments upstream of the Trent-Derwent confluence at Aston and Potlock (Chapter 4.7.3; Loveday 2004). The riverine location of these monuments invites comparison with many other interrupted-ditch enclosures in the Midlands, notably in the Thames and Nene Valleys, while monument pairing may also be observed in neighbouring valleys such as the Nene and the Welland (ibid. 112–3). In addition, the location of both sets of monuments close to the Tame-Trent confluence reinforces the notion that confluence zones may have carried special significance in the later prehistory of the Trent Valley.

Causewayed enclosures vary significantly in terms of their internal areas, morphology and topographic locations, and probably also their functions (Oswald et al. 2001) and without excavation few positive conclusions may be drawn regarding the purpose of the Alrewas and Mavesyn Ridware enclosures. Some fieldwalking has been carried out on these sites, but this has yielded no finds which could shed light upon their date. With this proviso, comparisons with other sites in southern and central England would suggest an earlier Neolithic origin and a range of primarily non-domestic functions – perhaps as foci for dispersed and relatively mobile communities, within which a wide variety

Fig.4.11 *Neolithic causewayed enclosure at Mavesyn Ridware, Staffordshire (source: Oswald et al. 2001. © English Heritage. NMR. Base map data reproduced by permission of the Ordnance Survey on behalf of The Controller of Her Majesty's Stationery Office. © Crown Copyright 100020618)*

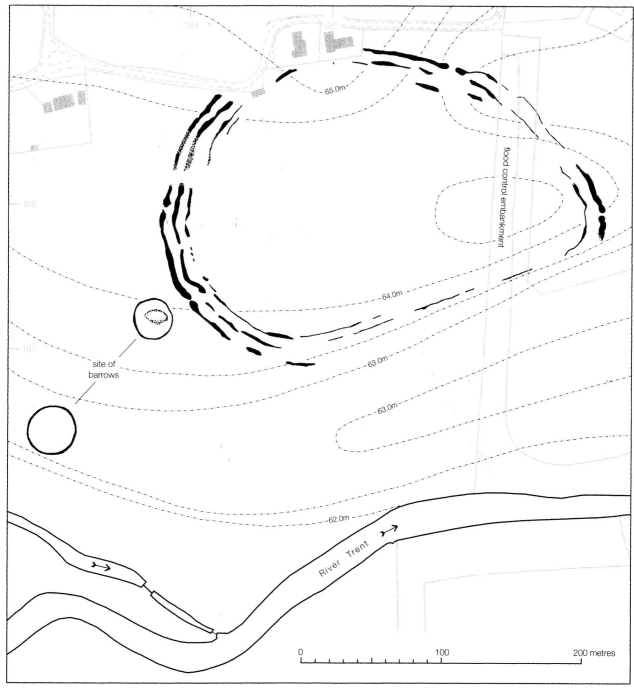

of ceremonial, funerary, exchange and other social or economic transactions could have been conducted (Oswald *et al.* 2001, 120–32). Occupation cannot be ruled out, but evidence from excavated sites elsewhere in Britain suggests that any settlement activity may have been episodic and of limited extent (*ibid.* 124–6).

Several examples have also been recorded in the Trent Valley of possible henges, although again none has been investigated by excavation. Potentially the best preserved example survives close to the Trent near Gunthorpe (Bishop 2001, 1; Nottinghamshire SMR 01820a). This enclosure is defined by a partially surviving ditch and an outer bank, and if genuinely of Neolithic or Bronze Age date would

be a remarkable survival for the Trent Valley. Other sites worth noting include Round Hill, Twyford, which preserves a massive mound some 4m high within a circular ditched enclosure with two opposing entrances (Harding with Lee 1987, 116–7, 119; Loveday 2004, 4–5; O'Brien 1978, 8). The enclosure recalls strongly Class II henges, but so far the only detailed archaeological investigations comprise a detailed contour survey and geophysical survey. Finally, Harding and Lee (1987, 221–4) and Whimster (1989, 69, fig.39: B) have drawn attention to a penannular ditched enclosure at Cromwell which may be related to Class I henge monuments. The massive ditch of this horseshoe-shaped enclosure certainly invites close comparison with monuments of that kind, and hence might imply a later

Fig.4.12 *Double pit circle near East Stoke, Nottinghamshire, possibly marking the foundations of timber posts (source: Cambridge University Collection of Air Photographs; photograph reference DC 10)*

Neolithic/Early Bronze Age ritual or ceremonial focus, but again further archaeological investigations are required to test this hypothesis.

Attention should be drawn finally to rare examples of single or multiple pit circles, perhaps marking the foundations of circular arrangements of timber posts, which if indicative of monuments with open perimeters may represent a translation into timber of the stone circles that are distributed widely over neighbouring areas of upland Derbyshire (e.g. Barnatt 1990). Affinities have been suggested with henge monuments (e.g. Harding with Lee 1987, 26) and possible reconstructions include lintelled timber structures, rings of freestanding posts and perhaps even settings of inverted tree trunks representing an inversion of the normal world (Gibson 2002, 9). The several examples which have been recorded in the Valley are known entirely from crop-mark evidence, and have yet to be investigated by excavation. Notable examples include a double pit circle at East Stoke, Nottinghamshire (Fig. 4.12; Harding with Lee 1987, 28–9) and a remarkable structure with multiple rings of concentric pits near Catholme, Staffordshire (Coates 2002, 79; Harding with Lee 1987, 268–71: site 171). A complex variation upon this theme may be provided by an interrupted ring-ditch with radiating lines of pits located close to the Catholme multiple pit circle (*ibid.* 271), although excavations would be required to test this hypothesis. The Catholme monuments are of particular interest in view of their location close to the Tame–Trent confluence, which it is suggested below might have acted also as a focus for cursus construction. This may be coincidental, but the concentration of Neolithic and Bronze Age monuments is sufficiently striking to suggest that this confluence zone could have had a special significance to Valley communities in the third and early second millennia BC.

4.7.3 Channels of Movement: Cursus Monuments and Timber Avenues

Several examples of long, narrow ditched enclosures, traditionally grouped under the heading of 'cursus' monuments (Barclay and Harding eds 1999), have been noted in the Middle Trent Valley between the confluences of the Trent with the Rivers Derwent and Tame. The best known of these are two substantial monuments at Aston-upon-Trent (Fig. 4.13; Elliott and Garton 1995; Gibson and Loveday 1989; Reaney 1968) and Potlock (Guilbert 1996; Knight 1998; Wheeler 1970: 'Findern cursus'), which extend respectively for at least 1.7km and 1.56km along the valley. These monuments are located a mere 10km apart, immediately upstream of the wide confluence zone where the Rivers Trent, Derwent and Soar meet. This remarkably close spacing, near the confluence of three major rivers, has attracted much comment – especially in view of the unusually high density of ring-ditches and other Neolithic and Bronze Age monuments in this area (e.g. Loveday 2004). It is all the more interesting given that the only other cursus monuments from the Trent Valley may lie upstream of these sites at the Trent-Tame confluence. Aerial photographs of that area have revealed crop-marks suggestive of two cursus monuments near Catholme (Hodder 1982; Jones 1992; Palmer 1976), again in close proximity to other monuments which have been ascribed to the Neolithic or Early Bronze Age, including the multiple pit circle and circular enclosure with radiating lines of pits discussed in the previous section and a cluster of ring-ditches (Hughes 2002, 2). Further excavations are required to investigate the

Fig.4.13 *Plan of the cursus and neighbouring cropmarks near Aston-upon-Trent, Derbyshire (source: Loveday 2004; reproduced by courtesy of R. Loveday and the Derbyshire Archaeological Society; © J. Goddard)*

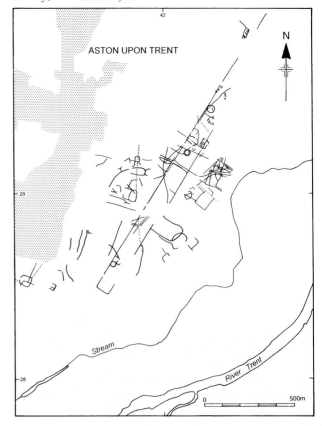

date and character of these sites, but there are suggestions of another major monument complex to rival that focused upon Aston and Potlock.

Excavations at the last two sites have enhanced our understanding of the morphology of cursus monuments in the Trent Valley, although the purpose and date of such enclosures remains unresolved. Trenches were cut across the Aston cursus ditches by Reaney (1968, 75) and Gibson and Loveday (1989), while more recently sections across the cursus ditches at Acre Lane and Weigh Lane have been cleaned and recorded (Elliott and Garton 1995). A trench was dug by Wheeler in 1969 across the Potlock cursus (Guilbert 1996; Wheeler 1970) and Guilbert has subsequently directed an extensive programme of fieldwalking, geophysical survey, test-pitting and excavation at this site. The latter work culminated in an extensive open-area excavation of the cursus-ditches and interior in advance of construction of the Derby Southern Bypass (Guilbert and Malone 1994; Knight 1998). The various ditch sections have demonstrated features of variable size and shape, dug up to c.1.2m beneath the level of the gravel and extending to a maximum of about 5m wide (e.g. Gibson and Loveday 1989, 38, figs 3:7, 3:8; 3:12). No surface traces of banks have survived, but banks formed from ditch upcast may be implied by a layer with high stone content recorded at Acre Lane, which it was suggested may have been spread from a bank by weathering or ploughing (Elliott and Garton 1995, 5), and by Reaney's (1968, 75) record of preferential silting from the interior of the cursus (see also Gibson and Loveday 1989, 27, fig.3.3). Archaeological investigations have shown that the ditches demarcating both cursuses were interrupted by entrance gaps, one at Potlock partially blocked by several small gullies (Guilbert 1996), but as at other cursus monuments their ends may well have been closed. Cropmarks have revealed a well-defined square terminal at the south-western extremity of the Aston cursus (Gibson and Loveday 1989, fig.3:1), providing unequivocal evidence for closure of the demarcated area, but the other cursus terminals have yet to be located. Excavations within the enclosed areas, which vary in width from c.75m at Potlock to c.100m at Aston, have yielded few clues as to their functions. The presence of ring-ditches within both cursuses, including two successive ring-ditches at Aston encircling a multi-phase funerary barrow (Reaney 1968, 70–74: Aston 1), may signify a link with sepulchral rituals but interpretation is complicated by the problem of demonstrating contemporaneity. At Aston, for example, Gibson and Loveday (1989, 38, 41) have argued that the cursus postdated one of the known ring-ditches, upon which the north-western cursus ditch may have been aligned.

The majority of radiocarbon dates from the primary levels of cursus ditches in other regions of Britain imply an earlier Neolithic origin for this monument class, with a major phase of construction in the second half of the fourth millennium cal BC (Barclay and Bayliss 1999; Harding and Barclay 1999, 5), but little evidence is so far available for the date of the Trent Valley examples. A trench across the northern ditch of the Potlock cursus revealed unweathered Peterborough Ware sherds at a low level in the ditch silts and Iron Age Scored Ware sherds in the uppermost fill of the same section.

Iron Age pottery was also recovered from other excavated sections, perhaps implying ploughing over the cursus during the later first millennium BC (Guilbert and Malone 1994, 17). A small fragment of a decorated Beaker pot and a sherd which it was suggested might be related to the Grooved Ware tradition were obtained from the 'very top' of one of the excavated ditch sections at Aston (Gibson and Loveday 1989, 42, fig.3:13, H and J), but in view of their stratigraphic locations both could postdate significantly the construction of the monument. Samples for radiocarbon dating have been taken from the cursus ditches at both Aston (Elliott and Garton 1995, 5) and Potlock, but the results of this work are not yet generally available.

The possible functions of cursus monuments have continued to fascinate prehistorians ever since Stukeley's (1740, 41) interpretation of the Amesbury cursus in Wiltshire as a 'course suitable for the racing of chariots by the ancient Britons', and convincing explanations of their role in later prehistoric society remain elusive. Their considerable lengths may imply a link with ceremonial processions, although the absence of obvious entrance gaps at the identified terminals of these monuments poses some obvious problems in accepting this hypothesis. The proximity of each of the identified cursus monuments to a host of Neolithic and Early Bronze Age funerary and ceremonial sites may imply a strong link with funerary and other ritual ceremonies (cf. Harding and Barclay 1999, 5–6). It has also been suggested that cursus monuments may have served to fix or formalise parts of some of the main routes of movement used by relatively mobile Neolithic communities (Last 1999, 94–5); if so, their presence at Aston and Potlock could provide important indirect evidence for the presumed role of the Trent and its tributaries as routes for the movement of people and commodities (Chapter 4.6). The proximity of these monuments to the Trent might reflect not only routes of movement but also strong symbolic links with water. Barclay and Hey (1999, 73) have noted the strong watery theme in the location of cursus monuments in the Upper Thames Valley and elsewhere, and have stressed the potential linkages between concepts of procession and running water and the possible symbolic importance of riverine locations to Neolithic communities (further implied in the Trent Valley by discoveries at sites such as Langford Lowfields: Chapter 4.6.2). It is interesting in this context to note that one of the breaks in the northern ditch of the Potlock cursus was shown by excavation to have been deliberately located to accommodate a stream which still crosses the monument immediately east of Potlock's House Farm (Guilbert 1996, 11). Finally, whatever their precise functions, their presence carries important implications for the extent of clearance during the period of their construction and use. Such major monuments imply extensive clearance of woodland, at least along the line of their route, and their presence at Aston and Potlock would support the evidence from nearby palaeochannels such as Chapel Farm and Hicken's Bridge for widespread clearance of some parts of the Trent-Derwent-Soar confluence during the Neolithic (Chapter 4.4.1).

Mention should be made finally of two lengths of a widely spaced double alignment of massive paired pits recorded to the north of South Muskham (SK791579) which

Fig. 4.14 Cropmarks of a possible timber avenue north of South Muskham, Nottinghamshire. Reproduced by permission of English Heritage (NMR) Derek Riley Collection (photograph reference DNR 1069/8, SK7958/72)

Whimster (1989, 80, fig. 60) has suggested could represent a timber-lined avenue of Neolithic or Early Bronze Age date (Fig. 4.14).Comparable monuments, distinguished by alignments of paired pits, have been postulated elsewhere in Nottinghamshire at Low Marnham (*ibid.* 30–1; fig.20: site 12) and Wilford (Jones 1998, 100) and in neighbouring areas such as the Lincolnshire Wolds and the Gwash Valley of Leicestershire (*ibid.* 100). It has been suggested that these might represent alternatives to cursus monuments (*ibid.* 101), and hence may provide further evidence for a growing preoccupation during the Neolithic with the control of movement through the landscape. Excavations at sites such as Thornborough and Dishforth (Harding and Johnson 2004, 26, 31; Tavener 1996, 184–6), both in North Yorkshire, have provided persuasive evidence for Neolithic or Early Bronze Age alignments of paired pits which may have contained upright timbers, but examples such as South Muskham are difficult to characterise without excavation. An alternative possibility at that site is a double alignment of open pits flanking a wide trackway, comparable to the pit alignments which developed later in this region as mechanisms of landscape division (Chapter 5.8.2).

4.8   Settlement and Population

Archaeological investigations of Neolithic and Bronze Age sites within the Trent Valley have focused traditionally upon burial monuments, and our knowledge of settlements of this period is therefore comparatively limited. Recent large-scale excavations in advance of quarrying, highway

development and other development threats, combined with systematic fieldwalking surveys of some stretches of the Valley, have partially redressed this imbalance, but even so many questions remain regarding the morphology, functions and spatial organisation of settlement. Attention is focused first upon the structural remains recovered during excavation, and the implications of this for an understanding of the character and functions of settlements. Later sections consider the evidence for increases in the density of settlements and their wider spatial organisation.

4.8.1   Settlement Morphology and Functions

Very few Neolithic or Early Bronze Age settlements have been excavated in the Trent Valley, and of these most have been revealed by accident during the investigation of other sites – for example, at Langford during the evaluation of a Roman agger (Holt *et al.* 2001) and at Willington during the excavation of a predominantly Iron Age and Romano-British crop-mark complex (Wheeler 1979). Settlements of the earlier Neolithic period are particularly elusive, and when located have yielded few insights into their morphology and functions. They are generally characterised by dispersed low-density scatters of pits, post-holes and gullies, mostly of unknown purpose and forming no obviously coherent plan, plus occasional hearths. Typical examples include scattered earlier Neolithic pits yielding pottery and flintwork in the vicinity of a ring-ditch at Holme Dyke, Gonalston (including a pit within which a virtually intact Neolithic bowl had been placed), several small pits and a hearth yielding earlier Neolithic sherds which survived beneath a multi-phased barrow with two associated Beaker burials at Aston-upon-Trent (Loveday 2000; 2004,10; Reaney 1968, 70–1), and a scatter of pits and post-holes forming 'no coherent plan' at Willington (Wheeler 1979, 65, fig.3: A). The absence of clearly defined residential structures may support the case for the mobile lifestyle favoured by many recent scholars of the period (Chapter 4.8.3) and could signify a pattern of widely dispersed temporary camps with shelter provided by skin tents or other temporary constructions which may have left few if any structural traces. Alternatively, as in later periods of prehistory, such limited structural remains could indicate the use of more permanent structural types that are unlikely to leave an archaeological signature. These could have included turf huts or perhaps stake-built constructions whose foundations had not penetrated deeply into the ground.

Appropriate emphasis should also be placed upon the particular difficulties of identifying earlier Neolithic features on the Trent terraces, particularly when dug into sandy subsoils. Experience has shown that earlier Neolithic feature fills, having suffered many millennia of disturbance by burrowing animals, worm action, leaching, root disturbance and other pedogenic processes are often virtually indistinguishable from the deposits into which they were dug, and hence their rarity may be due partly to the considerable difficulties of recognition (cf. Wheeler 1979, 60). A graphic illustration of this is provided by a shallow earlier Neolithic pit at Holme Dyke, Gonalston, which was invisible after cleaning of the sub-ploughsoil layers down to the level at which Late Bronze Age and earlier Iron Age features could be clearly discerned (Elliott and Knight in prep.). Only a surface concentration of heat-affected pebbles alerted the excavator to the possibility of an archaeological feature. Subsequent levelling of the surface in a series of 50mm spits revealed a shallow pit of irregular form, distinguishable mainly by the slightly more compacted character of its fill and by the deliberate placement near the base of a plain round-bottomed bowl which may have been intact at the time of deposition (Fig. 4.15). Excavations revealed a sparse and widely scattered distribution of Neolithic pits in its vicinity, but it is worth speculating how many more earlier Neolithic

Fig.4.15 Earlier Neolithic plain round-bottomed bowl placed in the bottom of a pit at Holme Dyke, Gonalston, Nottinghamshire (photograph: L. Elliott)

features might have eluded discovery, particularly during the watching briefs carried out adjacent to the carefully cleaned excavation trenches.

A number of informative contrasts may be drawn between the limited settlement data from the Trent Valley and rare examples of more substantial earlier Neolithic settlements in some neighbouring regions. The most notable of these is a settlement recorded to the north of the Trent in the Derbyshire Wye Valley at Lismore Fields, Buxton, dated by a series of five radiocarbon dates to between 3990 and 3105 cal BC (Garton 1991, 11–14). Excavations at this site revealed a hitherto unknown later Mesolithic and earlier Neolithic occupation focus, the latter comprising at least two rectangular post-built buildings and a scatter of pits and post-holes. Charred plant remains of emmer wheat, chaff and flax were retrieved from the post-holes of the earlier Neolithic buildings, and provided clear evidence for the use of cereals. Some other finds, however, including crab apples and hazelnuts, indicate that hunting and gathering may still have formed an important element of the local economy (Jones 2000, 81–2). This settlement is unique in the Peak District and unparalleled in the Trent Valley, but its discovery by chance in an area not previously thought to have been settled in the Neolithic provides a salutary warning that the known structural remains from the Valley may represent only part of the picture. The range of structural, artefactual and environmental data from Lismore Fields also sits uneasily with the hypothesis of mobile settlements, discussed in greater detail below (Chapter 4.8.3), suggesting that in some areas more permanent occupation recalling traditional models of settled Neolithic agricultural groups may have formed one element of the settlement system.

Significantly more settlements of the later Neolithic and Early Bronze Age periods have been recorded in the Trent Valley, but again none of the examples has preserved an imposing range of structural remains. The only exception to this are burnt mounds, which it has been argued above may form a component of some later Neolithic and Early Bronze Age settlements in the Trent Valley (Chapter 4.6.3). At one end of the scale are such perplexing sites as Castle Donington, where an isolated pit yielding Grooved Ware pottery and flintwork was recovered (Coward and Ripper 1999), or Holme Pierrepont, where extensive excavations revealed a single pit yielding small fragments of 'Early Bronze Age' pottery and flint flakes (O'Brien, 1979b, 2: Site 4). Other sites have yielded a broader range of structural evidence, although this is rarely particularly informative. The norm for settlements of this period is a variable but generally low density of widely dispersed pits, post-holes and hearths indicative of scattered houses and other buildings, as recorded at Fisherwick (Miles 1969) and Willington (Wheeler 1979, 65–73, fig.3; 69–73, fig.5) and in the vicinity of ring-ditches at Fatholme (Losco-Bradley 1984), Holme Dyke, Gonalston (Elliott and Knight 1998,16, fig.2: A) and Great Briggs, Holme Pierrepont (Guilbert, undated). Of these, potentially one of the most coherent plans was provided by a roughly trapezoidal arrangement of twelve post-holes, some yielding Grooved Ware sherds, which was postulated at Willington alongside

Fig.4.16 *Late Neolithic settlement at Willington, Derbyshire (source: Wheeler 1979; reproduced by courtesy of H. Salisbury and the Derbyshire Archaeological Society)*

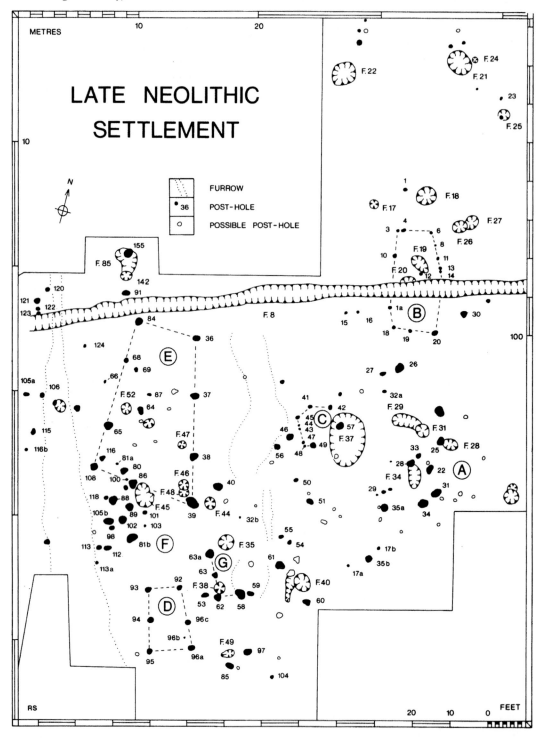

a wider scatter of later Neolithic pits and post-holes (Fig. 4.16; Wheeler 1979, 65–6, fig.3: B; *cf.* Beamish 2001, 10). These might mark the walls or internal roof-supports of a small rectangular building, at least 8m long by 3.0–3.8m wide, but it is doubtful whether all of these features genuinely relate to the same structure.

Some of the best-preserved occupation remains have been recorded beneath barrows and other earthworks, notably from beneath barrows at Swarkestone Lowes (Greenfield 1960) and Aston-upon-Trent (Loveday 2004, 10; Reaney 1968, 70–1) and from below the agger of the Roman

Fosse Way near Langford (Holt *et al.* 2001). The level of preservation of these sites is significantly better than most river-terrace sites, as they had not been exposed prior to discovery to the destructive effects of modern ploughing. Again, however, the prevailing image is of widely scattered jumbles of pits, post-holes and occasionally hearths and gullies forming no obvious pattern. This is exemplified at Swarkestone Lowes, where excavations by Greenfield (1960) of Barrow IV revealed beneath the mound an occupation layer incorporating Beaker pottery and flintwork, together with several pits, a remarkable density of features interpreted as post- and stake-holes,

Fig.4.17 *Beaker occupation level beneath Barrow IV at Swarkestone Lowes, Derbyshire, showing features attributed by the excavator to this phase and a large robber trench extending from left foreground.   Pit 11 is shown fully excavated (between the ranging rods) but pit 10 (to right of robber trench terminal) is unexcavated; the hearths are not visible in this photograph (source: Greenfield 1960; reproduced by courtesy of the Derbyshire Archaeological Society)*

and two burnt patches which may represent hearths (Fig. 4.17; *ibid.* 11–15, figs 5–6, plates IV–VI). Some doubt the interpretation of the 'stake-holes' which formed a series of curious alignments beneath the mound (*ibid.* fig.5), but the sealed pits and hearths and the associated occupation debris provide persuasive evidence for pre-barrow occupation. This layer also yielded the first certain examples of earlier Neolithic Grimston Ware from Derbyshire, raising the possibility of a yet earlier phase of activity reaching back perhaps to the fourth millennium BC. At Langford, excavations beneath the agger of a Roman road revealed an uneven scatter of pits and possibly post-holes yielding Peterborough Ware and Beaker sherds, flintwork and charred barley, spelt and hazelnut shells (Holt *et al.* 2001), but insufficient evidence survived to permit discussion of the settlement morphology.

4.8.2   Settlement and Population Densities

Assessment of the density of settlement in the Trent Valley during the Neolithic and Early Bronze Age relies heavily upon the evidence of systematic fieldwalking, supported by the results of large-scale excavations and watching briefs conducted during the stripping of terrace and floodplain environments in advance of sand and gravel extraction. Recent fieldwalking surveys in the region, such as have been conducted along the Fosse Way between East Stoke and Newark (Kinsley and Knight, 1992, fig.38) and elsewhere in Nottinghamshire around South Muskham (Garton 2002) and near Collingham (Knight and Kennett 1994), have revealed extensive spreads of Neolithic and Bronze Age lithic tools and waste material over the gravel

terraces. This is in sharp contrast to floodplain zones where the accumulation of more recent alluvium has buried traces of pre-Roman activity (Garton 2002, 26–7, 32, fig.5). The latter phenomenon is especially pronounced in the lower reaches of the Trent, particularly to the north of Gainsborough, where deep alluvial deposits extend far beyond the modern river channel. In addition, quarrying has demonstrated extensive sub-alluvial spreads of Neolithic and Early Bronze finds and the remains of structures such as burnt mounds, providing convincing evidence for Neolithic activity in valley-bottom locations once thought to have been avoided by settlement.

Interpretation of the fieldwalking data is complicated by the difficulty of establishing the character, date and duration of activity represented by surface lithic scatters. The character of the sites represented by these stone concentrations can of course only be established by excavation, although even then many questions may remain regarding their functions. Many concentrations could preserve sub-ploughsoil features indicative of settlement or task-specific activities, but few sites within the region have yet been sampled by excavation. Small-scale excavations have been carried out on a few prehistoric lithic scatters, notably at South Clifton, Nottinghamshire (Phillips 1975, 20) and Newton Cliffs, Lincolnshire (Garton *et al.* 1989). The former yielded no evidence of structural remains, and was interpreted as probably a later Neolithic/Early Bronze Age knapping site. At Newton Cliffs, by contrast, more convincing evidence for occupation was provided by a wide scatter of pits, possible post-holes and other features yielding Neolithic and Early Bronze Age flintwork and pottery (*ibid.* 107–12, 146–7, 156–60). These imply multiple phases of activity, but little may be deduced regarding the morphology of the settlement from which the finds appear to have derived (*ibid.* 166–8).

Further problems arise from the imprecise dating of lithic artefacts, preventing accurate determination of the longevity of activity and hence the number of sites that may have been in use at any one time. The problem of elucidating temporal trends in site density and population levels is exacerbated by the particular difficulty of identifying earlier Neolithic sites, which it has been suggested may be characterised by more localised discard, commonly in pits (Clay 2002, 111–2; Healy 1992). These have proved extremely elusive in large-scale surveys using extensive collection strategies – such as the Fenland Survey (Hall and Coles 1994) – and together with Mesolithic sites have only emerged as significant components of the landscape in more intensive fieldwalking surveys (for example, those based upon fieldwalking along transects set 10m apart: e.g. Garton 2002.) Significant problems are also encountered in disentangling later Mesolithic from earlier Neolithic lithic collections, particularly in view of the possible continuation of Mesolithic blade technology well into the earlier Neolithic (Myers 2001b, 9–10; Pitts and Jacobi 1979) and the possibility of a preference for similar topographic locations. The latter is suggested in the Leicestershire claylands, where later Mesolithic and earlier Neolithic groups may have shared a preference for locations close to the headwaters of streams and rivers (Clay 2001b, 21; 2002, 109–12), and in the Trent Valley at terrace-edge locations such as Collingham (Knight 1994; Chapter 3.3.1).

Despite these problems, the contrast between the density and spatial extent of earlier and later Neolithic/Early Bronze Age lithic scatters is sufficiently marked to suggest an overall increase in the density of human activity within the Valley from the earlier Neolithic to Early Bronze Age, and hence possibly population levels. Full account must be taken of the typically higher proportion of chronologically diagnostic tools which occur in later Neolithic/Early Bronze Age assemblages (Garton 2002, 26), but with this proviso a general increase in the density of settlement may be postulated in areas within the Trent Valley such as South Muskham (*ibid.*, 26–7, fig.5) or along the Fosse Way to the south of Newark (Kinsley and Knight 1992, 43–4, fig.38). A similar trend towards higher levels of activity has been suggested in neighbouring areas, including the claylands of Leicestershire (Clay 2002, 112–4) and the Magnesian limestone escarpment near Creswell Crags, Derbyshire (Knight *et al.* 1998, 79). Further evidence for an expansion in the density of settlement may be provided by the palaeoenvironmental data indicative of progressive woodland clearance, although the exact extent of clearance by the end of the Early Bronze Age is debatable (Chapter 4.4). A case has been made in Chapter 4.4 for quite extensive clearance of some stretches of the Valley by the end of this period, notably in the vicinity of the monument complex centred upon the Aston and Potlock cursuses, but significant intra-regional differences in the extent of clearance and hence the density of activity may also be suggested.

4.8.3   The Spatial Organisation of Settlement: Mobile or Sedentary?

The exact impact of the shift from a hunter-gatherer to a predominantly agricultural subsistence economy upon community lifestyles, and in particular the spatial organisation of settlement, remains unclear. Recent scholars of the period have favoured a mobility model for the earliest agriculturalists, involving extensive long-fallow cultivation and pasture, mobile communities and impermanent settlements (e.g. Barrett 1994; Thomas 1991; Whittle 1997). In this model, a predominantly woodland environment is envisaged, exploited by small mobile communities herding domesticated stock (predominantly cattle) and cultivating cereals in clearings which could have been abandoned after harvesting or later revisited. It should be emphasised that this mobility model has been developed mainly within the context of southern England, and the applicability of it to the Trent Valley has yet to be demonstrated convincingly. It could provide a convenient explanation for the sparse and ephemeral structural remains of this period, and in particular the extreme paucity of earlier Neolithic settlement evidence. However, the possibility cannot be discounted of more permanent structures which have eluded discovery or which employed constructional techniques liable to leave few, if any, archaeological traces (Chapter 4.8.1). It is also worth recalling the salutary evidence from the earlier Neolithic settlement at Lismore Fields for cereal storage (Jones 2000) and hence for a more settled community than would be expected within the framework of prevailing mobility models. This evidence cannot be translated directly to the Trent Valley, but it is worth emphasising as confirmation of the dangers of transferring models of social organisation between areas which may have differed significantly in terms of their environmental and socio-economic restraints.

Similar doubts on the subject of mobile versus sedentary lifestyles must be expressed for settlements of the later Neolithic and Early Bronze Age. Investigations in some areas of southern England have suggested a transition during the Neolithic from long-fallow to more intensive short-fallow systems, and for a progression towards more permanent settlements (Whittle 1997). Unfortunately, insufficient evidence is available from sites in the Trent Valley to establish whether a similar sequence might have prevailed in this region. These periods undoubtedly witnessed significant woodland clearance (Chapter 4.4) but the continuing emphasis in the settlement record upon small, unenclosed settlements or specialised activity foci characterised mainly by sparsely distributed pits and post-holes provides no indication of a progression towards such permanent settlements as dominated the Valley during the first millennium BC (Chapter 5). Rare discoveries have been made of post-hole arrangements which might imply more substantial buildings, such as the trapezoidal post-built structures postulated by Wheeler (1979, 65–6) at Willington, but none of these structures is without ambiguity. Major problems of interpretation also attend burnt mounds, early examples of which have been noted above at Willington and Holme Dyke, Gonalston. It has been suggested that such monuments could have served as foci for dispersed communities, the members of which might have congregated at these sites for purposes such as feasting or bathing, but whether these communities were mobile or sedentary is a matter which can only be resolved by further research.

 Whatever the solution to this problem, there can be little doubt that the Neolithic and Early Bronze Age communities who had utilised the resources of the Trent Valley had access to a range of commodities whose production sources may have lain well beyond the confines of the river catchment. These far-flung links are exemplified by the distribution within the Valley of a variety of non–local objects, including Great Langdale (GroupVI) and Charnwood (Group XX) polished stone axes (Clough and Cummins 1988; Cummins and Moore 1973; Loveday 2004), pottery

vessels whose fabrics may have incorporated non-local inclusions (e.g. Woodward 2000, 48–9), and by certain exotic Early Bronze Age metal products – such as the long copper dagger with Armorican parallels from a barrow at Lockington, which Needham (2000, 40) has suggested may have derived ultimately from Brittany. As argued above, some exchange and other social transactions may have been co-ordinated at monuments such as causewayed enclosures and henges, while cursus monuments may even have served to formalise key routes of movement (Chapter 4.7.3). Together, this rather fragmentary evidence implies a complex network of social relationships uniting widely dispersed mobile or sedentary groups, both within the Valley and farther afield, and provides an essential background for the spatial linkages we consider in the following chapter.

Fig.4.18 *Neolithic and Early Bronze Age sites referred to in the text, compiled by S. Baker*
(1.Aldwincle; 2.Alrewas; 3.Aston-upon-Trent; 4.Attenborough; 5.Barrow-upon-Trent; 6.Barton-under-Needwood; 7.Besthorpe; 8.Bole Ings; 9.Castle Donington; 10.Catholme; 11.Clifton; 12.Collingham; 13.Colwick; 14.Cottam; 15.Creswell Crags; 16.Croft; 17.Cromwell; 18.East Stoke; 19.Elvaston; 20.Eye Kettleby; 21.Fatholme; 22.Fisherwick; 23.Fiskerton; 24.Flag Fen; 25.Girton; 26.Gonalston; 27.Grendon; 28.Gunthorpe; 29.Hickens Bridge; 30.Holme Pierrepont; 31.Langford, Newark; 32.Langford Lowfields; 33.Lismore Fields, Buxton; 34.Lockington; 35.Low Marnham; 36.Mavesyn Ridware; 37.Newark; 38.Newington; 39.Newton Cliffs; 40.Nottingham; 41.Potlock; 42.Raunds; 43.Round Hill, Twyford; 44.Shardlow; 45.Shelford; 46.South Clifton; 47.South Muskham; 48.Stanwick; 49.Staythorpe; 50.Swarkestone Lowes; 51.Weston-on-Trent; 52.Whitemoor Haye; 53.Wigber Low; 54.Wilford; 55.Willington)

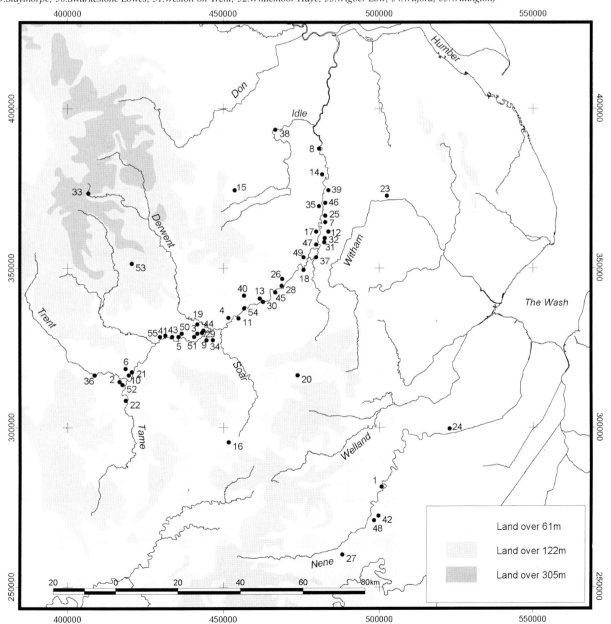

REFERENCES

Allen, C.S.M., Harman, M. and Wheeler, H. 1987. Bronze Age cremation cemeteries in the East Midlands, *Proc. Prehist. Soc.* **53**, 187–221.

Allen, C., Salisbury, H. and Sheppard, R. 1994. A Bronze Age burial site at Clifton, Nottinghamshire, *Trans. Thoroton Soc. Nottinghamshire* **98**, 130–133.

Alvey, R.C. 1964. Charred Cereals from Aston-on-Trent, Derbyshire. Unpublished archive report, Derby Museum.

Atkinson, R.J.C., Piggott, S.M. and Sanders, N.K. 1951. *Excavations at Dorchester, Oxon.* Oxford: printed for the visitors and sold at the Ashmolean Museum.

Barber, K.E., Chambers, F.M., Maddy, D., Stoneman, R. and Brew, J.S. 1994. A sensitive high-resolution record of late Holocene climatic change from a raised bog in northern England, *The Holocene* **4**, 198–205.

Barber, K.E., Maddy, D., Rose, N., Stevenson, A.C., Stoneman, R. and Thompson, R. 2000. Replicated proxy-climate signals over the last 2000 yr from two distant UK peat bogs: new evidence for regional palaeoclimatic teleconnections, *Quat. Sci. Rev.* **19**, 481–487.

Barber, M. 2003. Neolithic enclosures and landscapes in the West Midlands, *West Midlands Regional Research Framework for Archaeology, Seminar 1*. http://www.arch-ant.bham.ac.uk/wmrrfa/sem1.htm

Barclay, A. and Bayliss, A. 1999. Cursus monuments and the radiocarbon problem, in A. Barclay and J. Harding (eds), *Pathways and Ceremonies: the Cursus Monuments of Britain and Ireland*, 11–29.

Barclay, A. and Harding, J. (eds) 1999. *Pathways and Ceremonies: the Cursus Monuments of Britain and Ireland*. Neolithic Studies Group Seminar Papers **4**. Oxford: Oxbow Books.

Barclay, A. and Hey, G. 1999. Cattle, cursus monuments and the river – the upper Thames, in A. Barclay and J. Harding (eds), *Pathways and Ceremonies: the Cursus Monuments of Britain and Ireland*, 67–76.

Barfield, L.H. 1991. Hot stones: hot food or hot baths?, in M.A. Hodder and L.H. Barfield (eds), *Burnt Mounds and Hot Stone Technology*, 59–67.

Barfield, L. H. and Hodder, M.A. 1987. Burnt mounds as saunas, and the prehistory of bathing, *Antiquity* **61**, 370–379.

Barfield, L.H. and Hodder, M.A. 1989. Burnt mounds in the West Midlands: survey and excavation, in A. Gibson (ed), *Midlands Prehistory*, 5–13.

Barnatt, J. 1990. *The Henges, Stone Circles and Ringcairns of the Peak District*. Sheffield Archaeol. Monogr. **1**. Department of Archaeology and Prehistory, University of Sheffield.

Barnatt, J. 1996. Barrows in the Peak District: a review and interpretation of extant remains and past excavations, in J. Barnatt and J. Collis (eds), *Barrows in the Peak District*, 3–94.

Barnatt, J. 2000. To each their own: later prehistoric farming communities and their monuments in the Peak, *Derbyshire Archaeol. J.* **120**, 1–86.

Barnatt, J. and Collis, J. (eds) 1996. *Barrows in the Peak District*. Sheffield: J.R. Collis Publications.

Barnatt, J. and Smith, K. 1991. The Peak District in the Bronze Age: recent research and changes in interpretation, in R. Hodges and K. Smith (eds), *Recent Developments in the Archaeology of the Peak District*, 23–36.

Barrett, J. 1994. *Fragments from Antiquity: an Archaeology of Social Life in Britain, 2900–1200 BC*. Oxford: Blackwell.

Beamish, M. 2001. Excavations at Willington, south Derbyshire. Interim report, *Derbyshire Archaeol. J.* **121**, 1–18.

Beamish, M. and Ripper, S. 2000. Burnt mounds in the East Midlands, *Antiquity* **74**, 37–38.

Bell, M. and Walker, M.J.C. 1992. *Late Quaternary Environmental Change. Physical and Human Perspectives*. Harlow: Longman.

Benito, G., Baker, V.R. and Gregory, K.J. (eds) 1998. *Palaeohydrology and Environmental Change*. Chichester: Wiley.

Bishop, M. 2001. An archaeological resource assessment of the Neolithic and Bronze Age in Nottinghamshire, *East Midlands Archaeological Research Framework*. http://www.le.ac.uk/archaeology/east_midlands_research_framework.htm

Bradley, R. 1984. *The Social Foundations of Prehistoric Britain*. London: Longman.

Bradley, R. and Gordon, K. 1988. Human skulls from the River Thames, their dating and significance, *Antiquity* **62**, 503–509.

Brayshay, B. and Dinnin, M.H. 1999. Integrated palaeoecological evidence for biodiversity at the floodplain-forest margin, *J. Biogeography* **26** (1), 115–131.

Brown, A.G. 1998. Fluvial evidence of the Medieval Warm Period and the late medieval climatic deterioration in Europe, in G. Benito, V.R. Baker and K.J. Gregory (eds), *Palaeohydrology and Environmental Change*, 43–52.

Brown, A.G. and Quine, T. (eds) 1999. *Fluvial Processes & Environmental Change*. Chichester: Wiley.

Buckley, V. (ed) 1990. *Burnt Offerings. International Contributions to Burnt Mound Archaeology*. Dublin: Worldwell Ltd – Academic Publications.

Canti, M.G. 1999. The production and preservation of faecal spherulites: animals, environment and taphonomy, *J. Archaeol. Sci.* **26**, 251–256.

Chambers, F.M., Barber, K.E., Maddy, D. and Brew, J. 1997. A 5500-year proxy-climate and vegetation record from Blanket mire at Talla Moss, Borders, Scotland, *The Holocene* **7** (4), 391–399.

Champion, T. 1999. The later Bronze Age, in J. Hunter and I. Ralston (eds), *The Archaeology of Britain*, 95–112.

Chapman, A. 2001. An archaeological resource assessment of the Neolithic and Bronze Age in Northamptonshire, *East Midlands Archaeological Research Framework*. http://www.le.ac.uk/archaeology/east_midlands_research_framework.htm

Clay, P. 1999.   The Neolithic and Bronze Age of Leicestershire and Rutland, *Trans. Leicestershire Archaeol. Hist. Soc.* **73**, 1–18.

Clay, P. 2001a.   An archaeological resource assessment of the Neolithic and Bronze Age of Leicestershire and Rutland, *East Midlands Archaeological Research Framework.* http://www.le.ac.uk/archaeology/east_midlands_research_framework.htm

Clay, P. 2001b.   An archaeological resource assessment and research agenda for the Neolithic and Early-Middle Bronze Age of the East Midlands, *East Midlands Archaeological Research Framework.* http://www.le.ac.uk/archaeology/east_midlands_research_framework.htm

Clay, P. 2002.   *The Prehistory of the East Midlands Claylands.* Leicester Archaeol. Monogr. **9**. School of Archaeology and Ancient History, University of Leicester.

Clay, P. and Salisbury, C.R. 1990.   A Norman mill dam and other sites at Hemington Fields, Castle Donington, Leicestershire, *Archaeol. J.* **147**, 276–307.

Clough, T.H.McK. and Cummins, W.A. 1988.   The petrological identification of stone implements from the East Midlands: third report, in T.H.McK. Clough and W.A. Cummins (eds), *Stone Axe Studies. Volume 2. The Petrology of Prehistoric Stone Implements from the British Isles*, 45–48.

Clough, T.H.McK. and Cummins, W.A. (eds) 1988.   *Stone Axe Studies. Volume 2. The Petrology of Prehistoric Stone Implements from the British Isles.* CBA Res. Rep. **67**.

Coates, G. 2002.   *A Prehistoric and Romano-British Landscape. Excavations at Whitemoor Haye Quarry, Staffordshire, 1997–1999.* BAR Brit. Ser. **340**.

Coles, B. 1992.   Further thoughts on the impact of beaver in temperate landscapes, in S. Needham and M.G. Macklin (eds), *Alluvial Archaeology in Britain*, 93–99.

Coles, B. 2001.   The impact of Western European beaver on stream channels: some implications for past stream conditions and human activity, *J. Wetland Archaeol.* **1**, 55–82.

Coles, J. and Coles, B. 1986.   *Sweet Track to Glastonbury.* London: Thames and Hudson.

Collis, J. 1983.   *Wigber Low, Derbyshire: a Bronze Age and Anglian Burial Site in the White Peak.* Department of Prehistory and Archaeology, University of Sheffield.

Cornwall, I.W. 1955.   Appendix II: soil samples, in M. Posnansky, The excavation of a Bronze-Age round barrow at Lockington, 25–27.

Coward, J. and Ripper, S. 1999.   Castle Donington. Willow Farm (SK 445 288), *Trans. Leicestershire Archaeol. Hist. Soc.* **73**, 87–91.

Cummins, W.A. and Moore, C.N. 1973.   Petrological identification of stone implements from Lincolnshire, Nottinghamshire and Rutland, *Proc. Prehist. Soc.* **39**, 219–255.

Cunliffe, B. and Rowley, T. (eds) 1978.   *Lowland Iron Age Communities in Europe.* BAR Int. Ser. **48**.

Darvill, T. and Thomas, J. (eds) 2001.   *Neolithic Enclosures in Atlantic Northwest Europe.* Neolithic Studies Group Seminar Papers **6**. Oxford: Oxbow Books.

Dauncey, K.D.M. and Hurrell, D.J. 1951.   The excavation of a round barrow at Cromwell, Nottinghamshire, *Trans. Thoroton Soc. Nottinghamshire* **55**, 1–2.

Davies, G. 2001.   Interim Statement on the Archaeological Works at Staythorpe Power Station. Unpublished report 438f, ARCUS, University of Sheffield.

Davis, R. 1999.   Bronze Age metalwork from the Trent Valley: Newark, Notts to Gainsborough, Lincs, *Trans. Thoroton Soc. Nottinghamshire* **103**, 25–47.

Davis, R. 2003.   A Bronze Age shield fragment and spearhead from Elvaston Quarry, Derbyshire, *Derbyshire Archaeol. J.* **123**, 63–70.

Dimbleby, G.W. 1960.   Appendix C. Charcoals, in E. Greenfield, The excavation of Barrow 4 at Swarkeston, Derbyshire, 47–48.

Elliott, L. and Garton, D. 1995.   Acre Lane, Aston: Recording of the Aston Cursus along a Newly-cut Storm Drain on the Line of the Derby Southern Bypass. Unpublished report, Trent & Peak Archaeological Trust, University Park, Nottingham.

Elliott, L. and Knight, D. 1998.   A burnt mound at Holme Dyke, Gonalston, Nottinghamshire, *Trans. Thoroton Soc. Nottinghamshire* **102**, 15–22.

Elliott, L. and Knight, D. 1999.   An early Mesolithic site and first millennium BC settlement and pit alignments at Swarkestone Lowes, Derbyshire, *Derbyshire Archaeol. J.* **119**, 79–153.

Elliott, L. and Knight, D. in prep.   Prehistoric and Romano-British settlement at Gonalston, Nottinghamshire.

Fairbairn, A.S. (ed) 2000.   *Plants in Neolithic Britain and Beyond.* Neolithic Studies Group Seminar Papers **5**. Oxford: Oxbow Books.

Field N. and Parker Pearson, M. 2003.   *Fiskerton. An Iron Age Timber Causeway with Iron Age and Roman Votive Offerings: the 1981 Excavations.* Oxford: Oxbow Books.

Finn, N. 1998.   Melton Mowbray, Eye Kettleby, Leicester Road (SK 731 180), *Trans. Leicestershire Archaeol. Hist. Soc.* **72**, 178.

Frodsham, P. (ed) 1996.   *Neolithic Studies in No-Man's Land. Papers on the Neolithic of Northern England from the Trent to the Tweed.* Northern Archaeology **13/14**. Newcastle-upon-Tyne: Northumberland Archaeological Group.

Garton, D. 1991.   Neolithic settlement in the Peak District: perspective and prospects, in R. Hodges and K. Smith (eds), *Recent Developments in the Archaeology of the Peak District*, 3–21.

Garton, D. 1993.   A burnt mound at Waycar Pasture, near Girton, Nottinghamshire: an interim report, *Trans. Thoroton Soc. Nottinghamshire* **97**, 148–149.

Garton, D. 2002.   Walking fields in South Muskham and its implications for Romano-British cropmark-landscapes in Nottinghamshire, *Trans. Thoroton Soc. Nottinghamshire* **106**, 17–39.

Garton, D. and Beswick, P. 1983.   The survey and excavation of a Neolithic settlement area at Mount Pleasant, Kenslow, 1980–1983, *Derbyshire Archaeol. J.* **103**, 7–40.

Garton, D. and Brown, J. 1999.   Flint, chert, quartzite and polished stone artefacts, in L. Elliott and D. Knight, An early Mesolithic site and first millennium BC settlement and pit alignments at Swarkestone Lowes, Derbyshire, 106–124.

Garton, D., Elliott, L. and Salisbury, C.R. 2001. Aston-upon-Trent, Argosy Washolme, *Derbyshire Archaeol. J.* **121**, 196–200.

Garton, D., Howard, A. and Pearce, M. 1996. Neolithic riverside ritual? Excavations at Langford Lowfields, Nottinghamshire, in R.J.A. Wilson (ed), *From River Trent to Raqqa*, 9–11.

Garton, D., Howard, A. and Pearce, M. 1997. Archaeological investigations at Langford Quarry, Nottinghamshire 1995–6, *Tarmac Papers* **1**, 29–40.

Garton, D., Morris, T. and Priest, V. 1994. Aston Cursus, in D. Knight (ed), A564(T) Derby Southern Bypass. Summary of Rescue Archaeological Works at Aston Cursus, Potlock Cursus and Swarkestone Lowes, 4–12.

Garton, D., Phillips, P. and Henson, D. 1989. Newton Cliffs: a flint-working and settlement site in the Trent Valley, in P. Phillips (ed), *Archaeology and Landscape Studies in North Lincolnshire*, 81–180.

Garwood, P. 2003. Early Bronze Age funerary monuments and burial traditions in the West Midlands, *West Midlands Regional Research Framework for Archaeology, Seminar 1*. http:// www.arch-ant.bham.ac.uk/wmrrfa/sem1.htm

Gearey, B. and Lillie, M. 2002. Palynology and Radiocarbon Assessment of Samples from Newington (NQ02) (SK 675943). Unpublished report 02/01 to Northern Archaeological Associates, Wetland Archaeology & Environments Research Centre, University of Hull.

Gibson, A. (ed) 1989. *Midlands Prehistory*. BAR Brit. Ser. **204**.

Gibson, A. (ed) 2002. *Behind Wooden Walls: Neolithic Palisaded Enclosures in Europe*. BAR Int. Ser. **1013**.

Gibson, A. and Loveday, R. 1989. Excavations at the cursus monument of Aston-upon-Trent, Derbyshire, in A. Gibson (ed), *Midlands Prehistory*, 27–50.

Gibson, A. and McCormick, A. 1985. Archaeology at Grendon Quarry, Northamptonshire. Part 1. Neolithic and Bronze Age sites excavated 1974–75, *Northamptonshire Archaeol.* **20**, 23–66.

Greenfield, E. 1960. The excavation of Barrow 4 at Swarkeston, Derbyshire, *Derbyshire Archaeol. J.* **80**, 1–48.

Greig, J. 1997. Pollen and plant macrofossils, in D. Knight and S. Malone, Evaluation of a Late Iron Age and Romano-British Settlement and Palaeochannels of the Trent at Chapel Farm, Shardlow and Great Wilne, Derbyshire (SK 455305), 34–35.

Greig, J. 2000. The pollen, in G. Hughes, *The Lockington Gold Hoard: an Early Bronze Age Barrow Cemetery at Lockington, Leicestershire*, 82–84.

Guilbert, G. undated. Great Briggs Ring-ditch, Holme Pierrepont, Notts. Unpublished summary report, Trent & Peak Archaeological Trust, University Park, Nottingham.

Guilbert, G. 1996. Findern is dead, long live Potlock – the story of a cursus on the Trent gravels, *Past* **24**, 10–12.

Guilbert, G. and Malone, S. 1994. Potlock cursus, in D. Knight (ed), A564(T) Derby Southern Bypass. Summary of Rescue Archaeological Works at Aston Cursus, Potlock Cursus and Swarkestone Lowes, 13–18.

Hall, D. and Coles, J. 1994. *Fenland Survey. An Essay in Landscape and Persistence*. London: English Heritage.

Harding, A.F. with Lee, G.E. 1987. *Henge Monuments and Related Sites of Great Britain*. BAR Brit. Ser. **175**.

Harding, J. 2003. *Henge Monuments of the British Isles*. Stroud: Tempus.

Harding, J. and Barclay, A. 1999. An introduction to the cursus monuments of Neolithic Britain and Ireland, in A. Barclay and J. Harding (eds), *Pathways and Ceremonies: the Cursus Monuments of Britain and Ireland*, 1–8.

Harding, J. and Johnson, B. 2004. Yorkshire's holy secret, *Brit. Archaeol.* **75**, 26–31.

Healy, F. 1992. Lithic material, in T. Lane, *Lincolnshire Survey. The Northern Fen Edge*, 98–106.

Healey, F. and Harding, J. forthcoming. *Raunds Area Project: the Neolithic and Bronze Age Landscapes at West Cotton, Stanwick and Irthlingborough, Northamptonshire*. London: English Heritage.

Healey, F. and Harding, J. 2003. Raunds. From hunters to farmers, *Brit. Archaeol.* **73**, 16–21.

Hedges, J. 1975. Excavation of two Orcadian burnt mounds at Liddle and Beaquoy, *Proc. Soc. Antiq. Scot.* **106**, 39–98.

Hillam, J. 1998. Tree-ring Analysis of Oaks from Langford Quarry, Newark-on-Trent, Nottinghamshire. Ancient Monuments Laboratory Report 7/98, English Heritage.

Hodder, M.A. 1982. The prehistory of the Lichfield area, *Trans. S. Staffordshire Archaeol. Hist. Soc.* **12**, 13–23.

Hodder, M.A. and Barfield, L.H. (eds) 1991. *Burnt Mounds and Hot Stone Technology. Papers from the Second International Burnt Mound Conference, Sandwell, 12th–14th October 1990*. West Bromwich: Sandwell Metropolitan Borough Council.

Hodges, R. and Smith, K. (eds) 1991. *Recent Developments in the Archaeology of the Peak District*. Sheffield Archaeol. Monogr. **2**. University of Sheffield.

Holt, R., Jones, H. and Knight, D. 2001. Evaluation Excavations on the Fosse Way, Langford, Nottinghamshire. Unpublished report, Trent & Peak Archaeological Unit, University Park, Nottingham.

Howard, A.J. 1992. *The Quaternary Geology and Geomorphology of the area between Newark and Lincoln*. Unpublished PhD thesis, Council for National Academic Awards.

Howard, A.J. and Knight, D. 2001. South Ings Close, Rampton, Nottinghamshire. Auger Survey of the Floodplain Deposits for LaFarge Aggregates Ltd. Unpublished report, Trent & Peak Archaeological Unit, University Park, Nottingham.

Howard, A.J., Corr, J., Smith, D.N., Smith, W. and Garton, D. 2003. Bulcote Farm, Gunthorpe, Nottinghamshire: Preliminary Environmental Assessment Report. Unpublished report, Trent & Peak Archaeological Unit, University Park, Nottingham.

Howard, A.J., Green, F.M., Hunt, C.O., Monkton, A., Smith, D.N. and Garton, D. Submitted. Middle to Late Holocene environmental change recorded in palaeochannels of the River Trent, Shardlow, Derbyshire, UK. *The Holocene*.

Howard, A.J., Hunt, C.O., Rushworth, G., Smith, D. and Smith, W. 1999a. Girton Quarry Northern Extension: Palaeobiological and Dating Assessment of Organic Samples collected during Stage 1 Geoarchaeological Investigations. Unpublished report, Trent & Peak Archaeological Trust, University Park, Nottingham.

Howard, A.J., Smith, D.N., Garton, D., Hilliam, J. and Pearce, M. 1999b.
Middle to Late Holocene environments in the Middle to Lower Trent Valley, in A.G. Brown and T. Quine (eds), *Fluvial Processes and Environmental Change*, 165–178.

Hughes, G. 2000.
The Lockington Gold Hoard: an Early Bronze Age Barrow Cemetery at Lockington, Leicestershire. Oxford: Oxbow Books.

Hughes, G. 2002.
Archaeology of the region, in G. Coates, *A Prehistoric and Romano-British Landscape. Excavations at Whitemoor Haye Quarry, Staffordshire, 1997–1999*, 2–3.

Hughes, G. and Roseff, R. 1995.
Excavations at Croft Quarry (SP 517 968), *Trans. Leicestershire Archaeol. Hist. Soc.* **69**, 100–108.

Hughes, P.D.M., Mauquoy, D., Barber, K.E. and Langdon, P.G. 2000.
Mire-development pathways and palaeoclimatic records from a full Holocene peat archive at Walton Moss, Cumbria, England, *The Holocene* **10**, 465–479.

Hunt, C.O. 1994.
Environmental Assessment, Cromwell Quarry, Nottinghamshire. Unpublished report, Trent & Peak Archaeological Unit, University Park, Nottingham.

Hunter, J. and Ralston, I. (eds) 1999.
The Archaeology of Britain. London: Routledge.

Jackson, D.A. 1976.
The excavation of Neolithic and Bronze Age sites at Aldwincle, Northants, 1967–71, *Northamptonshire Archaeol.* **11**, 12–64.

Jeffery, S. 1991.
Burnt mounds, fulling and early textiles, in M.A. Hodder and L.H. Barfield (eds), *Burnt Mounds and Hot Stone Technology*, 97–107.

Jones, A. 1992.
Catholme, Staffordshire: an Archaeological Evaluation. Unpublished report, Birmingham University Field Archaeology Unit.

Jones, D. 1998.
Long barrows and elongated enclosures in Lincolnshire: an analysis of the air photographic evidence, *Proc. Prehist. Soc.* **64**, 83–114.

Jones, G. 2000.
Evaluating the importance of cultivation and collecting in Neolithic Britain, in A.S. Fairbairn (ed), *Plants in Neolithic Britain and Beyond*, 79–84.

Keevill, G. 1992.
Life on the edge: archaeology and alluvium at Redlands Farm, Stanwick, Northants., in S. Needham and M.G. Macklin (eds), *Alluvial Archaeology in Britain*, 177–184.

Kinsley, A.G. and Knight, D. 1992.
Archaeology of the Fosse Way. Vol.2: Newark to Widmerpool. Unpublished report, Trent & Peak Archaeological Trust, University Park, Nottingham.

Knight, D. 1994.
Cromwell Quarry Extension, Notts: Summary Report on Trial Trenching and Test-pitting. Unpublished report, Trent & Peak Archaeological Unit, University Park, Nottingham.

Knight, D. (ed) 1994.
A564(T) Derby Southern Bypass. Summary of Rescue Archaeological Works at Aston Cursus, Potlock Cursus and Swarkestone Lowes. Unpublished report, Trent & Peak Archaeological Unit, University Park, Nottingham.

Knight, D. 1996.
Excavations at Fernello Sitch, Barrow-upon-Trent, Derbyshire, in R.J.A. Wilson (ed), *From River Trent to Raqqa*, 79–80.

Knight, D. 1998.
The Derby southern bypass, *Current Archaeology* **157**, 32–33.

Knight, D. and Beswick, P. 2000.
A possible Beaker burial at Rampton, Nottinghamshire, *Trans. Thoroton Soc. Nottinghamshire* **104**, 15–20.

Knight, D. and Howard, A.J. 1995.
Archaeology and Alluvium in the Trent Valley. Revised edition. Trent & Peak Archaeological Trust, University Park, Nottingham.

Knight, D. and Kennett, A. 1994.
Proposed Gravel Quarry at Collingham, Notts: Fieldwalking Survey. Summary Report and Recommendations for Further Work. Unpublished report, Trent & Peak Archaeological Unit, University Park, Nottingham.

Knight, D. and Malone, S. 1997.
Evaluation of a Late Iron Age and Romano-British Settlement and Palaeochannels of the Trent at Chapel Farm, Shardlow and Great Wilne, Derbyshire (SK 455305). Unpublished report, Trent & Peak Archaeological Trust, University Park, Nottingham.

Knight, D., Garton, D. and Leary, R. 1998.
The Elmton fieldwalking survey: prehistoric and Romano-British artefact scatters, *Derbyshire Archaeol. J.* **118**, 69–85.

Lane, T. 1992.
Lincolnshire Survey. The Northern Fen Edge. Sleaford: East Anglian Archaeology **66**.

Last, J. 1999.
Out of line: cursuses and monument typology in Eastern England, in A. Barclay and J. Harding (eds), *Pathways and Ceremonies: the Cursus Monuments of Britain and Ireland*, 86–97.

Leah, M. and Crowson, A. 1994.
The excavation of a potboiler mound at Feltwell Anchor, *Fenland Research* **9**, 46–50.

Lillie, M. 1998.
The palaeoenvironmental survey of the lower Trent valley and Winterton Beck, in R. Van de Noort and S. Ellis (eds), *Wetland Heritage of the Ancholme and Lower Trent Valleys: an Archaeological Survey*, 33–72.

Limbrey, S. 2000.
The buried soil and mound materials, in G. Hughes, *The Lockington Gold Hoard: an Early Bronze Age Barrow Cemetery at Lockington, Leicestershire*, 85–92.

Long, A.J., Innes, J.B., Kirby, J.R., Lloyd, J.M., Rutherford, M.M., Shennan, I. and Tooley, M.J. 1998.
Holocene sea-level change and coastal evolution in the Humber estuary, eastern England: an assessment of rapid coastal change, *The Holocene* **8**, 229–247.

Losco-Bradley, S. 1984.
Fatholme, Barton-under-Needwood, Staffordshire, *Proc. Prehist. Soc.* **50**, 402.

Loveday, R. 2000.
Aston: a barrow preserved, *Curr. Archaeol.* **167**, 438–439.

Loveday, R. 2001.
Dorchester-on-Thames – ritual complex or ritual landscape?, in A. Barclay and J. Harding (eds), *Pathways and Ceremonies: the Cursus Monuments of Britain and Ireland*, 49–63.

Loveday, R. 2004.
Contextualising Monuments. The Exceptional Potential of the Middle Trent Valley, *Derbyshire Archaeol. J.* **124**, 1–12.

Loveday, R. and Petchey, M. 1982.
Oblong ditches: a discussion and some new evidence, *Aerial Archaeol.* **8**, 17–24.

Macklin, M.G. 1999.
Holocene river environments in prehistoric Britain: human interaction and impact, *Quat. Proc.* **7**, 521–530.

Martin, A. and Allen, C. 2002. Two prehistoric ring ditches and an associated Bronze Age cremation cemetery at Tucklesholme Farm, Barton-under-Needwood, Staffordshire, *Trans. Staffordshire Archaeol. Hist. Soc.* **39**, 1–15.

Martin, E. 1988. Swales Fen, Suffolk: a Bronze Age cooking pit?, *Antiquity* **62**, 358–359.

Membery, S. 2001. An archaeological resource assessment of the Neolithic and Early Bronze Age in Lincolnshire, *East Midlands Archaeological Research Framework*. http://www.le.ac.uk/archaeology/east_midlands_research_framework.htm

Mercer, R.J. 1990. *Causewayed Enclosures*. Princes Risborough: Shire Publications.

Miles, N. 1969. Excavations at Fisherwick, Staffs., 1968 – a Romano-British farmstead and a Neolithic occupation site, *Trans. S. Staffordshire Archaeol. Hist. Soc.* **10**, 1–22.

Mithen, S. 1999. Hunter-gatherers of the Mesolithic, in J. Hunter and I. Ralston (eds), *The Archaeology of Britain*, 35–57.

Moffett, L. and Monckton, A. 2000. The charred plant remains, in G. Hughes, *The Lockington Gold Hoard: an Early Bronze Age Barrow Cemetery at Lockington, Leicestershire*, 78–81.

Monckton, A. 2003. An archaeological resource assessment and research agenda for environmental archaeology in the East Midlands, *East Midlands Archaeological Research Framework*. http://www.le.ac.uk/archaeology/east_midlands_research_framework.htm

Mullin, D. 2003. *The Bronze Age Landscape of the Northern English Midlands*. BAR Brit. Ser. **1351**.

Myers, A. 2001a. An archaeological resource assessment of the Neolithic and Early Bronze Age in Derbyshire, *East Midlands Archaeological Research Framework*. http://www.le.ac.uk/archaeology/east_midlands_research_framework.htm

Myers, A.M. 2001b. An archaeological resource assessment and research agenda for the Mesolithic in the East Midlands, *East Midlands Archaeological Research Framework*. http://www.le.ac.uk/archaeology/east_midlands_research_framework.htm

Needham, S.P. 1992. Holocene alluviation and interstratified settlement evidence in the Thames Valley at Runnymede Bridge, in S. Needham and M.G. Macklin (eds), *Alluvial Archaeology in Britain*, 249–260.

Needham, S.P. 1996. Chronology and periodisation in the British Bronze Age, *Acta Archaeologica* **67**, 121–140.

Needham, S.P. 1997. An independent chronology for British Bronze Age metalwork: the results of the Oxford radiocarbon accelerator programme, *Archaeol. J.* **154**, 55–107.

Needham, S. 2000. The gold and copper metalwork, in G. Hughes, *The Lockington Gold Hoard: an Early Bronze Age Barrow Cemetery at Lockington, Leicestershire*, 23–47.

Needham, S. and Macklin, M.G. (eds) 1992. *Alluvial Archaeology in Britain*. Oxbow Monogr. **27**. Oxford: Oxbow Books.

Northern Archaeological Associates. 2002. Newington Quarry, Nottinghamshire. Archaeological Evaluation of Phase 1 Extraction Area and Haul Road. Unpublished report NAA 02/77, Northern Archaeological Associates.

O'Brien, C. 1978. Land and settlement in Nottinghamshire and lowland Derbyshire, *E. Midland Archaeol. Bull.* **12**, Supp.

O'Brien, C. 1979a. The excavation of a ring ditch at Fiskerton, Nottinghamshire, *Trans. Thoroton Soc. Nottinghamshire* **83**, 80–82.

O'Brien, C. 1979b. Excavations at Holme Pierrepont Site 4. Unpublished report, Trent Valley Archaeological Research Committee, University Park, Nottingham.

O'Kelly, M. 1954. Excavations and experiments in ancient Irish cooking places, *J. Roy. Soc. Antiq. Ireland* **84**, 105–155.

Oswald, A., Dyer, C. and Barber, M. 2001. *The Creation of Monuments. Neolithic Causewayed Enclosures in the British Isles*. Swindon: English Heritage.

Palmer, R. 1976. Interrupted ditch enclosures in Britain: the use of aerial photography for comparative studies, *Proc. Prehist. Soc.* **46**, 161–186.

Parker-Pearson, M. 1999. The earlier Bronze Age, in J. Hunter and I. Ralston (eds), *The Archaeology of Britain*, 77–94.

Pasmore, A.H. and Pallister, J. 1967. Boiling mounds in the New Forest, *Proc. Hampshire Fld. Club Archaeol. Soc.* **24**, 14–19.

Pearson, L. 2003. Cows, beans and view: landscape and farming of the West Midlands in later prehistory, *West Midlands Regional Research Framework for Archaeology, Seminar 2*. http://www.arch-ant.bham.ac.uk/wmrrfa/sem2.htm

Pearson, M.C. 1956. A pollen analytical investigation of a Bronze Age barrow at Swarkeston, in M. Posnansky, The Bronze Age round barrow at Swarkeston, 23–25.

Phillips, C.W. 1941. Some recent finds from the Trent near Nottingham, *Antiq. J.* **21**, 133–143.

Phillips, P. 1975. A Neolithic flint workshop at South Clifton, Nottinghamshire, *Trans. Thoroton Soc. Nottinghamshire* **79**, 16–28.

Phillips, P. (ed) 1989. *Archaeology and Landscape Studies in North Lincolnshire. Aerial and Surface Survey on the Lincolnshire Wolds and Excavation at Newton Cliffs, North Lincolnshire*. BAR Brit. Ser. **208** (ii).

Piggott, S. 1938. The Early Bronze Age in Wessex, *Proc. Prehist. Soc.* **4**, 52–106.

Pitts, M.W. and Jacobi, R.M. 1979. Some aspects of change in flaked stone industries of the Mesolithic and Neolithic in southern Britain, *J. Archaeol. Sci.* **2**, 163–177.

Posnansky, M. 1955a. The Bronze Age round barrow at Swarkeston, *Derbyshire Archaeol. J.* **75**, 123–139.

Posnansky, M. 1955b. The excavation of a Bronze Age round barrow at Lockington, *Trans. Leicestershire Archaeol. Hist. Soc.* **31**, 17–29.

Posnansky, M. 1956a. Some Considerations of the Pleistocene Chronology and Prehistory of Part of the East Midlands. Unpublished PhD thesis, University of Nottingham.

Posnansky, M. 1956b. The Bronze Age round barrow at Swarkeston, *Derbyshire Archaeol. J.* **76**, 10–26.

Pryor, F. 1992. Special section: current research at Flag Fen, Peterborough, *Antiquity* **66**, 439–531.

Pryor, F. 1998. *Farmers in Prehistoric Britain*. Stroud: Tempus.

Pryor, F. 2001. *The Flag Fen Basin. Archaeology and Environment of a Fenland Landscape*. Swindon: English Heritage Archaeological Reports.

Rackham, J. 2002. Newington Quarry, Bawtry: Preliminary Assessment of Macroscopic Environmental Evidence. Unpublished report 33/02 to Northern Archaeological Associates, The Environmental Archaeological Consultancy.

Ray, K. 2003. The Neolithic in the West Midlands: an overview, *West Midlands Regional Research Framework for Archaeology, Seminar 1*. http:// www.arch-ant.bham. ac.uk/wmrrfa/sem1.htm

Reaney, D. 1968. Beaker burials in South Derbyshire, *Derbyshire Archaeol. J.* **88**, 68–81.

Revill, S. 1974. The excavation of a ring ditch at Shelford, Nottinghamshire, *Trans. Thoroton Soc. Nottinghamshire* **78**, 7–12.

Riley, D.N. 1987. *Air Photography and Archaeology*. London: Duckworth.

Royal Commission on Historical Monuments (England). 1960. *A Matter of Time. An Archaeological Survey of the River Gravels of England*. London: HMSO.

Salisbury, C.R., Whitley, P.J., Litton, C.D. and Fox, J.L. 1984. Flandrian courses of the River Trent at Colwick, Nottingham, *Mercian Geologist* **9** (4), 189–207.

Scaife, R.G. and Allen, M.J. 1999. A prehistoric vegetational history from the Trent Valley, near Cottam, Nottinghamshire, *Trans. Thoroton Soc. Nottinghamshire* **103**, 15–24.

Scurfield, C.J. 1997. Bronze Age metalwork from the River Trent in Nottinghamshire, *Trans. Thoroton Soc. Nottinghamshire* **101**, 29–57.

Smith, C.A. 1978. The landscape and natural history of Iron Age settlement on the Trent gravels, in B. Cunliffe and T. Rowley (eds), *Lowland Iron Age Communities in Europe*, 91–101.

Smith, D.N., Roseff, R., Bevan, L., Brown, A.G., Butler, S., Hughes, G. and Monckton, A. 2005. Archaeological and environmental investigations of a Late Glacial and Holocene river valley sequence on the River Soar at Croft, Leicestershire, *The Holocene* **15** (2).

Snelling, A. and Rackham, J. 2001. Environmental assessment, in R. Holt, H. Jones and D. Knight, Evaluation Excavations on the Fosse Way, Langford, Nottinghamshire, 20–23.

Stukeley, W. 1740. *Stonehenge: a Temple Restor'd to the British Druids*. London.

Tavener, N. 1996. Evidence of Neolithic activity near Marton-le-Moor, North Yorkshire, in P. Frodsham (ed) *Neolithic Studies in No-Man's Land*, 183–187.

Thomas, J. 1991. *Rethinking the Neolithic*. Cambridge University Press.

Topping, P. (ed) 1997. *Neolithic Landscapes*. Neolithic Studies Group Seminar Papers **2**. Oxbow Monogr. **86**. Oxford: Oxbow Books.

Tyers, I. 2003. Dendrochronological Spot Dates of Samples from Newington Quarry, near Misson (NQ 02), Nottinghamshire. Unpublished report 573B for Northern Archaeological Associates, ARCUS Dendrochronology Laboratory, University of Sheffield.

Van de Noort, R. and Davies, P. 1993. *Wetland Heritage: an archaeological assessment of the Humber Wetlands*. The Humber Wetlands Project, School of Geography and Earth Resources, University of Hull.

Van de Noort, R. and Ellis, S. (eds) 1998. *Wetland Heritage of the Ancholme and Lower Trent Valleys. An Archaeological Survey*. The Humber Wetlands Project, School of Geography and Earth Resources, University of Hull.

Vine, P.M. 1982. *The Neolithic and Bronze Age Cultures of the Middle and Upper Trent Basin*. BAR Brit. Ser. **105**.

Welch, C.M. 1994. A Bronze Age 'burnt mound' at Milwich, *Staffordshire Archaeol. Hist. Soc.* **36**, 1–15.

Wheeler, H. 1970. The Findern cursus, *Derbyshire Archaeol. J.* **90**, 4–7.

Wheeler, H. 1979. Excavation at Willington, Derbyshire, 1970–1972, *Derbyshire Archaeol. J.* **99**, 58–220.

Whimster, R. 1989. *The Emerging Past. Air Photography and the Buried Landscape*. London: RCHME.

Whittle, A. 1997. Moving on and moving around: Neolithic settlement mobility, in P. Topping (ed), *Neolithic Landscapes*, 15–22.

Whittle, A. 1999. The Neolithic period, c.4000–2500/2200 BC, in J. Hunter and I. Ralston (eds), *The Archaeology of Britain*, 58–76.

Whittle, A., Atkinson, R.J.C., Chambers, R. and Thomas, N. 1992. Excavations in the Neolithic and Bronze Age complex at Dorchester-on-Thames, Oxfordshire, 1947–1952 and 1981, *Proc. Prehist. Soc.* **58**, 143–201.

Wilson, R.J.A. (ed) 1996. *From River Trent to Raqqa*. Nottingham Studies in Archaeology **1**. Department of Archaeology, University of Nottingham.

Windell, D. 1989. A late Neolithic 'ritual focus' at West Cotton, Northamptonshire, in A. Gibson (ed), *Midlands Prehistory*, 85–94.

Woodward, A. 2000. The prehistoric pottery, in G. Hughes, *The Lockington Gold Hoard: an Early Bronze Age Barrow Cemetery at Lockington, Leicestershire*. Oxford: Oxbow Books.

Woodward, A. 2003. Pots, pits and monuments, *West Midlands Regional Research Framework for Archaeology, Seminar 1*. http://www.arch-ant.bham.ac.uk/wmrrfa/sem1.htm

Yates, D. forthcoming. *Land, Power and Prestige. Bronze Age Field Systems in Southern England*. Oxford: Oxbow Books.

Zvelebil, M. 1994. Plant use in the Mesolithic and its role in the transition to farming, *Proc. Prehist. Soc.* **60**, 35–74.

5 THE LATER BRONZE AND IRON AGES: TOWARDS AN ENCLOSED LANDSCAPE

DAVID KNIGHT AND ANDY J. HOWARD

5.1 Introduction

Discussion is focused in this chapter upon the later second and first millennia BC, from the Middle Bronze Age to the Late Iron Age – a period of significant social and economic change during which the Valley landscape was fundamentally transformed. This period witnesses the demise of the great ceremonial landscapes that dominated some stretches of the Trent in the later Neolithic and Early Bronze Age, together with a major expansion of settlement and a shift towards an increasingly bounded landscape. These developments are most pronounced in the latter half of the first millennium BC, which sees significant additional large-scale clearance of floodplain and terrace woodland and the emergence in some reaches of the Valley of landscapes whose salient features – rectilinear enclosures, field systems and major linear boundaries – imply a more tightly controlled environment with careful allocation of pasture, arable and other natural resources. Dating of these developments remains problematic, depending mainly upon discoveries of imprecisely dated pottery, rare items of metalwork, glass and other typologically diagnostic finds in settlement and boundary features, plus a small number of radiocarbon dates. These problems have been discussed at length in a recent review of the later Bronze Age and Iron Age ceramic sequence of the East Midlands (Knight 2002) and the chronological framework proposed in that study provides the foundation for the present chapter (*ibid.* fig.12.2).

It was long assumed that the Trent Valley had remained as densely wooded and sparsely occupied in the Late Bronze Age and Iron Age as was imagined for earlier periods (Kenyon 1952; Piggott 1958) but over the last forty years our perceptions of this period have changed as dramatically as those of earlier periods of prehistory. The traditional model of a thinly settled and largely sylvan environment received its first significant challenge with the publication in 1960 of the RCHME volume *A Matter of Time*. This review of the English river gravels highlighted the dense pattern of cropmarks in the Trent Valley around Newark in Nottinghamshire (RCHME 1960, 12–15, 37–42, fig. 5; e.g. plate 4c) and raised the possibility of an unexpectedly high density of Iron Age activity in some stretches of the Valley during a period when settlement was hitherto imagined to have been both 'scanty' and 'transient' (Piggott 1958, 13). Subsequent excavations at key sites such as Willington in Derbyshire (Wheeler 1979), Holme Pierrepont in Nottinghamshire (O'Brien 1978b, 301–5) and Catholme (Losco-Bradley and Kinsley 2002) and Fisherwick in Staffordshire (Smith ed. 1979) confirmed this view and provided the foundation for the pioneering syntheses of Iron Age and Romano-British settlement by O'Brien (1978a; 1979) and Smith (1977; 1978). More recent reviews of the air photographic evidence

have drawn attention to some remarkable cropmark palimpsests, including the elaborate coaxial field systems and enclosures on the gravel terraces near Newark that may have originated in the Late Iron Age (Whimster 1989; 1992). In addition, further large-scale excavations at sites such as Gamston (Knight 1992), Gonalston (Elliott and Knight 1997; 2002; 2003) and Rampton (Knight 2000a; 2000b) in Nottinghamshire, Swarkestone Lowes (Elliott and Knight 1999) and Barrow-upon-Trent (Knight and Southgate 2001) in Derbyshire, Castle Donington (Coward and Ripper 1999) and Lockington (Hughes 2000, 17; Meek 1995) in Leicestershire and Whitemoor Haye (Coates 2002) in Staffordshire have enhanced significantly the settlement record and have emphasised the potential of the alluvial zone for the survival of well-preserved structural and palaeoenvironmental data.

Much of the above work has been reviewed by Willis (2001) as part of the East Midlands Research Frameworks Project, drawing upon County assessments by Barrett (2001), Bishop (2001), Clay (2001) and Membury (2001). In addition, papers incorporating useful reviews of the later Bronze Age and Iron Age in the Staffordshire Trent Valley have been prepared recently by Wardle (2003) and Wigley (2003) as part of the West Midlands Research Frameworks Project. These syntheses have emphasised the uneven spread of archaeological data for this period along the Valley, with particularly sparse distributions of known sites downstream of Gainsborough in Lincolnshire (Van de Noort and Ellis eds 1998, 289–96) and in the uppermost reaches of the Valley beyond the Tame-Trent confluence (Wardle 2003). This reflects to a large extent spatial variations in the density of archaeological fieldwork and towards the Humber Estuary the particular difficulty of locating sites buried beneath deep alluvium and post-medieval warp deposits (Van de Noort and Ellis eds 1998, 292), and must urge caution in extrapolating too widely from data obtained from the more intensively studied middle reaches of the Valley.

Attention is focused first upon the evidence for climatic change and the developing fluvial landscape, with particular emphasis upon channel development, the spread of floodplain wetlands and the closely related processes of alluviation and colluviation. Subsequent sections will consider the accumulating evidence for the role of the river as an economic and social resource, the changing balance between woodland, pasture and arable, and the trend towards a more densely settled and enclosed landscape. The latter may be regarded as the most significant landscape development of the period, and is manifested most clearly by changes in the spatial organisation of settlement and by the development of a progressively bounded landscape of fields and territorial boundaries.

5.2   The Climatic Background

There is a general consensus that the climate of Britain became significantly cooler and wetter from the latter half of the second millennium BC into the succeeding millennium, although the detail of these fluctuations is far less clear. Recent work has emphasised the importance of records of bog surface wetness, deduced from analyses of cores recovered from ombrotrophic mires, as high-resolution data indicative of synchronous sub-continental scale variations in climate (Barber *et al.* 1994; 2000). Records have been obtained from the uplands of northern Britain which provide compelling evidence for periods of wetter and/or cooler climate during the later Bronze Age and Iron Age. At Bolton Fell Moss, Cumbria, for example, Barber *et al.* (1994) identified climatic deteriorations spanning the periods between 1550–1050 cal BC and 850–550 cal BC, while at the nearby Walton Moss Hughes *et al.* (2000) identified the same 1550 cal BC deterioration as well as climatic downturns between 1290–910 cal BC and 370–90 cal BC. Farther north, at Coom Rigg Moss and Felecia Moss in the Scottish borders, Mauquoy and Barber (1999) have identified wetter and cooler periods between 760–710 cal BC, 590–520 cal BC, 180–130 cal BC and 30 cal BC – cal AD 80, implying a complex and as yet poorly understood sequence of climatic fluctuations spanning the mid to late first millennium BC. Also in the Scottish Borders, Chambers *et al.* (1997) have identified shifts towards a wetter climate at around 1883–1641 cal BC and 823–599 cal BC, whilst Anderson *et al.* (1998) have identified a yet earlier climatic deterioration in the northwest Scottish Highlands between 1950 and 1550 cal BC. In addition to the evidence for climatic deterioration obtained from analyses of peat cores, Baillie (1995) has noted the dendrochronological data for a catastrophic downturn in climate in northern Europe around 1159 BC, which he has linked to increased volcanic activity. This hypothesis is not without controversy (Buckland *et al.* 1997), but the possible contribution of catastrophic events to processes of climatic change should not be underestimated when studying the palaeoenvironmental archive, including that of lowland river valleys such as the Trent (*cf.* Monckton 2003).

The establishment of high-resolution climatic records for lowland peat deposits must rank as a high research priority, for although the above records accurately reflect climatic trends in the uplands of northern Britain, their use as climatic indicators for southerly lowland environments such as the Trent Valley may be debated. Despite these reservations, researchers such as Barber have argued that regional palaeoclimatic teleconnections can be demonstrated between the signals recorded in the uplands and raised mires in lowland contexts (Barber *et al.* 2000). In addition, from the perspective of fluvial geomorphology, Macklin (1999) has argued that periods of enhanced fluvial activity across Britain can be linked with periods of climatic deterioration such as those identified from the record at Bolton Fell Moss. In the Tyne basin, for example, Macklin (1999) has correlated a peak in alluvial sedimentation and incision between 1400 and 500 cal BC with wetter and cooler conditions, although he has noted that this

response was restricted to the middle and lower reaches of the system. Assuming that the effects of a wetter and/or cooler climate were experienced at lower altitudes such as the Trent Valley, the increased precipitation levels during these periods may have contributed to the development of floodplain wetlands and are likely to have affected the frequency and magnitude of flooding within the Trent catchment. This is particularly likely to have occurred as the Rivers Derwent and Dove drain extensive parts of the south Pennine uplands (Chapter 5.3). In agriculturally marginal areas of Britain, these changes may also have affected adversely the length of the growing season and the viability of the food-producing economy, but their impact upon the well-drained and fertile river-gravels of the Trent Valley is more debatable. Some changes in regional crop husbandry practices or in the balance between arable and pastoral activity may have occurred as a result of these changes, but the limited palaeobotanical data from Bronze Age or Iron Age sites within the region (Monckton 2003) currently prevent further discussion of this issue.

5.3   The Fluvial Landscape

As in the second millennium BC, a rich wetland mosaic dissected by a network of major and minor channels flowing across the Valley floor may be postulated. Continued clearance of woodland from the floodplain, gravel terraces and adjacent upland areas would have created a progressively open landscape (Chapter 5.5) which in turn would have been more vulnerable to soil erosion and the redeposition by colluviation and alluviation of fine-grained sediments. Close to the main channels, the river remained laterally mobile, while in minor streams or abandoned channels fringed by reedswamp, minerogenic and organic sediments would have accumulated under lower energy conditions. An anastomosing system of multiple stable channels may be suggested from the available evidence, although it should be emphasised that this is mainly based on evidence from the lower and middle reaches of the Trent. At Waycar Pasture, Girton, Nottinghamshire, for example, radiocarbon dates indicate that several of the channels may have been in use and infilling at the same time (Howard *et al.* 1999). A similar scenario may be suggested for two channels in the Middle Trent Valley at Willow Farm, Castle Donington, which diverged around a burnt mound. Three radiocarbon dates from silty peat in the first channel span the period from 1740–830 cal BC (Beta-119551, 2940 ± 80 BP, 1400–900 cal BC; Beta-119552, 2840 ± 60 BP, 1210–830 cal BC; Beta-119553, 3280 ± 70 BP, 1740–1410 cal BC). A single date of 2830 ± 60 BP (Beta-119648, 1210–830 cal BC) was obtained from silty peat in the second channel (Smith and Howard 2004).

Significant lateral channel mobility may be demonstrated at a number of sites, including Holme Pierrepont, immediately downstream of Nottingham (MacCormick *et al.* 1968; Musty and MacCormick 1973). Excavations near Holme Pierrepont Hall of an abandoned river channel revealed a complex association between three log boats, one dated to 2180 ± 110 BP (Birm-132, 410 cal BC–cal AD 60) by a sample from its oak gunwale, a 12-spoke wooden wheel of probable Romano-British date, and a large morticed beam interpreted as possibly part of a bridge, raft, floating jetty or trackway. Considerable research was undertaken on the geological context of the boats, which were wedged between large tree-trunks lying upon or within sands and gravels above Mercia Mudstone bedrock (Cummins and Rundle 1969). The overlying sands and gravels were interpreted as point bar deposits laid down by a meandering river migrating to the south and east. Sedimentological calculations suggested that the channel was approximately 3m deep and 30m wide, while molluscan analyses of a coeval calcareous unit (shell bed 1) demonstrated that the bottom of the channel was muddy and covered in weed (Cummins and Rundle 1969). Analyses of two other calcareous units higher up the stratigraphic sequence (shell beds 2 and 3) recorded the abandonment of the meander and encroachment by reedswamp. The excellent state of preservation of the Holme Pierrepont boats, together with the associated sedimentological data, has been used to suggest that they were sunk, caught within a log jam and buried rapidly, most probably during a flood event (MacCormick et al.1968; Cummins and Rundle 1969).

Away from the river, the continued expansion of floodplain wetlands may be demonstrated at sites such as South Ings Close, Rampton, approximately 10km north of Girton. An auger survey of an area of floodplain enclosed by a meander of the Trent led to the identification of a peat bed, mainly 1–2m thick, forming a well-preserved continuous surface across the valley floor, blanketed beneath around 3m of inorganic alluvium (Howard and Knight 2001). This peat bed was dated by radiocarbon to between 3130 ± 70 BP (Beta-159224, 1530–1210 cal BC) and 2900 ± 70 BP (Beta-159222, 1370–900 cal BC). Palaeobiological analysis of the peat indicates a local alder carr with a small element of old mature woodland, while nearby pastoral activity is indicated by the presence of dung beetles and ribwort plantain. Such wetland areas may well have expanded in the earlier first millennium BC as the result of a combination of increased precipitation levels, run-off and possibly rising groundwater levels, the latter two exacerbated by progressive woodland clearance.

Attention should be drawn finally to the related processes of alluviation and colluviation. Many questions remain regarding the chronology of these depositional processes, but there are suggestions of significant changes in the character and rate of alluviation from as early perhaps as the Late Iron Age. This is particularly the case in the Trent Valley to the north of Newark, at Late Iron Age and Romano-British sites such as Ferry Lane Farm, Collingham (Walker 2001; Zeepvat 2000, 109–10, 115–6), Rampton (Knight 2000a; 2000b; Ponsford 1992) and Littleborough (Riley, Buckland and Wade 1995) in Nottinghamshire and in the Idle marshlands at sites such as Sandtoft, North Lincolnshire (Samuels and Buckland 1978). A stratigraphic progression is indicated on many of these sites from anaerobic organically rich silts and clays to oxidised red-brown silty clays. Where datable, these later deposits appear to be Roman or later in date (Chapter 6.3.2), although an earlier origin cannot be ruled out. Comparisons may be drawn with the progressive accumulation of colluvial

deposits, which on a number of sites may be shown to have sealed Iron Age or Romano-British features, as at Foxcovert Farm, Aston-upon-Trent, Derbyshire (Hughes 1999, 179–80, 186, fig.3) and at Kelham, Nottinghamshire, at the interface between the Holme Pierrepont Terrace and floodplain (Knight and Priest 1998), although the chronology of these deposits is even less certain. The observed changes in the rate and character of alluviation were linked originally to soil erosion caused by Roman agricultural innovations such as deeper ploughing and the cultivation of winter cereals, which would have exposed bare soils to weathering and erosion during the wetter and colder winter months (Buckland and Sadler 1985). It is worth speculating, however, whether the origins of these processes might lie in the more intensive farming regimes which it is suggested later in this chapter may have developed in this region during the later Iron Age. Such geomorphic processes could in turn have placed increasing pressures upon land resources and hence might have contributed towards the development of the more tightly managed landscape implied by the evidence discussed in later sections of this chapter.

5.4 The Role of the River

A number of localities along the Middle and Lower Trent have provided evidence for the role of the river as a key route of movement, in the form of log boats, and as a focus for the ceremonial or ritual deposition of metalwork and possibly burials. Rare discoveries have also been made of wooden posts, stakes and other structural remains that might signify waterside structures or causeways across marshy ground, thus recalling such well-known Bronze Age sites as Flag Fen, Cambridgeshire (Pryor 1992; 2001) and Iron Age sites such as Fiskerton, Lincolnshire (Field and Parker Pearson 2003). None of the sites in the Trent Valley, however, has been fully investigated by excavation, and the character of these must remain in doubt. Attention should be drawn also to riverside burnt mounds, which continued in use in this region during the second millennium BC and possibly beyond. These are discussed in detail in a later section of this chapter, within the framework of the model of dispersed unenclosed settlement which is proposed for the later second and early first millennia BC (Chapter 5.7.1).

5.4.1 River Transport and Riverine Structures

The first direct archaeological evidence from the Valley for river traffic may be traced as far back as the Middle Bronze Age, with the discovery at sites such as Clifton and Holme Pierrepont in Nottinghamshire and Aston-upon-Trent in Derbyshire of log boats attributable with variable degrees of certainty to the later Bronze Age and Iron Age periods. Two of these boats, from Argosy Washolme, have been discussed above (Chapter 4.6.5), together with nearby structural remains which span the time periods considered in this and the preceding chapter. Detailed discussion of these is not necessary here, but it is worth emphasising the Middle Bronze Age date implied by the radiocarbon evidence from one boat and the preservation *in situ* in this vessel of a possible cargo of sandstone blocks obtained from a source at least 3km upstream. These stones, which may have been intended as construction material for the foundations of a nearby brushwood trackway dated to the Early and Middle Bronze Ages, provide a unique insight into the types of goods that may have been moved along the Trent by boat.

Fig. 5.1 *View of stern ends of log boats from the River Trent at Clifton, Nottinghamshire (source: Phillips 1941; reproduced from the Antiquaries Journal by permission of the Society of Antiquaries and the Nottingham Evening Post; © Evening Post)*

One of the earliest and most intriguing discoveries of log boats in the Trent Valley was made during dredging of the river at Clifton near Nottingham (Fig.5.1; McGrail 1978,178–83, figs 12–13, 40–41, 87; Phillips 1941). A large number of oak stakes, spaced 'about a yard apart' was observed in the river bed, while from the same area were recovered three log boats, six human skulls and an outstanding collection of Middle and Late Bronze Age metalwork (including ten socketed spearheads, two rapiers, a dirk, two swords and two knives); other finds recovered during dredging of the site and 'its close neighbourhood' (*ibid.* 140) included a Neolithic stone axe and axe-hammer, a few Roman coins and some pottery, an Anglo-Saxon shield boss and cruciform brooch and an undated stone crucible and bronze bowl, suggesting a complex depositional sequence. Phillips interpreted the oak stakes as a Bronze Age 'pile structure – possibly a dwelling' (*ibid.* 134) but alternative interpretations include a wooden causeway comparable to that excavated at Fiskerton in the Witham Valley (Parker-Pearson 2003, 184). Phillips suggested that the Bronze Age metalwork provided a reasonable guide to the date of the boats, but although a Middle or Late Bronze Age date would be entirely possible in view of recent discoveries at Aston-upon-Trent (Chapter 4.6.5), close dating is frustrated by the lack of direct artefact associations and radiocarbon determinations.

Further important discoveries of log boats were made during quarrying at Holme Pierrepont, where three boats were found stratified near the base of the gravels beneath *c.*3m of clean gravel and almost 2m of overlying alluvial topsoil (Cummins and Rundle 1969; MacCormick *et al.* 1968; McGrail 1978, 205–12, figs 20–22; Musty and MacCormick 1973). The cross-bedding of the gravels in which they were buried suggested incorporation subsequent to their deposition within a southwards migrating point bar, indicative of a south-eastwardly migrating river course

(Cummins and Rundle 1969, figs 1 and 2). All except Boat 1 were reported to be in good condition, and it was argued that they had been rapidly buried, possibly during flood. Boats 1 and 2 were entangled with tree trunks, possibly indicating that they had floated downstream to a point where further movement had been impeded by tree trunks, although the boats and trunks need not relate to a single event. Dating hinges upon a radiocarbon date of 2180 ±110 BP (Birm-132, 410 cal BC–cal AD 60) obtained from part of the oak gunwale of Boat 1 (Musty and MacCormick 1973, 276), suggesting a later Iron Age date for at least one vessel. Too much emphasis cannot of course be placed upon a single date, while further caution must be urged as the sample was not obtained from the outermost sapwood and hence may overestimate the age of the boat. A similar date was suggested for the other vessels in view of their comparable stratigraphic positions, but the discovery beneath Boat 1 of a 12-spoked wooden wheel compared by MacCormick to Roman examples emphasises the difficulty of equating the initial date of deposition with the recorded stratigraphic position. Reference should also be made to the discovery at this location of a large morticed beam, interpreted as possibly part of a bridge, raft, floating jetty or trackway (MacCormick *et al.*1968).

5.4.2 Metalwork Deposits

The Trent, in common with other lowland rivers such as the Thames or the Nene, has yielded substantial quantities of bronze tools and weapons attributable on typological grounds mainly to the Middle and Late Bronze Ages – notably at the Nottinghamshire sites of Clifton (Philips 1941), Holme Pierrepont (e.g. *East Midlands Archaeological Bulletin* 11, 1977, 46), Langford (Fig.5.2; Knight 1997) and Carlton (Davis 1999, 45, plate 1), the Lower Trent in Lincolnshire (van de Noort and Ellis eds 1998, 126–7) and upstream of the Trent-Soar confluence in Derbyshire (e.g. Elvaston and Shardlow Quarries: Davies 2003; C. Salisbury: pers. comm.). Some of these were retrieved from the river during fishing or dredging, but most have been obtained during quarrying of sub-alluvial gravel deposits. The original circumstances of deposition can no longer be ascertained, but many could have been deposited singly or together with other finds in contemporary river channels, lakes or other wet or marshy locations, possibly as ceremonial or ritual offerings, as goods accompanying burials, mechanisms for defining social territories or as a result of processes such as casual loss or erosion from bankside settlements (*cf.* Bradley 1998, 97–154). The distribution of such finds is extremely uneven, with notable concentrations between the Trent-Soar confluence and Bleasby, Nottinghamshire (Scurfield 1997), and between Newark and Gainsborough (Davis 1999). Several locations characterised by unusually high densities of metalwork may be identified within the Valley – for example, near Aston-upon-Trent, where recent work at Shardlow Quarry in the vicinity of the two log boats discussed in Chapter 4.6.5 has at the time of writing exposed twelve Middle to Late Bronze Age spearheads, rapiers, palstaves and socketed axes, possibly deposited mainly at the interface between contemporary lacustrine and dry-land contexts (C. Salisbury: pers. comm.; Davis 2003). This spatial patterning may reflect genuine variations in the level of activity, but there is every

Fig. 5.2 *Middle Bronze Age rapier recovered during quarrying at Langford Lowfields, Nottinghamshire; length 470 mm (source: Knight 1997; reproduced by permission of the Thoroton Society of Nottinghamshire)*

likelihood that the distribution has been severely skewed by non-archaeological factors such as the extent of quarrying, the vigilance of quarry workers, the use on some conveyor belts of metal detectors (as at Shardlow Quarry) and the level of archaeological reconnaissance.

This pattern of deposition continues into the Iron Age, although considerably fewer Iron Age items have been recorded. This may indicate a genuine decline in the practice of deliberate deposition in watery contexts, providing thereby an interesting contrast with the nearby Witham Valley where the contrast between Bronze Age and Iron Age artefact densities in wet locations is far less apparent (Field and Parker Pearson 2003, 171–2). Alternatively, this contrast could reflect at least in part the emphasis in this later period upon iron tools and weapons which are less likely to survive. Notable examples of riverine deposits include two Hallstatt-derived bronze swords from Holme Pierrepont (Cowen 1967, 444, plate LIX.5 and plate LXI.2; Meyer 1984, 75; *East Midlands Archaeological Bulletin* 9, 1966, 36–7, fig.7.7–8), a decorated La Tène shield boss from near the Trent-Soar confluence (Watkin *et al.* 1996), an Early/Middle La Tène bronze sword scabbard from Sutton Reach in Nottinghamshire (May 1976, 128–9, plate 3) and two bronze discs from Newark which have been compared to continental Hallstatt cheek piece ornaments (Meyer 1984, 75). In common with much other Bronze and Iron Age metalwork from watery contexts, these items could have been deposited ceremonially, but as noted above the exact circumstances of deposition must remain obscure.

The possibility of a link between the deposition of metalwork in riverine or other watery locations and human burials is an interesting one, given that burial monuments appear to have figured significantly less prominently in the landscape in the later Bronze Age (except perhaps as reminders of past traditions of monumental burial). It could provide one explanation for the comparative dearth of known funerary sites of the later Bronze Age and Iron Age, although as argued above the case for riverine burial is not easily proved (Chapter 4.6.2). Later Bronze Age burial evidence is in fact extremely sparse in the Trent Valley, and is limited to rare flat-grave cremation cemeteries attributable to the Deverel-Rimbury funerary tradition, particularly at Hoveringham (Allen *et al.* 1987) and Barton-under-Needwood, Staffordshire (Martin and Allen 2002). Some of these burials may have been denoted by grave markers, but there is a clear contrast with the monumental funerary architecture of the later Neolithic and Early Bronze Age. Burials of the Iron Age are no less elusive, and the possibility of a link with riverine deposition of metalwork (and possibly other material) should be borne in mind when assessing this paucity of evidence. Attention should also be drawn to rare discoveries at riverside locations of sub-square ditched enclosures which it is suggested later in this chapter may be related to the Arras burial tradition of eastern Yorkshire. Further work is required to characterise more precisely these monuments, but it is worth emphasising here the preference of barrow-builders in eastern Yorkshire for valley locations close to water (*cf.* Bevan 1999, 137–8). This provides an interesting comparison with the Trent Valley, and emphasises the potential symbolic role of the river in contemporary funerary practices.

5.5 Woodland Clearance, Regeneration and Management

Persuasive evidence may be cited for continued woodland clearance, in some areas on a very extensive scale, although occasional evidence for woodland regeneration emphasises the complexity of this process. Attention should also be drawn to the growing evidence for management of the woodland by techniques such as coppicing and pollarding, without which the resource would no doubt have been very seriously depleted.

Away from the river itself, the long-established palaeochannel sequences at Bole Ings and Girton in Nottinghamshire offer valuable insights into the process of woodland clearance. At Bole Ings, peat from the upper part of the organic-rich palaeochannel fill provides significant palynological evidence for arable and pastoral agriculture after 2690 ± 100 BP (Beta-75270, 1050–540 cal BC), including cereal pollen (Brayshay and Dinnin 1999; Dinnin 1997). At Girton, peat from the upper part of the channel fill has been dated by radiocarbon to 2890 ± 60 BP (AA-29321, 1290–900 cal BC) and indicates a landscape which, at the transition from the second to first millennium BC, had been cleared of woodland and shrubs and was instead dominated by grasses and sedges. Elsewhere in the Lower Trent Valley, coring and biological analyses of a series of palaeochannels immediately north of Girton at Waycar Pasture provide a record of arable farming from early in the second millennium BC through to the Romano-British period (Howard *et al.* 1999). Pastoral activity is also suggested by the presence of dung beetles, while charcoal and burnt clay fragments indicate fire within the landscape. Farther north, in the tributary valley of the River Idle, palynological studies of peat deposits in the floodplain at Misson, Nottinghamshire, indicate a decline in woodland after 2690 ± 60 BP (Beta-68363, 980–790 cal BC) and the spread of dense fenland habitat. Although it is assumed that human impact is the cause, there is no supporting evidence within the palynological or archaeological record.

These discoveries, together with the evidence from Staythorpe which was discussed in an earlier section (Chapter 4.4.1; Davies 2001), suggest extensive clearance and an expansion of both arable and pasture in much of the Lower Trent from the earlier Bronze Age through into the Iron Age. Farther upstream, in the Middle Trent Valley, pollen contained within the waterlogged basal fills of two pits at Hoveringham Quarry, Gonalston provide evidence for a similar cleared environment with both pasture and arable cultivation (Fig.5.3; Scaife 1999). Hazel twigs from the lower fill of one pit yielded a radiocarbon date of 2960 ± 50 BP (Beta-104494, 970–790 cal BC) while part of a sharpened hazel post from near the bottom of another pit provided a *terminus post quem* for the deposit of 3220 ± 80BP (Beta-104493, 1690–1310 cal BC). Analyses by Scaife (1999) of associated organic deposits from both pits identified pollen indicative of a predominantly oak and hazel woodland, with a lower representation of lime, beech, ash, holly and alder. Grasses and grassland indicators were also well represented, together with some cereal pollen and taxa indicative of disturbed ground. This picture of a largely cleared, cultivated landscape with distant woodland and floodplain pasture is supported by the environmental data from the Derbyshire sites of Hicken's Bridge and Shardlow, discussed in Chapter 4.4.1, and by organic samples obtained from palaeochannel fills at the above-mentioned site near Willow Farm, Castle Donington (chapter 5.3). The palaeochannel sequence at Willow Farm extends from the second millennium cal BC until around 800 cal BC, and implies during this period a landscape with very sparse woodland cover; the samples are dominated by waterside plant species typical of slowly flowing water, together with numerous terrestrial beetles indicative of grassland and pastoral activities in the riparian corridor (Smith and Howard 2004, 114, table 4).

Yet farther upstream, in the Tame Valley south of its confluence with the Trent, palaeoenvironmental data from ditch fills on the Middle to Late Iron Age settlement at Fisherwick (Smith ed. 1979) indicate that by the Late Iron Age the proportion of arboreal pollen in sampled contexts had plummeted to around 35% of the total record, implying extensive clearance of the gravel terraces for grassland and arable farming (*ibid.* 95). The arboreal pollen was dominated by tree and shrub species typical of secondary forest or hedges, including elder and willow (*ibid.* 83), suggesting that little primeval woodland survived in the vicinity of the site. Alder was particularly well represented, comprising approximately 41% of the arboreal pollen and 58% of the waterlogged wood retrieved from archaeological contexts,

and may have been particularly prevalent on the alluvial floodplain and in other damp environments. Hazel was also well represented in the pollen record (approximately 24% of arboreal pollen) and it was suggested that it may well have been managed as a coppice, perhaps even within enclosures designed to prevent browsing by livestock (Smith 1978, 95; ed. 1979, 102). The floodplain, within this model, would have provided rich summer pastures as well as hay for winter fodder and a wide range of resources such as reeds for thatch or the raw materials for wattlework, basketry and hurdles (*ibid.* 102). A comparable cleared landscape has been postulated at Whitemoor Haye, where detailed analyses of preserved insects (Smith 2002), charred and waterlogged plant remains (Ciaraldi 2002; Greig 2002) and charcoal residues (Gale 2002) from Iron Age contexts have demonstrated a mixture of arable and grassland with limited woodland cover (Coates and Woodward 2002, 79). Study of associated charcoal residues has indicated a fairly wide range of trees and shrubs in the vicinity of the site, despite extensive clearance for arable and grassland, including oak, maple, alder, hazel, ash, willow/poplar and probably birch (Gale 2002, 75). A predominance of oak was argued probably to reflect its use as fuel rather than its dominance as a species (Coates and Woodward 2002, 79).

It should be emphasised, despite the persuasive evidence for progressive clearance, that not all of the Trent Valley was intensively cultivated by the Late Bronze Age. At Yoxall in the Upper Trent Valley of Staffordshire, for example, analysis of an organically rich palaeochannel fill dated by associated hazel to 2780 ± 60 BP (Beta-73350, 1110–800 cal BC) suggested that the landscape was still well forested with dense sedges, rushes and alder close to the channel, and dense mixed oak, hazel, lime and birch woodland on the higher terraces (Smith *et al.* 2001). Evidence for human activity is provided in the upper part of the sequence by plants indicative of disturbed and open ground, including sorrel, ribwort plantain and goosefoots as well as oat or wheat grains. There is also some evidence from associated insects and pollen for the development of dry, acid heathland at unknown locations in the vicinity of the site.

The full extent of clearance in the Trent Valley by the end of the first millennium BC remains, therefore, a vexed issue, which only sustained research aimed at elucidating local variability in the vegetation sequence can hope to elucidate. Further problems arise with attempts to determine the ratio of primeval to regenerated woodland. There is persuasive evidence from several sites in the Trent Valley and neighbouring areas for woodland regeneration during the first millennium BC. A notable example was recorded in the Idle marshlands near Scaftworth, Nottinghamshire, where fluctuations in the ratio of arboreal to non-arboreal pollen within organic deposits beneath and above the timber foundations of a Roman road were argued to imply one or possibly two phases of forest regeneration subsequent to Bronze Age clearance (McElearney 1991). Such discoveries emphasise the complexity of the relationship between Late Bronze Age and Iron Age farming communities and their landscape, which in many areas may have passed through successive phases of clearance and woodland regeneration.

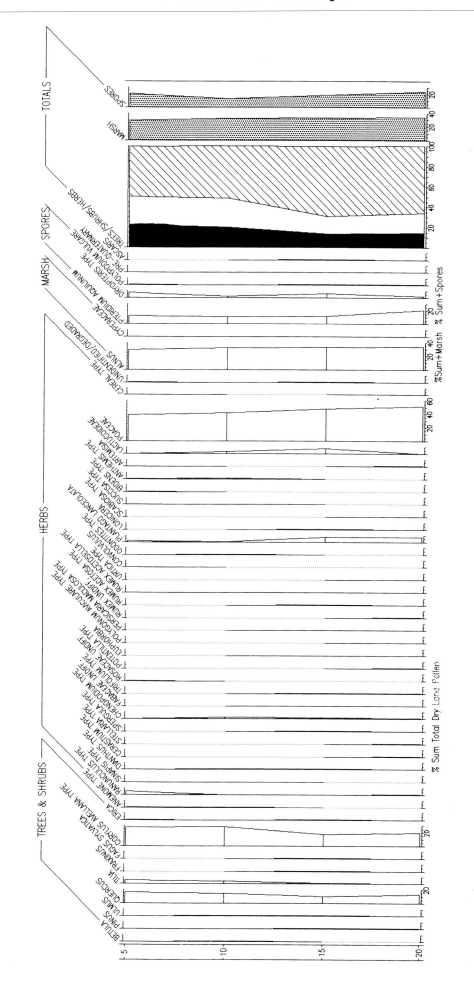

Fig. 5.3 *Pollen percentages in organic material from later Bronze Age pit (0108) at Gonalston, Nottinghamshire; vertical axis: spot samples; horizontal axis: percentage of total dry land pollen (source: Scaife 1999; reproduced by permission of Dr R. Scaife)*

Gonalston 108

5.6 The Agricultural Landscape

Agricultural expansion is suggested not only by the aforementioned changes in the proportion of arboreal to non-arboreal pollen but also by increased frequencies of cultivated grains, weeds of cultivation and pasture indicators within dated assemblages of pollen, plant macrofossils and charred plants, notably at Gamston (Moffett 1992) and Aslockton (Moffett 1993) in Nottinghamshire, Fisherwick (Smith ed. 1979) and Whitemoor Haye (Ciaraldi 2002; Greig 2002) in Staffordshire and Barrow-upon-Trent in Derbyshire (Knight and Southgate 2001; analyses by J. Rackham in progress). There are indications from the palaeobotanical remains recovered from a number of sites of extensive pasture in some stretches of the Valley, although more detailed assessments of the relationship between crop and animal husbandry must await further analyses of palaeobotanical assemblages (*cf.* Monckton 2003, 11). Grazed grasslands may also be deduced from analyses of insect remains from waterlogged deposits – notably at Fisherwick (Smith ed. 1979, 96, 100) and Whitemoor Haye (Smith 2002, 68), where the high representation of dung beetles provides particularly eloquent testimony to the presence of livestock. Further more detailed discussion of the animal husbandry regime is frustrated by the poor preservation of faunal remains in the acidic terrace gravels of the Trent. Thus, although small quantities of bone from cattle, sheep or goat, horse and pig are commonly retrieved, the relative significance of these species, the uses to which they were put and the extent to which husbandry practices varied over time or space remain far from clear.

Detailed information on the range of crops and crop husbandry practices is also sparse at present, despite much palaeoenvironmental sampling of river terrace sites in recent years. Emmer and spelt wheat have been identified in a small number of securely dated Middle and Late Bronze Age contexts – notably at Lockington Site V, where a pit yielding charcoal dated to 3039 ± 80 BP (Beta-83722, 1500–1010 cal BC) incorporated a high concentration of charred plant remains including emmer grains and chaff plus spelt glumes (Moffett and Monckton 2000, 79: Pit F182); it was suggested that the high proportion of chaff in this context could indicate waste from the preparation of glume wheat for consumption (*ibid.*). Barley was also cultivated, as demonstrated by the discovery of charred barley and emmer with hazelnut shells in samples obtained from a Middle to Late Bronze Age burnt mound at Castle Donington (Monckton 2003, 11). Iron Age charred plant assemblages are more common, and have regularly yielded spelt, emmer and hulled barley, and more rarely legumes such as the bean or pea (*ibid.* 13). Again, however, the relative significance of these crops and the balance on individual sites between crop production and processing remain uncertain (e.g. Gamston: Moffett 1992; Aslockton: Moffett 1993; Whitemoor Haye: Ciaraldi 2002; Coates and Woodward 2002, 88). Arable intensification, demonstrated in other parts of the Midlands and southern England during the later Iron Age (e.g. Lambrick 1992, 84–5), may be implied by the increased representation of crops such as spelt which may be sown in both autumn and spring and by higher densities on some later Iron Age sites of charred

cereal remains (e.g. Gamston: Monckton 2003, 15–16). In addition, increases may also be observed on some sites in the density of pits which could have been used for grain storage (e.g. Knight 1992, 38), although the significance of this trend is difficult to assess in view of the wide range of alternative functions that such features might have performed (e.g. Reynolds 1974).

5.7 From Open to Enclosed Settlement

5.7.1 The Later Second and Early First Millennia BC

Occupation sites of this early period are significantly more elusive than those of the later first millennium BC, despite the evidence for progressive woodland clearance and the consequent likelihood of quite extensive settlement, and have been revealed mainly by chance during excavations of later Iron Age or Romano-British enclosures such as Gamston (Knight 1992), Gonalston (Elliott and Knight 2002) and Willington (Wheeler 1979). Rare associations have been recorded with Deverel-Rimbury pottery and post Deverel-Rimbury (PDR) plainwares, dated respectively from the latter half of the second millennium BC and the final centuries of the second millennium BC to the tenth or ninth centuries cal BC (Knight 2002, 123–6). Associations with Deverel-Rimbury pottery are especially scarce, and comprise sparse scatters of pits or post-holes forming no obvious pattern – notably at Gonalston, where scattered pits and post-holes within an area occupied by a later Iron Age enclosure yielded fragments of Deverel-Rimbury bucket urn (Elliott and Knight 2002). This is in sharp contrast to some neighbouring regions, such as south Lincolnshire, where rare enclosures of this period have been recognised (e.g. Billingborough: Chowne *et al.* 2001; Kirmond le Mire: Field and Knight 1992). Settlements yielding PDR plainwares are little easier to interpret. Notable examples of the latter include Catholme, where the discovery of several timber roundhouses suggests an early unenclosed phase of settlement (Losco-Bradley and Kinsley 2002, 15; A.G. Kinsley & G. Guilbert: pers. comm). Several four- and six-post structures on this site could also belong to this early phase, but unfortunately none may be closely dated. In addition, excavations at Willow Farm, Castle Donington, revealed an extensive open settlement incorporating at least one post-built round-house, dated by associated PDR plainwares (Coward and Ripper 1999; P. Marsden: pers. comm.), while at Lockington Site V a scatter of pits, some yielding plain PDR sherds, was recorded immediately to the west of an earlier Bronze Age barrow (Hughes 2000, 17, 56–7, fig.31.15–17; Meek 1995). Associations between domestic structures and Late Bronze Age–Earlier Iron Age (LBA-EIA) pottery of the ninth to fifth/fourth centuries BC are more common, although it should be emphasised that pottery attributable to this ceramic tradition is still rare by comparison with the ubiquitous Earlier and Late La Tène wares of the Middle and Late Iron Ages. Many of the settlements yielding LBA-EIA pottery also preserve stratigraphic evidence for a progression from an early open settlement to an enclosure phase associated with Earlier or Late La Tène pottery, hence echoing a trend observed elsewhere in the Midlands and indeed in southern Britain generally (*cf.* Thomas 1997, 211–3). Examples include Gamston, where a Middle to Late Iron Age enclosure ditch cut an earlier semi-circular structure, a palisade trench and several pits (Fig. 5.4; Fig.5.5: Phase 2 enclosure; Knight 1992, 23–27), Fleak Close, Barrow-upon-Trent, where the bedding trench of at least one timber round-house and several widely dispersed pits, post-holes and gullies were truncated by a later enclosure ditch or by features cut by this ditch (Fig.5.10; Knight and Southgate 2001, 201) and Gonalston, where the north-eastern boundary ditch of a substantial Middle to Late Iron Age enclosure cut a scatter of pits, post-holes and gullies, some conceivably part of the same phase of activity as a severely truncated round-house located in their vicinity (Fig.5.17: D; Elliott and Knight 2002).

The structural elements of these early sites generally form low-density scatters with no discernible spatial patterning, often much truncated by later activity. A particularly extensive spread of features was recorded at Gonalston, where structural remains associated with PDR plainwares and LBA-EIA pottery, including scattered pits, post-holes and possibly the truncated foundations of timber round-houses were spread thinly and intermittently over an elongated gravel island (Elliott and Knight 2002; Fig.5.17). This pattern of scattered unenclosed features is repeated at other quarries that have been extensively investigated, including Barrow-upon-Trent (Knight and Southgate 2001), Willington (Wheeler 1979, 78–86) and Castle

Fig. 5.4 *Semicircular structure (foreground) truncated by Iron Age enclosure ditch at Gamston, Nottinghamshire (photograph: D.Knight)*

Donington (Beamish and Ripper 2000), and raises the possibility of extensive but thinly spread settlement of the river terraces from this early period. The general absence of archaeologically detectable boundaries, which provides such a striking contrast with settlements of the Middle and Late Iron Ages, could imply a largely unbounded landscape during the early first millennium – and by implication perhaps comparatively unrestricted access to land resources (*cf.* Pryor 1998, 144–5). This in turn might support the suggestion by some that early Valley communities had been bound into complex cycles of short- and long-distance transhumance (Bishop 2001, 4), conceivably with an emphasis upon a system of shifting agriculture rather than the more permanent cultivation implied by the extensive field systems of the later Iron Age (*cf.* Smith 1978, 98). Such widely ranging communities may have had little need for boundaries, which it is suggested below might have emerged at a later date as population, livestock and settlement densities increased, and especially as access to traditional pastures became more restricted and pressures mounted for the more intensive exploitation of arable resources. More speculatively, contacts between widely dispersed communities could have provided a spur to the development of the medium and long-distance exchange networks in basic commodities such as pottery, salt and querns or precious items such as glass beads or fine metalwork which are particularly evident in the later Iron Age of the Trent Valley (e.g. Knight 1992, 85, fig.30; 2002, 137–41; Knight *et al.* 2003).

This model of dispersed unenclosed settlement should be adapted to take account of two other classes of monument that have emerged recently as significant components of the later prehistoric settlement pattern. The most widespread of these are burnt mounds, which it was suggested in the previous chapter may have developed in this region during the later Neolithic period – as cooking sites, for example, or as saunas, foci for textile production and locations of other craft or industrial activities (Chapter 4.6.3). Current evidence would favour a predominantly later Neolithic to Bronze Age date range for these monuments, raising the possibility that they had continued in use as social foci for widely dispersed communities throughout the second millennium BC. However, dating is currently extremely imprecise, and significant investment in radiometric dating is required before the chronology of these monuments can be established with reasonable certainty.

A particularly well preserved burnt mound, on present evidence possibly dating to the later Bronze Age, was recorded during excavations at Willington, on the edge of a contemporary river channel which had later filled with silts (Fig 4.5: Burnt Mound II; Beamish 2001, 13; Beamish and Ripper 2000, 37, fig. 2). The most remarkable discovery was a rectangular trough of some 400 litres capacity with a round wood lining comprising a basal arrangement of thirteen timbers laid side by side plus stacked timbers along each side which had been retained by corner stakes (Fig.5.6). A deposit of cut branches and logs in the channel silts adjacent to the trough was interpreted as evidence perhaps for the consolidation of marshy ground next to the mound. Evidence for an association with cooking activities

Fig. 5.5 *Iron Age structural sequence at Gamston, Nottinghamshire (source: Knight 1992; reproduced by permission of the Thoroton Society of Nottinghamshire)*

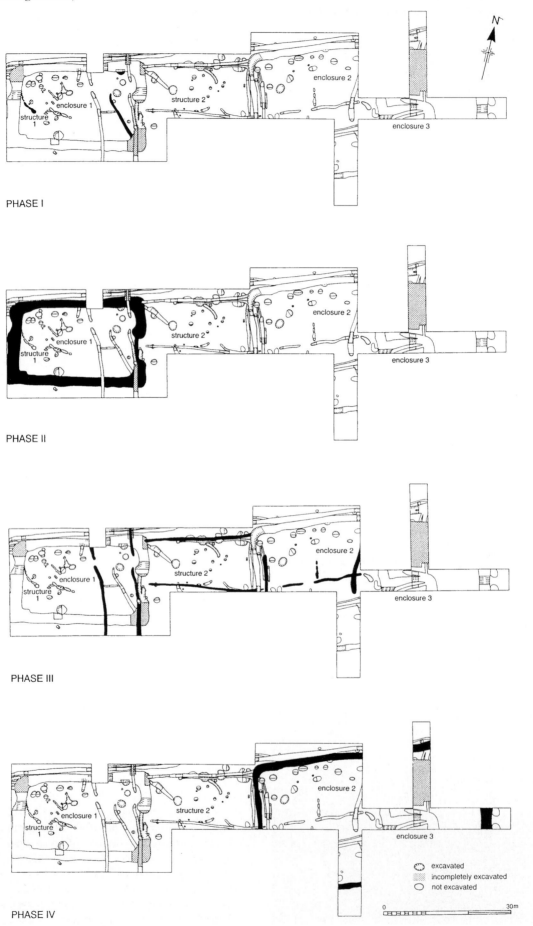

Fig. 5.6 *Wood-lined trough of burnt mound at Willington, Derbyshire (photograph: M. Beamish)*

may be provided by discoveries in the nearby channel fills of rare fragments of ox and possibly horse. Assessment of the wood from the trough revealed tool-marks created by metal blades, suggesting to the excavator a Bronze Age or later date for this structure, while a base sherd ascribed to the Middle or Late Bronze Age was retrieved some 25m to the south of the mound. Radiocarbon dates are planned for the associated timbers (M. Beamish: pers. comm.), and firm conclusions on the date range of this site must be reserved until receipt of these.

The date of demise of burnt mounds as regular components of the Valley landscape is unclear, but it is possible that some had continued in use into the early centuries of the following millennium. Unequivocal evidence for such late dating has yet to be obtained from the region, but there is a hint on at least one site of continuation into the earlier first millennium. At Gonalston, one of several linear ditches (Fig.5.17: K) forming part of a boundary system which may have originated in the mid-first millennium BC appears to have been deliberately diverted to run into the trough of one of several burnt mounds recorded during gravel extraction (Fig.5.7; Fig.5.17: F). This may relate to the final use of a monument designed originally for other purposes and perhaps long decayed, but at the very least it implies that the trough had remained as a clearly visible feature well into the first millennium BC.

Another indicator of Late Bronze Age or Early Iron Age settlement, as yet unparalleled elsewhere within the Trent Valley, was located during excavations at Girton, to the south of the burnt mound at Waycar Pasture which was noted in the previous chapter. This was represented by a remarkable concentration of almost 600 plain and decorated LBA-EIA sherds, many in fresh condition, associated with a thin layer of dark loamy sand incorporating charcoal,

fragmentary burnt bone and abundant heat-shattered pebbles (Fig.5.8; Kinsley 1998, 43–7; H. Jones & A.G. Kinsley: pers. comm.). One side of this deposit had been truncated during machining, but it may have extended originally over a roughly circular area at least 7m in diameter. The dense concentration of burnt stones initially evoked comparisons with burnt mounds, but the association with abundant pottery, bone and other finds would be highly unusual for such monuments. Comparisons should be sought instead with Late Bronze Age or Early Iron Age middens, which are rare in the Midlands (e.g. Stickford, Lincolnshire: Lane forthcoming) but widely distributed in Wessex and neighbouring regions. Notable examples include the Wiltshire midden complexes at Potterne (Lawson 2000), East Chisenbury (Brown *et al.* 1994) and All Cannings Cross (Cunnington 1923), although it should be stressed that all of these extended over far larger areas and preserved significantly deeper and more complex stratigraphy than the comparatively modest mound at Girton. All of the known examples from southern England have provided associations with Late Bronze Age or Early Iron Age pottery, suggesting a restricted period of usage, and provide a key source of evidence for early first millennium BC domestic activity. As with other middens of this period, however, the possibility of ritual or ceremonial activities associated with food preparation and consumption should also be considered (*cf.* Brown *et al.* 1994). In the case of Girton, evidence for associated settlement may be provided

Fig. 5.7 *Remains of wood-lined trough associated with burnt mound at Gonalston, Nottinghamshire (photograph: L.Elliott)*

Fig. 5.8 *Section across midden at Girton, Nottinghamshire, showing thin layer of dark midden material beneath layer of blown sand (photograph: H. Jones)*

by a scatter of stratigraphically unrelated pits, ditches and gullies yielding LBA-EIA sherds that was recorded during machine-stripping adjacent to this deposit.

5.7.2 The Later First Millennium BC

Significant changes in the spatial organisation of settlement in the Trent Valley may be discerned from the mid-first millennium BC, with the progressive enclosure of occupation foci and specialised activity areas by ditches and other barriers to movement, including earthen banks, palisades and probably hedges (*cf.* Smith 1978, 95, 98). Associations with Earlier and Late La Tène pottery, combined with rare finds of datable metalwork and occasional radiocarbon dates, suggest an origin for this process probably no earlier than the fifth or fourth centuries BC, with a rapid gathering of momentum in the Late Iron Age and Romano-British periods (e.g. Fisherwick: Smith ed. 1979; Barrow-upon-Trent: Knight and Southgate 2001; Gamston: Knight 1992). This trend towards enclosure was accompanied in some areas by the development of field systems and the construction of more substantial land boundaries such as pit alignments, implying a new concern with the stricter control of land resources.

The enclosures that may be shown to have dominated much of the Trent Valley in the final centuries of the first millennium BC form part of a morphologically diverse monument class, defined by the presence of one or more continuous or discontinuous circuits of ditch, bank or palisade (*cf.* Whimster 1989, 28). In contrast to field boundaries, which emerged during the same period as a means of dividing outlying pasture and arable resources, enclosures may be regarded as foci for specialised activities associated closely with occupation or, in rare cases perhaps, with burial. Significant variations may be observed in the form, scale and spatial configuration of enclosure boundaries, the size and shape of the enclosed area, arrangements for access and the range of associated structural, artefactual and palaeoenvironmental remains (*ibid.* 28–9, 66–7). These in turn imply a wide range of functions connected not only with the everyday, such as occupation, the sorting and housing of livestock and the processing and storage of grain, but also with ceremony, ritual and burial.

Enclosure morphology

A small number of Iron Age enclosures may have been demarcated by a palisade set in a continuous bedding trench, as was proposed at Willington (Wheeler 1979, 103, fig.18: F352/3 & F367) and Holme Pierrepont Site 4 (O'Brien 1979, 1, fig.1), but most enclosures of this period are represented in the archaeological record solely by a single circuit of ditch, often recut on many occasions. Very few multiple-ditched enclosures have been recorded, with the most notable exception of an elongated curvilinear enclosure which is postulated at Aslockton (Fig.5.11), although recutting of ditches adjacent to their original alignment may create complex ground plans bearing a superficial resemblance to complex multiple-ditched enclosures. At Fleak Close, Barrow-upon-Trent, for example, excavations of a postulated double-ditched

cropmark enclosure revealed up to three stratigraphically successive enclosure ditches created by progressive recutting of the enclosure ditch on its outer side (Fig.5.10; Knight and Southgate 2001).

An internal or external bank may sometimes be deduced, either from zones of preferential silting within the ditch fill, discontinuities in the distribution of features within enclosures or, in rare cases, by the discovery of the denuded remains of an earthen bank. At Aslockton, for example, a wide and largely ploughed-out earthwork was observed flanking the north-eastern edge of the outermost of two parallel ditches visible as cropmarks to the west of Mill Lane and as substantial features in an evaluation trench dug along the roadside verge (Palmer-Brown and Knight 1993; Fig.5.11). Some ditches may have been flanked by hedges set on the ground surface or upon an associated bank, although the case for these must be argued from indirect evidence such as the discovery in waterlogged ditch fills at Fisherwick of cut twigs from blackthorn, willow and other typical hedgerow species (Smith 1978, 98–9; Smith ed. 1979, 24, 96). Similar problems attend the identification of associated fences, although at Fisherwick these were suggested on the basis of fragments of trimmed and sharpened oak and alder stakes which might have formed part of an associated fence (*ibid.* 76–7) and the discovery on the inner side of one enclosure ditch of a narrow gully interpreted rather optimistically by the excavator as an associated palisade trench (*ibid.* 24, 154, fig.10: feature 19).

Attention should also be drawn to a small number of undated earthwork enclosures within or on the fringes of the Valley which have been interpreted in the past as Iron Age hillforts or their lowland equivalents. These include a partially destroyed 3ha enclosure on a gravel terrace at Borough Hill, Walton-on-Trent, Derbyshire, which has been interpreted as a univallate Iron Age hillfort (Challis and Harding 1975, 47; Hogg 1979, 155; *Victoria County History Derbyshire* I, 1905, 786–7), an impressive univallate earthwork enclosure of *c.*1.7ha overlooking the Trent Valley at Bury Bank, near Stone, Staffordshire (Darlington 1994, 14–17, figs 15,16,127; Hogg 1979, 155; *Victoria County History Staffordshire* I, 332, 342–4), a sub-rectangular enclosure of *c.*1.5ha at Crow Wood, Styrrup, Nottinghamshire, which has been compared to Iron Age 'marsh forts' such as Sutton Common, South Yorkshire (Badcock and Symonds 1994; *cf.* Parker-Pearson and Sydes 1997) and a heterogeneous group of earthwork enclosures on the Mercia Mudstone claylands fringing the northern edge of the Trent Valley east of Nottingham (O'Brien 1978a, 10–11, fig.8; Simmons 1963). Serious doubts have been raised regarding the interpretation of the Borough Hill earthworks as evidence of a later prehistoric hillfort (Guilbert 2004), and judgement on the character of this perplexing site is best deferred until opportunities arise for more detailed archaeological investigations. Similarly, a recent reassessment of the 'hillforts' of central Nottinghamshire has emphasised the likelihood of widely varying origins and functions (Bishop 2001, 3), while neither of the remaining enclosures may be attributed with certainty to the period of our enquiry.

The internal areas of those enclosures which may be dated with confidence to the first millennium BC varied dramatically, reflecting in part probably variations in function. Known examples range from miniscule enclosures of less than 0.01ha at Gonalston (Elliott and Knight 2003, 201; Fig.5.9) and Brough-on-Fosse, Nottinghamshire (Fig.5.16:A) to as much as *c*.20ha at Aslockton (Fig.5.11), although doubts remain at the last of these sites regarding the full spatial extent of the boundary works. The emphasis lies firmly upon rectilinear shapes, in sharp contrast to the preference for circularity in domestic architecture, although Iron Age enclosures of curvilinear or polygonal form have also been recorded at sites such as Potlock, Derbyshire (Guilbert and Malone 1994, 13, 17–18, fig.3.1), Fisherwick (Smith ed. 1979, fig.3; *cf.* also Whimster 1989, 66) and Whitemoor Haye (Coates 2002, 33, fig.25: Area C). The ditch circuits were interrupted by one or more rarely two entrances, represented either by directly opposed ditch terminals (e.g. Gamston: Knight 1992, fig.3: enclosure 1) or occasionally by more elaborate arrangements of in-turned terminals or entrance outworks which in some cases may have facilitated the movement of stock (e.g. Fleak Close: Fig.5.10). Post-hole settings suggestive of associated gate structures sometimes survive – as at Fisherwick, where post-hole alignments suggested a gated fenced passage which it was argued might have served to sort livestock entering or leaving the enclosure (Smith ed. 1979, 24–6, 96, fig.7). Another link with stock handling may be provided by the occasional provision of corner entrances, which it has been suggested might have helped funnel stock contained within an enclosure towards the entrance (Pryor 1996, 318–9; e.g. Whitemoor Haye Area B: Coates 2002, 31, fig. 22). Attention has also been drawn by a number of scholars to the easterly orientation of some enclosure entrances, which it has been suggested might signify an orientation upon the rising sun – notably at Gamston (Fig.5.5), Fisherwick (Fig.5.13) and Whitemoor Haye (Coates and Woodward 2002, 8; *cf.* Willis 1999, 93). A significantly larger sample of excavated enclosures would be required, however, to establish whether the preferred easterly orientation of Iron Age enclosure entrances which has been noted in other areas of Britain (*ibid.* 93) had also prevailed in the Trent Valley, while doubts must also be expressed regarding the cosmological significance of this observation.

The purpose of enclosure

A significant number of enclosure boundaries would have provided impressive barriers to movement, seemingly well in excess of that required for purely utilitarian purposes such as stock control and drainage, and we may speculate therefore whether many boundaries might have fulfilled important social as well as economic functions. Much emphasis has been placed in recent studies of Iron Age enclosures upon the symbolic role of boundaries, the construction and maintenance of which has been linked to strategies designed to emphasise group identity and enhance social cohesion (e.g. Bevan 1997; 1999; Chadwick 1999; Hingley 1990). These strategies could represent reactions to increasing pressures upon land resources, and in their most extreme manifestation could have resulted in the

Fig. 5.9 *Iron Age ditched enclosure at Gonalston, Nottinghamshire; entrance top left (photograph: L. Elliott)*

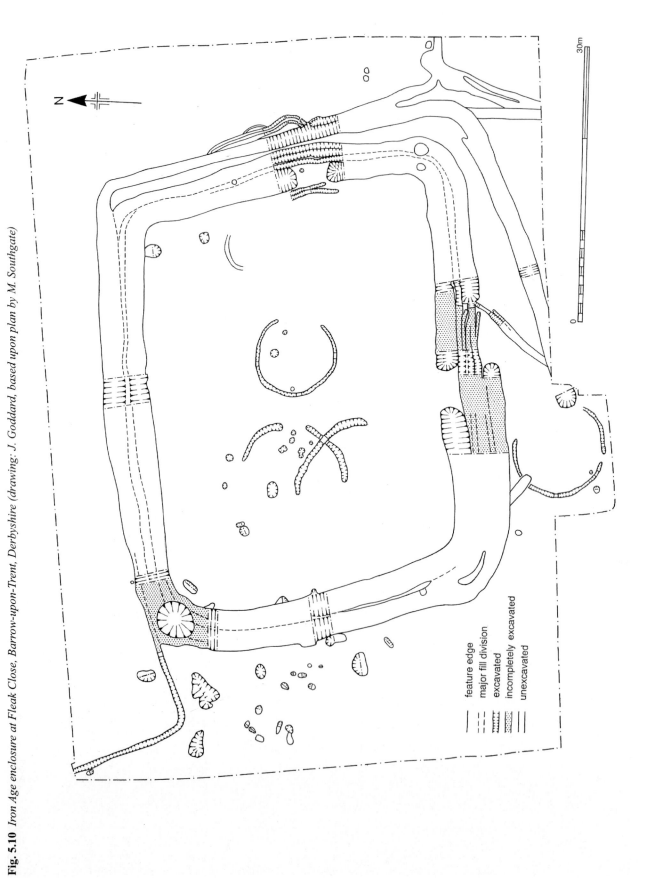

Fig. 5.10 *Iron Age enclosure at Fleak Close, Barrow-upon-Trent, Derbyshire (drawing: J. Goddard, based upon plan by M. Southgate)*

feature edge
major fill division
excavated
incompletely excavated
unexcavated

30m

construction of sites such as Aslockton, where an evaluation trench across part of a cropmark site reminiscent of some of the complex multiple-ditched sites of Lincolnshire (Winton 1998) revealed substantial boundary works which may originally have been of defensive proportions (Hampton, 1975, 122; Palmer-Brown and Knight 1993; Fig.5.11). This site lies just beyond the edge of the Trent Valley, on the crest of a low drift-covered interfluve separating the River Smite and the Car Dyke, and is defined on its north-eastern and north-western sides by single or multiple ditches clearly visible as cropmarks. There are suggestions of single or multiple ditches demarcating south-eastern and south-western boundaries to the site, although the linear cropmarks marking these features are intermittent and need not necessarily represent an originally continuous boundary. A trench along the western roadside verge of Mill Lane revealed two closely spaced and possibly contemporary ditches, up to 6m wide by at least 2m deep, flanked by a levelled bank between the two ditch alignments and a second denuded bank along the outer edge of the external ditch (*ibid.* 146: Phase 2). A post-hole cut through the bank could imply some kind of timber strengthening, but significantly more of the earthwork would need to be excavated to determine this. The site was not placed in an obviously defensive location, but the scale of the remains implies a formidable barrier to movement which at the very least would have represented a potent symbol of prestige and display. Similar arguments may be applied to several other Iron Age enclosures within the region, some on hill-top or promontory locations reminiscent of those favoured by hillfort-builders. These include a substantial curvilinear ditch at Swarkestone Lowes, which may have defined a Middle to Late Iron Age ridge-top enclosure of approximately 8ha (Fig.5.12; Elliott and Knight 1999) and a smaller enclosure near Chapel Farm, Shardlow (Knight and Malone 1997; 1998). A gradiometer survey of the latter site revealed an irregular curvilinear ditch demarcating a roughly semi-circular area of at least 0.5ha at the end of a gravel promontory elevated slightly above the Trent floodplain. Evaluation trenches across this feature suggested a substantial multi-phased ditch which on the basis of associated pottery may have originated towards the end of the Late Iron Age and continued in use into the second century. A dense pattern of Late Iron Age/Romano-British gullies, pits and possible post-holes was recorded during evaluation excavations inside the enclosure, but more extensive excavations would be required to clarify the structural sequence and the extent and character of pre-Roman activity.

The above examples are distinguished by their large internal areas, well above the average for enclosures of this period. However, many much smaller enclosures display a similar emphasis upon boundary constructions which would seem excessive if they had been intended solely for purposes such as stock control. At Brough-on-Fosse, for example, excavations uncovered a small sub-oval enclosure demarcated by an impressive V-shaped ditch, dug originally to a depth of approximately 1.4m and almost 2m wide at the mouth (H. Jones: pers. comm.: Fig.5.16: A). This seems wholly out of proportion to the size of the enclosed area (<0.01ha) and as at Aslockton or Swarkestone Lowes

prompts consideration of the role of factors such as prestige and display in its construction.

Further questions on the social significance of enclosure are prompted by consideration of the complex and often bewildering sequences of ditch recutting which have emerged during the excavation of many Iron Age sites within the region. This is exemplified at Fleak Close (Fig.5.10), where the Iron Age boundary ditch had been recut repeatedly along its outer edge, causing a gradual but significant expansion of the enclosed area, and may be demonstrated also on many Romano-British enclosures within the region – notably at Gonalston, where a subrectangular ditched enclosure had been repeatedly recut along its inner edge, thus reducing progressively the internal area (Elliott and Knight 2003, 202; Fig.17: E). Such sequences could have a simple functional explanation, reflecting the need for repeated cleaning out of silted enclosure ditches, although it would seem that this essential activity could have been achieved far more easily by removing accumulated ditch silts rather than by re-digging beside a previous alignment. In the face of such evidence, some researchers have speculated whether protracted recutting sequences should be viewed in part as symbolic acts, aimed at emphasising, by means of successive re-inscriptions upon the landscape, the strong links between communities and the lands they farmed (*cf.* Chadwick 1999, 161–4; Hingley 1990). In the context of the Trent Valley, with ever-growing pressures during the later first millennium BC upon limited land resources, community activities which reinforced the rights of ownership or which served to reinforce group identity and bind individual members more closely together may well have assumed ever growing significance.

The above arguments may be strengthened by the discovery in Iron Age enclosure ditches of structured deposits, particularly of animal or human remains, which could imply ceremonial deposition focused upon settlement boundaries (e.g. Gwilt 1997; Hill 1995; Willis 1999, 96–9). Such evidence is extremely rare in the Trent, due to the poor preservation of bone in the acidic sands and gravels of the river terraces, but occasional discoveries in Iron Age ditches hint that in this region too such practices may have been more common than can be demonstrated at present. At Fleak Close, Barrow-upon-Trent, for example, a large assemblage of red deer antler and a pig jaw had been deposited in the bottom of a large pit dug into the filling of an Iron Age enclosure ditch in the exact centre of one of its corners (Knight and Southgate 2001). The coincidence is striking, raising the option of a deliberate act of deposition while the corner of the largely infilled enclosure ditch was still remembered and respected, thus providing perhaps some symbolic link with earlier land divisions (*cf.* Proctor 2002).

Enclosure functions

Whatever the exact motivations for their construction, enclosures are likely to have embraced a wide range of functions and, in the case of occupied sites, the size and status of the population grouping may have varied significantly. The possibility of differentiation in terms of

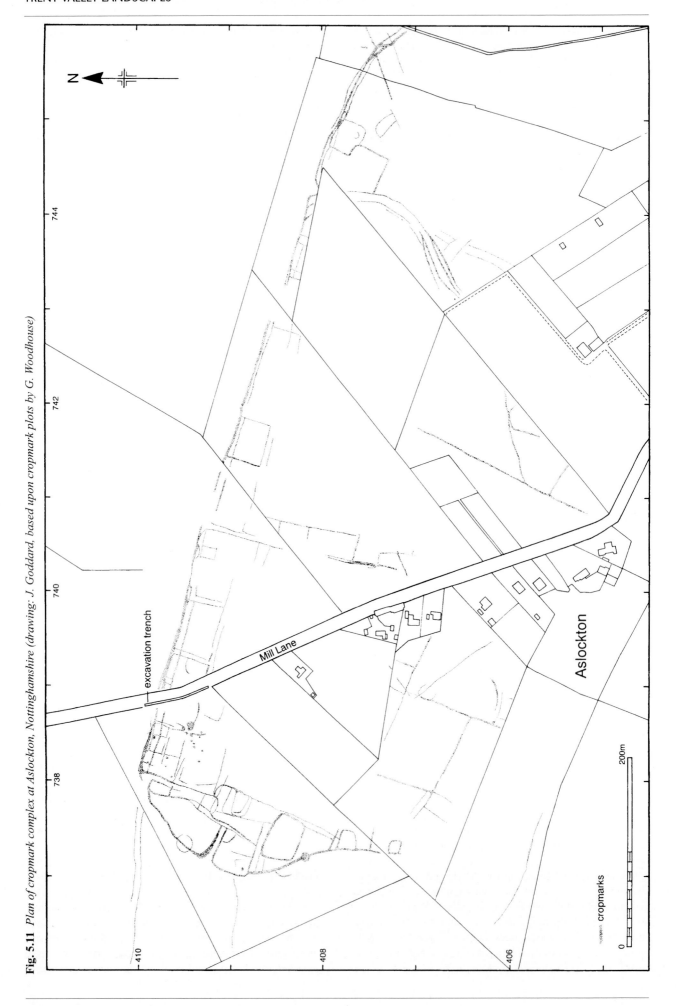

Fig. 5.11 *Plan of cropmark complex at Aslockton, Nottinghamshire (drawing: J. Goddard, based upon cropmark plots by G. Woodhouse)*

Mill Lane

excavation trench

Aslockton

cropmarks

0　　　　　　　　200m

N

410

408

406

738

740

742

744

community size and status is illustrated most strongly by the sites at Aslockton and Swarkestone Lowes, which it has been suggested above may represent substantial enclosures up to about 8ha and 20ha respectively. These stand out from all other Iron Age enclosures within the region on the grounds of their massive internal areas and raise the possibility of significant variations in community size, functions and perhaps status. Both have yielded structural and artefactual remains that could signify contemporary occupation, although as only tiny portions of each site have been excavated any conclusions on the subject of their functions and spatial organisation must remain tentative. Major difficulties also arise on these and other sites because of the loss of structural remains as a result of ploughing and other destructive activities, together with the possible use of constructional techniques which are likely to leave few if any physical traces, and hence appropriate caution must be exercised when interpreting archaeologically blank areas.

At Aslockton, cropmarks suggest a large elongated curvilinear enclosure which may have been divided by ditches constructed on a north-east to south-west alignment into two main compartments, each possibly edged by a series of sub-rectangular ditched enclosures positioned around a central open space (Fig.5.11). As noted above, a trench across the north-eastern enclosure boundary revealed two parallel ditches, up to 6m wide by 2m deep, each flanked originally by substantial banks. The trench extended southwards for about 125m beyond these ditches, revealing dense Middle Iron Age to Romano-British structural and artefactual remains within a broad 50m-wide zone adjacent to the enclosure boundary, but otherwise no traces of activity, conceivably implying that the area beyond had been reserved for purposes such as stock grazing. Support for a link with stock management is provided by the unusually abundant faunal remains which survived, particularly of cattle and sheep/goat, with a lower representation of pig, horse and dog, although it should be emphasised that that the soil conditions on this low drift-covered interfluve were more conducive to the preservation of bone than the acidic gravels of the river terraces. Further indirect evidence for an association with animal husbandry is provided by finds of fired clay triangular loomweights, bone weaving combs and other worked bone artefacts (Hamshaw-Thomas 1992). Charred chaff, cereal grains and seeds included spelt, emmer/spelt, hulled barley and various weeds of cultivation, suggesting crop-processing activities on site (Moffett 1992).

In contrast perhaps to Aslockton, occupation at Swarkestone Lowes may have been dispersed widely within the area demarcated by the curvilinear ditch (Fig. 5.12). The discovery during excavation of quite extensive areas yielding no evidence of structural or artefactual remains indicative of occupation raises the possibility that large parts of the enclosed area might have been reserved for purposes such as stock grazing, with the obvious proviso that structural remains may in some areas have eluded discovery. Associated pollen, plant macrofossils and insect remains would support the case for extensive pasture (Elliott and Knight 1999, 139–49), although detailed discussion of the animal husbandry regime is prevented by the poor survival of bone in the acidic

soils. General parallels may be suggested with the pattern of Iron Age land-use postulated in the Thames Valley at Stanton Harcourt, Oxfordshire, where dispersed terrace-edge communities with juxtaposed arable land may have encircled a zone of communal pasture (Lambrick 1992, 90–3). This 'pastoral' core was dominated by an extant henge and a Bronze Age barrow cemetery, recalling the demarcation by the curvilinear Iron Age ditch at Swarkestone of a ridge-top barrow cemetery (Fig.5.12). Similar monument 'associations' have been observed elsewhere in Britain and Ireland (e.g. Hingley 1999), and have been cited as evidence of the use of earlier funerary and ritual sites as foci in the laying out of later agricultural settlements, possibly as a mechanism for defining and reinforcing group identity by reference to ancestry (*ibid.* 246–8).

Most other enclosures within the Trent Valley fall within the size range of *c.*1.5ha (e.g. Potlock: Guilbert and Malone 1994, 13, 17–18, fig. 3.1) to 0.01ha (e.g. Brough-on-Fosse: Fig.5.16: A; Vyner ed. forthcoming) and of these the vast majority enclose areas of less than 0.5ha. The evidence of internal structures and associated finds and palaeoenvironmental remains would suggest a wide variety of functions. The interiors of a significant number of the smaller enclosures preserved structural remains that might signify contemporary occupation, and in view of their size may have served as habitation foci for extended family or kin groups. Associated finds provide little evidence of status variations between these settlements, which apart from occasional items of metalwork (e.g. Knight 1992, 66) or objects such as glass beads (e.g. Henderson 1992) show little evidence of material wealth. This provides an intriguing contrast with the quantities of rich metalwork obtained from the Trent (Chapter 5.4.2), which as yet find no counterpart in the artefact records recovered from settlements within the Valley.

The archaeological record relating to the majority of enclosed settlements is characterised in fact by a remarkable level of homogeneity. We might almost imagine an enclosure template, for time and again we encounter rectilinear ditched enclosures up to approximately 0.3ha in area with traces of one or more circular structures which may have served as dwellings, scatters of pits for purposes such as grain storage or cooking and various ancillary structures such as four-post structures, some of which could represent raised granaries (*cf.* Ellison and Drewett 1971; Gent 1983). Typical examples include a sub-square ditched enclosure at Fisherwick, preserving at least one multi-phased internal round-house which could have been contemporary with its use (Fig.5.13), Fleak Close, where a sub-rectangular ditched enclosure preserved three centrally placed round-houses, two of which could have been in contemporary use (Fig.5.10), and Whitemoor Haye, where excavations revealed two subrectangular enclosures incorporating multiple round-houses and scattered pits (Coates 2002, 21–33, figs 17 and 22: Areas A and B). Only rarely, however, can a stratigraphic link be demonstrated between the enclosure ditch and internal structures, and the case for contemporary occupation generally rests upon the less secure grounds of their spatial relationships – thus warning against over-elaborate interpretations of intra-enclosure spatial patterning. The problem is exemplified by the discovery inside a Middle to

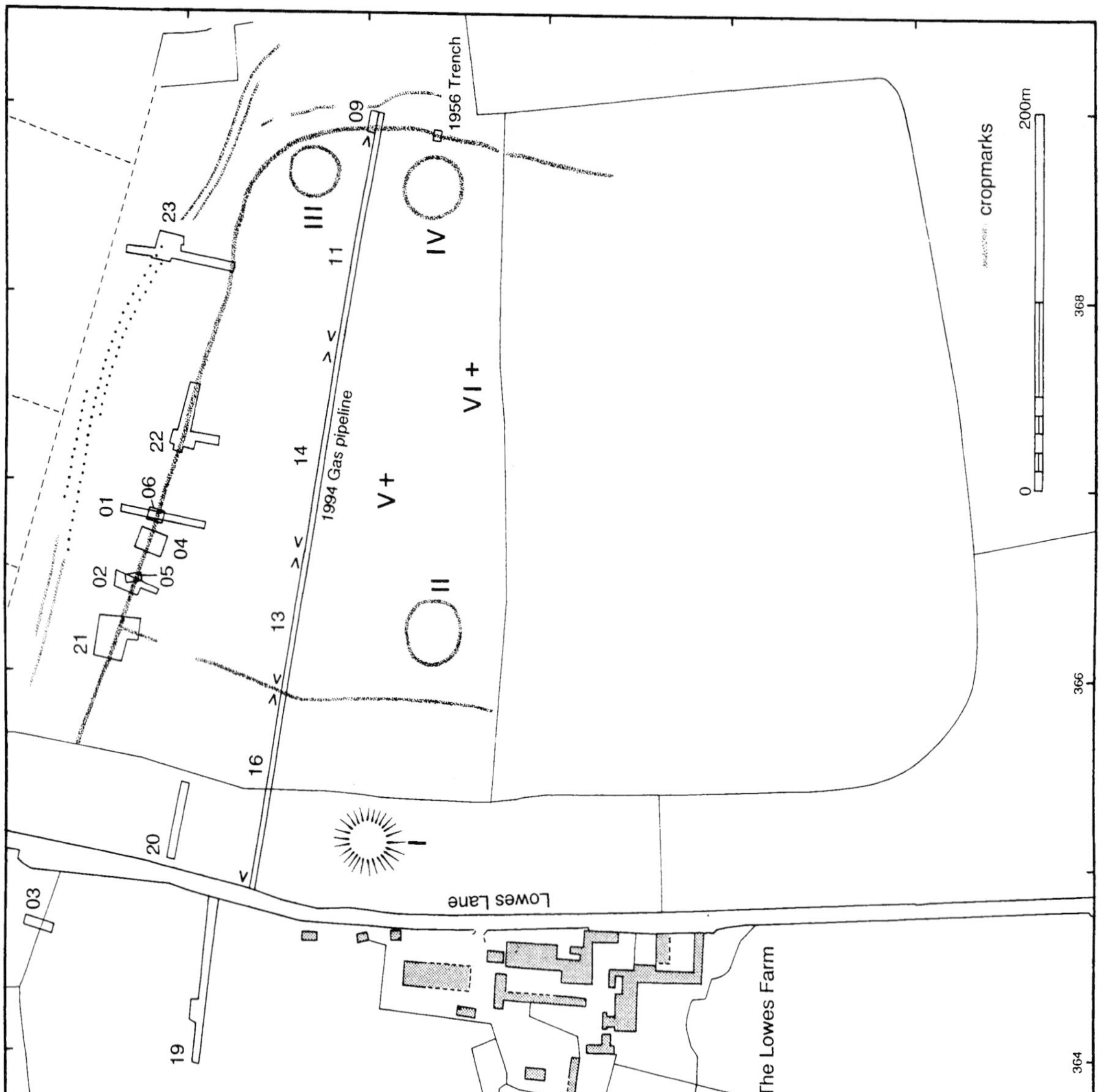

Fig. 5.12 Plan of Bronze Age barrow cemetery; Iron Age curvilinear 'enclosure' and triple pit alignment at Swarkestone Lowes, Derbyshire (drawing: J. Goddard, based upon plan in Elliott and Knight 1999)

Fig. 5.13 *Iron Age enclosures and associated field systems at Fisherwick, Staffordshire (drawing: J. Goddard, based upon drawings in Smith ed. 1978)*

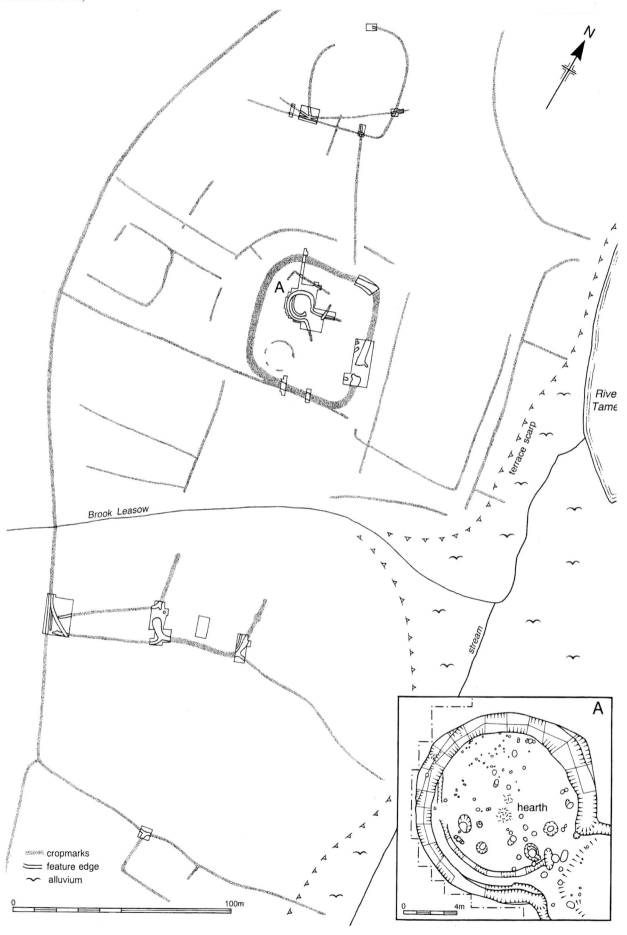

Fig. 5.14 *Multi-phase Iron Age round-house at Gonalston, Nottinghamshire, showing two phases of bedding trench and later post-hole ring (photograph: L. Elliott)*

Late Iron Age subrectangular ditched enclosure at Gonalston of a remarkable round-house defined by two phases of bedding trench, 11m and 12m in diameter, and by a slightly larger ring of post-holes partially cutting the outermost bedding trench (Elliott and Knight 2002, 149; Fig.5.14). Its spatial location, towards the centre of the enclosure and roughly equidistant from the south-western and north-eastern enclosure ditches, suggests that it might have been carefully positioned relative to these boundaries. However, the retrieval of diagnostic LBA-EIA pottery sherds from the recut entrance posts on the south-eastern side of the structure raises the possibility that at least the earlier phases of the round-house had preceded construction of the enclosure.

Another major problem arises from the difficulty in many cases of establishing whether occupation was permanent or seasonal in nature. Many lower-lying sites, particularly on the edges of gravel terraces, might have been particularly prone to flood, and, in common with sites in other Midlands river valleys, may have been occupied only in the summer months (*cf.* Farmoor, Oxfordshire: Lambrick and Robinson 1978). Much emphasis has been placed in recent years upon the development of palaeoenvironmental sampling programmes, notably at Gonalston and Barrow-upon-Trent, and it is to be hoped that completion of this work will permit eventually a more informed assessment of this issue.

The evidence for contemporary internal occupation, either permanent or seasonal, is rarely unequivocal, and it is likely that some enclosures had performed specialised functions connected only indirectly with occupation.

Possible functions include paddocks for purposes such as controlled grazing or the intensive care of stock during periods of lambing or calving (Ciaraldi 2002, 63; Lambrick 1992, 100–1), fodder and crop stores (Knight 1992, 84) or even coppice enclosures (Smith 1978, 95), while there are possibilities also of a strong link in some cases with ritual. Particular attention should be drawn in this latter respect to a small group of typologically distinct square-ditched enclosures, up to around 10m in diameter internally, which it has been suggested may be related to the square barrows of the Arras tradition of eastern Yorkshire (Whimster 1989, 25, 33; *cf.* Bevan 1999; Stead 1991). Small clusters of these enclosures have been recorded in Nottinghamshire, most notably at North Muskham (Fig. 5.15; Whimster 1989, 25, plate 17) and Gonalston (Woodhouse 1993, 12–13; Fig.5.17: C), and are known as far upstream as Aston-upon-Trent (May 1970) and Barrow-upon-Trent (Derbyshire SMR 16709b) in Derbyshire. The enclosures bear a striking resemblance to the square-ditched barrows of the Arras tradition, although none of the cropmarks preserves traces of the central pit which is such a distinctive feature of many Arras burials (Stead 1991, figs 5–17). Three examples within the Trent Valley have been excavated, including an 8 x 8m enclosure at Acre Lane, Aston-upon-Trent, and two 10 x 10m enclosures at Gonalston. Small quantities of Iron Age sherds were retrieved from the fill of each of these enclosures, thus supporting the case for a later Iron Age origin, but none yielded positive evidence for an associated mound or burials. Approximately half of the interior of the Aston enclosure was excavated, revealing only a small pit with no associated finds near one corner (May 1970, fig.2). The absence of a grave pit is not necessarily a problem, as some burials of the Arras tradition were placed directly on the ground surface (Stead 1991, 179–80). Similarly, any traces of the inhumation burials which are a hallmark of this tradition are unlikely to have survived the acidic soil conditions. The Gonalston enclosures were investigated by a single evaluation trench cutting across each enclosure ditch and a small part of the enclosed area, and hence any traces of associated burials or grave goods could well survive within the areas which as part of the planning permission for the quarry were not examined; both enclosures are now preserved *in situ*.

Despite the inconclusive results of these excavations, a link between some square-ditched enclosures and barrows of the Arras tradition remains likely. The typological parallels are striking, while the tight clustering of enclosures which is particularly evident at both Aston and North Muskham strongly suggests cemetery complexes. In addition, the valley locations, close to water, recall the topographical preferences of barrow-builders in eastern Yorkshire (Bevan 1999, 137–8). Whatever their functions, their presence emphasises the need to consider ritual as well as everyday processes when contemplating the origins of enclosures. Furthermore, were the Arras connection to be vindicated, the presence of these potentially high-status burials would provide important additional evidence for social ranking. It would serve also to emphasise the role of the Trent as an important artery for the movement not only of materials (Knight 1992, fig.30) but also of novel concepts of burial

(through the interchange of ideas or, more controversially, movements of population groups).

The growth of nucleated settlements

Although some enclosures might represent discrete entities, excavations generally unveil a complex landscape in which many of these smaller enclosures had formed only one component of a significantly more elaborate settlement plan. These possibilities have been explored for a variety of sites within the region, including the smaller of two sub-rectangular ditched enclosures that were excavated at Gamston (Fig.5.5: Enclosure 1; Knight 1992, 28–31). This enclosure contained a variety of features that on stratigraphic grounds mainly predated or followed the period of its use and yielded no convincing evidence for contemporary internal dwellings. With the proviso that houses of turf or other structures lacking deeply dug foundations might have eluded discovery, it was proposed that the enclosure could have served another purpose, perhaps as a stock corral or a protected grain or fodder store, with occupation restricted to the area outside the enclosure. Similar conclusions may be drawn from a host of sites in the Trent Valley, suggesting that the concept of the 'agglomerated' settlement, which has been applied to extensive and long-lived sites such as Twywell (Jackson 1975) or Crick (Hughes 1998) in Northamptonshire, should be extended to this region. Other notable examples from the Trent Valley in which occupation had extended beyond areas enclosed for this or other purposes include Willington, where later Iron Age

Fig. 5.15 *Square-ditched enclosure cluster flanking palaeochannels adjacent to the River Trent at North Muskham, Nottinghamshire. Reproduced by permission of English Heritage (NMR) Derek Riley Collection (photograph reference DNR 427/24, SK 8060/5)*

occupation was represented by scattered round-houses, pits, hearths and a curvilinear palisade trench interpreted by the excavator as possibly a 'cattle pound' (Wheeler 1979, 103: F367), and Holme Dyke, Gonalston, where pits and other structural remains yielding Scored Ware and other later Iron Age pottery extended northwards beyond a Middle to Late Iron Age ditched enclosure (Fig.5.17: D; Elliott and Knight 2002). Interpretation is complicated on all of these sites by the difficulty of establishing which features had been in contemporary use. But with this proviso, there are hints that some of these settlements had extended over quite large areas – for example, at Lockington, where fieldwalking, geophysical survey and trial excavations of an extensive cropmark complex incorporating possible roundhouses, rectilinear enclosures and trackways may indicate a major Iron Age settlement that had continued in use into the Roman period (Clay 1985; 2001, 3). This in turn raises the possibility of population groupings beyond the level of the extended family unit. There are suggestions also of a chronological dimension to this development, derived from the results of recent excavations of major Late Iron Age to Roman settlements such as Ferry Lane Farm, Collingham, for long regarded as exceptional on the grounds of its polyfocal cropmark plan (Whimster 1989, 77; Zeepvat 2000; P. Connolly: pers. comm.), Rampton (Knight 2000a; 2000b; Ponsford 1992) and Brough-on-Fosse, immediately north of the Roman town of *Crococalana* (Jones 2002; Vyner ed. forthcoming; Fig.5.16). There are hints at all of these sites of sizeable communities, seemingly

Fig.5.16 *Later Iron Age and Saxon settlement immediately north of the Roman town of Crococolana, Brough-on-Fosse, Nottinghamshire (drawing: D. Gilbert)*

beyond the level of the single farmstead, and anticipating perhaps the major nucleated settlements which it is argued in the following chapter developed in the Trent Valley in the post-Conquest period (Chapter 6.7.2). Comparisons may be suggested between these larger 'agglomerated' sites and the Late Iron Age 'nucleated' or 'complex' settlements that have been identified in neighbouring areas such as Lincolnshire, including Dragonby (May 1996), Old Sleaford (Elsdon 1997) and Owmby (May 1984, 21; *cf.* Winton 1998). In contrast to those sites, however, many of which have yielded substantial quantities of Iron Age coins, brooches and other rich artefacts (including, at Old Sleaford, a vast quantity of clay moulds indicative of local coin production), there is little evidence from the artefacts recovered from these or other Trent Valley Iron Age sites for significant status variations. Occasional copper alloy or iron brooches and rare exotic items such as La Tène glass beads (e.g. Henderson 1992) imply limited access to high value commodities, but the current artefact assemblages from these sites conjure no clear image of significant material wealth or sharp social stratification.

5.8   The Wider Landscape

5.8.1 Field Systems

A significant number of later Iron Age enclosures along the Valley may be shown to have been closely integrated with systems of predominantly sub-rectangular fields and linear trackways, providing clear evidence therefore for a link between the development of enclosures and field systems. Examples include Fisherwick, where Smith proposed an infield-outfield system centred upon a block of permanent annually cultivated arable fields and paddocks adjacent to the habitation focus (Smith ed. 1979, 101), and Gonalston, where several ditches aligned from north-west to south-east divided an elongated gravel promontory raised slightly above the alluvial floodplain (Fig.5.17: G-L; Elliott and Knight 2002; 2003). Dating of these systems is complicated by the paucity of finds obtained from many field ditches and by the likelihood that repeated scouring of these features may have biased the artefact record towards later periods. With these provisos, however, an origin in the mid-first millennium BC contemporary with the earliest enclosures may be suggested for some field systems. This is in sharp contrast, therefore, to many areas of eastern England and the Midlands, where the origins of field systems may be traced well into the Bronze Age, if not earlier (e.g. Lambrick 1992; Pryor 1996; Yates forthcoming).

One of the earliest ceramic associations from the Trent Valley was recovered during excavations at Gonalston, where the terminal of one of several roughly parallel ditches running from north-west to south-east across an elongated 'island' of gravel (Fig.5.17: L) yielded a deposit of largely unabraded pottery sherds. This included fragments of a pot with a high, everted neck and internal corrugations recalling several LBA-EIA vessels from Gretton, Northamptonshire (Jackson and Knight 1985, fig.6.24; fig.8.55, 58, 65, 73) and Fiskerton, Lincolnshire (Elsdon and Knight 2003, fig.5.1,1, fig.5.2,3 & 5; *cf.* Knight 2002, 130) and hence possibly signifying construction from at least the mid-

Fig. 5.17 *Prehistoric and Roman features recorded during excavations at Gonalston, Nottinghamshire (drawing: J. Goddard)*

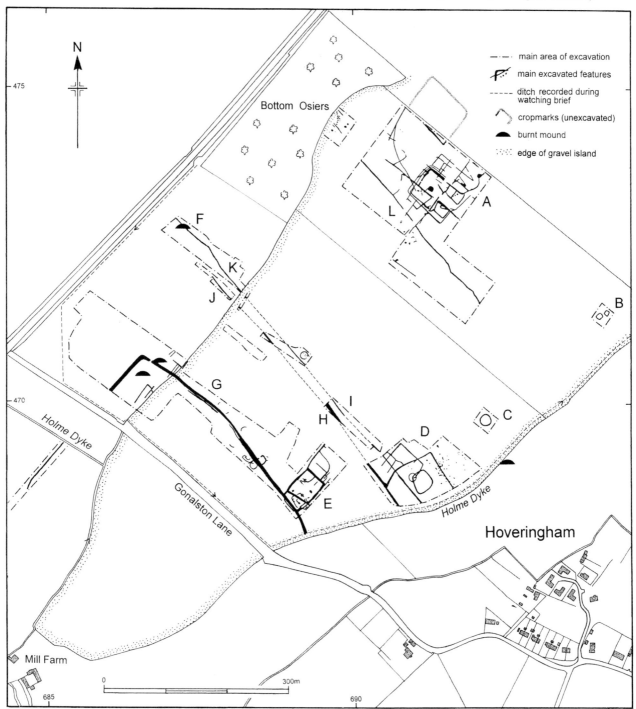

first millennium BC. Other ditches running parallel with this feature yielded Middle and Late Iron Age pottery, including Scored Ware and wheel-made Late La Tène sherds, suggesting continued use of components of this system throughout the later Iron Age. A similarly early origin may be suggested for several of the linear ditches which were recorded at Willington (Wheeler 1979). Four linear ditches were attributed by the excavator to the Iron Age (*ibid*. 86: F1200; 94–6: F1, F8, F295/431) of which at least one could have overlapped the period of use of LBA-EIA ceramics. One ditch with a dark humic fill yielded a substantial group of large LBA-EIA sherds and animal bones, mainly towards the bottom of the ditch, although it should be noted that very small and abraded Romano-

British sherds were retrieved from the upper fills (*ibid*. 86, 165, fig.2: F1200; fig.69.21–29). In addition, two phases of one of three intersecting ditches some 300m to the east of this feature had disturbed a pit yielding an assemblage of classic LBA-EIA vessels (F421; *ibid*. 165, fig.69.13–15) while the ditch itself yielded a small collection of LBA-EIA and later Iron Age pottery (*ibid*. fig 69, 19–20); the values of these associations, however, are much reduced by the protracted sequence of recuts and the likelihood of significant redeposition from earlier features (*ibid*. 94–6).

Although the origins of field systems may be traced, therefore, at least to the mid-first millennium BC, the evidence which is currently available would suggest a significantly later origin for the majority of field boundaries. Dating is complicated, however, by the likelihood that only the latest episodes of activity may register in the records of associated artefacts. In much of Nottinghamshire, large tracts of the Valley preserve extensive field systems whose components may currently be dated from no earlier than the later first century BC or early first century AD, inviting comparison in this respect with the well known 'brickwork-plan' field systems which appear to have developed at broadly the same time on the Sherwood Sandstones of north Nottinghamshire and South Yorkshire (Chapter 6.8.1; Chadwick 1999, 154–5; Garton 1987; Riley 1980). One such system was revealed at Gamston, where excavations uncovered a rectilinear system of ditched boundaries dated stratigraphically and by associated Late La Tène sherds from no earlier than the early or mid first century AD (Fig.5.5: Phase 3; Knight 1992, 31–3). A similarly late origin may be suggested on the basis of current ceramic associations for components of the remarkable coaxial field systems which extend along the Nottinghamshire stretch of the Trent Valley to the north of Newark, notably at Kelham, where excavated field ditches yielded small numbers of Late La Tène as well as Romano-British sherds (Knight and Priest 1998), although more extensive excavations may demonstrate eventually a rather earlier origin for these systems. These coaxial systems extended over large expanses of the Holme Pierrepont Terrace to the north of Newark, and provide an image of a highly organised landscape in which densely distributed rectilinear enclosures were tied in to a well planned landscape of coaxial fields, trackways and pit alignments (Fig.5.18; cf. Whimster 1989, figs 60–61). The limited excavations which have been carried out in this area, combined with the results of systematic fieldwalking, suggest that some elements of this system, which appears to have developed fully only in the Roman period, may be traced to the Late Iron Age. Significantly more work is required before the contribution of Iron Age farmers to this tightly constrained rural landscape may be quantified precisely (Garton 2002). There seems little doubt, however, in view of the marked regularities which may be discerned in the spacing of enclosures and the organisation of adjacent field areas, that the fully developed landscape had incorporated a dense network of broadly contemporary settlements set within a tightly managed agricultural landscape (see also Chapter 6.8.1 – 6.8.3).

5.8.2   Pit Alignments

Attention should also be drawn to the close relationship between many rectilinear field systems and networks of pit alignments (cf. Whimster 1989, figs 60–61; Boutwood 1998; Willis 2001, 43–4). The latter may in some cases represent merely another manifestation of field or trackway boundaries – as perhaps at Lockington, where a trackway which may have formed the focus of an agglomerated Iron Age settlement was represented for much of its length by a double line of pits (Clay 1985, 17, fig.3), and at Kings Bromley in Staffordshire, where a rectilinear arrangement of pit alignments has been interpreted as evidence for a field system laid out carefully to avoid a group of ring-

ditches which at the time of its construction may have demarcated visible barrows (Wardle 2003, 9). Mostly, however, their wide spacing and orientation suggest a division of the landscape into larger blocks, in some cases possibly indicating the boundaries between competing groups. This phenomenon is demonstrated particularly clearly by the spatial arrangements of pit alignments within the coaxial field systems around South and North Muskham, where certain striking coincidences with later boundaries – for example, the continuation of the line of a double pit alignment near North Muskham by the boundary of Cromwell parish (Whimster 1989, fig.61: SK793603) – raise some intriguing questions on the subject of landscape continuity. Similar spatial patterning is apparent at other locations elsewhere in the Trent Valley, including Barrow-upon-Trent immediately upstream of the Trent-Derwent confluence (Fig.5.19). Extensive excavations at this site prior to gravel quarrying revealed lengths of a seemingly rectilinear pattern of pit alignments, possibly defining blocks of land associated with excavated Iron Age enclosures, although dating evidence is currently restricted to rare scraps of Iron Age pottery from the upper pit fills or from stratigraphically later ditches (Knight and Morris 1998; Knight and Southgate 2001).

Most excavated pit alignments in the Trent Valley have yielded few if any associated finds, reflecting presumably their positioning away from contemporary settlement foci generating domestic rubbish, and hence dating is extremely difficult (e.g. Besthorpe Quarry, Nottinghamshire: Southgate et al. 1998; Ward et al. 1999; Barrow-upon-Trent: Knight and Morris 1998; Knight and Southgate 2001; Area T, Whitemoor Haye: Coates 2002, 15–16). Small quantities of Iron Age pottery have been recovered from some pit alignments, including examples at Catholme (Losco-Bradley and Kinsley 2002, 20), Swarkestone Lowes (Elliott and Knight 1999, 101), Aston Hill, Aston-upon-Trent (Abbott and Garton 1995; Garton and Abbot 1998) and Whitemoor Haye (Fig. 5.20; Coates 2002, 13–15: Area S). Only rarely, however, have typologically diagnostic sherds attributable to a particular ceramic phase been recovered from primary contexts.

Origins for this boundary type in the mid or early first millennium BC may possibly be implied by a small collection of pottery recovered from several pits forming an alignment at Aston Hill (Abbott and Garton ibid. 7, fig.2: Pit 1003), although the excavators concluded that the sherds were more likely to have been residual from an earlier phase of activity (Garton and Abbott 1998). 106 coarse quartz-gritted sherds were recovered during surface cleaning of the pits and from various depths within their fills, together with another nine typologically related sherds from a nearby ditch and gully. The sherds, which derive wholly from hand-made vessels, include fragments of pots with carinated and pronounced rounded girths, sometimes embellished with a row of finger-nail incisions, and thin-walled vessels with finely tapered rims; all invite close comparison with typical LBA-EIA ceramic assemblages from the region (cf. Knight 2002, 126–131). Sherd condition varies considerably, from abraded to unabraded, providing few clues to the depositional history of this collection, but the possibility

Fig. 5.18 *Cropmarks of coaxial field systems in the Trent Valley to the north of Newark, Nottinghamshire (source: Whimster 1989).* © *Crown Copyright. NMR. Base map data reproduced by permission of the Ordnance Survey on behalf of The Controller of Her Majesty's Stationery Office.* © *Crown Copyright 100020618*

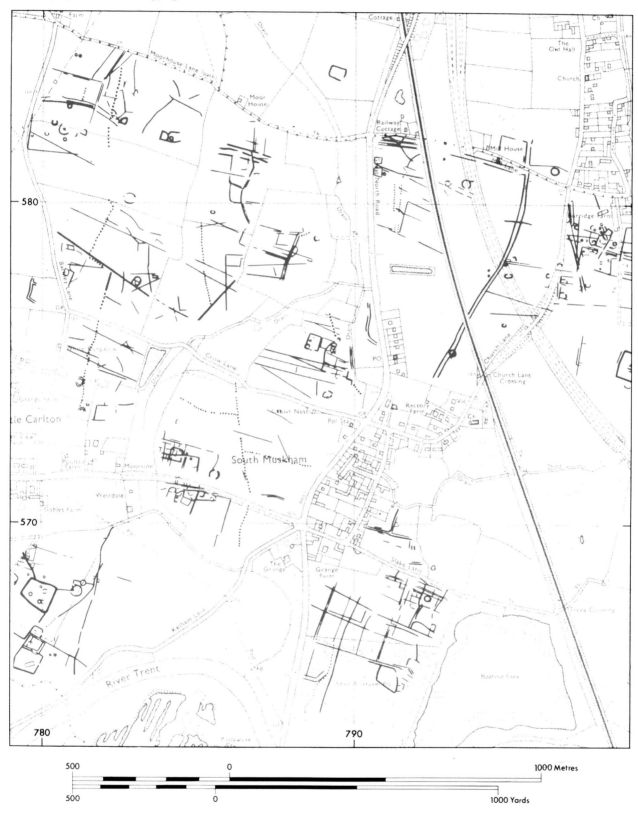

of an origin for this monument during the proposed ninth to fifth/fourth century BC date range of LBA-EIA ceramics from the region cannot be ruled out.

With the possible exception of Aston Hill, the limited ceramic evidence from the Trent Valley would support a later Iron Age origin for pit alignments, broadly contemporary therefore with the proposed shift in emphasis from open to enclosed settlement in the latter half of the first millennium BC. Several of the most informative ceramic associations have been recovered from the components of a double line of staggered circular pits at Whitemoor

Fig. 5.19 *Iron Age pit alignment at Fleak Close, Barrow-upon-Trent, Derbyshire (photograph: D. Knight)*

Haye (Fig. 5.20; Coates 2002, 13–15). Most excavated pits on this site had been recut at least once, but one feature yielded parts of the rim and base of two hand-made Iron Age ellipsoid jars in a secondary silt-sand deposit which had accumulated in the original bowl-shaped cut (*ibid.* 13, fig.10: F509, layer 5018; pottery: fig.36.1–2). Iron Age pottery was also retrieved from F519 (recut of F533), F534 (recut of F538) and F526 (recut of F548; pottery: fig.35.1–3), together with a granite rubber from F519. The pottery from F526 comprised a group of three ellipsoid or globular vessels represented by large moderately abraded sherds with many conjoins and, together with the 'large chunks' retrieved from F509, was interpreted as probably a deliberate placement recalling structured deposits in a number of pit alignments elsewhere in the Midlands and eastern England (Coates and Woodward 2002, 81–2; Pollard 1996). All of the pottery may be paralleled in later Iron Age assemblages in the East Midlands, and would suggest a date of deposition in the Middle or Late Iron Ages. Support for a later Iron Age date was provided by a radiocarbon determination of 2230 ± 60 BP (Beta-135227, 400–110 cal BC) from charcoal in pit F526 (Coates 2002, 15; Appendix 1). Important evidence for the late continuation of some pit alignment systems is provided by the discovery at Rampton of a line of pits forming one side of a large rectilinear enclosure dated firmly to the Roman period (Fig.6.16; Chapter 6.8.4). A Roman date for the alignment may be postulated on the grounds of its spatial relationship to the ditches forming the remainder

Fig. 5.20 *Iron Age double pit alignment and Romano-British enclosure at Whitemoor Haye, Staffordshire (source: Coates 2002; reproduced by permission of Birmingham Archaeology)*

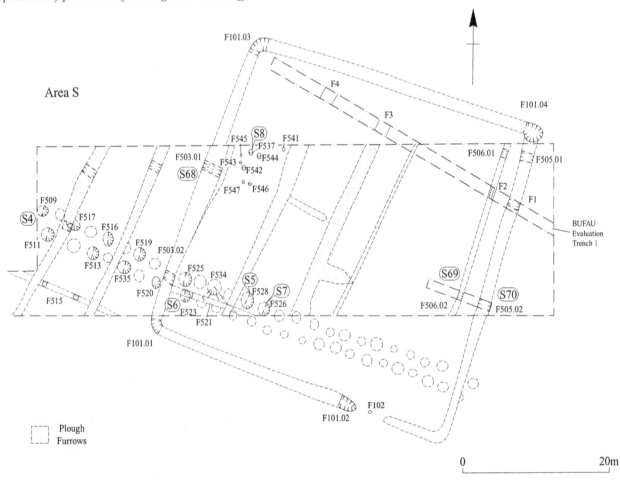

of this enclosure and the discovery at various levels in the fills of several pits of small quantities of Romano-British sherds. The discovery is of particular interest in view of the common association of pit alignments with the coaxial fields of the Trent Valley near Newark, which it is has been suggested above may have developed mainly in the Roman period, and provides useful support for the argument that pit alignments had formed an integral element of the Roman boundary system in this area.

The late dating for pit alignments which is implied by the limited evidence of ceramic associations and radiocarbon determinations stands in sharp contrast to areas such as the Nene Valley, where at Wollaston, Grendon and elsewhere in Northamptonshire pit alignments, arranged sometimes in coaxial fashion, were an important component of the early first millennium BC landscape (Meadows 1995; e.g. Gretton: Jackson 1974; Ringstead: Jackson 1978). Further excavations may necessitate further reappraisal of the chronology of pit alignments within the Trent Valley, but until new evidence is obtained a significantly later development may be postulated in this region by comparison with areas such as the Nene or Thames Valleys – coinciding perhaps with the general progression from the mid-first millennium BC towards an enclosed landscape.

5.8.3   Linear Earthworks and Ditches

Attention may be drawn first to two enigmatic linear earthworks, lying just beyond the eastern edge of the Trent Valley, which might support the case for the imposition of territorial boundaries from the later Iron Age. Recent archaeological investigations along the Roman Fosse Way prior to dualling of the A46 between Newark and Lincoln have identified two linear earthworks which may have been truncated by the Roman road – at Gallows Nooking Common, North Collingham, Nottinghamshire, within an area of predominantly Middle to Late Iron Age settlement, and at Sheep Walk Lodge, near Swinderby in Lincolnshire (Vyner ed. forthcoming). Investigations at both of these sites have revealed linear earthworks followed by county or parish boundaries, which at both sites might correlate with pre-Roman land divisions.

Archaeological investigations at Gallows Nooking Common prior to road construction revealed a low earthen bank coinciding with the boundary between Nottinghamshire and Lincolnshire and the boundaries of North Collingham, Norton Disney and Swinderby parishes (Knight 1991, 52–3, fig.25). This somewhat sinuous bank converged towards the south-west with the Fosse Way, but to the north-east it diverged gradually from the road before turning abruptly through *c*.90° to form a perpendicular alignment with the road. This curious arrangement, which isolated a narrow irregularly shaped strip of North Collingham parish from the remainder of this parish, suggested that the boundary may have been laid out prior to construction of the Fosse Way, and spurred excavations aimed at investigating the character and date of the bank and its relationship to the Roman road. An evaluation trench across the bank revealed a fairly slight construction, much disturbed by burrowing and root activity, flanked on its south-eastern side by a recut

ditch yielding fragments of three Late Iron Age wheel-made vessels which in view of the large size and comparatively fresh condition of many of the sherds would appear to have been deliberately deposited (Kinsley 1993; Vyner ed. forthcoming). The close spatial relationship between the bank and ditch may indicate that they had formed elements of a contemporary boundary work, although as only a few unstratified Iron Age and later sherds were recovered from the bank it cannot be closely dated. More recent excavations have recovered Late Iron Age sherds from other sections across the flanking ditch, and have shown the bank to overlie ditches and gullies forming part of a Middle to Late Iron Age system of enclosures aligned obliquely to the bank. It was not possible to investigate the relationship of these sub-bank features to the flanking ditch. However, if the latter had formed an integral component of the boundary, both bank and ditch might be argued to relate to a phase of late Iron Age landscape reorganisation preceding construction of the Roman road (Vyner ed. forthcoming).

The linear earthwork at Sheep Walk Lodge, which survives on the north-western side of the A46 some 4km north-east of Gallows Nooking Common, also raises some difficult questions of interpretation (Knight 1991, 58–9, fig.28; Vyner ed. forthcoming). A low earthwork flanked for part of its course by a ditch may be observed running through woodland for some 370m along the north-western edge of the Fosse Way, where it forms the boundary between the Lincolnshire parishes of Thurlby and Thorpe-on-the-Hill. A largely infilled ditch projecting roughly at right angles to this earthwork near its north-eastern end is also followed by a parish boundary, and creates a tiny triangle of land between the Fosse Way and the earthwork which makes little sense except as evidence of truncation by the Roman road of an earlier land boundary. An evaluation trench across the earthwork at its northern end, where it turns through a right angle to head north-westwards away from the Fosse, revealed an earthen bank associated with an outer ditch. No evidence of date was obtained during this work, and the case for a pre-Roman origin must rest for the present upon its curious spatial relationship to the Fosse Way.

An Iron Age origin has also been suggested for a variety of multiple ditched boundaries which have been identified from aerial photographic surveys of the Trent Valley and neighbouring regions, including examples at Newton-on-Trent, Lincolnshire, between the Rivers Eau and Trent at Scotter and Scotton in Lincolnshire (Boutwood 1998, 30–1) and at Whitemoor Haye (Coates 2002, 18–21, figs 4 and 15; Coates and Woodward 2002, 81). An Iron Age or earlier date for some of the linear boundary systems in the Valley may be implied by evidence obtained during recent excavations at Whitemoor Haye, although even here the evidence is equivocal. One of several evaluation trenches across an east-west triple-ditch alignment at this site showed it to predate stratigraphically a Romano-British trackway (Coates 2002, 18–20; fig.4: trench 18), raising the possibility of a pre-Roman origin, but none of the excavated features yielded associated datable finds. Later more extensive excavations of the triple ditch system also failed to recover associated artefacts. However, the spatial positioning of these ditches parallel to and between a pair of double pit alignments, one dated by associated pottery and radiocarbon determinations to the later first millennium BC (Chapter 5.8.2), would favour the excavator's interpretation of these as part of a contemporary system of land allotment (Coates and Woodward 2002, 81–2).

The case for an Iron Age, or perhaps earlier, origin for at least some major linear boundaries within the region is

strengthened by discoveries in neighbouring areas, where single, double, triple or quadruple-ditched boundaries, occasionally associated with earthworks, have been assigned dates from the later Bronze Age to Late Iron Ages (Boutwood 1998, 37–9; Willis 2001, 44–7). Notable examples include a triple-ditch system at Ketton, Rutland, which on the basis of associated pottery and metalwork may have experienced a long period of use commencing in the Late Bronze Age or Early Iron Age (Mackie 1993), and a pair of very substantial ditches near Gretton, within

Fig. 5.21 Later Bronze Age and Iron Age sites referred to in the text; compiled by S. Baker
(1.Aslockton; 2.Aston-upon-Trent; 3.Barrow-upon-Trent; 4.Barton-under-Needwood; 5.Besthorpe; 6.Billingborough; 7.Birstall; 8.Bleasby; 9.Bole Ings; 10.Brough; 11.Carlton-on-Trent; 12.Castle Donington; 13.Catholme; 14.Clifton; 15.Collingham; 16.Crick; 17.Dragonby; 18.Fisherwick; 19.Fiskerton; 20.Flag Fen; 21.Gallows Nooking Common; 22.Gainsborough; 23.Gamston; 24.Girton; 25.Gonalston; 26.Grendon; 27.Gretton; 28.Hicken's Bridge; 29.Holme Pierrepont; 30.Kelham; 31.Ketton; 32.Kings Bromley; 33.Kirmond le Mire; 34.Langford; 35.Lincoln; 36.Littleborough; 37.Lockington; 38.Misson; 39.Newark; 40.Newton-on-Trent; 41.North Muskham; 42.Old Sleaford; 43.Owmby; 44.Potlock; 45.Rampton; 46.Ringstead; 47.Sandtoft; 48.Scaftworth; 49.Scotter; 50.Scotton; 51.Shardlow; 52.Sheepwalk Lodge; 53.South Muskham; 54.Staythorpe; 55.Stickford; 56.Stone; 57.Styrrup; 58.Sutton Common; 59.Sutton Reach; 60.Swarkestone Lowes; 61.Twywell; 62.Walton-on-Trent; 63.Whitemoor Haye; 64.Willington; 65.Wollaston; 66.Yoxall)

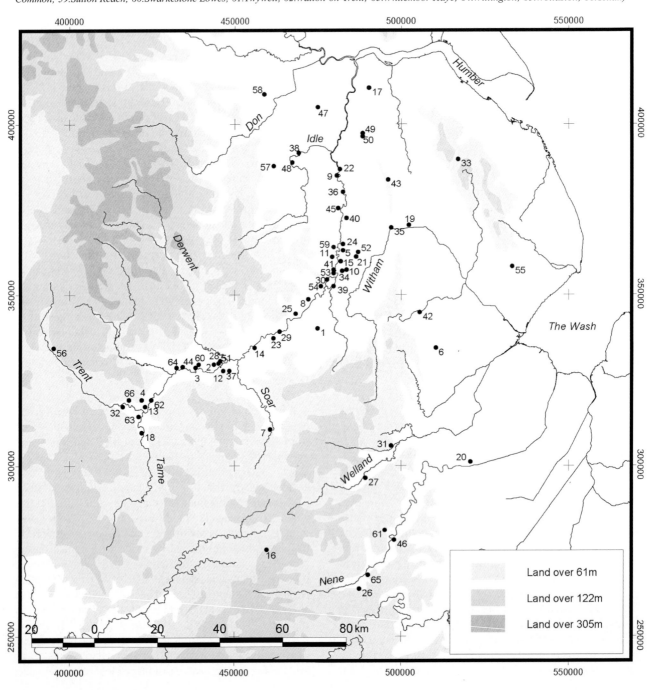

which had been deposited a remarkable collection of pottery spanning the transition from the LBA-EIA to Earlier La Tène ceramic traditions (Jackson and Knight 1985). A defensive role seems inappropriate for monuments of this type, which would appear to have been designed instead to control and in some cases possibly also to channel movement (Boutwood 1998, 41). The concept of a dual function is particularly attractive in the context of the Gretton linear ditches, which would seem excessively deep if they had served only as trackways (Jackson and Knight 1998, fig.5), and we might speculate whether they had served both as routes of movement and as the physical manifestation of a boundary between neighbouring communities, perhaps symbolising and reinforcing group identity.

5.9   Conclusions: the Mechanisms of Change

It has been suggested in this chapter that enclosures, rectilinear field systems and networks of pit alignments and other linear boundaries are interrelated phenomena, signifying increasing pressures upon finite pasture and arable resources and a growing demand for tighter control of the Valley environment. The root causes of these pressures remain uncertain, but there are suggestions of a strong link with population growth, and in particular with the demands for increased grazing. It has long been accepted that the population in many areas of lowland Britain increased significantly during the course of the first millennium BC, leading to infilling within established core areas and the colonisation of areas which in the early part of the millennium may not have been so favoured for settlement (e.g. Haselgrove 1999, 271–2; Lambrick 1992, 80; Smith 1977; 1978). These included areas such as the extensive heavy boulder clays of the Nene-Ouse watershed (Knight 1984, 304) and the claylands of Leicestershire (Clay 2002), the exploitation of which may have been facilitated by the introduction of crops more suitable for damp and heavy ground (Cunliffe 1991, 372) and changes in agricultural technology following the progressive adoption of iron tools for tillage. Comparisons of the numbers of pottery collections obtained from sites in the Trent Valley that may be attributed to the Deverel-Rimbury, Post Deverel

Rimbury, LBA-EIA, Earlier La Tène and Late La Tène ceramic traditions would seem to support this view (*cf.* Bishop 2001, 2; data in www.arch.soton.ac.uk/Research/ PotteryGazetteer). The possibility must be borne in mind that in earlier periods pottery may have been less widely used or may survive less frequently, but the contrasts in the densities of sites attributable to each ceramic phase are sufficiently striking to suggest that this is a genuine trend. The well-ordered systems of rectilinear fields and closely spaced enclosures that may be postulated in some parts of the Valley by the end of the Late Iron Age, most notably in the area to the north of Newark, provide a striking contrast with the thin scatters of seemingly amorphous unenclosed settlements which characterise the earlier first millennium BC. It would be unwise to speculate on total population levels, but there seems little reason to doubt a significant increase in relative population densities. However, in the Trent Valley, where pasture may have represented the key agrarian resource, pressure on space may ultimately represent more a function of increasing stock levels and spiralling grazing needs than expansion of the human population (*cf.* Lambrick 1992, 85).

Finally, and more speculatively, consideration should be given to the possible impact upon carrying capacity of climatic deterioration (Chapter 5.2), progressive woodland clearance (Chapter 5.5) and intensified agricultural activity (Chapter 5.6). Increasing climatic wetness has been linked above to changes in surface run-off rates and the expansion of valley wetlands (Chapter 5.3), and together with progressive removal of the protective forest canopy and the intensification of arable farming may have contributed to significantly higher rates of soil erosion in the river catchment. This in turn may have spurred the accumulation of alluvial and colluvial deposits, which although apparently mainly of Roman or later date could have begun to accumulate from the Late Iron Age. Significant additional research is required on the chronology of alluviation and colluviation to investigate further this hypothesis, but to Iron Age communities faced with deteriorating land resources, careful demarcation and rationalisation of these may have seemed the most sensible option.

REFERENCES

Abbott, C. and Garton, D. 1995. Report on the Archaeological Evaluations on the Proposed Site of a Borrow Pit on Aston Hill, Aston-upon-Trent, Derbyshire. July edition. Unpublished report, Trent & Peak Archaeological Trust, University Park, Nottingham.

Allen, C.S.M., Harman, M. and Wheeler, H. 1987. Bronze Age cremation cemeteries in the East Midlands, *Proc. Prehist. Soc.* **53**, 187–221.

Anderson, D.E., Binney, H.A. and Smith, M.A. 1998. Evidence of abrupt climatic change in northern Scotland between 3900 and 3500 calendar years BP, *The Holocene* **8**, 97–103.

Ashworth, A.C., Buckland, P.C. and Sadler, J.P. (eds) 1997. *Studies in Quaternary Entomology. An Inordinate Fondness for Insects.* Quaternary Proceedings **5**. London: Quaternary Research Association.

Badcock, A. and Symonds, J. 1994. Archaeological Field Evaluation of Land at Styrrup Hall Farm, Styrrup, Nottinghamshire. Unpublished report, ARCUS, University of Sheffield.

Baillie, M.G.L. 1995. A *Slice Through Time.* London: Batsford.

Barber, K.E., Chambers, F.M., Maddy, D., Stoneman, R. and Brew, J.S. 1994. A sensitive high-resolution record of late Holocene climatic change from a raised bog in northern England, *The Holocene* **4**, 198–205.

Barber, K.E., Maddy, D., Rose, N., Stevenson, A.C., Stoneman, R. and Thompson, R. 2000. Replicated proxy-climate signals over the last 2000 yr from two distant UK peat bogs: new evidence for regional palaeoclimatic teleconnections, *Quat. Sci. Rev.* **19**, 481–487.

Barnatt, J. 1987. Bronze Age settlement on the East Moors of the Peak District of Derbyshire and South Yorkshire, *Proc. Prehist. Soc.* **53**, 393–418.

Barnatt, J., Bevan, B. and Edmonds, M. 2002. Gardom's Edge: a landscape through time, *Antiquity* **76**, 51–56.

Barrett, D. 2001. An archaeological resource assessment of the later Bronze and Iron Ages (the first millennium BC) in Derbyshire, *East Midlands Archaeological Research Framework Project*. http://www.le.ac.uk/ archaeology/east_midlands_research_framework. htm

Beamish, M. and Ripper, S. 2000. Burnt mounds in the East Midlands, *Antiquity* **74**, 37–38.

Bevan, B. 1997. Bounding the landscape: place and identity during the Yorkshire Wolds Iron Age, in A. Gwilt and C.C. Haselgrove (eds), *Reconstructing Iron Age Societies*, 181–191.

Bevan, B. 1999. Land-life-death-regeneration: interpreting a middle Iron Age landscape in eastern Yorkshire, in B. Bevan (ed), *Northern Exposure: Interpretative Devolution and the Iron Ages in Britain*, 123–147.

Bevan, B. (ed) 1999. *Northern Exposure: Interpretative Devolution and the Iron Ages in Britain*. Leicester University Press.

Bewley, R.H. (ed) 1998. *Lincolnshire's Archaeology from the Air*. Lincolnshire History and Archaeology Occ. Pap. **11**. Lincoln: Society for Lincolnshire History and Archaeology.

Bishop, M. 2001. An archaeological resource assessment of the first millennium BC in Nottinghamshire, *East Midlands Archaeological Research Framework Project*. http://www.le.ac.uk/archaeology/east_midlands_ research_framework.htm

Boutwood, Y. 1998. Prehistoric linear boundaries in Lincolnshire and its fringes, in R.H. Bewley (ed), *Lincolnshire's Archaeology from the Air*, 29–46.

Bradley, R. 1998. *The Passage of Arms. An Archaeological Analysis of Prehistoric Hoards and Votive Processes*. 2nd edition. Oxford: Oxbow.

Brayshay, B. and Dinnin, M.H. 1999. Integrated palaeoecological evidence for biodiversity at the floodplain-forest margin, *J. Biogeography* **26** (1), 115–131.

Brindley, A.L. and Lanting, J.N. 1990. The dating of fulachta fiadh, in V.M. Buckley (ed), *Burnt Offerings: International Contributions to Burnt Mound Archaeology*, 55–56.

Brown, G., Field, D. and McOmish, D. 1994. East Chisenbury midden complex, in A.P. Fitzpatrick and E.L. Morris (eds), *The Iron Age in Wessex: Recent Work*, 46–49.

Buckland, P.C. and Sadler, J. 1985. The nature of Late Flandrian alluviation in the Humberhead Levels, *E. Midlands Geogr.* **8**, 239–251.

Buckland, P.C., Dugmore, A.J. and Edwards, K.J. 1997. Bronze Age myths? Volcanic activity and human response in the Mediterranean and North Atlantic regions, *Antiquity* **71**, 581–593.

Buckley, V. M. (ed) 1990. *Burnt Offerings: International Contributions to Burnt Mound Archaeology*. Dublin: Worldwell Ltd – Academic Publications.

Burnham, B.C. and Johnson, H.B. (eds) 1979. *Invasion and Response. The Case of Roman Britain*. BAR Brit. Ser. **73**.

Chadwick, A. 1999. Digging ditches, but missing riches? Ways into the Iron Age and Romano-British cropmark landscapes of the North Midlands, in B. Bevan (ed), *Northern Exposure: Interpretative Devolution and the Iron Ages in Britain*, 149–171.

Challis, A.J. and Harding, D.W. 1975. *Later Prehistory from the Trent to the Tyne*. BAR Brit. Ser. **20**.

Chambers, F.M., Barber, K.E., Maddy, D. and Brew, J. 1997. A 5500-year proxy-climate and vegetation record from blanket mire at Talla Moss, Borders, Scotland, *The Holocene* **7**, 391–399.

Charles, B.M., Parkinson, A. and Foreman, S. 2000. A Bronze Age ditch and Iron Age settlement at Elms Farm, Humberstone, Leicester, *Trans. Leicestershire Archaeol. Hist. Soc.* **74**, 113–220.

Chowne, P., Cleal, R.M. and Fitzpatrick, A.P. with Andrews, P. 2001. Excavations at Billingborough, Lincolnshire, 1975–8. A Bronze-Iron Age settlement and salt-working site, *E. Anglian Archaeol.* **94**.

Ciaraldi, M. 2002. Plant macroremains, in G. Coates, *A Prehistoric and Romano-British Landscape. Excavations at Whitemoor Haye Quarry, Staffordshire, 1997–1999*, 62–66.

Clay, P. 1985. A survey of two cropmark sites at Lockington-Hemington, Leicestershire, *Trans. Leicestershire Archaeol. Hist. Soc.* **59**, 17–26.

Clay, P. 1992. An Iron Age farmstead at Grove Farm, Enderby, Leicestershire, *Trans. Leicestershire Archaeol. Hist. Soc.* **66**, 1–82.

Clay, P. 2001. An archaeological resource assessment of the later Bronze and Iron Age (first millennium BC) in Leicestershire and Rutland, *East Midlands Archaeological Research Framework Project*. http://www.le.ac.uk/archaeology/east_midlands_ research_framework.htm

Clay, P. 2002. *The Prehistory of the East Midlands Claylands*. Leicester Archaeol. Monogr. **9**. School of Archaeological Studies, University of Leicester.

Coates, G. 2002. *A Prehistoric and Romano-British Landscape. Excavations at Whitemoor Haye Quarry, Staffordshire, 1997–1999*. BAR Brit. Ser. **340**.

Coates, G. and Woodward, A. 2002. Discussion, in G. Coates, *A Prehistoric and Romano-British Landscape. Excavations at Whitemoor Haye Quarry, Staffordshire, 1997–1999*, 79–90.

Collis, J.R. (ed) 1977. *The Iron Age in Britain: a Review*. Department of Archaeology and Prehistory, University of Sheffield.

Coombs, D.G. and Thompson, F.H. 1979. Excavation of the hillfort of Mam Tor, Derbyshire, 1965–69, *Derbyshire Archaeol. J.* **99**, 7–51.

Coward, J. and Ripper, S. 1999. Castle Donington. Willow Farm (SK 445 288), *Trans. Leicestershire Archaeol. Hist. Soc.* **73**, 87–91.

Cowen, J.D. 1967. The Hallstatt sword of bronze: on the Continent and in Britain, *Proc. Prehist. Soc.* **33**, 377–454.

Cummins, W.A. and Rundle, A.J. 1969. The geological environment of the dug-out canoes from Holme Pierrepont, Nottinghamshire, *Mercian Geol.* **3**, 177–188.

Cunliffe, B.W. 1991. *Iron Age Communities in Britain.* 3rd edition. London: Routledge.

Cunliffe, B. and Rowley, T. (eds) 1978. *Lowland Iron Age Communities in Europe.* BAR Int. Ser. **48**.

Cunnington, M.E. 1923. *The Early Iron Age Inhabited Site at All Cannings Cross Farm, Wiltshire.* Devizes: George Simpson & Co. Ltd.

Darlington, J. 1994. *Stafford Past. A Guide to the Archaeological and Historical Sites of the Stafford Area.* Stafford: Stafford Borough Council.

Davies, G. 2001. Interim Statement on the Archaeological Works at Staythorpe Power Station. Unpublished report 438f, ARCUS, University of Sheffield.

Davis, R. 1999. Bronze Age metalwork from the Trent Valley: Newark, Notts to Gainsborough, Lincs, *Trans. Thoroton Soc. Nottinghamshire* **103**, 25–47.

Davis, R. 2003. A Bronze Age shield fragment and spearhead from Elvaston Quarry, Derbyshire, *Derbyshire Archaeol. J.* **123**, 63–70.

Dinnin, M. 1997. Holocene beetle assemblages from the Lower Trent floodplain at Bole Ings, Nottinghamshire, UK, in A.C. Ashworth, P.C. Buckland and J.P. Sadler (eds), *Studies in Quaternary Entomology. An Inordinate Fondness for Insects,* 83–104.

Eccles, J., Caldwell, P. and Mincher, R. 1988. Salvage excavation at a Romano-British site at Chainbridge Lane, Lound, Nottinghamshire, 1985, *Trans. Thoroton Soc. Nottinghamshire* **92**, 15–21.

Elliott, L. and Knight, D. 1997. Further excavations of an Iron Age and Romano-British settlement near Gonalston, Nottinghamshire, *Trans. Thoroton Soc. Nottinghamshire* **101**, 65–72.

Elliott, L. and Knight, D. 1998. A burnt mound at Holme Dyke, Gonalston, Nottinghamshire, *Trans. Thoroton Soc. Nottinghamshire* **102**, 15–22.

Elliott, L. and Knight, D. 1999. An early Mesolithic site and first millennium BC settlement and pit alignments at Swarkstone Lowes, Derbyshire, *Derbyshire Archaeol. J.* **119**, 79–153.

Elliott, L. and Knight, D. 2002. Gonalston Holme Dyke, *Trans. Thoroton Soc. Nottinghamshire* **106**, 14–89.

Elliott, L. and Knight, D. 2003. Hoveringham Gonalston Lane, *Trans. Thoroton Soc. Nottinghamshire* **107**, 20–22.

Ellison, A.E. and Drewett, P.L. 1971. Pits and post holes in the British early Iron Age: some alternative explanations, *Proc. Prehist. Soc.* **37**, 183–194.

Elsdon, S. 1997. *Old Sleaford Revealed.* Oxbow Monogr. **78**. Oxford: Oxbow Books.

Elsdon, S. and Knight, D. 2003. The Iron Age pottery, in N. Field and M. Parker Pearson, *Fiskerton. An Iron Age Timber Causeway with Iron Age and Roman Votive Offerings: the 1981 Excavations,* 87–92.

Enright, D. and Thomas, A. 1998. Wellingborough, land off Wilby Way, *S. Midlands Archaeol.* **28**, 31–32.

Field, N. and Knight, D. 1992. A Later Bronze Age site at Kirmond le Mire, *Lincolnshire Hist. Archaeol.* **27**, 43–45.

Field, N. and Parker Pearson, M. 2003. *Fiskerton. An Iron Age Timber Causeway with Iron Age and Roman Votive Offerings: the 1981 Excavations.* Oxford: Oxbow Books.

Field, N. and White, A. (eds) 1984. *A Prospect of Lincolnshire.* Lincoln: F.N. Field and A.J. White.

Fitzpatrick, A.P. and Morris, E.L. (eds) 1994. *The Iron Age in Wessex: Recent Work.* Salisbury: Association Française d'Etude de l'Age du Fer and Wessex Archaeology.

Fulford, M. and Nichols, E. (eds) 1992. *Developing Landscapes of Lowland Britain. The Archaeology of the British Gravels: a Review.* Soc. Antiq. Occ. Pap. **14**.

Gale, R. 2002. Charcoal, in G. Coates, *A Prehistoric and Romano-British Landscape. Excavations at Whitemoor Haye Quarry, Staffordshire, 1997–1999,* 74–78.

Garton, D. 1987. Dunston's Clump and the brickwork plan field systems at Babworth, Nottinghamshire: excavations 1981, *Trans. Thoroton Soc. Nottinghamshire* **91**, 16–73.

Garton, D. 1993. A burnt mound at Waycar Pasture, Girton, Nottinghamshire: an interim report, *Trans. Thoroton Soc. Nottinghamshire* **97**, 148–149.

Garton, D. 2002. Walking fields in South Muskham and its implications for Romano-British cropmark-landscapes in Nottinghamshire, *Trans. Thoroton Soc. Nottinghamshire* **106**, 17–39.

Garton, D. and Abbott, C. 1998. Aston Hill, *Derbyshire Archaeol. J.* **118**, 150.

Garton, D. and Salisbury, C.R. 1995. A Romano-British wood-lined well at Wild Goose Cottage, Lound, Nottinghamshire, *Trans. Thoroton Soc. Nottinghamshire* **99**, 15–43.

Gent, H. 1983. Centralised storage in later prehistoric Britain, *Proc. Prehist. Soc.* **49**, 243–267.

Gibson, A. (ed) 2003. *Prehistoric Pottery. People, Pattern and Purpose.* BAR Int. Ser. **1156**.

Greig, J.R.A. 1979. Seeds and pollen from Site SK187072, in C.A. Smith (ed), *Fisherwick. The Reconstruction of an Iron Age Landscape,* 81–87.

Greig, J. 2002. Waterlogged seeds, in G. Coates, *A Prehistoric and Romano-British Landscape. Excavations at Whitemoor Haye Quarry, Staffordshire, 1997–1999,* 72–74.

Guilbert, G. 2004. Borough Hill, Walton-upon-Trent – if not a hill fort, then what? *Derbyshire Archaeol. J.* **124**, 248–257.

Guilbert, G. and Malone, S. 1994. Potlock cursus, in D. Knight (ed), A564(T) Derby Southern Bypass. Summary of Rescue Archaeological Works at Aston Cursus, Potlock Cursus and Swarkestone Lowes, 13–18, figs 3.1–3.4.

Gwilt, A. 1997. Popular practices from material culture: a case study of the Iron Age settlement at Wakerley, in A. Gwilt and C.C. Haselgrove (eds), *Reconstructing Iron Age Societies,* 153–166.

Gwilt, A. and Haselgrove, C.C. (eds) 1997. *Reconstructing Iron Age Societies.* Oxbow Monogr. **71**. Oxford: Oxbow Books.

Hampton, J. 1975. The organization of aerial photography in Britain, in D.R. Wilson (ed), *Aerial Reconnaissance for Archaeology*, 118–125.

Hamshaw-Thomas, J. 1992. Aslockton, Nottinghamshire: Faunal Analysis. Unpublished report, Trent & Peak Archaeological Unit, University Park, Nottingham.

Haselgrove, C.C. 1999. Iron Age societies in central Britain: retrospect and prospect, in B. Bevan (ed), *Northern Exposure: Interpretative Devolution and the Iron Ages in Britain*, 253–275.

Henderson, J. 1992. Glass bead, in D. Knight, Excavations of an Iron Age settlement at Gamston, Nottinghamshire, 68–70.

Hill, J.D. 1995. *Ritual and Rubbish in the Iron Age of Wessex*. BAR Brit. Ser. **242**.

Hingley, R. 1989. Pit Alignment Boundaries. Unpublished Monuments Protection Programme Class Description, English Heritage.

Hingley, R. 1990. Boundaries surrounding Iron Age and Romano-British settlements, *Scottish Archaeol. Rev.* **7**, 96–103.

Hingley, R. 1999. The creation of later prehistoric landscapes and the context of reuse of Neolithic and earlier Bronze Age monuments in Britain and Ireland, in B. Bevan (ed), *Northern Exposure: Interpretative Devolution and the Iron Ages in Britain*, 233–251.

Hodder, M.A. and Barfield, L.H. (eds) 1991. *Burnt Mounds and Hot Stone Technology. Papers from the Second International Burnt Mound Conference, Sandwell, 12th–14th October 1990*. West Bromwich: Sandwell Metropolitan Borough Council.

Hogg, A.H.A. 1979. *British Hill-forts: an Index*. BAR Brit. Ser. **62**.

Howard, A.J. and Knight, D. 2001. South Ing Close, Rampton, Nottinghamshire. Auger Survey of the Floodplain Deposits. Unpublished report, Trent & Peak Archaeological Unit, University Park, Nottingham.

Howard, A.J., Hunt, C.O., Rushworth, G., Smith, D. and Smith, W. 1999. Girton Quarry Northern Extension: Palaeobiological and Dating Assessment of Organic Samples collected during Stage 1 Geoarchaeological Evaluations. Unpublished report, Trent & Peak Archaeological Unit, University Park, Nottingham.

Hughes, G. 1998. The Excavation of an Iron Age Settlement at Covert Farm (DIRFT East), Crick, Northamptonshire. Post-excavation Assessment and Updated Research Design. Unpublished report, Birmingham University Field Archaeology Unit.

Hughes, G. 1999. The excavation of an Iron Age cropmark site at Foxcovert Farm, Aston-on-Trent 1994, *Derbyshire Archaeol. J.* **119**, 176–188.

Hughes, G. 2000. *The Lockington Gold Hoard. An Early Bronze Age Barrow Cemetery at Lockington, Leicestershire*. Oxford: Oxbow Books.

Hughes, P.D.M., Mauquoy, D., Barber, K.E. and Langdon, P.G. 2000. Mire-development pathways and palaeoclimatic records from a full Holocene peat archive at Walton Moss, Cumbria, England, *The Holocene* **10**, 465–479.

Hull, G. 2001. A Late Bronze Age ringwork, pits and later features at Thrapston, Northamptonshire, *Northamptonshire Archaeol.* **29**, 73–92.

Jackson, D.A. 1974. Two new pit alignments and a hoard of currency bars from Northamptonshire, *Northamptonshire Archaeol.* **9**, 13–45.

Jackson, D.A. 1975. An Iron Age site at Twywell, Northamptonshire, *Northamptonshire Archaeol.* **10**, 31–93.

Jackson, D.A. 1976. Two Iron Age sites north of Kettering, Northamptonshire, *Northamptonshire Archaeol.* **11**, 71–88.

Jackson, D.A. 1978. A late Bronze Age – early Iron Age vessel from a pit alignment at Ringstead, *Northamptonshire Archaeol.* **13**, 168.

Jackson, D.A. and Knight, D. 1985. An early Iron Age and Beaker site near Gretton, Northants, *Northamptonshire Archaeol.* **20**, 67–85.

Jones, H. 2002. Brough, Glebe Farm, *Trans. Thoroton Soc. Nottinghamshire* **106**, 147–148.

Kenyon, K. M. 1952. A survey of the evidence concerning the chronology and origins of Iron Age 'A' in southern and midland Britain, *Bull. Inst. Archaeol. Univ. London* **8**, 29–78.

Kinsley, G. 1993. Evaluation Excavations at Gallows Nooking Common, Nottinghamshire: Summary Report. Unpublished report, Trent & Peak Archaeological Trust, University Park, Nottingham.

Kinsley G. 1998. Interim report on archaeological watching briefs and excavations at Girton Quarry extension, Newark, *Tarmac Papers* **2**, 41–49.

Knight, D. 1984. *Late Bronze Age and Iron Age Settlement in the Nene and Great Ouse Basins*. BAR Brit. Ser. **130**.

Knight, D. 1991. Archaeology of the Fosse Way. Implications of the Proposed Dualling of the A46 between Newark and Lincoln. Unpublished report, Trent & Peak Archaeological Trust, University Park, Nottingham.

Knight, D. 1992. Excavations of an Iron Age settlement at Gamston, Nottinghamshire, *Trans. Thoroton Soc. Nottinghamshire* **96**, 16–90.

Knight, D. (ed) 1994. A564(T) Derby Southern Bypass. Summary of Rescue Archaeological Works at Aston Cursus, Potlock Cursus and Swarkestone Lowes. Unpublished report, Trent & Peak Archaeological Trust, University Park, Nottingham.

Knight, D. 1997. A Middle Bronze Age rapier from Langford, Nottinghamshire, *Trans. Thoroton Soc. Nottinghamshire* **101**, 59–61.

Knight, D. 2000a. An Iron Age and Romano-British Settlement at Moor Pool Close, Rampton, Nottinghamshire. Unpublished report, Trent & Peak Archaeological Unit, University Park, Nottingham.

Knight, D. 2000b. Rampton, Moor Pool Close, *Trans. Thoroton Soc. Nottinghamshire* **104**, 159–160.

Knight, D. 2002. A regional ceramic sequence: pottery of the first millennium BC between the Humber and the Nene, in A. Woodward and J.D. Hill (eds), *Prehistoric Britain. The Ceramic Basis*, 119–142.

Knight, D. and Howard, A. J. 1995. *Archaeology and Alluvium in the Trent Valley: an Archaeological Assessment of the Floodplain and Gravel Terraces.* Trent & Peak Archaeological Trust, University Park, Nottingham.

Knight, D. and Malone, S. 1997. Evaluation of a Late Iron Age and Romano-British Settlement and Palaeochannels of the Trent at Chapel Farm, Shardlow and Great Wilne, Derbyshire. Unpublished report, Trent & Peak Archaeological Trust, University Park, Nottingham.

Knight, D. and Malone, S. 1998. Further Evaluations of an Iron Age and Romano-British Settlement and Fluvial Features at Chapel Farm, Shardlow and Great Wilne, Derbyshire. Unpublished report, Trent & Peak Archaeological Trust, University Park, Nottingham.

Knight, D and Morris, T. 1998. Fernello Sitch, *Derbyshire Archaeol. J.* **118**, 156–157.

Knight, D. and Priest, V. 1998. Excavations of a Romano-British field system at Lamb's Close, Kelham, Nottinghamshire, *Trans. Thoroton Soc. Nottinghamshire* **102**, 27–37.

Knight, D. and Southgate, M. 2001. Barrow-upon-Trent: Fleak Close and Captain's Pingle, *Derbyshire Archaeol. J.* **121**, 201–202.

Knight, D., Hunt, C.O. and Malone, S. 1999. Auger Survey of Crown Estate Lands near Bingham, Nottinghamshire. Unpublished report, Trent & Peak Archaeological Unit, University Park, Nottingham.

Knight, D., Marsden, P. and Carney, J. 2003. Local or non-local? Prehistoric granodiorite-tempered pottery in the East Midlands, in A. Gibson (ed), *Prehistoric Pottery. People, Pattern and Purpose*, 111–125.

Lambrick, G. 1992. The development of late prehistoric and Roman farming on the Thames gravels, in M. Fulford and E. Nichols (eds), *Developing Landscapes of Lowland Britain. The Archaeology of the British Gravels: a Review*, 78–105.

Lambrick, G. and Robinson, M. 1979. *Iron Age and Roman Riverside Settlements at Farmoor, Oxfordshire.* CBA Res. Rep. **32**. London: Oxfordshire Archaeological Unit and Council for British Archaeology.

Lane, T.W. forthcoming. *Prehistoric Sites from the Fenland Management Project in Lincolnshire.* Lincolnshire Archaeology Heritage Report Series.

Lawson, A. J. 2000. *Potterne 1982–5: Animal Husbandry in Prehistoric Wiltshire.* Salisbury: Trust for Wessex Archaeology.

Losco-Bradley, S. and Kinsley, G. 2002. *Catholme. An Anglo-Saxon Settlement on the Trent Gravels in Staffordshire.* Nottingham Studies in Archaeology 3. Department of Archaeology, University of Nottingham.

MacCormick, A.G., Dickson, J.H., Ransom, M. and Alvey, R.C. 1968. Three dug-out canoes and a wheel from Holme Pierrepont, Nottinghamshire, *Trans. Thoroton Soc. Nottinghamshire* **72**, 14–31.

McElearney, G. 1991. Pollen Analysis from Scaftworth Roman Road Excavations, 1991. Unpublished report, University of Sheffield Archaeological Services.

McGrail, S. 1978. *Logboats of England and Wales.* BAR Brit. Ser. **51**.

Machin, M.L. and Beswick P. 1975. Further excavations of the enclosure at Swine Sty, Big Moor, Baslow, and a report on the shale industry at Swine Sty, *Trans. Hunter Archaeol. Soc.* **10**, 204–211.

Mackie, D. 1993. Prehistoric ditch systems at Ketton and Tixover, Rutland, *Trans. Leicestershire Archaeol. Hist. Soc.* **67**, 1–14.

Macklin, M.G. 1999. Holocene river environments in prehistoric Britain: human interaction and impact, *Quat. Proc.* 7, 521–530.

Martin, A. and Allen, C. 2002. Two prehistoric ring ditches and an associated Bronze Age cremation cemetery at Tucklesholme Farm, Barton-under-Needwood, Staffordshire, *Trans. Staffordshire Archaeol. Hist. Soc.* **39**, 1–15.

Mauquoy, D. and Barber, K.E. 1999. A replicated 3000 yr proxy-climate record from Coom Rigg Moss and Felecia Moss, the Border Mires, northern England, *J. Quat. Sci.* **14**, 263–275.

May, J. 1970. An Iron Age square enclosure at Aston-upon-Trent, Derbyshire: a report on excavations in 1967, *Derbyshire Archaeol. J.* **90**, 10–21.

May, J. 1976. *Prehistoric Lincolnshire.* History of Lincolnshire **1**. Lincoln: History of Lincolnshire Committee.

May, J. 1984. The major settlements of the later Iron Age in Lincolnshire, in N. Field and A. White (eds), *A Prospect of Lincolnshire*, 18–22.

May, J. 1996. *Dragonby. Report on Excavations at an Iron Age and Romano-British Settlement in North Lincolnshire.* Oxbow Monogr. **61**. Oxford: Oxbow Books.

Meadows, I. 1995. Wollaston, *S. Midlands Archaeol.* **25**, 41–45.

Meek, J. 1995. The Excavation of a Pit Complex at Lockington-Hemington, Leicestershire. Unpublished report 95/981, Leicestershire Archaeological Unit.

Membury, S. 2001. An archaeological resource assessment of the later Bronze and Iron Age (first millennium BC) in Lincolnshire, *East Midlands Archaeological Research Framework Project.* http://www.le.ac.uk/archaeology/east_midlands_research_framework.htm

Meyer, M. 1984. Hallstatt imports in Britain, *Bull. Inst. Archaeol. London* **21**, 69–84.

Moffett, L. 1992. Charred plant remains, in D. Knight, *Excavations of an Iron Age settlement at Gamston, Nottinghamshire*, 79–82.

Moffett, L. 1993. Plant Remains from Aslockton. Unpublished report in Nottinghamshire SMR.

Moffett, L. and Monckton, A. 2000. The charred plant remains, in G. Hughes, *The Lockington Gold Hoard: an Early Bronze Age Barrow Cemetery at Lockington, Leicestershire*, 78–81.

Monckton, A. 2003. An archaeological resource assessment and research agenda for environmental archaeology in the East Midlands, *East Midlands Archaeological Research Framework.* http://www.le.ac.uk/archaeology/east_midlands_research_framework.htm

Musty, J. and MacCormick, A.G. 1973. An early Iron Age wheel from Holme Pierrepont, Notts., *Antiq. J.* **53**, 275–277.

O'Brien, C. 1978a. Land and settlement in Nottinghamshire and lowland Derbyshire. An archaeological review, *E. Midlands Archaeol. Bull.* **12**, Supplement.

O'Brien, C. 1978b. Excavations at Holme Pierrepont, *Trans. Thoroton Soc. Nottinghamshire* **82**, 76.

O'Brien, C. 1979. Iron Age and Romano-British settlement in the Trent basin, in B.C. Burnham and H.B. Johnson (eds), *Invasion and Response. The Case of Roman Britain*, 299–313.

Palmer-Brown, C. and Knight, D. 1993. Excavations of an Iron Age and Romano-British settlement at Aslockton, Nottinghamshire: interim report, *Trans. Thoroton Soc. Nottinghamshire* **97**, 146–147.

Parker Pearson, M. 2003. The British and European context of Fiskerton, in N. Field and M. Parker Pearson, *Fiskerton. An Iron Age Timber Causeway with Iron Age and Roman Votive Offerings: the 1981 Excavations*, 179–188.

Parker Pearson, M. and Sydes, R.E. 1997. The Iron Age enclosures and prehistoric landscape of Sutton Common, South Yorkshire, *Proc. Prehist. Soc.* **63**, 221–259.

Phillips, C.W. 1941. Some recent finds from the Trent near Nottingham, *Antiq. J.* **21**, 133–143.

Piggott, S. 1958. Native economies and the Roman occupation of north Britain, in I.A. Richmond (ed), *Roman and Native in North Britain*, 1–27.

Pollard, J. 1996. Iron Age riverside pit alignments at St Ives, Cambridgeshire, *Proc. Prehist. Soc.* **62**, 93–115.

Ponsford, M.W. 1992. A late Iron Age and Romano-British settlement at Rampton, Nottinghamshire, *Trans. Thoroton Soc. Nottinghamshire* **96**, 91–122.

Proctor, J. 2002. Late Bronze Age/Early Iron Age placed deposits from Westcroft Road, Carshalton: their meaning and interpretation, *Surrey Archaeol. Collect.* **89**, 65–103.

Pryor, F. 1992. Special section: current research at Flag Fen, Peterborough, *Antiquity* **66**, 439–531.

Pryor, F. 1996. Sheep stockyards and field systems: Bronze Age livestock populations in the Fenlands of eastern England, *Antiquity* **70**, 313–324.

Pryor, F. 1998. *Farmers in Prehistoric Britain*. Stroud: Tempus.

Pryor, F. 2001. *The Flag Fen Basin: Archaeology and Environment of a Fenland Landscape*. Swindon: English Heritage.

Reynolds, P.J. 1974. Experimental Iron Age storage pits: an interim report, *Proc. Prehist. Soc.* **40**, 118–131.

Richmond, I.A. (ed) 1958. *Roman and Native in North Britain*. London: Nelson.

Riley, D.N. 1980. *Early Landscape from the Air: Studies of Cropmarks in South Yorkshire and North Nottinghamshire*. Department of Prehistory and Archaeology, University of Sheffield.

Riley, D.N., Buckland, P.C. and Wade, J.S. 1995. Aerial reconnaissance and excavation at Littleborough-on-Trent, Notts, *Britannia* **26**, 253–284.

Royal Commission on Historical Monuments (England). 1960. *A Matter of Time. An Archaeological Survey of the River Gravels of England*. London: HMSO.

Samuels, J. and Buckland, P.C. 1978. A Romano-British settlement at Sandtoft, South Humberside, *Yorkshire Archaeol. J.* **50**, 65–75.

Scaife, R. 1999. Gonalston: Pollen Analysis of the Bronze Age and Romano-British Features. Unpublished report in Nottinghamshire SMR.

Scurfield, C.J. 1997. Bronze Age metalwork from the River Trent in Nottinghamshire, *Trans. Thoroton Soc. Nottinghamshire* **101**, 29–57.

Simmons, B.B. 1963. Iron Age hill forts in Nottinghamshire, *Trans. Thoroton Soc. Nottinghamshire* **67**, 9–20.

Smith, C.A. 1977. The valleys of the Tame and middle Trent – their populations and ecology during the late first millennium BC, in J.R. Collis (ed), *The Iron Age in Britain: a Review*, 51–61.

Smith, C.A. 1978. The landscape and natural history of Iron Age settlement on the Trent gravels, in B. Cunliffe and T. Rowley (eds), *Lowland Iron Age Communities in Europe*, 91–101.

Smith, C.A. (ed) 1979. *Fisherwick. The Reconstruction of an Iron Age Landscape*. BAR Brit. Ser. **61**.

Smith, D. 2002. Insect remains, in G. Coates, *A Prehistoric and Romano-British Landscape. Excavations at Whitemoor Haye Quarry, Staffordshire, 1997–1999*, 67–72.

Smith, D.N. and Howard, A.J. 2004. Identifying changing fluvial conditions in low gradient alluvial archaeological landscapes: can coleoptera provide insights into changing discharge rates and floodplain evolution, *J. Archaeol. Sci.* **31**, 109–120.

Smith, D.N., Roseff, R. and Butler, S. 2001. The sediments, pollen, plant macrofossils and insects from a Bronze Age channel fill at Yoxall Bridge, Staffordshire, *Environmental Archaeol.* **6**, 1–12.

Southgate, M., Garton, D., Morris, T. and Priest, V. 1998. Besthorpe Quarry, *Trans. Thoroton Soc. Nottinghamshire* **102**, 138.

Stanley, J. 1954. An Iron Age fort at Ball Cross Farm, Bakewell, *Derbyshire Archaeol. J.* **74**, 85–99.

Stead, I.M. 1991. *Iron Age Cemeteries in East Yorkshire: Excavations at Burton Fleming, Rudston, Garton-on-the-Wolds and Kirkburn*. English Heritage Archaeol. Rep. **22**. London: English Heritage in association with British Museum Press.

Thomas, R. 1997. Land, kinship relations and the rise of enclosed settlement in first millennium BC Britain, *Oxford J. Archaeol.* **16**, 211–217.

Van de Noort, R. and Ellis, S. (eds) 1998. *Wetland Heritage of the Ancholme and Lower Trent Valleys. An Archaeological Survey*. The Humber Wetlands Project, School of Geography and Earth Resources, University of Hull.

Vyner, B. (ed) forthcoming. *Archaeology on the A46 Fosse Way: Newark–Lincoln*. CBA Res. Rep.

Walker, J. 2001. Besthorpe Quarry, *Trans. Thoroton Soc. Nottinghamshire* **105**, 185.

Ward, A., Garton, D., and Snelling, A. 1999. Besthorpe Quarry, *Trans. Thoroton Soc. Nottinghamshire* **103**, 87.

Wardle, C. 2003. The Late Bronze Age & Iron Age in Staffordshire: the torc of the Midlands?, *West Midlands Regional Research Framework for Archaeology*. http://www.arch-ant.bham.ac.uk/wmrrfa/sem2.htm

Watkin, J., Stead, I., Hook, D. and Palmer, S. 1996.
A decorated shield boss from the River Trent, near Ratcliffe on Soar, *Antiq. J.* **76**, 17–30.

Wheeler, H. 1979.
Excavations at Willington, Derbyshire, 1970–2, *Derbyshire Archaeol. J.* **99**, 58–220.

Whimster, R.P. 1989.
The Emerging Past. Air Photography and the Buried Landscape. London: RCHME.

Whimster, R.P. 1992.
Aerial photography and the British gravels: an agenda for the 1990's, in M. Fulford and E. Nichols (eds), *Developing Landscapes of Lowland Britain. The Archaeology of the British Gravels: a Review,* 1–14.

Wigley, A. 2003.
Touching the void: Iron Age landscapes and settlement in the West Midlands, *West Midlands Regional Research Framework for Archaeology.* http://www.arch-ant.bham.ac.uk/wmrrfa/sem2.htm

Willis, S.H. 1999.
Without and within: aspects of culture and community in the Iron Age of north-eastern England, in B. Bevan (ed), *Northern Exposure: Interpretative Devolution and the Iron Ages in Britain,* 81–110.

Willis, S.H. 2001.
An archaeological resource assessment and research agenda for the later Bronze Age and Iron Age (the first millennium BC) in the East Midlands, *East Midlands Archaeological Research Framework.* http://www.le.ac.uk/archaeology/pdf_files/emidiron.pdf.

Wilson, D.R. (ed) 1975.
Aerial Reconnaissance for Archaeology. CBA Res. Rep.**12**.

Winton, H. 1998.
The cropmark evidence for prehistoric and Roman settlement in west Lincolnshire, in R. Bewley (ed), *Lincolnshire's Archaeology from the Air,* 47–68.

Woodhouse, G. 1993.
Tarmac Hoveringham (THM): Archive Report. Unpublished report, Trent & Peak Archaeological Trust, University Park, Nottingham.

Woodward, A. and Hill, J.D. (eds) 2002.
Prehistoric Britain. The Ceramic Basis. Oxford: Oxbow Books.

Yates, D. forthcoming.
Land, Power and Prestige. Bronze Age Field Systems in Southern England. Oxford: Oxbow Books.

Zeepvat, R. J. 2000.
Three Iron Age and Romano-British Rural Settlements on English Gravels: Excavations at Hatford (Oxfordshire), Besthorpe (Nottinghamshire) and Eardington (Shropshire) undertaken by Tempvs Reparatvm between 1991 and 1993. BAR Brit. Ser. **312**.

6   THE ROMANO-BRITISH LANDSCAPE

DAVID KNIGHT, ANDY J. HOWARD AND RUTH LEARY

6.1   Introduction

This chapter focuses upon changes in the landscape of the Trent Valley between the initial advance of the Roman army into the region between the late AD 40's and AD 50's and the final abandonment of the province in the early fifth century. Further large-scale clearance may be demonstrated within this period, with significant expansion and intensification of arable cultivation and pasture in the Valley and in neighbouring regions such as the Sherwood Sandstones of north Nottinghamshire and South Yorkshire. These processes, accentuated by further climatic deterioration from the second and third centuries, contributed towards the accumulation in low-lying areas of thick alluvial and colluvial deposits, the progression towards a fluvial regime of multiple or single stable channels and an expansion of wetlands, leading in some parts of the Middle and Lower Trent to further peat formation.

The Roman occupation also impacted profoundly upon prevailing forms of socio-political and economic organisation, with the imposition of new administrative systems, the growth of a market economy, the imposition of a new and alien government on the existing social order, further significant expansion of settlement and population, and the growth of a hierarchical settlement structure including 'small towns', villas, nucleated 'villages' and single farmsteads. These changes were accompanied by the growth of a sophisticated road network, complementing transport routes along the Trent and other waterways, and increased human utilisation of riverine resources. There is also an increasing body of documentary and artefactual evidence relating to social divisions within the landscape that were first hinted at in the Late Iron Age with the recognition from documentary and numismatic sources of tribal divisions within the region. These provided the basis for the Roman division of the region through which the Trent flowed into two civitates, correlating with the Cornovii in a vaguely defined area of the Upper Trent (Webster 1991), and with the Corieltauvi (Tomlin 1983) for most of its course eastwards to the Humber Estuary (Todd 1991; Whitwell 1982). Roman ceramic and numismatic evidence suggests that the Trent may have flowed through a border zone between the Corieltauvi and the north-westerly upland tribes grouped loosely by the Romans under the heading of Brigantes, or perhaps between broad sub-divisions (septs) of the Corieltauvi, thus emphasising the possible role of the river in this period not only as a boundary between highland and lowland zone but also as a fundamental social divide.

In terms of chronology, dating of sites attributable to this period hinges largely upon discoveries of fine and coarse pottery, detailed analysis of which generally permits reasonably close dating to the following broad time periods: mid-late first century, early-mid second century, late second century, late second-early third century, mid-late third century and fourth century. This dating does not, however, permit articulation of the processes of conquest with any precision. Particular problems arise from the slow adoption of Roman pottery in the area outside of military sites such as Rocester, Staffordshire (Leary 1996a, 49), Derby (Birss 1985; Brassington 1971; 1980; cf. Willis 1996), and *Margidunum,* East Bridgford, Nottinghamshire (Todd 1969), and the continued use of Late Iron Age coarse wares as components of pottery assemblages as late as the second century even at Lincoln (Darling 1984, 86). However, by comparison with earlier periods a fairly refined chronological framework may be employed in the analysis of landscape change. Finds of associated metalwork, coins and other typologically diagnostic artefacts are significantly rarer, especially on lower status rural settlements, and in the case of higher value items can pose particular problems of interpretation due to their long periods of circulation. The latter problem should also be borne in mind when considering the possible life histories of imported samian, arretine or other fine pottery.

Sites of the Roman period in the Trent Valley and neighbouring areas attracted considerable antiquarian interest, due largely to the preservation on some higher status town and villa sites of conspicuous earthworks and the remains of stone building foundations, tessellated pavements and other visually striking structural remains. Notable sites in this respect include the extant earthwork enclosure at *Margidunum,* where Stukeley (1776, 105, plate 90) observed building foundations and floors within a Roman town which was later extensively excavated by Oswald (1927; 1941; 1948; 1952; 1956) and Todd (1969), and Southwell, Nottinghamshire, where excavations in 1959 of an area known since the eighteenth century as a source of *tesserae,* painted wall plaster, tile and other building debris revealed the stone foundations of a bath structure and 'villa' with impressive mosaic floors (Daniels 1966; Whitwell 1982, 101–2). Considerably less attention has been focused traditionally upon the lower-status rural settlements that appear to have been spread densely across the Romano-British countryside, although excavations on a variety of settlements over the last thirty years have done much to redress this imbalance. The first large-scale excavations of Roman rural settlements were carried out in the 1970's on sites such as Willington in Derbyshire (Wheeler 1979) and Holme Pierrepont in Nottinghamshire (O'Brien 1979, 301–5) and provided the foundations for the important syntheses of Iron Age and Romano-British settlement in the Trent Valley by O'Brien (1978a; 1979) and Smith (1977; 1978). These supplemented earlier reviews of the evidence for Corieltauvian settlement by Todd (1973) and of settlement in the Lower Trent Valley by Whitwell (1970) as part of his survey of Roman Lincolnshire. Considerably more open-area excavations of Roman settlements have been carried out subsequently, particularly since 1990 with the rapid growth of developer-funding, but the number of extensively excavated and published sites of this period still remains lamentably low by comparison with other Midlands river valleys such as the Upper Thames and Nene (e.g. Fulford and Nichols eds 1992).

Knowledge of the Roman landscape of the Trent Valley has been enhanced significantly in more recent years not only by the expansion of developer-funded excavations but also by increased investment in aerial photographic surveys and systematic fieldwalking. The publication in 1960 of the RCHME volume *A Matter of Time* first focused attention upon the dense pattern of cropmarks in the Trent Valley around Newark, many of which, it was suggested, could relate to Roman activity (*RCHME* 1960, 12–15, 37–42, fig.5; e.g. Plate 4c). More recent assessments of the aerial photographic evidence have highlighted some remarkable cropmark palimpsests on the Trent river-gravels and in neighbouring areas, significant elements of which may relate to Roman activity. Particular attention should be drawn to Whimster's aerial photographic survey of the Lower Trent Valley north of Newark, which revealed a dense pattern of predominantly rectilinear ditched enclosures and a system of linear ditches running roughly parallel and orthogonally to the River Trent (Whimster 1989; 1992, 11–14). Most of the components of this landscape remain undated, but limited excavations suggest currently a predominantly Late Iron Age to Roman date (Chapter 6.8.2). Further valuable insights into this period have been provided by Riley's aerial surveys, mainly to the north and west of the Trent Valley on the Sherwood Sandstones of north Nottinghamshire and South Yorkshire (Riley 1980). The 'brickwork-plan' field systems revealed during this work also appear to have developed during the Late Iron Age and Roman periods (*cf.* Chadwick 1999) and hence may provide further evidence for a significant expansion of settlements and field systems during this period. A similar impression of expanding settlement is conveyed by the several systematic fieldwalking surveys that have been conducted within the region, including those carried out in the vicinity of South Muskham, Nottinghamshire (Garton 2002), along the Fosse Way between Newark and Widmerpool, Leicestershire (Kinsley and Knight 1992), and in the Trent Valley south of Derby (Myers 2001, 9–10; Palfreyman 2001, 150–6). The density of Roman surface finds is often quite low, as around South Muskham, but the broad spread of material would support the case for a general expansion of settlement.

Our knowledge of this period in the Trent Valley is enhanced finally by rare fragments of documentary evidence. The Trent itself enters history following a reference by Ptolemy to *Trisantonis fluvii ostia* (the mouth or outlet of the River *Trisantona*), which significantly carries clear implications of flooding (Rivet and Smith 1979, 477; Chapter 6.3.2). Urban settlements and roads also enter the historic record via the Antonine Itinerary, some of the former with clear implications of riverine structures which have left no discernible archaeological trace and of rapid or violent flows which would accord well with the archaeological and environmental evidence for an increasingly flood-prone river. In addition, the evidence of epigraphy and inscriptions

on objects such as lead pigs and fine bronze objects permit unprecedented insights into subjects such as trade, the use of the river and the socio-economic status of settlements. Meanwhile the documentary evidence for tribal divisions provides an important source for assessing the possible role of the Trent as a key social as well as physical boundary during this period.

Important general reviews of the Corieltauvi have been published by Todd (1973; 1991) and Whitwell (1982), while Webster's (1973; 1991) account of the Cornovii includes a useful synthesis of the evidence for Romano-British activity in the Upper Trent. General discussions of the Roman impact upon the Lower Trent are also incorporated in studies of Roman Lincoln and Lincolnshire by Whitwell (1970; 1992) and more recently by Jones (Jones M.J. 2002). These works may be supplemented by a series of overview papers prepared as part of the East and West Midlands Research Frameworks project. These include general reviews of the East Midlands by Taylor (2001), building upon County reviews by Bennet (2001), Bishop (2001), Liddle (2001) and Myers (2001), and a useful synthesis of the evidence for Romano-British Staffordshire by Wardle (2003).

6.2   Climatic Change

There is an accumulating body of evidence to imply that the climate of Britain was both warmer and drier in the early Roman period, becoming cooler and wetter during the course of the Roman occupation, although as in preceding periods the evidence is heavily biased towards upland zones preserving records in ombrotrophic mires of variations in bog surface wetness (Barber *et al.* 1994; 2000). A number of cores recovered from such contexts in the uplands of northern Britain have provided persuasive evidence for periods of wetter and/or cooler climate, particularly through the latter part of the Roman occupation. At Bolton Fell Moss, Cumbria, for example, Barber *et al.* (1994) identified a wetter shift between cal AD 50–150, whilst at Walton Moss, approximately 5km to the south-east, Hughes *et al.* (2000) identified wetter shifts around cal AD 200 and cal AD 500. Further examples may be cited at Coom Rigg Moss and Felecia Moss in the Scottish borders, where Mauquoy and Barber (1999) identified a wet and cool period between cal AD 210–360. Farther south, and hence arguably of more direct relevance to the Trent Valley, work by Chiverrell (2001) on the North Yorkshire Moors identified a wet shift from cal AD 260–540.

Macklin (1999) has argued that periods of increased flood frequency, magnitude and fluvial deposition across Britain around cal AD 100 and between cal AD 200–500 can be correlated with these periods of climatic deterioration. Assuming that the effects of a wetter and/or cooler climate were experienced at lower altitudes such as the Trent Valley, the increased precipitation levels during these periods may well have affected the frequency and magnitude of flooding throughout the Trent catchment. This is implied by the upper clay fills of features dating to the late second century or later at sites such as Bottom Osiers, Gonalston, Nottinghamshire (Elliott and Knight 1997) and Moor Pool Close, Rampton,

Nottinghamshire (Knight 2000; Ponsford 1992) and by the deep alluvium burying Roman remains at sites such as Ferry Lane Farm, Collingham, Nottinghamshire (Bourn *et al.* 2000) and Littleborough, Nottinghamshire (Riley *et al.* 1995). Changing hydrological conditions would have had major implications for settlements located on or adjacent to the Trent floodplain, as at Rampton or Gonalston, and could explain the apparent shift in the medieval period to higher sand and gravel islands elevated above the threat of all but the highest flood inundations (Chapter 7.7.6).

Changes in precipitation and temperature are also likely to have affected the length of the growing season, although their effects may have been felt mainly in more marginal upland areas such as the Derbyshire East Moors rather than the richer farmlands of the Trent Valley. Such changes could, however, have affected the relative proportions of crops and, at least on the floodplain, the balance between arable and pasture. Increasing wetness could well have spurred further emphasis upon pastoral land-use in floodplain and other low-lying environments, as well perhaps as favouring crops such as spelt or bread wheat that were more tolerant of cooler and damper conditions (Jones 1981, 109). The subject of agriculture is pursued further in a later section of this chapter, where the charred grain and other palaeobotanical data from Roman sites within the region are reviewed.

6.3   Fluvial geomorphology

6.3.1   Channel Morphology

Current evidence suggests a progressive concentration of river flow during this period into a limited number of major channels and the infilling of secondary channels with fine-grained alluvium, thus continuing the trend towards more stable meandering and anastomosing fluvial systems which has been postulated for the first millennium BC (Chapter 5.3). Immediately downstream of Nottingham, for example, Salisbury *et al.* (1984) have argued for restriction of the Iron Age and Roman Trent to a line close to the present Polser Brook, citing in support of this claim the available borehole evidence and the discovery of Iron Age and possibly Romano-British log boats and associated finds (Chapter 5.4.1; Cummins and Rundle 1969; MacCormick *et al.* 1968). As discussed in the previous chapter, these archaeological remains were buried within the deposits of a laterally migrating point bar of a meandering river approximately 3m deep and 30m wide. In addition, dating of unidentified plant macrofossils recovered during coring of two sinuous palaeochannels of the Trent at Barton-in-Fabis, Nottinghamshire, suggests that organic sediments were accumulating in a well-developed meandering river between cal AD 390 and 660 (1450 ± 26 BP, Oxa-12780, cal AD 540–660; 1609 ± 27 BP, Oxa-12781, cal AD 390–540; 1550 ± 27 BP, Oxa-12782, cal AD 420–600). Farther downstream in the Lower Trent Valley, coring and dating of peaty palaeochannel sediments at Waycar Pasture, Girton, Nottinghamshire, indicated the infilling of two channels during the later Iron Age and Roman periods, from 160 cal BC to cal AD 240 (1940 ± 60BP, Beta-129962, 50 cal BC–cal AD 240; 1980 ± 60BP, Beta-129964, 160 cal BC–cal AD 140), suggesting that an anastomosing network

may have characterised this part of the valley floor (Howard *et al.* 1999). Channels need not, however, be viewed as essentially static elements of the floodplain during this period, for rapid movements (or 'avulsions') during flood may often have impacted upon the channel pattern. Such movements may have impacted significantly upon low-lying Roman settlements, as perhaps at the riverside town of *Segelocum*, Littleborough (Riley *et al.* 1995). Thick alluvial deposits on this site, interstratified with Roman structural remains, have demonstrated extensive flooding from the second or early third centuries (Chapter 6.3.2). Riley *et al.* (1995, 263) have speculated whether the abandonment of an early channel of the Trent immediately west of *Segelocum*, and the restriction of river flow to the current single channel running along the eastern edge of the site, might reflect channel change following flooding in this or a later period. Such changes could have impacted significantly upon the role of the settlement as a major crossing point of the Trent, either in this period or later, and could have contributed to the replacement of Littleborough by Gainsborough as the key crossing point of this reach of the Trent during the medieval period (*ibid.* 263).

6.3.2   Alluviation and Colluviation

Fluvial studies elsewhere within the English Midlands have demonstrated how the concentration of flow into major channels and the infilling of secondary channels with alluvium are probably linked to the increasing inputs of fine-grained sediments into these fluvial systems, causing increased bank cohesion and decreased lateral channel mobility (*cf.* Brown's 'Stable Beds Aggrading Banks' model: Brown 1997, 24–5; Brown *et al.* 1994). Within the Trent catchment, there is ample evidence for accelerating fine-grained sediment delivery to the valley floor during the Roman period as a consequence of alluvial and presumably also colluvial processes.

Evidence of alluviation associated with increased overbank flooding has been recorded from investigations at a number of Roman sites distributed mainly along the Middle and Lower Trent. This process appears to have accelerated in the later Roman period, as demonstrated at Bottom Osiers, Gonalston (Elliott and Knight 1997), Rampton (Knight 2000), Staythorpe, Nottinghamshire (Heritage Lincolnshire 1992a; 1992b), Littleborough (Riley *et al.* 1995) and Ferry Lane Farm (Bourn *et al.* 2000, 109–10, fig.28; Rackham 2000, 115) by the infilling and/or sealing of Roman features and the incorporation within and above Roman deposits of silts and clays interpreted as flood deposits. However, at Ferry Lane Farm the burial of Roman features beneath *c.*0.3 m of sand which was interpreted as a flood horizon or plough wash (Bourn *et al.* 2000, 99) may equally reflect the reworking of extensive tracts of blown sand.

The stratigraphic sequence revealed during excavations at Rampton provides a useful model for consideration (Fig.6.1; Knight 2000). The Roman site was located adjacent to a major palaeochannel of the Trent that would probably have formed a contemporary low-lying marshy area with rich pasture and other wetland resources, the proximity of which may well have been an important factor

Fig.6.1 *Romano-British pit sealed by light grey alluvial clay and cutting sub-alluvial palaeochannel deposits at Rampton, Nottinghamshire; base of pit sealed originally by alluvium in centre foreground (photograph: D.Knight)*

in the choice of site location. Numerous Romano-British ditches and pits, including several post-pits, had been cut through the upper channel deposits, providing a valuable *terminus ante quem* for the infilling of this former river channel (*ibid.* 11–12, fig.5). These features were sealed by alluvial clay deposits up to a maximum of about 2.5m thick, incorporating a *c.*0.1–0.4m thickness of very dark grey alluvial clays which merged upwards with a sequence of light grey beneath oxidised brown alluvial clays, reflecting presumably the variable impact with depth of groundwater levels and weathering processes (*cf.* Lamb's Close, Kelham, Nottinghamshire: Knight and Priest 1998, 32). The grey alluvial clays petered out within a narrow zone following the edge of the terrace, but the upper oxidised brown clays extended farther across the terrace, sealing a large number of Romano-British terrace-edge features. The stratigraphic sequence would support the hypothesis of increased flooding and overbank alluviation, which in turn may have prompted a retreat towards higher and drier areas of the terrace in the later Roman period as the area became increasingly prone to flood. The area may have been abandoned altogether towards the end of the Roman period for reasons of increasing wetness. The only evidence for post-Roman activity prior to post-medieval drainage of the area is an iron seax (large thick-backed knife) which it has been suggested may mark the location of a Saxon burial (Jones and Knight 2002). This was retrieved from a riverside location some distance perhaps from the main focus of contemporary habitation, which might lie beneath the modern village of Rampton.

A similar model of progressive overbank flooding may be proposed for other sites in the Lower Trent and along some of its major tributary valleys, including a settlement at Sandtoft, North Lincolnshire, on the banks of the Old Idle near its confluence with the River Don (Samuels and

Buckland 1978). At that site, Romano-British features and artefacts were recorded in contexts sealed within and beneath alluvium, while the focus of occupation appears to have moved progressively eastwards to a marginally higher sand ridge during the fourth century – presumably in response to increased flooding. In addition, at the Roman town of *Segelocum*, several kilometres downstream of Rampton, excavations revealed a sequence of alluvial deposits up to a maximum of 1.5m thick overlying and interstratified with Roman structural remains (Fig.6.2; Riley *et al.* 1995). The stratigraphic sequence is best illustrated in a trench excavated by Wade in the garden of Vicarage Farm, where deposits of clean orange-brown clay silts beneath dark brown silts containing much late Roman pottery and animal bone overlay and were interleaved with Roman structural remains. These silts were interpreted as flood deposits, indicative of a major phase of alluviation, which on the basis of associated artefacts was argued probably to have commenced in the later second or early third century (*ibid.* 257–63, fig.5). Riley *et al.* also speculated whether flooding might have prompted not only a shift in the focus of occupation towards slightly higher ground but also a change in settlement plan (*ibid.* 256, 263), although large-scale excavations would be required to test this hypothesis.

Roman flood deposits may also be identified farther upstream in the Middle Trent Valley, including sites at Willington (Wheeler 1979, 110, 116–7, 121, 125), Whitemoor Haye, Staffordshire (Coates and Woodward 2002, 79) and Bottom Osiers, Gonalston (Elliott and Knight 1997), and as argued at Willington may in some case provide an explanation for observed changes in landscape organisation (Wheeler 1979, 125). The upper fills of many features at Bottom Osiers were filled with particularly thick alluvial clays that have been interpreted

Fig.6.2 *Section across Roman features at Segelocum, Littleborough, Nottinghamshire, showing features and structural remains sealed by and interstratified with flood deposits (source: Riley et al. 1995; reproduced by permission of the Society for the Promotion of Roman Studies)*

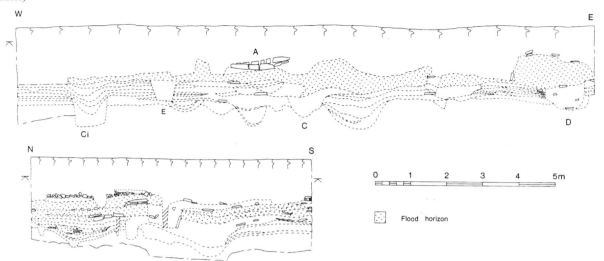

as evidence for increased flooding, possibly from an as yet undated palaeochannel to the west of the site. These features included a large pond incorporating substantial quantities of second century pottery and other artefacts, including querns, textiles and objects of wood and leather, which appear to have been deliberately dumped after the feature had fallen out of use (Elliott and Knight 1997, 69). The artefact evidence from this and other features suggests strongly that occupation had not continued significantly beyond the second century, and abandonment due to increased flooding remains an attractive hypothesis.

Additional evidence for flooding may be provided by the evidence of Roman place names. Brief reference has been made above to Ptolemy's description of *Trisantonis fluvii ostia* – the mouth or outlet of the river Trisantona (Rivet and Smith 1979, 477). The *santon* element of the name may be related to the British *sento*, meaning a path, and in the context of a river might mean a trespasser or one liable to flood. *Tri* intensifies that which follows, and hence would imply a very vigorous flooder. The derivation from *sento* could mean alternatively a wanderer or meanderer, which would fit well with the evidence above for stable meandering or anastomosing channels. The root could derive alternatively from *sem,* meaning to draw water, and in the context of river names would signify water pouring out or flooding. In Yugoslavia an inscription records a dedication to a Goddess Sentona (CIL III.3026) so the name may also carry implications of an associated deity. Further evidence for the Romans' appreciation of the tempestuous qualities of the river can be found in their name for the Roman small town at Littleborough – *Segelocum* (Rivet and Smith 1979, 453). This is derived from the British words *sego* (power or force) and *loc* (loch or pool), implying a 'violent' pool (Rivet and Smith 1979, 453) or, as suggested by Jackson (1970, 79), 'a pool on the Trent with a rapid current' (*cf.* Riley *et al.* 1995, 253).

Significantly more work is required to clarify more precisely the impact within the region of changes in flood frequency, which might be imagined to have impacted most seriously upon terrace-edge and floodplain sites in areas

characterised by subdued relief and/or subject to unusually high river discharges. Areas at risk would most likely have included the expansive confluence zone of the Rivers Trent, Derwent and Soar and the broad alluvial floodplain and subdued gravel islands of the Lower Trent immediately downstream of Newark. Key questions also remain regarding the long-term impact of these proposed changes in flood frequency, although comparisons between the distributions of Roman and medieval settlements suggest a general trend during the course of the first millennium AD towards the location of settlement foci on higher and drier gravel terraces. Medieval villages are generally located significantly farther from the river and in more elevated locations than their Roman predecessors (Chapter 7.7.6). This suggests, therefore, that the Roman period may mark the beginning of a protracted process of retreat from the floodplain which may only have been reversed with the development from post-medieval times of more effective river management strategies.

The anthropogenic processes which led to increased alluviation on the floodplain, namely woodland clearance, soil erosion and increased slope-channel coupling, may also have resulted in the deposition of significant depths of colluvial sediment at the floodplain edge. In contrast, however, to the widespread evidence for alluviation, unequivocal evidence for Roman colluviation is not readily forthcoming. Possible evidence for late Roman or post-Roman colluviation was obtained from a Late Iron Age and Roman settlement at Lamb's Close, Kelham, which was associated with a rectilinear system of ditched field boundaries extending across the Holme Pierrepont Terrace onto the floodplain (Knight and Priest 1998). An evaluation trench was excavated across the interface between these two terrain units to establish whether the field boundaries extended beneath alluvium, and revealed an approximately 0.2–0.3m thick layer of sandy clay which was interpreted as a colluvial deposit formed from the erosion of ploughsoil, although a Roman date is not unequivocal. Another example of significant colluvial accumulations has been recorded in the vicinity of *Margidunum* on the Mercia Mudstone escarpment immediately east of the Trent

Valley. Here, a variety of Roman and Iron Age features were shown to be sealed beneath colluvium derived from slopes of surprisingly gentle gradient, including probably the edge of a major villa complex (Appleton *et al.* 2004; Knight and Malone 1993), but more detailed dating must await the completion of on-going fieldwork.

Researchers across Britain in the 1970s and 1980s were keen to explain the causes of accelerated alluviation and colluviation from the Bronze Age onwards as either a response to climatic change or a result of anthropogenic activity (Macklin and Lewin 1993; Robinson and Lambrick 1984; Shotton 1978). It is now generally accepted, however, that these factors are inextricably linked (Macklin 1999, 523). The expansion of agriculture into areas which may not hitherto have been extensively exploited, such as the Sherwood Sandstones of north Nottinghamshire and South Yorkshire (Garton 1987; Riley 1980), together with changing agricultural practices such as the sowing of winter cereals and the introduction of new deep ploughing technologies capable of severing the root mat, may be isolated as significant causal factors (*cf.* Buckland and Sadler 1985, 248; Didsbury 1992). These changes may, however, have been accentuated by increasing climatic wetness, which would have increased rates of surface runoff and hence soil erosion. Increased fine-grained sediment accumulation generated by these processes may be assumed to have impacted upon the number of primary channels within the floodplain and hence the discharge capacity of the river system; this in turn may have contributed to increased overbank flooding and alluviation.

6.3.3 Peat Formation

Additional evidence for the progressive waterlogging of valley floors is provided by the discovery in parts of the Middle and Lower Trent Valley of extensive peat deposits dating from the Roman period. A notable example of late Roman peat accumulation has been investigated at East Carr, Mattersey, Nottinghamshire, where an extensive rectilinear field system was partially buried beneath peat extending across the floodplain of the Idle Valley (Fig.6.17; Garton *et al.* 1995; Morris and Garton 1998a; 1998b). In addition, farther downstream at Adlingfleet near Trent Falls, peat formed from a mixed alder carr woodland was dated to cal AD 420–1220, indicating continued formation of peat in the lowermost reaches of the Trent well into the later first millennium AD (Lillie 1998, 54). The latter discovery also raises some awkward questions regarding the mechanisms of formation of these deposits. Some peat layers may reflect the combined impact upon surface runoff and groundwater levels of anthropogenic processes and increasing climatic wetness, as discussed above. In the Lower Trent Valley and the Humberhead Levels, the period from AD100–400 was also a time of marine transgression (Van de Noort and Davies 1993, 18) and explanations of increased peat formation in areas such as the Idle Valley should also take account of the impact upon the catchment of fluctuations in sea-level. Marine transgressions in the Lower Trent have been inferred from borehole studies undertaken in the wider Humber Estuary and neighbouring valleys such as the Ancholme and the Foulness (Gaunt and

Tooley 1974; Long *et al.* 1998). Although potentially of major significance, the precise implications of these data for the Lower Trent region can only be established after further significant research.

6.3.4 Blown Sand

It is worth speculating finally whether some of the extensive blown sand deposits which blanket the Holme Pierrepont Terrace on the western and eastern margins of the valley floor in the Trent Valley north of Newark might have been reworked during this period. In addition, clearance of the protective woodland canopy from the Sherwood Sandstones during the laying out of the 'brickwork plan' fields may also have caused extensive redeposition of wind-borne material. Observations during open-area excavations at Rampton (Knight 2000), discussed in greater detail below, provided striking evidence for the remarkable speed with which substantial depths of sand could accumulate against hedges or in other sheltered environments in severely windy conditions (*c.*100–200mm overnight). Such contemporary aeolian activity is not unusual and has been noted in other areas where extensive coversands are mapped, such as the Vale of York (Radley and Simms 1967).

Aeolian deposits which may be dated unequivocally to the Roman period have not yet been recorded in the Valley, but excavations at Girton revealed extensive blown sand deposits which on stratigraphic grounds would fit most comfortably within a Roman or perhaps early medieval context (Kinsley 1998; H. Jones and G. Kinsley: pers. comm.). Substantial thicknesses of blown sand were recorded on this site, stratified above the LBA-EIA midden described in the previous chapter (Chapter 5.7.1) and above a pit alignment yielding in one of the pits the base of a typologically undiagnostic hand-made Iron Age pot, but cut into by late Anglo-Saxon or later medieval ridge and furrow. The deposits were interstratified with a variety of cut features, none as yet closely dated, but it is hoped that full post-excavation analysis will permit eventually more precise dating of these important deposits.

6.4   River Management and Transport

Evidence has been obtained from several neighbouring regions of bridges, including crossings of the Witham at Lincoln (Jones, M.J. 2002, 107–12) and the Nene at Aldwincle in Northamptonshire (Jackson and Ambrose 1976), and of docks or quays (e.g. Lincoln: Jones, M.J. 2002, 107–9), mills (e.g. Wood Burcote, Northamptonshire: Turland 1977) and other structures indicative of significant advances in the control and exploitation of river resources. As yet, however, no examples of bridges or other riverine structures of this period have been recorded in the Trent Valley, with the possible exception of a stone-paved ford which was removed from the river-bed during navigation improvements at Littleborough in 1820 (Riley *et al.* 1995, 253–6). This was located adjacent to the Roman town of *Segelocum,* at the point where the Roman road from Lincoln to Doncaster may have crossed the Trent (Fig.6.3; *ibid.* figs 1–2), although the structure could date from a

Fig.6.3 *Plan of Romano-British small town of Segelocum, Littleborough, Nottinghamshire (source: Riley et al. 1995; reproduced by permission of the Society for the Promotion of Roman Studies)*

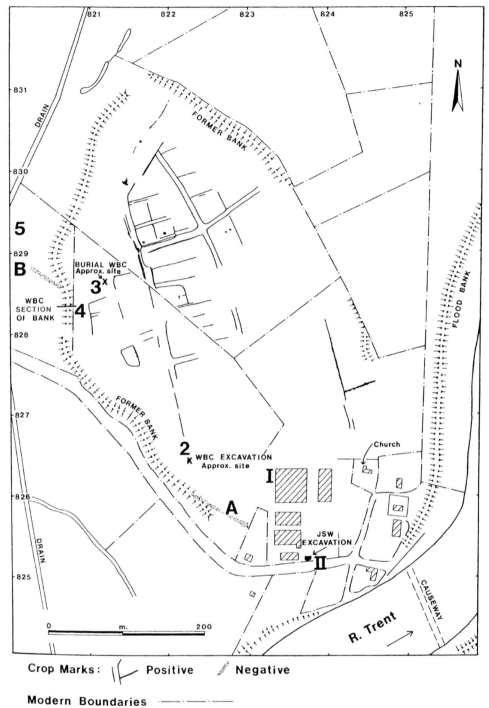

later period of use. The place name evidence implies a river crossing near the small town at *Ad Pontem*, Thorpe, whose name ('at the bridge') may refer to a structure destroyed by the eastwards meander migration that has since truncated the western edge of the town defences (Burnham and Wacher 1990, 273; Rivet and Smith 1979, 241). Other bridges are suspected elsewhere along the river where alignments of known or suspected Roman roads demand river crossings (Whitwell 1982, 67), including locations in Nottinghamshire near Gunthorpe (Todd 1969, 13) and below Red Hill, Ratcliffe-on-Soar (Elsdon, 1982; Palfreyman and Ebbins 2003, 26–7). The elaborate timber bridge at Cromwell, Nottinghamshire, merits particular

mention, as this was for long regarded as a tribute to Roman engineering skills. Recent radiocarbon dating of preserved timbers, however, has shown that this structure dates from the early medieval period (Salisbury 1995).

The Romans were well aware of the advantages of water transport, and the Trent would most likely have served as an important route for the transport of raw materials and finished products (Whitwell 1982, 67–8). Particular significance may be attached in this respect to the cluster of second to fourth century pottery kilns which have been recorded in the river valley at a series of closely spaced sites at Torksey, Knaith, Lea, Newton-on-Trent and Little London,

Lincolnshire, and possibly at Meering, Nottinghamshire (Field 1984; Field and Palmer-Brown 1991). These sites were located close to small towns, presumably because of their proximity to market opportunities, but appear also to have been positioned with an eye for riverine transport. The recent recognition of Redcliff on the northern shore of the Humber as an entrepot of some importance for pottery importation (Willis 1996, 217) would fit well with this model of river-based trade although north-south distribution (for example, of Nene Valley colour-coated wares) would necessarily have relied more heavily upon overland transport. Other commodities which may have been traded along the river include lead from production sites in the Peak District (implied by the discovery in the vicinity of Brough-on-Humber, East Yorkshire, of inscribed lead ingots from unknown sources in the Peak District: Sitch 1990, 166–8, table 12.1), wine (Whitwell 1982, 140), products of the Durobrivan mosaic workshops (Smith 1969) and a variety of other bulky commodities such as stone, brick, tile and perhaps even salt.

The importance of the Trent as a transport route may have been enhanced in its lowermost reaches by construction of the Fossdyke Canal, which may have been dug in Roman times as a link between the Trent at Torksey and navigable reaches of the Witham (Jones, M.J. 2002, 95; Whitwell 1982, 66, 133, 140). Construction of this waterway involved the canalisation of the River Till, which flows into the Brayford Pool at Lincoln, and an old channel flowing east from the Trent at Torksey; a new cutting linking these was dug between between Odder and Drinsey Nook. The canal would have expedited the cross-country movement of goods southwards to Lincoln from centres such as York and from production sites upstream of Torksey, particularly bulky raw materials such as building stone from the Pennines (Jones, M.J. 2002, 95). Doubts remain, however, regarding the date of construction of this canal, despite the retrieval from the watercourse of a bronze statuette of Mars and other Roman material (Jones, M.J. 2002, plate 29; Oswald 1937, 13; Phillips 1934, 117), and an Anglo-Scandinavian origin for the watercourse is also possible (Jones, M.J. 2002, 95).

6.5 Woodland Clearance and Management

Continued clearance of woodland on the floodplain and gravel terraces is implied by a variety of palaeobiological evidence, although the number of environmental records spanning this time period is low by comparison with some earlier periods (Monckton 2003). Augmentation of the available records, particularly with data from rural contexts, may be highlighted therefore as a key research priority for the future.

A particularly useful palaeoenvironmental sequence was recorded at Croft, Leicestershire, just south of the study area in the Soar Valley. Environmental investigations prior to quarrying identified a series of organic channels, one of which yielded hazel dated to 1880–1440 cal BC (Beta-75197, 3360 ± 80 BP) and peat dated to 200 cal BC–cal

AD 320 (Beta-78005, 1960 ± 100 BP). Pollen remains showed a transition from a heavily wooded landscape comprising alder, oak, lime and hazel to an environment with sparse woodland. Alder pollen, for example, was observed to decline from c.70 % to c.6 % of the total land pollen (Smith et al. submitted). This woodland was replaced in the Romano-British period by herbaceous flora, reflecting an expansion of grassland (up to 40 %) and other herbaceous species such as ribwort plantain (up to 15 %). The pollen evidence is echoed by the identification of insects which feed typically on docks and clover and of dung beetles characteristic of pastoral contexts. Arable activity is implied by cereal pollen and other plants typical of cultivated or disturbed ground, such as nettle, goosefoot, fat hen, chickweed and dock.

Additional important evidence for woodland clearance has been obtained from analyses of pollen preserved in a variety of mid-first to second century pits, ponds and ditches revealed during excavations at Bottom Osiers, Gonalston (Fig.6.4; Scaife 1999). Pollen remains from mid- to late first century contexts demonstrate an expansion of herb flora, particularly grasses, suggesting that pasture/grassland was locally important. Cereals were also present in significant quantities (up to 10% of total dry land pollen in one sample; Chapter 6.6), suggesting to Scaife a mixed arable and pastoral economy. Fewer trees were represented than in the Bronze Age sample described in the previous chapter, but sufficient oak and hazel pollen was retrieved to suggest the continuity of these species after the clearance of other woodland types such as lime and elm. A comparatively poor representation of holly, lime and elm pollen suggests isolated or sporadic examples of these species. Alder was also present, but reduced values in comparison with the Bronze Age suggest a change in the character of the floodplain, with increased waterlogging (reflecting higher ground water-table and surface run-off) or progressive woodland clearance, or both. Pollen from second century contexts implies a further reduction in the number of trees and a corresponding increase in herbs of agriculture, suggesting yet further expansion of human activity. Small percentages of oak and hazel, plus even smaller quantities of ash, lime, beech and holly, provide an insight into the character of the remaining regional woodland. The herbaceous flora is extremely diverse, and is dominated by grasses with evidence for the cultivation or processing of cereals, together with one grain of flax (Chapter 6.6).

In the Lower Trent Valley, at Girton, two palaeochannels at Waycar Pasture are known from associated peat deposits to have been infilling from 160 cal BC (1940 ± 60 BP, Beta-129962, 50 cal BC–cal AD 240; 1980 ± 60 BP, Beta-129964, 160 cal BC–cal AD 140; Garton 1999; Howard et al. 1999). As at Croft, pollen and insect remains indicate a largely cleared pastoral landscape, with limited deciduous woodland probably at some distance on the higher terraces (including pine, lime, birch and oak). Arable cultivation is indicated by the presence of cereal pollen (some certainly of barley type). High counts of fern spores, which were also identified at Croft, were argued to imply soil erosion from arable fields; these taxa are very resistant to breakdown in soil profiles, and hence tend to be heavily represented in

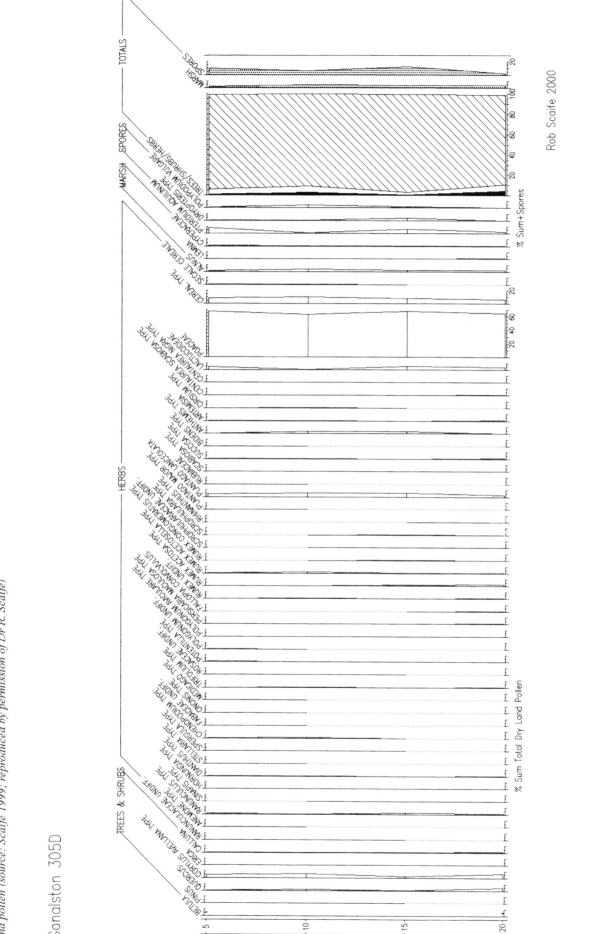

Fig.6.4 *Pollen percentages in organic material from Romano-British pond (0305) at Bottom Osiers, Gonalston, Nottinghamshire; vertical axis: spot samples; horizontal axis: percentage of total dry land pollen (source: Scaife 1999; reproduced by permission of Dr R. Scaife)*

depositional environments receiving inputs of eroded soil (*ibid.* 9). Fragments of burnt clay and charcoal indicate the use of fire, reflecting either clearance or natural burning. A largely cleared landscape with both pasture and arable farming may also be deduced from the environmental evidence recovered at Sandtoft in the Idle Valley (Samuels and Buckland 1978). Organic sediments filling the adjacent palaeochannel and settlement ditches preserved insect remains indicative of a cleared landscape and a mixed farming economy, with pastoral activity indicated by a considerable dung beetle fauna.

Overall, the available data suggest an extensively cleared environment during the Romano-British period along much of the Trent Valley, although additional large-scale sampling may demonstrate eventually significant intra-regional variations in the extent and character of the surviving woodland resource. The available palaeoenvironmental data imply in fact a very complex landscape, possibly with areas of wildwood and zones of secondary woodland growth interspersed amongst land cleared for pasture and arable usage. In the Idle marshlands near Scaftworth, Nottinghamshire, for example, fluctuations in the ratio of arboreal to non-arboreal pollen within organic deposits beneath and above the timber foundations of a Roman road were argued to imply one or possibly two phases of forest regeneration subsequent to Bronze Age clearance (McElearney 1991). In contrast, excavations by Oswald within the defended core of the Romano-British 'small town' of *Margidunum* uncovered a late first century plank-lined well constructed from mature forest oaks argued to derive from a 'wildwood' source (Garton and Salisbury 1995, 27–31, 40–1, fig.8). The trees from which the planks derived were of variable age and displayed signs of slow growth, and were argued to have grown up in a competitive woodland environment characteristic of an unmanaged 'wildwood' location. The authors speculated whether these might have derived from ancient woodland surviving in the area around *Margidunum (ibid.* 41), although the site's position astride the Fosse Way would have ensured easy access to non-local timber sources.

Another issue that should be addressed briefly here is the extent of clearance on the adjacent interfluves. Information from these areas is less extensive, reflecting the historic bias of archaeological investigations towards the gravel terraces. Discoveries in upland areas that *have* been examined, however, suggest that many areas away from the Valley may have been fairly densely settled and intensively farmed in the Roman period – notably around *Margidunum* and at Laxton, Nottinghamshire, where fieldwalking and casual finds suggest a dense distribution of sites (Appleton *et al.* 2004; Bishop 2001, 2; Kinsley and Knight 1992), and in Staffordshire, where the striking contrast between 236 Romano-British and five Iron Age findspots in the County Sites and Monuments Record has been argued to reflect significant increases in both wealth and population (Wardle 2003, 24). This compares well with the evidence from adjacent areas, such as Leicestershire and Northamptonshire, for more intensive cultivation of clay soils (Clay 2002; Monckton 2003, 18). It would also support the argument that further development of the 'brickwork plan' field systems

to the north of the Trent Valley in the Roman period may have been partly a response to increased pressure upon land resources (Chapter 6.8.1).

As in the first millennium BC, woodland management would have been essential if the expansion of pasture and arable resources were not to deplete seriously the woodland resource. Evidence for coppicing has been recovered from a number of sites along the Trent Valley and in adjacent upland areas – notably at Menagerie Wood, Worksop, Nottinghamshire, where fragments of hazel with axe-trimmed and broken ends probably deriving from coppice poles were recovered (Garton *et al.* 1988, 29, 32, table 1). Further important evidence for woodland management was obtained from analysis of the oak planks lining a third century well at Wildgoose Cottage, Lound, Nottinghamshire (Figs 6.5 and 6.6; Garton and Salisbury 1995). The fast growth and curving grain of the timbers from this well were argued to imply derivation from open woodland or hedges rather than dense 'wildwood', in contrast therefore to the above-mentioned first century well from *Margidunum*. None of the timbers was over 75 years old, implying regular felling, while samples of two trees preserved features suggestive of coppicing (*ibid.* 40). This would fit well with the insect evidence for a 'landscape of established grassland, virtually devoid of trees' (*ibid.*19), the scarce woodland resources of which may have been carefully nurtured within intensively managed coppices.

6.6   Arable and Pasture

Although the case for extensive clearance of substantial tracts of the Trent Valley would seem firmly founded, key questions remain regarding the balance between pastoral and arable land use, details of farming practices and the issue of intra-regional contrasts in land use. The balance between pasture and arable is unlikely to have remained constant over time or space, and may well have varied significantly between the various topographic zones of the Upper, Middle and Lower Trent. In addition, conclusions drawn from palaeoenvironmental studies of other Midlands river valleys, most notably the Upper Thames, raise the possibility of fundamental differences in land-use between floodplain and terrace environments, and quite possibly between the lower and higher gravel terraces (*cf.* Lambrick 1992). Work in other areas of Britain has also highlighted the evidence for agricultural expansion and intensification during this period, in response probably to demographic growth and the need to produce a surplus to cater for an increasing number of people not directly involved in agriculture, especially the Roman army and the growing urban population (Van der Veen and O'Connor 1998). Such developments may also have affected the Trent Valley (*cf.* Coates and Woodward 2002, 88), and in this section the limited range of evidence for reconstruction of the agricultural economy is briefly reviewed.

Considerable effort has been expended in recent years upon the implementation of sampling strategies aimed at obtaining palaeoenvironmental data capable of elucidating the Romano-British agricultural economy, particularly

Fig.6.5 *Axiometric reconstruction of plank-lined Romano-British well at Wild Goose Cottage, Lound, Nottinghamshire (source: Garton and Salisbury 1995; reproduced by permission of D. Garton, Dr C. Salisbury and the Thoroton Society of Nottinghamshire)*

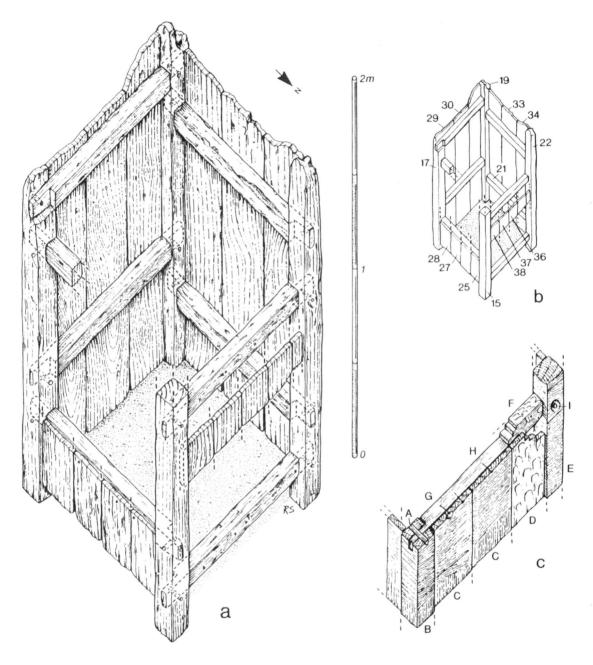

6.6.1 Animal Bones

Study of the pastoral economy is frustrated, as in earlier periods, by the poor preservation of animal bone in features cut into the acidic soils of the river terraces, and discussion of animal husbandry practices must rest at present upon a limited number of small and generally poorly preserved faunal assemblages (*cf.* Monckton 2003: Appendix). Thus, although palaeobotanical and insect remains provide persuasive evidence for a steady expansion of pasture throughout the period (Chapter 6.5), discussion of the range and proportions of animal breeds or more sophisticated questions such as the balance by age or sex, husbandry practices and butchery techniques cannot yet be pursued in any detail. Just beyond the Valley, larger and more useful bone assemblages have been recovered from rural sites with depositional environments more favourable to the preservation of bone, notably on a low ridge of fluvio-glacial sand and gravel at Aslockton, Nottinghamshire, immediately east of the Trent Valley (Hamshaw-Thomas 1992; Palmer-Brown and Knight 1993), and at several towns such as *Margidunum* (Harman 1969), on the Mercia

at large quarry sites such as Whitemoor Haye (Coates 2002), Gonalston (Elliott and Knight 1997) and East Carr, Mattersey (Morris and Garton 1998a; 1998b). Much of the information gained from this work lies buried in unpublished archive reports or is the subject of on-going post-excavation programmes, but sufficient data are available to permit some general conclusions on the role of pasture and arable and the character of the agricultural landscape. The main sources of information are discussed below, with consideration in turn of the available faunal and palaeobotanical data.

Fig.6.6 *Grey ware narrow-necked jar from Wild Goose Cottage, Lound, preserving extensive areas of abrasion and vertical scratch marks on its surface, probably used to retrieve water from the wood-lined well (source: Garton and Salisbury 1995; reproduced by permission of D. Garton, Dr C. Salisbury and the Thoroton Society of Nottinghamshire)*

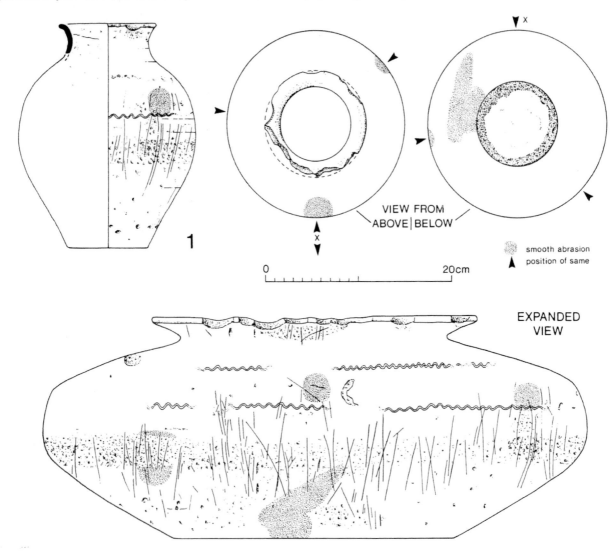

Mudstone escarpment east of the Valley, and Little Chester, on the east bank of the Derwent at Derby (Harman and Weinstock 2002). However, the applicability to the Trent Valley of conclusions drawn from sites in these different topographic zones is debatable, and the results of such work must be applied with caution. There is also every likelihood that the animal husbandry regime on urban or villa sites had differed significantly from that of the smaller rural settlements.

In the Trent Valley, small faunal assemblages from rural settlements on the gravel terraces such as Barrow-upon-Trent (Knight and Southgate 2001), Chapel Farm, Shardlow (Elliott 1997) and Willington (Harman 1979) in Derbyshire and Gonalston (Elliott and Knight 1997; 2003) and Ferry Lane Farm (Locker 2000) in Nottinghamshire provide limited evidence for the range of domestic species. Rather better preserved collections have been obtained from several low-lying sites where faunal remains have been preserved within waterlogged ditch, pit or pond fills, notably at Chainbridge Lane, Lound (Eccles *et al.* 1988) and in sub-alluvial contexts at Rampton (Knight 2000), but the numbers of identifiable bone fragments recovered are

still too small to permit detailed quantitative analyses. With this proviso, there are suggestions of a general emphasis upon cattle and sheep/goat, with variable proportions of horse and pig, although the relative importance of these and the uses to which they were put could obviously have varied significantly between sites and over time. Occasional discoveries of faunal remains which appear to have been deliberately and carefully placed within enclosure ditches or other features hint at the continuation of ceremonial practices postulated on some Iron Age sites within the region (Chapter 5.7.1) – as at Chainbridge Lane, where excavations revealed a Romano-British enclosure ditch containing two virtually complete animal skeletons. These included most of a large adult pig, deposited in the bottom of the ditch 'with its backbone bent round, and its front and back feet close together, as if they had been bound' (Eccles *et al.* 1988, 17). The animal would appear to have been deposited whole, perhaps because of disease (*ibid.*17) or possibly as a ritual or ceremonial offering.

A rare insight into husbandry practices within the region is provided by a collection of animal bones obtained from several phases of excavation inside and outside the defended core of the town at Little Chester. This has demonstrated a consistent emphasis upon cattle and sheep, with smaller numbers of pig, horse, dog and domestic fowl (Harman 1985; Harman 2000; Harman and Weinstock 2002). The proportions of these animals varied over time (*ibid.* fig.90), but throughout the period of occupation cattle and sheep remained the dominant domesticates. Most cattle and sheep bones derived from mature animals, suggesting use for wool and milk as well as meat, while cattle could obviously also have been used for traction. The cattle bones obtained during excavations of the south-eastern defences and an area of extra-mural occupation to the east were particularly informative. These consisted mainly of waste from slaughtering and butchering, with a comparative scarcity of bones from the best parts of the carcass, and could signify that they had been exported elsewhere (*ibid.* 309). Interesting comparisons may be drawn with bone assemblages from inside the town at the Pickford's Garage and Nursery sites, where most bone waste was interpreted as evidence of on-site slaughtering and butchering, principally of mature beef cattle which could have been consumed on site or exported (Harman 2000, 276).

Similar evidence for an emphasis upon cattle and sheep/ goat, with significantly lower proportions of pig, horse and dog, is provided by faunal assemblages recovered from the Romano-British rural settlement at Aslockton (Hamshaw-Thomas 1992) and from first to fourth century contexts at *Margidunum* (Harman 1969). Analysis of the faunal remains obtained from stratigraphic deposits at *Margidunum* emphasises the fluid nature of the animal husbandry regime, which at this site might have shifted over time from an emphasis upon sheep/goat to cattle (Harman 1969, tables 2–3). Evidence was obtained for a multiplicity of economic uses, and perhaps for changes in the pattern of use over time. Meat production was clearly important in view of the volume of waste bones, which it was suggested could indicate the sale of the better joints after slaughtering and butchering and the retention of those with less meat, recalling therefore the evidence from Little Chester. However, changes in the age ranges of sheep/goat between stratified deposits of Periods I–IV could signify an increasing emphasis upon their role as providers of wool and milk, while the identification of significant proportions of cattle over five years old would imply that many may also have been kept for milking, breeding and draught purposes.

6.6.2 Palaeobotanical Remains

Although considerable efforts have been focused in recent years upon the retrieval of charred plants, pollen and plant macrofossils, the great bulk of this evidence remains the subject of post-excavation analysis. Evidence from elsewhere in the West and East Midlands would suggest an emphasis in this period upon spelt wheat, with some emmer/bread wheat and hulled barley, together with smaller proportions of crops such as oats, rye and flax (Monckton 2003, 17–18, Appendix). However, although some of these crops have been identified on Valley sites, research on this subject is currently far less advanced than in other Midlands river valleys such as the Thames.

A particularly rich charred plant assemblage was recovered from a Roman sample at Whitemoor Haye, where it was interpreted as the waste from different stages of cereal processing (Ciaraldi 2002). This was dominated by chaff (recalling the general dominance on Roman sites of burnt wheat chaff, which is generally interpreted as processing waste or fuel from processing: Monckton 2003, 17) and comprised mainly spelt glume bases with small quantities of barley, rye and a single seed of wild or cultivated flax. Further evidence for an emphasis upon spelt wheat is provided by charred plant assemblages retrieved during the excavation of a stone aisled building at Ockbrook, Derbyshire, which it is suggested below may have formed part of a comparatively high status rural settlement. (Chapter 6.7.2; Wagner 2001). Charred grain was recovered from various contexts dating between the first and third centuries, including a corn drier (H1) and hearth deposits, and apart from a dominance of spelt included some bread wheat, possibly emmer wheat, oats and hulled barley.

Farther downstream, surprisingly abundant pollen evidence indicative of local cereal cultivation and/or crop processing was obtained from a variety of late first and second century ditches, pits and ponds at Bottom Osiers, Gonalston (Scaife 1999). These features, which it is suggested probably had a limited pollen catchment, yielded pollen from herbs indicative of arable and disturbed ground and from cereals, including wheat/ barley and rye. It was stressed, however, that this arable component could derive from secondary sources such as that liberated from cereal processing (winnowing and threshing) and/or from human and animal waste (including faecal material), and hence local cultivation cannot be assumed. A single pollen record of flax was also identified, but it was argued that even a single grain could indicate local growth or retting in the pond from which it derived.

6.6.3 Structural Remains

The complex spatial arrangements of ditched enclosures, trackways and ponds which are characteristic of many Roman rural settlements within the region are strongly resonant of an association with the management of livestock, and provide important indirect evidence for the central role of animal husbandry within the agricultural economy. This is well demonstrated at Bottom Osiers, Gonalston, where large-scale excavations have revealed a complete settlement plan focused upon a multiple ditched enclosure linked via a ditched trackway to a system of peripheral ditched enclosures, fields and ponds (Elliott and Knight 1997). The dominant feature of the multiple-ditched enclosure was a large pond with slopes of shallow gradient, the basal fills of which appeared to have been churned up by trampling, possibly by stock. A strong association with livestock would support the available pollen evidence for extensive grassland (Chapter 6.5; Scaife 1999). Another site which could indicate a strong link with the channelling and holding of stock was discovered during excavations at Whitemoor Haye, where two rectilinear ditched enclosures yielding no internal features or traces of substantial domestic activity were interpreted as possibly stock enclosures; these were positioned either side of a ditched trackway, interpreted as probably a droveway, to which one of them was physically joined (Coates and Woodward 2002, 85–7; fig.45: Areas A & S). However, the discovery of spelt wheat grains and crop processing waste in one of the enclosure ditches suggested to the excavator that the enclosure in Area S might also have been used for the processing of crops. A similar association with stock management has been argued for enclosures at Fisherwick, Staffordshire (Miles 1969, 7–13), where again a relationship with a droveway has been postulated, and a link with the rearing of either cattle or horses has been suggested (*ibid.* 11).

Attention should also be drawn to the discovery of several classes of structure which could signify a connection with hay or fodder production. The most common of these are represented by small annular enclosures up to about 5m in diameter, typified by examples recorded during excavations of the Nottinghamshire sites of Rampton (Fig.6.7; Knight 2000), Brough-on-Fosse (Fig.5.16: B-E; Jones, H. 2002, 147) and Ferry Lane Farm (Walker 2001). The shallow continuous gullies which characterise these structures appear to have been open during use, and although of uncertain function are generally assumed to have drained the areas around stacks of hay, fodder or other materials (e.g. Walker 2001). The earliest examples could date from the Late Iron Age, to judge by discoveries of small numbers of Iron Age sherds in the fills of several annular ditches at Brough-on-Fosse (H. Jones: pers. comm.), but the great majority apparently relate to Romano-British activity. The predominance of Roman examples is of particular interest in view of the possible link with hay production, which it has been suggested may have developed in Britain only

during the Roman period (e.g. Lambrick 1992, 101–3; Van der Veen and O'Connor 1998, 134), but we should beware of underestimating the potential range of functions.

Another class of specialised pastoral structure may be represented by around 70 curious subrectangular ditched enclosures which were recorded in the Idle Valley during quarrying at East Carr, Mattersey (Fig.6.8; Morris and Garton 1998b, fig.2). These vary significantly in size, from 2–4m wide by 2–14m long, while in one instance an outer rectangular post-hole setting was recorded (*ibid.* fig. 2B). The continuous steep-sided gullies which define these structures appear to have been open during use, in common with the annular gullies described above, and it has been suggested that they could have served to drain the areas around stacks of material such as hay, reeds, peat, wood or withies (*ibid.*). Occasional discoveries of Romano-British sherds in the ditch fills suggest a Roman date, while the cutting of three enclosures by Roman field ditches suggested to the excavators the possibility of a change in land use immediately before the area was divided and drained by a rectilinear system of field ditches (Chapter 6.8.1).

6.7   Settlement Expansion and Retreat

A model of significant population growth may be postulated for this period, with infilling in established settlement 'core' areas, the colonisation of hitherto marginal zones and the growth of large nucleated settlements. This appears to have accompanied a gradual retreat from many lower-lying regions, possibly in response to increased flooding (Chapter 6.3), creating thereby a complex picture of advance and retreat. Away from the flood-prone zone, there

Fig.6.7 *Rampton, Nottinghamshire: Romano-British annular enclosure, possibly a stackstand (background), cut by a square ditched enclosure (foreground) containing a square setting of four post-holes, possibly a granary (photograph: D. Knight)*

Fig.6.8 *Subrectangular ditched enclosure at East Carr, Mattersey, Nottinghamshire, cut by Romano-British field ditch (photograph: T. Morris)*

are clear indications of an increasingly densely settled and enclosed landscape, the character of which may have varied significantly regionally – as witnessed, for example, by the uneven spread of known coaxial field systems. Variations may be postulated between the Upper, Middle and Lower Trent and, most significantly, between areas north and south of the river – thus reinforcing a contrast which first becomes apparent in the archaeological record in the later Iron Age (Chapter 5.1).

6.7.1 Population Growth

A significant increase in settlement density and hence population levels may be postulated in some parts of the Trent Valley in the four centuries following the Roman Conquest, although the pace of population growth may have varied significantly over both time and space. Considerably less certainty may be attached to population estimates for the fifth century and beyond, during which period population levels may have followed a downwards spiral, but this is a question which is better addressed in the following chapter. The levels of population growth prior to this period are disputed, but a recent review of the Nottinghamshire evidence has led Bishop (2001, 2) to suggest that in the second and third centuries population levels in some areas could have equalled or even exceeded those postulated from data contained in the Domesday Survey of 1086. It is suggested below that such burgeoning population levels, if vindicated by future work, may have placed even greater strains upon carrying capacity than in

the later Iron Age, and hence may have represented major forces of socio-economic and environmental change. Fieldwalking and excavation in many neighbouring areas, including the less easily cultivated claylands to the south of the Trent, suggest similar demographic pressures (e.g. Clay 2002).

The arguments for significant population growth are supported first by the evidence of settlement distributions, assessment of which suggests expansion within established 'core' zones and the colonisation of areas that may have been largely unexploited in the Iron Age. Due regard must be paid to the problem of establishing which sites had been in contemporary use, but with this proviso there is persuasive evidence that some areas with long histories of occupation had witnessed significant increases in the density of settlement during the Roman occupation. This process of infilling may be demonstrated most convincingly by investigations at several large quarry sites where open-area excavations have permitted the assignation of dates to a broad range of features, mainly on the basis of associated pottery. These include Gonalston, where three Romano-British settlements overlapping broadly in date were excavated within an area of around 25ha, and Holme Pierrepont, where a cluster of four enclosure complexes spanning the Iron Age and Roman periods was exposed during excavations over an area of 1sq km (O'Brien 1979, fig.2). These settlements may be argued to have overlapped chronologically on the basis of associated finds, and hence cannot be interpreted as evidence merely of temporal shifts in the focus of occupation. They provide, therefore, a graphic impression of the density of settlement in this period, although this level of activity may not have been maintained throughout the entire length of the valley.

The case for increased settlement densities within established 'core' areas may be supported by the higher frequencies of Romano-British relative to Iron Age sites which have been recorded during systematic fieldwalking. Assessments of the greater abundance of Roman pottery should take account of its greater visibility and durability in comparison to much prehistoric pottery and, most crucially, the increased availability of mass-produced ceramic products. Interpretation is complicated further by uncertainties regarding the circumstances of deposition of this material and by the problem of establishing contemporaneity. In the latter case, however, the comparative precision which may be attained in the dating of Roman ceramics, commonly to half-century periods, renders this less of a problem than in earlier periods. Key surveys within the Trent Valley include the area around South Muskham, where systematic fieldwalking of an area of dense cropmarks plotted originally by Whimster (1989) suggested that a significant proportion of these could relate to Roman activity (Garton 2002). The regular layouts of fields and the close spacing of predominantly rectilinear ditched enclosures imply an element of deliberate planning, but the presence of earlier settlement foci suggests also that we should interpret these systems as evidence for large-scale reorganisation of an already settled landscape rather than wholesale colonisation (cf. Whimster 1989, 84–6). Other fieldwalking surveys within the region have prompted similar conclusions, as in the Trent Valley to the south of Derby. Extensive fieldwalking in that area by members of the Ockbrook and Borrowash Historical Society across a variety of geologies, including Mercia Mudstone and boulder clay, has demonstrated a hitherto unknown density of Roman activity within an area of known prehistoric settlement (Myers 2001, 9–10; Palfreyman 2001, 150–6). An average spacing of farmsteads broadly comparable to the modern distribution of post-Enclosure farms in the area has been postulated (ibid. 151), although it is debatable how many of these would have been in contemporary use.

There is, in addition, persuasive evidence to suggest the expansion of settlement into areas that may not have been occupied on a large scale during the first millennium BC. This is particularly apparent to the north of the Trent, where extensive blocks of 'brickwork plan' fields have been plotted (Garton 1987; Riley 1980). It was suggested in the previous chapter that the origins of this process may lie in the Late Iron Age, and hence the developments of the Roman period should perhaps be seen as a culmination of processes begun at a rather earlier date (Chapter 5.8.1; e.g. Dunston's Clump, Babworth, Nottinghamshire: Garton 1987; Pickburn Leys, South Yorkshire: Sydes and Symonds 1985). In the case of the 'brickwork plan' field systems, the evidence may signify expansion to areas which were previously regarded as marginal. Expansion to such areas, which are characterised by comparatively poor sandy soils particularly vulnerable to wind erosion once cleared of their protective woodland canopy, may reflect land shortages in long-settled areas such as the Trent Valley, although other factors such as improved farming techniques, new breeds of livestock and changes in the system of taxation may also have prompted the exploitation of hitherto marginal resources (Chapter 6.8.1).

One other important strand of evidence for significant population growth is an apparent increase in the spatial extent and structural complexity of many settlement units, together with pronounced increases in the quantity and diversity of associated artefacts. Appropriate consideration should be given in such cases to the possible impact of temporal shifts in the focus of occupation due to processes such as the decay and abandonment of dwellings, for such settlement drift could obviously create a wholly false impression of settlement size (cf. Bradley 1978, 21). In addition, caution should be urged in assuming a close correlation between artefact totals and population levels, for as noted above many other factors could have influenced the quantity and range of artefacts entering the archaeological record. These and other problems are discussed in greater detail in the following section, where the demographic implications of the processes of urbanisation and nucleation are considered.

6.7.2   The Spatial Organisation of Settlement

The pattern of settlement changed in several fundamental respects during the Roman period, with the superimposition of an elaborate network of roads and fortifications aimed primarily at expediting the military conquest of the province, the founding of local centres responsible for implementing provincial policies and the growth of a complex system of closely interrelated small towns, high-status villa complexes, nucleated agricultural settlements and enclosed farmsteads. The origins of enclosed farms and possibly nucleated settlements may be traced to the Late Iron Age (Chapter 5.7.2), but towns and villas represent entirely novel departures for the Trent Valley. This is in sharp contrast to areas farther south, where enclosed and territorial 'oppida' are well known components of the Late Iron Age landscape (Millett 1990, 21–8). At the same time, it is possible to demonstrate significant continuity with Late Iron Age traditions of settlement. Many urban and villa sites appear to have developed from Iron Age occupation foci, some of which could conceivably have coincided with the residences of the high-status groups implied by certain classes of Iron Age artefact but currently invisible within the settlement record. In addition, excavations and aerial photographic surveys throughout the valley have identified a high density of predominantly enclosed Romano-British settlements which in morphological terms differ little if at all from their Iron Age antecedents. These morphological similarities conceal some fundamental changes in their socio-economic status, for there is clear evidence that, to some extent, the Roman market economy impacted upon all categories of settlement from an early date, prompting the development of a complex network of social, political and economic links between communities within the valley and farther afield. These themes are discussed in greater detail below, commencing first with the imposition of military installations and the growth of towns and villa complexes. The discussion concludes with an assessment of the sizeable substratum of enclosed settlements which without excavation could so easily be mistaken for their Iron Age predecessors and the evidence for the transformation of some of these into nucleated settlements.

The military impact

The location of the Trent Valley, at the interface between the lowland and highland zones, ensured its importance as a key location for the launching of campaigns against the unruly upland tribes of the north and west; these comprised a socially heterogeneous mixture of indigenous tribes, grouped together by the Romans under the general heading of 'Brigantes'. The Trent is skirted to the east by the Fosse Way, constructed by the advancing army between the legionary fortresses of Exeter (*Isca*) and Lincoln (*Lindum*), while the Valley is crossed by an elaborate network of other Roman roads which originally would have linked a series of forts extending along the Trent and north-westwards into Brigantia (Todd 1969, 39–42; Whitwell 1982, 36–9, 44–7, fig.5). The major military route along the Fosse Way, immediately east of the Trent, provided links with an early fort at *Ad Pontem* (Burnham and Wacher 1990, 270–6; Forcey 1994; Whitwell 1982, 38) and possibly also forts at *Margidunum* (Kinsley and Knight 1992; Todd 1969; Whitwell 1982, 37–8) and *Crococalana*, Brough-on-Fosse (Vyner ed. forthcoming; Whitwell 1982, 39), although the nature of the military presence at the latter two sites is uncertain. Along the Trent itself, a possible military origin has been postulated on rather tenuous grounds for the town of *Segelocum* (Riley *et al.* 1995, 262), while in the upper reaches of the Trent early forts are known at Trent Vale and Chesterton, near the urban site of Holditch in Staffordshire (Burnham and Wacher 1990, 217–22). Beside the Derwent at Derby, immediately north of the river's confluence with the Trent, two successive forts may be identified – at Strutts Park, built in the AD 50's (Forrest 1967), and Little Chester, constructed in the AD 70's (Dool and Wheeler 1985). Elsewhere in the Trent Valley, unexplored forts have been recorded from the air in the alluvial floodplain at Holme, Nottinghamshire (McWhirr 1970, 12, plates 2–3; St Joseph 1961, 120; Whitwell 1982, 35), commanding a key crossing point of the Trent, and in riverside locations at Marton (St Joseph 1977, 128–9, fig.3; Whitwell 1982, 35–6) and Newton-on-Trent in Lincolnshire (St Joseph 1965, 74–5, fig.2, plate 10,1; Whitwell 1982, 35). In addition, at Sawley, Derbyshire, a small subrectangular earthwork enclosure on the Trent floodplain has been identified as a possible fortlet (Todd 1967). North and west of the Trent, an extensive network of early forts, marching camps and vexillation fortresses may be reconstructed (Whitwell 1982, 44–7), including the Nottinghamshire sites of Osmanthorpe (Bishop and Freeman 1993), Broxtowe (*Thoroton Soc. Excavation Section* 3, 1938, 6–17; Mackreth 1965; Whitwell 1982, 45), Farnsfield (Riley 1977), Calverton (*Britannia* 14, 1983, 270–1) and Gleadthorpe (*Britannia* 11, 1980, 330–5), Pentrich, Chesterfield and Brough-on-Noe in Derbyshire, and Rocester in Staffordshire (Dearne ed. 1993, 1–5).

The existing archaeological evidence for military installations ends in the late first century over most of the Trent Valley and immediately adjacent areas (probably in the AD 70's), except at Little Chester where military activity continued into the second century AD (*cf.* Dool and Wheeler 1985, table 24). Despite their short life as fortifications, however, these sites exerted a profound impact upon the social and economic organisation of the region. Several forts formed foci for later civilian settlements, and hence contributed to the progress of urbanisation – notably at *Ad Pontem* (Burnham and Wacher 1990, 270–6; Forcey 1994), Little Chester (Dool and Wheeler 1985; Sparey-Green 2002) and possibly *Segelocum* (Riley *et al.* 1995, 262). Reference should also be made at this point to the important small town of *Margidunum*, on the Mercia Mudstone escarpment immediately east of the Trent Valley, for although there may not necessarily have been a fort on this site its early phases display a strong military element (Todd 1969).

The economic and social impact of the military occupation is well illustrated by the ceramic evidence, for, as Willis (1996) has demonstrated, these early forts were crucial to the adoption of Roman pottery styles and traditions within a region which was otherwise slow to adopt ceramic change. This is reflected by the clear evidence for the importation of pots at Redcliff and Lincoln and the importation of foreign potters into the region to supply such forts as Rocester (Leary 1996a, 49) and Derby (Birss 1985; Brassington 1971; 1980). At *Margidunum,* fine wares of the first century seem to have been supplied from elsewhere in Britain and the Continent and by 'imported' potters, while coarse ware was provided locally in the form of 'Trent Valley Ware' (Todd 1968a). The latter shares many characteristics with local 'native' wares, but the consistently grey fabric identified by Todd is far harder than that found on neighbouring farmsteads such as Holme Pierrepont and Gonalston. This fabric was used for a distinctive range of coarse-ware jars with cordoned and corrugated bodies, contrasting with the Late Iron Age jars with simple bead and everted rims or cordoned neck jars with upright, flat-topped rims; it could have been made by potters brought from farther south, whose presence may be assumed to have impacted significantly upon established ceramic traditions. A similar situation can be detected at Littleborough, where Lyons Ware is attested alongside red slipped wares, probably from Lincoln, and 'Trent Valley' coarse wares (Riley *et al.* 1995, 272–3).

The spread of urbanisation

Several sites listed as towns in the Antonine Itinerary may be identified in the Trent Valley (*cf.* Whitwell 1982, table 3). These included many at former fort sites, including the above-mentioned riverbank settlements at *Ad Pontem* (Fig.6.9; Burnham and Wacher 1990; Forcey 1994; Inskeep 1965) and possibly *Segelocum* (Fig.6.2; Riley *et al.* 1995). Other named sites of particular significance for an understanding of the progress of urbanisation in the Trent Valley include *Margidunum* (Todd 1969), on the Mercia Mudstone escarpment flanking the eastern edge of the Valley, *Crococalana* (Vyner ed., forthcoming; Wooley 1910), on the broad fluvial terrace extending north-east of Newark, and the town of Little Chester, referred to in the

Fig.6.9 *Air photograph of Ad Pontem Roman town, Thorpe, Nottinghamshire, showing the truncation by fluvial erosion of the terrace-edge town defences; River Trent top left (copyright reserved Cambridge University Collection of Air Photographs; photograph reference BYL 10)*

seventh century Ravenna Cosmography as *Derbentione* after the adjacent River Derwent (Fig.6.10; Dool and Wheeler 1985; Sparey–Green 2002). It is suggested below that these named sites, in common with other 'small towns' in Britain (Burnham and Wacher, 1990, 1–6; Millett 1990, 143–56), may have housed significant population concentrations and are likely to have embraced a wide range of administrative, religious, industrial and trading functions which differentiate them from the primarily agricultural nucleated settlements and enclosed farmsteads that were scattered densely over their hinterlands.

Additional urban settlements, not referred to in the Antonine Itinerary or other documentary sources, have been identified in the upper reaches of the Trent Valley

at Holditch in Staffordshire (Burnham and Wacher 1990, 217–22) and possibly at Red Hill and Newark in Nottinghamshire, although interpretation of the latter two sites is particularly problematic. At Newark, evaluation excavations at the Warwick and Richardson's Brewery site to the north of the town centre revealed a wide spread of structural and artefactual remains which, in view of the deep stratigraphy and dense finds distributions observed in some trenches, would be more typical of an urban site such as *Margidunum* or *Crococolana* than a standard rural settlement (Kinsley *et al.* 1997). Comparable arguments may be advanced for the site at Red Hill, located on the Mercia Mudstone escarpment overlooking the Trent-Soar confluence. Archaeological investigations have revealed an extensive Romano-British site incorporating structures

Fig.6.10. *Plan of small town of Little Chester, Derby, and neighbouring sites (Canterbury Archaeological Trust: Peter Atkinson; source: Sparey-Green et al. 2002; reproduced by courtesy of C. Sparey-Green and the Derbyshire Archaeological Society)*

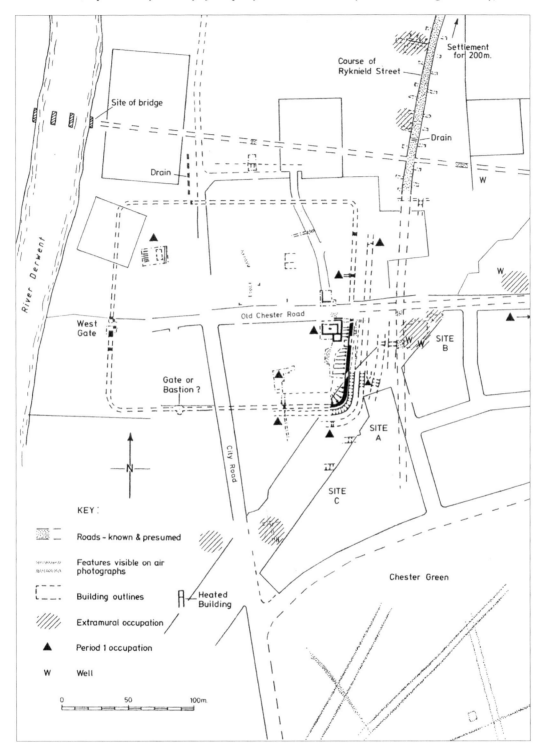

interpreted as a villa and temple, together with inhumation and cremation burials (e.g. Leary 1996b) and a rich artefact record indicative of extensive craft, industrial and trading activities (including metalwork, slag and other debris deriving from iron smithing and the working of copper alloy and lead, coins and pottery: Elsdon 1982; Palfreyman and Ebbins 2003). A recent reassessment of the evidence from this site has suggested a comparison with 'small towns' (*op. cit.*), and has reinterpreted the 'villa' as possibly a *mansio* comparable to that which it is suggested below may have serviced travelling Imperial officials at *Margidunum*.

The process of town development was clearly complex. As argued in the previous section, convincing evidence has been obtained from *Ad Pontem* and Little Chester for early fort phases, while Holditch was sited only 1km to the east of the fort at Chesterton (Burnham and Wacher 1990, 217). Claims for early forts at *Margidunum, Crococalana* and *Segelocum* have yet to be verified by excavation, although the artefact data provide compelling evidence for a significant military presence at the first of these sites. There is also a gradually accumulating body of evidence to suggest that some towns had developed on the sites of pre-Roman settlements. At *Ad Pontem,* excavations by Wacher revealed Late Iron Age structural remains sealed beneath the south-east rampart of the fort, including part of a of a curving gully interpreted by the excavator as the foundation trench of a circular hut with a cobbled floor (Wacher 1964, 160, fig.12). In addition, aerial photographs of the Roman town of *Crococalana* suggest that the town defences may overlie an earlier settlement focused upon a series of small ditched enclosures aligned along a trackway running obliquely across the defended area (Whimster 1989, 76, fig.55). This could signify an early Roman roadside settlement, preceding construction of the town defences, but the oblique alignment of the axial trackway relative to the Fosse Way must raise also the possibility of a pre-Roman origin for this settlement. Other evidence for early settlement near the Roman town was provided by the discovery during recent excavations immediately north of *Crococalana* of part of a large and complex later Iron Age settlement (Fig.5.16; Chapter 5.7.2). The relationship between this settlement and the pre-Roman remains which may be implied by aerial photographs of *Crococalana* remains uncertain, but its existence close to the later town emphasises at the very least the antiquity of settlement in its immediate hinterland. Reference should also be made to the discovery of several scatters of plain handmade Iron Age sherds during fieldwalking north-east and south-west of the defended core of *Margidunum* (Appleton *et al.* 2004, 9–10; Kinsley and Knight 1992, 24–5). In addition, 130 probable Iron Age sherds (including one fragment of Scored Ware) were retrieved from area-stratified deposits and a linear hollow in an evaluation trench dug to the south-west of the town (plus small numbers of redeposited Iron Age sherds in two other trenches: Kinsley and Knight 1992, 26–32: areas 01, 02 and 06). The discovery of Iron Age material hints at foci of pre-Roman activity in the vicinity of the defended core of the town, but the date and character of this activity remain uncertain.

Finds from *Margidunum* and other excavated sites within the region provide clear evidence of settlement growth from the immediate post-Conquest period, but the main period of urban expansion within the region appears generally to date from the later second century onwards. The reasons for this are not fully understood, but it has been suggested that changes in the nature of the imperial administrative structure may have been largely responsible for the burgeoning of both small towns and villas from the end of the second century (Millett 1990, 127–51). A change from cash taxation collected by the *civitates* to compulsory requisition, together with inflation, may have disadvantaged the *civitas* capitals and major towns. However, a shift to decentralised tax collection, together with a decline in the role of the major towns, would have benefited the small towns and may have prompted some movement of artisans and traders from the major to small towns.

The core areas of many of the small towns within the region were demarcated from as early as the late second century by ditches and ramparts, followed in succeeding centuries by impressive stone walls – as demonstrated, for example, by excavations at Little Chester and *Margidunum.* This could imply growing security concerns, although this development could also reflect in part competition between urban centres during the major period of their growth (Millett 1990, 139). These defended nuclei commonly formed only a small part of a far more extensive settlement, implying a sizeable population concentration. Excavations, combined with fieldwalking and geophysical survey, have revealed structural remains and artefact spreads extending far beyond the defended nuclei of many sites. At *Margidunum*, for example, these extended as ribbon development for at least half a kilometre along the Fosse Way either side of the defended core, and north-westwards along a Roman road followed today by Bridgford Street (Burnham and Wacher 1990, 260–4; Kinsley and Knight 1992). Few major public buildings have been recorded within these areas. The most notable exceptions include a complex of buildings at *Margidunum,* which it is suggested below might represent a *mansio,* and a temple and another possible *mansio* at Red Hill. Again, this comparative dearth of public buildings may reflect wider developments within the province and Empire-wide developments generally. The third and fourth centuries witnessed increasing discouragements to the curial class in terms of the financing of extensive public building works (Millett 1990, 130–1, 139). During this period, the display of wealth was focused upon villas rather than municipal buildings, although town security remained a concern and a curial burden. Although there is good evidence that Lincoln continued to fulfil an important role in provincial affairs, these developments clearly impacted on the small towns along the Trent Valley, which it appears had developed from the late second to fourth centuries in parallel with the enlargement and elaboration of nearby villas. The emphasis in the archaeological record of these small towns appears rather to have been upon dwellings and craft or industrial workshops (such as smithies), although discoveries of window glass, plain or painted wall plaster, brick, tile and *tesserae* from towns such as *Crococalana, Margidunum* and *Segelocum* suggest that buildings of pretension were present amongst the artisan households.

The small towns are likely to have performed a very wide range of functions, including key administrative roles such as the collection of taxation and service as imperial post stations. The latter may be demonstrated at *Margidunum,* where reassessment of Oswald's excavation plans suggests a structural complex comprising a building with hypocausts and other structures grouped around a courtyard that has recently been interpreted as probably part of a *mansio* (Burnham and Wacher 1990; *cf.* Red Hill: Palfreyman and Ebbins 2003). This would have served as an inn for the accommodation of individuals engaged in official duties on behalf of the imperial postal service (the *cursus publicus*). Finds of styli, inkpots and inscriptions provide measures of literacy at these centres, even if this were restricted only to the official and curial classes. The administrative as well as economic functions of these small towns are reflected also in the quantity of coinage recovered, which completely eclipses the very small numbers obtained from villas and rural sites (unpublished coin collections from *Crococalana* and *Margidunum* in Newark Museum and University of Nottingham Museum; also Ponting forthcoming). Links with religious activities are implied by the temple at Red Hill, assuming that this site is correctly interpreted as a small town, and by a wide variety of finds. We may note in particular the discovery at *Segelocum* of a stone altar inscribed ...../...../...*E.../lib(ertus) aram C*[. .] A (... freedman [set up] this altar), which illustrates the religious life of the settlement and conveys some impression of the wealth and status of some of the inhabitants (*Victoria County History Nottinghamshire* II, 1910, 22; RIB 277). In addition, excavations at *Margidunum* unearthed a variety of second century Central Gaulish votive pipe-clay figurines (Todd 1969, 93, plate 5), implying an associated temple or shrine, while the recovery of two head pots from a pool to the east of the putative *mansio* complex (Oswald 1956, plate V) may imply an association with ritual activity.

Marketing and production roles are emphasised by finds of artefacts and other material indicative of extensive craft and industrial activities, together with far-reaching trade connections facilitated probably by their ready access to riverine as well as road-based transport networks. Industrial activities are implied by finds indicative of activities such as iron smithing and smelting (e.g. at Little Chester, Holditch and *Margidunum*) or pottery production, including the early military pottery production at Little Chester (Langley and Drage 2000; Sparey-Green 2002) and *Margidunum* (Todd 1969). In addition, discoveries of imported goods such as pottery, tile, non-local building stone and querns imply an elaborate network of exchange links connecting these sites with neighbouring villas and other rural settlements as well as many other areas of Britain and the Continent. There is increasing evidence for the integration of towns with neighbouring rural sites, ranging from villas to enclosed settlements, although it remains unclear whether towns had acted as redistribution centres for goods or whether rural sites had benefited from passing riverine trade serving urban centres. Analysis of the artefacts from the nucleated settlement at Ferry Lane Farm, for example, has revealed an articulation with the exchange networks represented at *Crococalana*. Preliminary analysis of part of the assemblage has identified small numbers of traded fine wares such as samian and white ware flagons from as early as the first century and much higher levels of traded wares by the third and fourth centuries, drawing on sources at Lincoln, the Nene Valley, Mancetter-Hartshill and farther north along the Trent, together with imported goods such as Gaulish samian and Spanish amphorae. Future work is planned to compare the nature of the assemblages of the groups from Ferry Lane Farm and the villa at Norton Disney, Lincolnshire, with the aim of tracing similarities in the supply patterns which might substantiate the case for socio-economic articulation. On a wider scale, frequent discoveries of material such as Central Gaulish samian and imported amphorae provide clear evidence for the broader Continental connections of these sites, while detailed analyses of the proportions of such types provide the option of defining more closely the differences between individual sites. Amphorae, for example, are particularly well represented at Little Chester, where a considerable immigrant population might be expected because of the lengthy military occupation, and comparatively poorly represented at *Margidunum* and *Crococalana* where the military input may have been less pronounced and much shorter.

Villa complexes

Archaeological investigations have revealed a small number of rural settlements in the Middle and Lower Trent characterised by Romanised dwellings with rectangular ground-plans, stone walls and various combinations of 'Roman' structural elements such as solid floors, tessellated pavements, hypocausts and baths, which in accordance with convention may be classified as villas (see Hingley 1989, 20–2; Millett 1990, 91–8; Todd 1991, 84–102; Whitwell 1982, 93–6). Several examples have been recorded on the Trent terraces, notably at Cromwell in Nottinghamshire (Fig.6.11; Whimster 1989, 78–9; Whitwell 1982, 107–8) and Lockington in Leicestershire (Fig.6.12; Clay 1985; Whitwell 1982, 106–7), but most villas in the region have been recorded away from the Trent terraces. These include examples in valley locations at Barton-in-Fabis (Thompson 1951), plus examples along the Fosse Way at Newton (Appleton *et al.* 2004; Todd 1969, 12) and Car Colston in Nottinghamshire (Todd 1969, 71–2) and at Norton Disney (Oswald and Buxton 1937); north of the river, prestigious villas have been excavated at Southwell (Daniels 1966) and Mansfield Woodhouse (Oswald 1949) in Nottinghamshire. The few excavated examples of high status Romanised buildings within the region include both corridor and courtyard plans (*cf.* Hingley 1989, 45–54; Whitwell 1982, 94–110, table 5) and would have formed imposing buildings, resonant of wealth and social status.

Fig.6.11 *Aerial photograph of Cromwell villa, Nottinghamshire, with the River Trent in the background; villa building in centre of double-ditched enclosure. Reproduced by permission of English Heritage (NMR) Derek Riley Collection (photograph reference DNR 426/23, SK 8062/24)*

Fig.6.12 *Cropmark plan of Lockington villa, Leicestershire, and adjacent settlement (source: Clay 1985; reproduced by courtesy of Leicestershire County Council Environment and Heritage Services, Dr P. Clay and the Leicestershire Archaeological and Historical Society)*

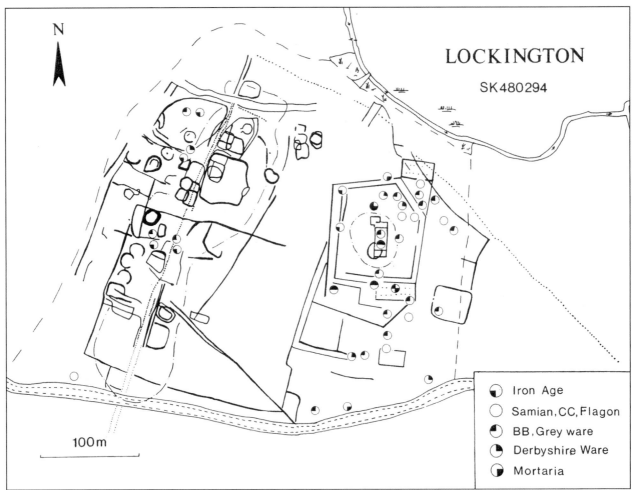

The concept of the villa carries significant connotations of the display of wealth (Millett 1990, 93–7) and attribution of a site to this category is not always a straightforward procedure (*cf.* Hingley 1989, 21). The problem of definition is aptly illustrated by the discovery of a mid-second to third century stone aisled building adjacent to a cobbled courtyard at Little Hay Grange, Ockbrook (Palfreyman 2001). Surface finds adjacent to the building, which was interpreted by the excavator as most probably a barn with storage and accommodation facilities, could signify a more extensive settlement complex. The building compares well with Romano-British aisled buildings recorded elsewhere in Britain (Hingley 1989, 39–45), including examples from elsewhere in the Trent Valley and neighbouring areas (e.g. Epperstone, Nottinghamshire; Whitwell 1982, 110–4, fig.19). Many of these have been recorded alongside winged corridor and courtyard villa buildings, but although the Ockbrook building is undoubtedly of Romanised form there are insufficient signs of surplus wealth for the term 'villa' to be applied with confidence.

Comparatively few of the small number of villas which have been positively identified in the Trent Valley or in immediately neighbouring areas have been extensively excavated, and hence details of their internal arrangements, relationship to adjacent structures, functions and chronological development are generally poorly known. Despite such difficulties, these impressive constructions may reasonably be viewed as the residences of the social elite, including probably the aristocracy involved in the administration of the pagus and towns. Finds such as the stylus from Norton Disney (Oswald and Buxton 1937, fig.4.55A) provide evidence of the level of education and sophistication to be expected from members of this class, while the range of rich artefacts and elaborate structural remains can leave no doubt of the high social and political status of their inhabitants. Many may have formed part of quite extensive settlements, to judge by the complex cropmark plots of the Cromwell (Fig.6.11; Whimster 1989 fig. 59) and Lockington (Fig.6.12; Clay 1985, fig.2) villas and the results of recent geophysical investigations and fieldwalking immediately south-west of *Margidunum* on the site of the Newton villa (Appleton *et al.* 2004). These surveys suggest very extensive villa complexes, possibly with a variety of building types, within which the villa building may have occupied only a relatively small part, and hence may imply quite large population groupings extending beyond the single extended family (*cf.* Hingley 1989, 59–71). Dating is problematic, but current evidence would suggest that some at least may have developed from pre-Roman occupation foci – as perhaps at Cromwell (Whimster 1989, 78–9) or, just outside the study area, at

Fig.6.13 *Plan of Romano-British enclosures and trackway at Whitemoor Haye, Staffordshire (source: Coates 2002; reproduced by permission of Birmingham Archaeology)*

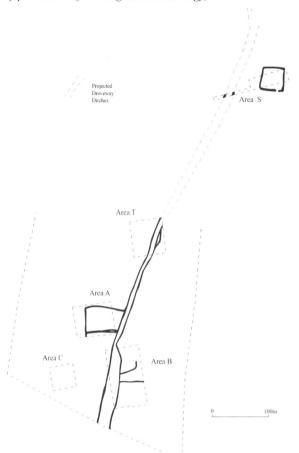

This relationship extended also to other categories of site, including the above-mentioned aisled building at Ockbrook. The pattern of Black Burnished (BB1) pottery at Derby compared with that from the nearby Romanised site at Ockbrook is so close as to suggest that some sites had a close relationship with the small town from a relatively early date.

Enclosed farmsteads

Forts, towns and villas were superimposed upon a landscape of single- or multiple-ditched rectilinear enclosures, commonly integrated with extensive systems of fields, paddocks, ponds and trackways, which in morphological terms appear to have differed little from those which came to dominate the Valley landscape during the later first millennium BC (Chapter 5.7.2). Such enclosures compare closely in terms of their layout, shape and size with their later Iron Age predecessors, and hence cannot realistically be distinguished from these without excavation. The problem of differentiation is illustrated by a sub-rectangular ditched enclosure at Gamston, Nottinghamshire, which may be distinguished typologically from a nearby Iron Age enclosure only by its greater internal area (Knight 1992, 28–34: Enclosures 1 and 2), two multi-phase enclosure complexes at Willington (Wheeler 1979, 105–25: Farmsteads I and II) and, either side of a ditched 'droveway' at Whitemoor Haye, two Romano-British subrectangular ditched enclosures which on typological grounds could equally well date from the Iron Age (Fig.6.13; Coates and Woodward 2002, 85–7).

Comparatively few Romano-British enclosed settlements within the region have been extensively excavated, but current evidence would suggest that a significant proportion correlate with the habitation foci of small farming communities on the scale of an extended family group – with the proviso that, as on many Iron Age sites, occupation could also have extended significantly beyond the enclosed area. Typical examples include the above-mentioned subrectangular ditched enclosure at Gamston, an enclosure complex at Bottom Osiers, Gonalston (Elliott and Knight 1997) and an enclosed settlement at Captain's Pingle, Barrow-upon-Trent (Knight and Southgate 2001). The first of these was only partially excavated, but revealed in one quadrant a significant cluster of pits, some possibly contemporary with its use, which may have been utilised for purposes such as grain storage. No structural remains indicative of internal occupation were obtained, although such evidence could have survived within the unexcavated area. The site at Bottom Osiers, by contrast, was fully excavated ahead of gravel extraction, permitting reconstruction of an unusually complete plan of the settlement and its associated field system. Developing from Iron Age roots, this site was characterised in the later second century AD by a large multiple-ditched enclosure linked via a ditched trackway to an extensive system of paddocks and fields (Fig.6.14; Elliott and Knight 1997, fig.2c). Little evidence was obtained for internal domestic structures, apart from several penannular gullies that may have drained the areas of timber roundhouses. These gullies yielded few associated artefacts and could represent Iron

Norton Disney (Oswald and Buxton 1937). The main period of their development, however, may have been from the late second century, contemporary therefore with the major phase of expansion of small towns.

Close links are implied with small towns, around which many villas were clustered. It has long been noted how some villas along the Fosse Way were concentrated around small towns. This is particularly evident in the vicinity of *Margidunum* (Todd 1969, 71–3), which is located centrally to the nearby Nottinghamshire villas of Car Colston, Newton, Shelford and Bingham. The relationship of the villa at Norton Disney with the small town at *Crococalana* may be similar, while analysis of pottery collected during recent fieldwalking at Sturton-le-Steeple outside *Segelocum* suggests a community with access to significant amounts of traded wares in the third and fourth centuries (at a comparable level to villas and small towns, but more than might be expected of a farmstead (Leary 2003). The elaboration of villas may be linked to the growth in activity at the small towns, and similar materials were sometimes used to embellish buildings in both. At *Margidunum*, for example, Oswald's 'late house' was provided with Charnwood slate roof-tiles comparable to those recovered during recent fieldwalking of the nearest villa at Newton (Appleton *et al.* 2004). In addition, available data suggest that villas around the towns were able to access a range of table-wares and traded goods not dissimilar to those supplied to towns by at least the late second century.

Fig.6.14 *Plan of early Romano-British enclosure complex at Bottom Osiers, Gonalston, Nottinghamshire; early Roman features denoted by black shading (source: Elliott and Knight 1997; reproduced by permission of the Thoroton Society of Nottinghamshire)*

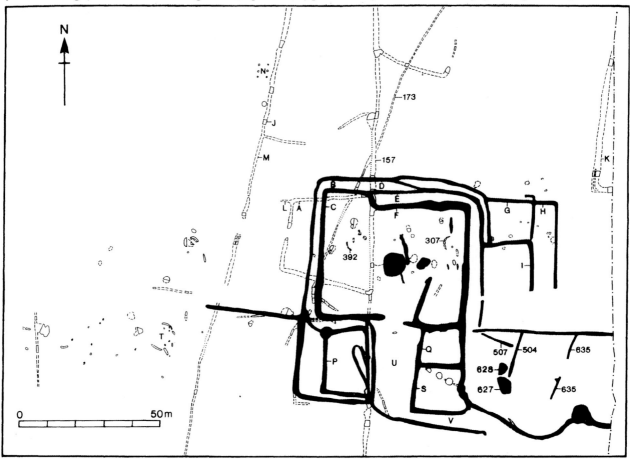

Age rather than Roman activity. As elsewhere within the region, however, there is every possibility that on this site Iron Age architectural traditions had lingered long into the Roman period. At Captain's Pingle, excavations revealed three sides of a probable subrectangular ditched enclosure linked stratigraphically to an extensive system of field boundaries continuing beyond the focus of excavation. Occupation is implied by extensive quantities of domestic rubbish, including pottery, *tegulae* and other tiles, querns, rare coins and objects of iron, copper alloy and lead. However, the only structural remains which could have been contemporary with the period of use of the enclosure include several hearth bases, at least one floored with *tegulae*, fragmentary fired clay ovens, scattered pits and post-holes and a small annular ditched enclosure, only *c*.4m in diameter, which has been interpreted as possibly a drainage gully associated with a stack-stand.

Although some enclosures fully or partially demarcated habitation areas, others may have performed more specialised roles connected with activities such as the maintenance of stock, grain storage and the cultivation of small garden plots. Specialised agricultural functions have been suggested for enclosures at sites such as Whitemoor Haye (Coates and Woodward 2002, 87–88), Fisherwick (Miles 1969, 7–13) and Willington (Wheeler 1979, 117, 121), where a range of ditched and palisaded enclosures have been variously interpreted as compounds linked with stock management and as areas demarcated for the processing and storage of crops. It should be emphasised

also that a significant number of sites may have comprised several contemporary enclosures performing a variety of functions, recalling therefore the model proposed for many later first millennium BC settlements within the region (Chapter 5.7.2).

Agriculture was undoubtedly the mainstay of these communities, although as emphasised previously, many questions remain regarding the balance between arable and pasture and the nature of the crop and animal husbandry regimes. It is possible that many settlements within the Valley, particularly sites such as Gonalston or Captain's Pingle which were located on low river terraces with ready access to potentially rich pasture resources, had performed specialised pastoral functions. Some of these might have been occupied only during the drier summer months, perhaps within the framework of a system of transhumance linking sites in low-lying and flood-prone environments with permanent home bases on the higher and drier gravel terraces and beyond (*cf.* Coates and Woodward 2002, 88–90). This recalls the landscape model that was proposed long ago in the Upper Thames on the basis of excavations at Iron Age and Roman sites such as Farmoor, Oxfordshire (Lambrick and Robinson 1979), but only now are excavations in the Trent Valley amassing a body of palaeoenvironmental data that should permit testing of this hypothesis. It is hoped that forthcoming analyses of the palaeobotanical assemblages obtained from major quarry sites such as Barrow-upon-Trent, Gonalston and East Carr, Mattersey will help elucidate this question, and hence permit more accurate assessment not only of the agrarian economy but also the probable density of permanent settlements and hence population levels.

Many of the above sites have yielded evidence for engagement in a wide range of craft and industrial activities, geared apparently towards both local and regional consumption (*cf.* Bishop 2001, 6–7; Taylor 2001, 15–18; Whitwell 1982, 130–40). The site at Captain's Pingle, for example, yielded extensive evidence for iron-working in the form of smithing slag, plano-convex hearth bottoms and part of a fired clay tuyère, while non-ferrous metal droplets suggest the working of copper alloy (Knight and Southgate 2001). Such settlements seem to have been bound into an extensive network of social and economic links connecting towns, villas and rural settlements. Comparative quantitative studies of the artefact assemblages recovered from these sites have great potential for characterising the relationships between elements of the town and country in the Trent Valley. There is some evidence that rural sites were able to purchase the range of available traded wares, although in rather lower quantities than the higher status villa and town sites, even in the second century. This may be demonstrated by the small quantities of early second century Black Burnished (BB1) wares and Roman fine wares such as samian which have been found at Holme Pierrepont, Gonalston and other Trent Valley rural settlements (e.g. Elliott and Knight 1997, 71, fig.3). Further evidence for widespread and regular access to traded commodities is provided by regular discoveries of quernstones, many of Millstone Grit deriving from Pennine production sources, which have been noted on enclosed farmsteads such as Gonalston (*ibid.* 71; Elliott and Knight 2003, 202), Holme Pierrepont (*East Midlands Archaeological Bulletin* 10, 1974, 43), Captain's Pingle (Knight and Southgate 2001) and other sites dispersed widely over the river-terraces.

Nucleated settlements

A small number of rural settlements stand out from the majority of sites by merit of the complexity and spatial extent of their structural remains, and raise the possibility of nucleated villages serving as habitation foci for multiple family groups (*cf.* Millett 1990, 205–11). These typically comprise clusters of multi-phased ditched enclosures and dense structural remains, spreading over several hectares, which are integrated closely with ditched trackways and field systems. The transition from 'farmstead' to 'village' is not easily defined, but the sheer density of archaeological remains at some settlements within the Valley suggests strongly that we should identify a distinct class of 'agglomerated' or 'nucleated' settlement. A number of nucleated settlements may extend over areas at least as large as some 'small towns', and in common with some of these may yield significant evidence for craft, industrial and trading activities and may exhibit regularity in their planning. These include Ferry Lane Farm (Fig.6.15), where a regular layout of trackways and enclosures resembling the late Roman plan postulated at *Segelocum* (Riley *et al.* 1995, 254–6, fig.2) has been suggested (Bishop 2001, 5), and Rampton, where the later phases of the settlement incorporated a massive subrectangular ditched enclosure divided into a series of smaller subrectangular enclosures separated and linked by trackways (Knight 2000).

It was suggested in the previous chapter that the roots of nucleation might lie in the Late Iron Age, at sites such as Ferry Lane Farm (Bourn *et al.* 2000), Rampton (Knight 2000), Brough-on-Fosse (Vyner ed., forthcoming) and Lockington, Leicestershire (Clay 185; 2001, 3; Chapter 5.7.2). The progress from Iron Age open settlement to late Roman nucleated settlement is perhaps best illustrated by the complex stratigraphic sequence recorded during recent excavations at Rampton, although final judgement on the proposed sequence of development must await full publication of the results of excavation. Archaeological investigations in advance of gravel quarrying revealed an extensive Iron Age and Romano-British settlement extending for approximately six hectares across the Holme Pierrepont Terrace and several low-lying alluvial depressions (Fig.6.16). The lower-lying parts of the site were buried beneath thick alluvium, suggesting that it may have been abandoned eventually in response to rising water levels and increases in flooding (Chapter 6.3.2). The site stands out from most other excavated rural settlements of this period in the Trent Valley on the grounds of its considerable spatial extent, structural complexity and exceptional wealth of finds. Even more remarkable was the preservation within the main occupation focus of a significant depth of stratified deposits, up to about 0.5m thick, rich in pottery and other artefacts, material derived from domestic or industrial hearths (layers of black, grey and orange ash, concentrations of charcoal and spreads of smithing slag), demolished buildings (*tegulae*, other tile fragments, stone rubble and daub) and domestic middens (incorporating pottery, broken querns, animal bone and other rubbish). These were interleaved with *in situ* domestic or industrial hearths and clay floors, recorded at various stratigraphic levels, implying a complex sequence of activity within the core area. Preliminary assessment of the stratigraphic relationships between features suggests a sequence of at least five main phases, commencing probably with an Early or Middle Iron Age open settlement including a post-built roundhouse and a scatter of pits and post-holes (Phase 1). Later stratigraphic phases, spanning the Late Iron Age to late Roman periods, witness the development of a rectilinear boundary system (Phase 2), followed by the construction of two large sub-rectangular ditched enclosures divided internally into smaller enclosed units (Phases 3–4). A pit alignment running northwards towards a palaeochannel of the Trent, which at the time of occupation probably formed a marshy depression, may have formed an eastern boundary during Phases 3 and 4. Several of the pit fills yielded Roman sherds, adding some weight to the suggestion that the pit alignment was an integral component of the Roman settlement plan. A final late Roman phase (5) may be represented, more speculatively, by a series of rectilinear fenced enclosures overlying the Phase 4 enclosure. The foundations of numerous roundhouses and other circular or rectilinear structures (including several annular gullies which might have drained stacks of hay or fodder and a four-post setting which might mark the foundations of a granary) were also recorded, but few of these may be related stratigraphically to features of the above phases. An exceptionally large quantity of Iron Age and Romano-British pottery was recovered (totalling some 15,000 sherds), together with daub, fired clay, *tegulae* and

Fig.6.15 *Cropmark complex at Ferry Lane Farm, Collingham, Nottinghamshire (copyright reserved Cambridge University Collection of Air Photographs; photograph reference CJO 33)*

other tile fragments, smithing slag, rotary querns, ironwork, copper alloy brooches, coins and occasional exotic items such as a gilded jadeite pin, indicating unusually intensive activity. Comparisons with other site assemblages should, however, take account of the preservation beneath alluvium of much of the settlement and the possibility that this may have exaggerated to some extent the richness of the artefact assemblage in comparison with plough-denuded sites.

6.8   Systems of Land Allotment

Excavation and crop-mark data suggest a significant expansion of field systems in the Trent Valley and neighbouring areas during the Roman period, creating in some areas vast landscapes of enclosure. These include the well-ordered 'brickwork-plan' field systems of north Nottinghamshire and South Yorkshire which were first

identified by Riley (1980; Garton 1987) and the extensive pattern of coaxial fields which was highlighted by Whimster (1989) in his aerial photographic survey of the lower Trent Valley to the north of Newark. These systems are discussed below in turn, followed by consideration of the evidence obtained from elsewhere in the region for field systems and possible territorial boundaries of this period.

6.8.1   Brickwork Plan Field Systems

These systems were first identified by Riley, who allocated the term 'brickwork' as a graphic description of the dense patterns of elongated rectilinear fields which show as crop- and soil-marks over extensive tracts of the Sherwood Sandstone outcrop in north Nottinghamshire and South Yorkshire (Riley 1980). These systems are known to penetrate eastwards as far as the Idle Valley (at East Carr,

Fig. 6.16 *Simplified plan of Romano-British nucleated settlement at Moor Pool Close, Rampton, Nottinghamshire, showing features revealed by excavation and their relationship to overlying alluvium and pre-Roman palaeochannel deposits; brown and grey sand not distinguished in pipeline corridor (source: Knight 2000; revised by S. Baker and D. Gilbert)*

Mattersey: Morris and Garton 1998a; 1998b; Fig.6.17–18) and southwards as far as Ramsdale, immediately north of Nottingham (Garton *et al.* 2000), but appear not to have extended into the Trent Valley. The processes leading to their formation are nonetheless of fundamental significance for an understanding of landscape developments in the Valley, and hence merit consideration here.

It was suggested in the previous chapter that the origins of 'brickwork-plan' field systems may lie in the Late Iron Age (*cf.* Chadwick 1999), together with a limited number of rectilinear field systems in the Trent Valley that may be related distantly to these systems (e.g. Gamston: Knight 1992; Lamb's Close, Kelham: Knight and Priest 1998). The bulk of the dating evidence, however, would support a Roman date (e.g. Garton 1987), although considerable doubts remain regarding the longevity of these systems. The origins and functions of 'brickwork plan' fields have spurred much debate, but it seems reasonable to interpret them as evidence for continuing and probably growing pressures upon the landscape. We have explored earlier in this chapter the evidence for population growth and the possibility of retreat during the later Roman period from some well-established areas as a result of increasing flooding and the expansion of valley wetlands. This may have prompted expansion to new areas, and could explain

the colonisation of areas such as the Sherwood Sandstones whose thin sandy soils would have been especially prone to soil erosion. Excavations of some settlements which are closely related to these field systems have yielded charred remains of cereal crops, including at Dunston's Clump six-rowed hulled barley, rye, flax, spelt wheat, bread wheat, and possibly emmer wheat and cultivated oats (Jones 1987), which may imply the cultivation as well as the processing of crops. However, crop cultivation on the easily eroded sandy soils of the Sherwood Sandstones would have required a heavy investment in animal husbandry if productivity were to be maintained (Garton 1987, 65), and we might speculate whether the emphasis in these areas may have been upon livestock management.

6.8.2 Newark Coaxial Field Systems

Although originating possibly in the Late Iron Age (Chapter 5.8.1), a predominantly Roman date range may be suggested for the coaxial field systems which have been observed from the air along the Trent Valley to the north of Newark (Fig.6.19; Garton 2002; Whimster 1989, figs 60–61). These coaxial systems extend in some areas beyond the present terrace edge beneath alluvium or colluvium, as demonstrated during excavations of a rectilinear field system which may have straddled the Late Iron Age and

Fig.6.17 *Plan of rectilinear field system at East Carr, Mattersey, Nottinghamshire (drawing: J. Goddard, based upon plan in Garton et al. 1995)*

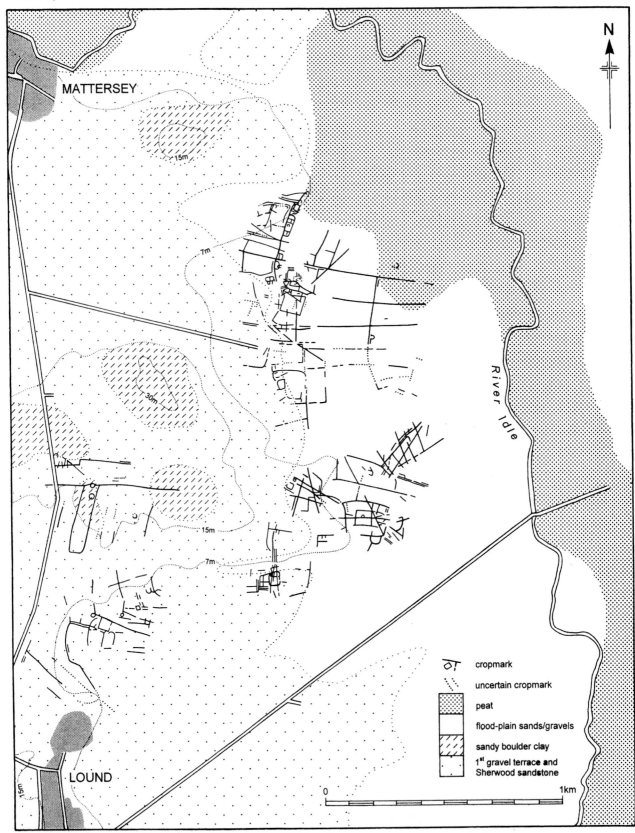

Fig.6.18 *Toolmarks formed during the excavation of field boundary ditches at East Carr, Mattersey, Nottinghamshire (photograph: T. Morris)*

Roman periods at Lamb's Close, Kelham (Knight and Priest 1998). They provide a graphic image of a highly organised landscape in which densely distributed rectilinear enclosures were tied in to a well-planned landscape of coaxial fields and trackways, reminiscent in general terms of the patterns of fields and enclosures which characterise the 'brickwork plan' field systems to their north and west (Garton 1987; Riley 1980).

In view of the marked regularities which may be discerned in the spacing of enclosures and the organisation of adjacent field areas, there seems little doubt that the fully developed landscape had incorporated a dense network of broadly contemporary settlements set within a tightly managed agricultural landscape. Considerably more palaeoenvironmental data are required before we can speculate on the relative roles of pasture and arable or on the possibility of functional differences between these valley systems and those prevailing on the Sherwood Sandstones. Significant differences may emerge, but we should beware at present of reading too much into the obvious typological contrasts between these systems. The Trent Valley presents a very different topography to the expansive Sherwood Sandstone uplands, with gravel islands of variable size and shape bounded and cut by intricate patterns of palaeochannels and active streams, and the observed morphological differences could well reflect in large part the variable spatial restraints imposed by topography.

6.8.3 Other Field Systems

Many Romano-British settlements in other parts of the Trent Valley preserve associated field systems, sometimes incorporating rectilinear arrangements of land plots reminiscent of those observed to the north of Newark, but as yet no other area of the Valley has yielded evidence for such an extensive landscape of coaxial fields and associated settlements. Some of these field systems have earlier origins, as at Gamston, where the Phase 3 rectilinear field system, dated by associated Late La Tène pottery to the mid-first century AD, could well have continued in use following the superimposition upon this system of a rectilinear ditched enclosure (Phase 4; Knight 1992, 31–3). Other field systems may represent innovations of the post-Conquest period, as at Bottom Osiers, Gonalston (Elliott and Knight 1997, fig.2c), Willington (Wheeler 1979, 116–7, 125, fig.42) and Whitemoor Haye (Coates and Woodward 2002, 88), where broadly rectilinear arrangements of field ditches dated by associated Roman pottery have been recorded over wide areas adjacent to excavated settlement foci. Taken together, this evidence would support the argument that the Roman landscape of much of the Trent Valley had been sub-divided between quite closely spaced settlements, separated by areas that may have been largely cleared and divided into field blocks. Areas of managed coppice or pollard and tracts of wild wood would still have survived on the floodplain and river terraces, as argued above (Chapter 6.5), but current evidence suggests that such areas were not especially extensive.

Attention should be drawn finally to the presence on several excavated settlements of clusters of small land parcels around the settlement focus, contrasting with more expansive field areas away from the main area of habitation. Such arrangements are hard to interpret, especially because of the difficulty of establishing which features were in contemporary use, but the smaller land units close to habitation areas might have been used for purposes such a stock pens or intensively cultivated vegetable plots. This contrast is especially pronounced at Rampton, where the settlement focus correlates with a complex arrangement of small ditched enclosures set within a system of large rectilinear fields covering an area of at least six hectares (Knight 2000). These small ditched enclosures coincided with the thick finds-rich layer described earlier in this chapter, a proportion of which might have been redeposited with the intention of building up and enhancing the soil adjacent to the main occupation focus. There is every likelihood that prolonged cultivation of the sandy soils of the Holme Pierrepont Terrace would have caused significant soil loss through erosion, and this may have encouraged the farming community to improve and deepen the soil by the addition of manure and other organic waste. This would have created, effectively, an infield area which could have been used for more intensive cultivation and for the stalling of animals whose manure would have enhanced yet further the soil fertility. The source of the sediment component of this putative artificial soil is more problematic, but one possibility is the incorporation of wind-blown sand. The recent excavations provided graphic evidence for the accumulation of substantial depths of wind-blown sand in

Fig.6.19 *Plan of coaxial field system at South Muskham, Nottinghamshire, and the distribution of Romano-British pottery recovered during systematic fieldwalking (source: Garton 2002; reproduced by permission of D. Garton and the Thoroton Society of Nottinghamshire)*

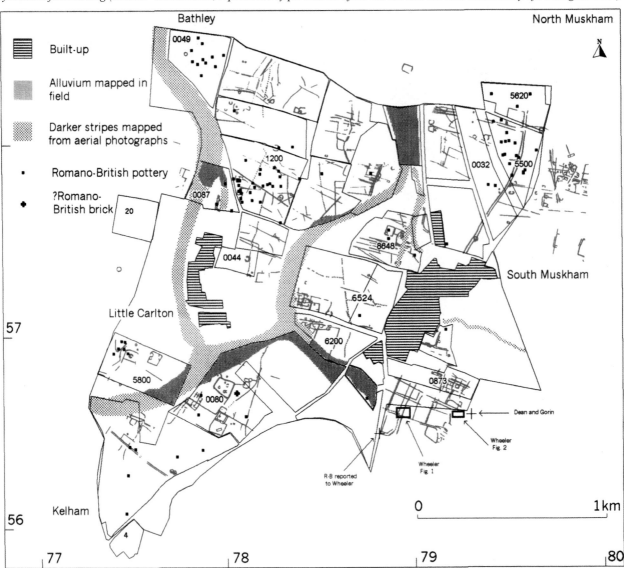

6.8.4 Pit Alignments

It was suggested in the previous chapter that pit alignments may have developed in the Trent Valley during the later first millennium BC, broadly contemporary with the proposed shift in emphasis from open to enclosed settlement, and may have continued to demarcate substantial blocks of land well into the Roman period (Chapter 5.8.2). The argument for a late continuation of these boundary monuments is supported strongly by the spatial arrangement of pit alignments within the coaxial field systems around the Nottinghamshire villages of North and South Muskham, which it was suggested earlier in this section may have developed mainly during the Roman period (Chapter 6.8.2; Whimster 1989, figs 60–61). Direct dating evidence in support of this argument is almost entirely absent, however, with the notable exception of an excavated pit alignment at Rampton (Knight 2000). Excavations at that site uncovered a pit alignment forming one side of a large rectilinear enclosure dated firmly to the Roman period on

the basis of associated pottery and its spatial relationship to the ditches forming the remainder of this enclosure. Further targeted excavations on pit alignments which appear to be closely integrated with Roman settlement complexes might clarify further the later history of this rather enigmatic monument class, although the general paucity of finds from excavated examples elsewhere in the region suggests that associated finds are likely to be retrieved only in exceptional circumstances.

6.9 Conclusions: the Trent as a Social Boundary?

One of the main themes to emerge from this study is the role of the Trent Valley as a zone of transition between the Romanised lowland zone towards the south and east, with its elaborate networks of Roman towns, roadside settlements, villas and other rural settlements, and the more militarised zone to the north and west. Few civilian settlements northwards of the Trent may be shown to have grown to any size, and as at key Pennine sites such as *Navio*, near Brough-on-Noe, their development was strongly

sheltered environments in windy conditions and, assuming extensive Romano-British cultivation, aeolian sands could have provided a steady source of sediment raw materials.

Fig.6.20 *Romano-British sites referred to in the text; compiled by S. Baker*
(1.Ad Pontem [Thorpe]; 2.Adlingfleet; 3.Aldwincle; 4.Aslockton; 5.Barrow-upon-Trent; 6.Barton-in-Fabis; 7.Belper; 8.Bingham; 9.Brough-on-Humber;
10.Broxtowe; 11.Calverton; 12.Car Colston; 13.Chesterfield; 14.Chesterton; 15.Crococolana [Brough-on-Fosse]; 16.Croft; 17.Cromwell; 18.Derby; 19.Dunston's
Clump; 20.Farnsfield; 21.Ferry Lane Farm [Collingham]; 22.Fisherwick; 23.Gainsborough; 24.Gamston; 25.Girton; 26.Gleadthorpe; 27.Gonalston; 28.Great
Wilne; 29.Gunthorpe; 30.Holditch; 31.Holme; 32.Holme Pierrepont; 33.Hoveringham; 34.Kelham; 35.Knaith; 36.Laxton; 37.Lea; 38.Lincoln; 39.Little Chester
[Derby]; 40.Little London; 41.Lockington; 42.Lound; 43.Mansfield Woodhouse; 44.Margidunum [East Bridgford]; 45.Marton; 46.Mattersey; 47.Meering;
48.Navio [Brough-on-Noe]; 49.Newark; 50.Newton; 51.Newton Cliffs; 52.Newton-on-Trent; 53.North Muskham; 54.Norton Disney; 55.Nottingham;
56.Ockbrook; 57.Osmanthorpe; 58.Pentrich; 59.Pickburn Leys; 60.Rampton; 61.Ramsdale; 62.Redcliff; 63.Redhill; 64.Rocester; 65.Sandtoft; 66.Sawley;
67.Scaftworth; 68.Segelocum [Littleborough]; 69.Shardlow; 70.Shelford; 71.South Ferriby; 72.South Muskham; 73.Southwell; 74.Staythorpe; 75.Sturton-le-
Steeple; 76.Swarkestone Lowes; 77.Sykehouse; 78.Torksey; 79.Trent Vale; 80.Vernemetum [Willoughby-on-the-Wolds]; 81.Whitemoor Haye; 82.Willington;
83.Winthorpe; 84.Wood Burcote; 85.Worksop)

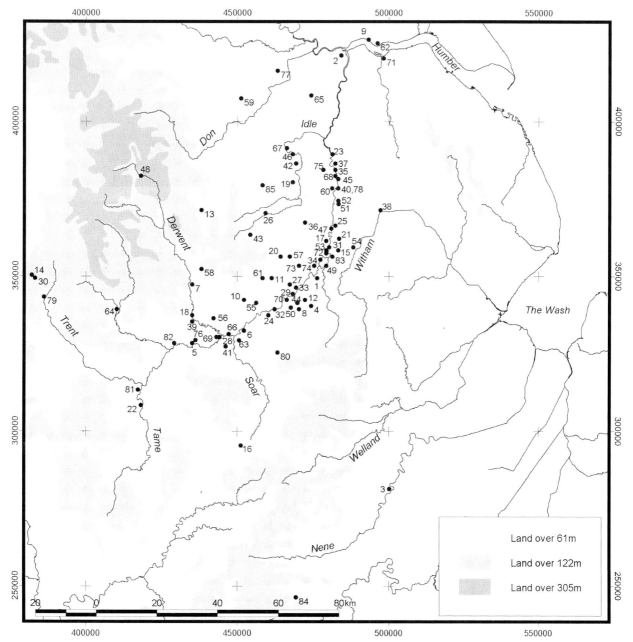

linked to neighbouring military establishments (Dearne ed. 1993). This contrasts starkly with areas to the south and east of the Trent, particularly along the Nottinghamshire Fosse Way, with its string of flourishing small towns such as *Margidunum, Ad Pontem, Crococalana, Vernemetum* and possibly Newark, and its hinterland of wealthy villas, nucleated settlements and enclosed farmsteads.

This spatial distinction between areas north and south of the Trent is reflected also in the distribution of Romano-British

pottery away from the early military sites, analysis of which provides interesting evidence for several stylistic zones respecting the river valley. These zones are particularly clearly defined in the first and early second centuries on civilian sites. First century assemblages south and east of the Trent are characterised by coarse bead-rim jars and large wide-mouthed bucket-shaped vessels plus fine cordoned carinated bowls, butt beakers and platters of Aylesford-Swarling affinity, while west and north of the river earlier Iron Age forms persisted alongside Late Iron

Age wheel-thrown jars with bead rims, upright flat-topped rims and neck cordons (Leary 1987 fig.17.1–5; Ponsford 1992, fig.19). This north-south contrast persisted into the later first century, when the civilian assemblages adjacent to and south of the Trent were dominated by coarse bead–rim jars and corrugated and cordoned jars with everted rims, plus a proportion of carinated and cordoned bowls and cups, platters and butt beaker type vessels. By contrast, site assemblages northwards of the Trent became progressively poorer and more restricted in range. From the end of the first century, the growing impact of Roman technology and a new distributive network can be seen in the civilian assemblages, with increased proportions of grey ware vessels and new Roman forms appearing on civilian sites along the Trent Valley. The ubiquitous rusticated ware spread both sides of the Trent and the regional zoning was overlaid with wares achieving wider distributions. From the mid to late second century onwards, four regional types of lid-seated jar developed. These comprised Dales ware and Dales ware type, made predominantly in Yorkshire and Lincolnshire, Derbyshire ware, produced around Belper, grey ware lid-seated jars made in South Yorkshire kilns, and a bifid rim jar manufactured in kilns in South Yorkshire and near Torksey at Little London. The geographical spread of these kilns and their core distribution zones seem to have maintained the stylistic zones noted earlier, but the distribution of finished products indicates changes in the nature of pottery distribution at some levels. The distribution of Dales ware, for example, crossed west of the Trent (Loughlin 1977, 116–25), while Derbyshire ware spread eastwards in small quantities. These wider distribution patterns suggest a breach in the Trent Valley border

argued for the earlier stylistic zones, but the more restricted distributions indicate the continuation of earlier patterns in some of the exchange networks. Although new forms such as the burnished ware jars and bowls were adopted across the region, other types may not have been distributed more widely and may retain those earlier stylistic boundaries – as Todd has suggested for East Midlands burnished ware (Todd 1968b). The extended distribution of traded coarse wares such as Dales and Derbyshire ware was matched by the increase of traded wares such as black burnished wares, Nene valley and Swanpool colour coated wares, Mancetter-Hartshill mortaria, flagons and samian.

Some intriguing parallels may be drawn between the stylistic zoning of Romano-British wares, described above, and the spatial patterning of later Iron Age La Tène-decorated pottery and Scored Ware (Knight 2002, fig.12.4; 12.5). Scored Ware rarely penetrates north or west of the Trent, while the La Tène-decorated wares of Lincolnshire have yet to be recorded beyond the Trent. A broadly similar pattern may be observed with the distribution of Corieltauvian coins, which are distributed mainly to the east and south of the Trent from the Humber to the Nene, thinning out significantly north and west of the river (May 1994; Whitwell 1982, fig.4). The spatial distribution of coins has suggested to some scholars that the Trent may well have formed a major political or economic boundary at this time (*ibid.* 19) and it is interesting to speculate whether the stylistic zoning of coins and pottery could reflect the role of the river valley as a border zone between social groupings corresponding broadly to the Corieltauvi and Brigantes.

REFERENCES

Appleton, E., Brown, J., Kinsley, G., Knight, D., Leary, R. and Johnson, T. 2004.
A46 Newark to Widmerpool Improvement. Geophysical survey, Fieldwalking and Landscape Interpretation at Margidunum, Nottinghamshire. Unpublished report, Trent & Peak Archaeological Unit, University Park, Nottingham.

Barber, K.E., Chambers, F.M., Maddy, D., Stoneman, R. and Brew, J.S. 1994.
A sensitive high-resolution record of late Holocene climatic change from a raised bog in northern England, *The Holocene* 4, 198–205.

Barber, K.E., Maddy, D., Rose, N., Stevenson, A.C., Stoneman, R. and Thompson, R. 2000.
Replicated proxy-climate signals over the last 2000 yr from two distant UK peat bogs: new evidence for regional palaeoclimatic teleconnections, *Quat. Sci. Rev.* 19, 481–487.

Bayley, J. (ed) 1998.
Science in Archaeology. London: English Heritage.

Bennett, M. 2001.
An archaeological resource assessment of Roman Lincolnshire, *East Midlands Archaeological Research Framework*. http://www.le.ac.uk/ archaeology/east_midlands_research_framework. htm

Bevan, B. (ed) 1999.
Northern Exposure: Interpretative Devolution and the Iron Ages in Britain. School of Archaeological Studies, University of Leicester.

Birss, R.S. 1985.
Coarse pottery, in J. Dool and H. Wheeler, Roman Derby: excavations 1968–1983, 90–124; 259– 267.

Bishop, M. 2001.
An archaeological resource assessment of Roman Nottinghamshire, *East Midlands Archaeological Research Framework*. http://www.le.ac.uk/ archaeology/east_midlands_research_framework. htm

Bishop, M.C. and Freeman, P.W.M. 1993.
Recent work at Osmanthorpe, Nottinghamshire, *Britannia* 24, 159–189.

Bourn, R., Hunn, J.R. and Symonds, J. 2000.
Besthorpe Quarry, Collingham, Nottinghamshire. A multi-period occupation site, in R. Zeepvat (ed), *Three Iron Age and Romano-British Settlements on English Gravels. Excavations at Hatford (Oxfordshire), Besthorpe (Nottinghamshire) and Eardington (Shropshire) undertaken by Tempus Reparatum between 1991 and 1993*, 71–117.

Bradley, R.J. 1978.
The Prehistoric Settlement of Britain. London: Routledge and Kegan Paul.

Brassington, M. 1971.
A Trajanic kiln complex near Little Chester, Derby, 1968, *Antiq. J.* 51, 36–69.

Brassington, M. 1980.
Derby Racecourse kiln excavations 1972–3, *Antiq. J.* 60, 8–47.

Brown, A.G. 1997. *Alluvial Geoarchaeology*. Cambridge University Press.

Brown, A.G. and Meadows, I. 2000. Roman vineyards in Britain: finds from the Nene Valley and new research, *Antiquity* **74**, 491–492.

Brown, A.G., Keough, M. and Rice, R.J. 1994. Floodplain evolution in the East Midlands, United Kingdom: the Lateglacial and Flandrian alluvial record from the Soar and Nene valleys, *Phil. Trans. Roy. Soc. London* **A348**, 261–293.

Buckland, P.C. and Sadler, J. 1985. The nature of Late Flandrian alluviation in the Humberhead Levels, *E. Midlands Geogr.* **8**, 239–251.

Burnham, B.C. and Johnson, H.B. (eds) 1979. *Invasion and Response. The Case of Roman Britain*. BAR Brit. Ser. **73**.

Burnham, B.C. and Wacher, J. 1990. *The 'Small Towns' of Roman Britain*. London: Batsford.

Chadwick, A. 1999. Digging ditches, but missing riches? Ways into the Iron Age and Romano-British cropmark landscapes of the North Midlands, in B. Bevan (ed), *Northern Exposure: Interpretative Devolution and the Iron Ages in Britain*, 149–171.

Chiverrell, R.C. 2001. A proxy record of late Holocene climate change from May Moss, northeast England, *J. Quat. Sci.* **16**, 9–29.

Ciaraldi, M. 2002. Plant macroremains, in G. Coates, *A Prehistoric and Romano-British Landscape. Excavations at Whitemoor Haye Quarry, Staffordshire, 1997–1999*, 62–66.

Clay, P. 1985. A survey of two cropmark sites at Lockington-Hemington, Leicestershire, *Trans. Leicestershire Archaeol. Hist. Soc.* **59**, 17–26.

Clay, P. 2002. *The Prehistory of the East Midlands Claylands*. Leicester Archaeol. Monogr. **9**. School of Archaeological Studies, University of Leicester.

Coates, G. 2002. *A Prehistoric and Romano-British Landscape. Excavations at Whitemoor Haye Quarry, Staffordshire, 1997–1999*. BAR Brit. Ser. **340.**

Coates, G. and Woodward, A. 2002. Discussion, in G. Coates, *A Prehistoric and Romano-British Landscape. Excavations at Whitemoor Haye Quarry, Staffordshire, 1997–1999*, 79–90.

Collis, J.R. (ed) 1977. *The Iron Age in Britain: a Review*. Department of Archaeology and Prehistory, University of Sheffield.

Cummins, W.A. and Rundle, A.J. 1969. The geological environment of the dug-out canoes from Holme Pierrepont, Nottinghamshire, *Mercian Geologist* **3**, 177–188.

Cunliffe, B. and Rowley, T. (eds) 1978. *Lowland Iron Age Communities in Europe*. BAR Int. Ser. **48**.

Daniels, C.M. 1966. Excavations on the site of the Roman villa at Southwell, 1959, *Trans. Thoroton Soc. Nottinghamshire* **70**, 13–54.

Darling, M. 1984. *Roman Pottery from the Upper Defences*. Lincoln Archaeological Trust Monogr. Ser. **16–2**. London: CBA for Lincoln Archaeological Trust.

Dearne, M.J. (ed) 1993. *Navio. The Fort and Vicus at Brough-on-Noe, Derbyshire*. BAR Brit. Ser. **234**.

Didsbury, P. 1992. Exploitation of the alluvium in the Lower Hull Valley in the Roman period, in S. Ellis and D.R. Crowther (eds), *Humber Perspectives*, 199–210.

Dool, J. and Wheeler, H. 1985. Roman Derby: excavations 1968–1983, *Derbyshire Archaeol. J.* **105**.

Douglas, I. and Hagedorn, J. (eds) 1993. *Geomorphology and Geoecology, Fluvial Geomorphology*. Zeitschrift für Geomorphologie (supplement) **85**.

Eccles, J., Caldwell, P. and Mincher, R. 1988. Salvage excavation at a Romano-British site at Chainbridge Lane, Lound, Nottinghamshire, 1985, *Trans. Thoroton Soc. Nottinghamshire* **92**, 15–21.

Elliott, L. 1997. Faunal remains, in D. Knight and S. Malone, Evaluation of a Late Iron Age and Romano-British Settlement and Palaeochannels of the Trent at Chapel Farm, Shardlow & Great Wilne, Derbyshire, 24.

Elliott, L. and Knight, D. 1997. Further excavations of an Iron Age and Romano-British settlement near Gonalston, Nottinghamshire, *Trans. Thoroton Soc. Nottinghamshire* **101**, 65–72.

Elliott, L. and Knight, D. 2002. Gonalston Holme Dyke, *Trans. Thoroton Soc. Nottinghamshire* **106**, 148–149.

Elliott, L. and Knight, D. 2003. Hoveringham Gonalston Lane, *Trans. Thoroton Soc. Nottinghamshire* **107**, 200–202.

Ellis, S. and Crowther, D.R. (eds), 1990. *Humber Perspectives: A Region Through the Ages*. Hull University Press.

Elsdon, S.M. 1982. Iron-Age and Roman sites at Red Hill, Ratcliffe-on-Soar, Nottinghamshire. Excavations of E. Greenfield, 1963, and previous finds, *Trans. Thoroton Soc. Nottinghamshire* **86**, 14–48.

Esmonde Cleary, A.S. 1989. *The Ending of Roman Britain*. London: Batsford.

Esmonde Cleary, A.S. and Ferris, I.M. 1996. Excavations at the new cemetery, Rocester, Staffordshire, 1985–1987, *Staffordshire Archaeol. Hist. Soc. Trans.* **35**.

Field, N. 1984. Romano-British kilns in the Trent Valley, *Lincolnshire Hist. Archaeol.* **19**, 100–102.

Field, F.N. and Palmer-Brown, C.P.H. 1991. New evidence for a Romano-British greyware industry in the Trent Valley, *Lincolnshire Hist. Archaeol.* **26**, 40–56.

Forcey, C. 1994. Excavations at Ad Pontem (Thorpe by Newark, Notts.), 1963 and 1965. Unpublished MA dissertation, University of Leicester.

Forrest, M. 1967. Recent work at Strutt's Park, Derby, *Derbyshire Archaeol. J.* **87**, 162–165.

Fulford, M. and Nichols, E. (eds) 1992. *Developing Landscapes of Lowland Britain. The Archaeology of the British Gravels: a Review*. Soc. Antiq. Occ. Pap. **14**. London: Society of Antiquaries.

Garton, D. 1987. Dunston's Clump and the brickwork plan field systems at Babworth, Nottinghamshire: excavations 1981, *Trans. Thoroton Soc. Nottinghamshire* **91**, 16–73.

Garton, D. 1999. Spalford Meadow, Spalford/Girton, *Trans. Thoroton Soc. Nottinghamshire* **103**, 101–105.

Garton, D. 2002. Walking fields in South Muskham and its implications for Romano-British cropmark landscapes in Nottinghamshire, *Trans. Thoroton Soc. Nottinghamshire.* **106**, 17–39.

Garton, D. and Salisbury, C.R. 1995. A Romano-British wood-lined well at Wild Goose Cottage, Lound, Nottinghamshire, *Trans. Thoroton Soc. Nottinghamshire* **99**, 15–43.

Garton, D., Elliott, L., Howard, A., Hunt, C. and Morris, T. 1995. Report for Stage 2 Evaluations on the Land East of Blaco Hill. Unpublished report, Trent & Peak Archaeological Trust, University Park, Nottingham.

Garton, D., Hunt, C.O., Jenkinson, R.D.S. and Leary, R.S. 1988. Excavations at a Romano-British cropmark enclosure near Menagerie Wood, Worksop, Nottinghamshire, *Trans. Thoroton Soc. Nottinghamshire* **92**, 22–33.

Garton, D., Southgate, M. and Leary, R. 2000. Archaeological evaluation of a proposed landfill site at Ramsdale, by Burntstump Waste Facility, Arnold, Nottinghamshire, *Tarmac Papers IV*, 31–43.

Gaunt, G.D. and Tooley, M.J. 1974. Evidence for Flandrian sea-level changes in the Humber Estuary and adjacent areas, *Bull. Geol. Survey GB* **48**, 25–41.

Hamshaw-Thomas, J. 1992. Aslockton, Nottinghamshire: Faunal Analysis. Unpublished report, Trent & Peak Archaeological Unit, University Park, Nottingham.

Harman, M. 1969. The animal bones, in M. Todd, Margidunum: excavations 1966–8, 96–103.

Harman, M. 1979. Animal bones, in H. Wheeler, Excavation at Willington, Derbyshire, 1970–1972, 215–217.

Harman, M. 1985. Derby north-west sector animal bone, appendix 2 in J. Dool and H. Wheeler, Roman Derby: excavations 1968–1983, 319–330.

Harman, M. 2000. The mammalian and bird bones, in R. Langley and C. Drage, Roman occupation at Little Chester, Derby: salvage excavation and recording by the Trent & Peak Archaeological Trust 1986–1990, 273–276.

Harman, M. and Weinstock, J. 2002. Mammal and bird bones, in C. Sparey-Green, Excavations on the south-eastern defences and extramural settlement of Little Chester, Derby 1971–2, 308–311.

Heritage Lincolnshire. 1992a. Archaeological Evaluation at the Electrical Sub-station, Staythorpe, Nottinghamshire, during January 1992. Unpublished report, Heritage Lincolnshire.

Heritage Lincolnshire. 1992b. Archaeological Evaluation at Staythorpe Electrical Sub-station during February and March 1992. Unpublished report, Heritage Lincolnshire.

Hingley, R. 1989. *Rural Settlement in Roman Britain.* London: Seaby.

Howard, A.J., Hunt, C.O., Rushworth, G., Smith, D. and Smith, W. 1999. Girton Quarry Northern Extension: Palaeobiological and Dating Assessment of Organic Samples collected during Stage 1 Geoarchaeological Evaluations. Unpublished report, Trent & Peak Archaeological Unit, University Park, Nottingham.

Hughes, P.D.M., Mauquoy, D., Barber, K.E. and Langdon, P.G. 2000. Mire-development pathways and palaeoclimatic records from a full Holocene peat archive at Walton Moss, Cumbria, England, *The Holocene* **10**, 465–479.

Inskeep, R.R. 1965. Excavations at Ad Pontem, Thorpe parish, Notts. *Trans. Thoroton Soc. Nottinghamshire* **69**, 19–39.

Jackson, D.A. and Ambrose, T.M. 1976. A Roman timber bridge at Aldwincle, Northamptonshire, *Britannia* **7**, 39–72.

Jackson, K. 1970. Romano-British names in the Antonine Itinerary, Appendix 2 in A.L.F. Rivet, The British section of the Antonine Itinerary, 68–82.

Jones, G. 1987. The plant remains, in D. Garton, Dunston's Clump and the brickwork plan field systems at Babworth, Nottinghamshire: excavations 1981, 58–61.

Jones, H. 2002. Brough, Glebe Farm, *Trans. Thoroton Soc. Nottinghamshire* **106**, 147–148.

Jones, H. and Knight, D. 2002. An Anglo-Saxon seax from Rampton, Nottinghamshire, *Trans. Thoroton Soc. Nottinghamshire* **106**, 47–51.

Jones, M.J. 2002. *Roman Lincoln.* Stroud: Tempus.

Jones, M.J., Stocker, D. and Vince, A. 2003. *The City by the Pool: Assessing the Archaeology of the City of Lincoln.* Oxford: Oxbow Books.

Jones, M.K. 1981. The development of crop husbandry, in M.K. Jones and G. Dimbleby (eds), *The Environment of Man: the Iron Age to the Saxon Period*, 95–127.

Jones, M.K. and Dimbleby, G (eds) 1981, *The Environment of Man: the Iron Age to the Saxon Period.* BAR Brit. Ser. **87**.

Kinsley, G. 1998. Interim report on archaeological watching briefs and excavations at Girton Quarry extension, Newark, 1997–98, *Tarmac Papers* **2**, 41–49.

Kinsley, G. and Knight, D. 1992. Archaeology of the Fosse Way. Volume 2. Implications of the Proposed Dualling of the A46 between Newark and Widmerpool. Unpublished report, Trent & Peak Archaeological Trust, University Park, Nottingham.

Kinsley, G., Leary, R., Priest, V. and Sheppard, R. 1997. Interim Report on Archaeological Evaluation at part of Warwick's and Richardson's Brewery Site and adjacent Land, Newark, Nottinghamshire. Unpublished report, Trent & Peak Archaeological Trust, University Park, Nottingham.

Knight, D. 1991. Archaeology of the Fosse Way. Implications of the Proposed Dualling of the A46 between Newark and Lincoln. Unpublished report, Trent & Peak Archaeological Trust, University Park, Nottingham.

Knight, D. 1992. Excavations of an Iron Age settlement at Gamston, Nottinghamshire, *Trans. Thoroton Soc. Nottinghamshire* **96**, 16–90.

Knight, D. 2000. An Iron Age and Romano-British Settlement at Moor Pool Close, Rampton, Nottinghamshire. Unpublished report, Trent & Peak Archaeological Unit, University Park, Nottingham.

Knight, D. 2002. A regional ceramic sequence: pottery of the first millennium BC between the Humber and the Nene, in A. Woodward and J.D. Hill (eds), *Prehistoric Britain. The Ceramic Basis*, 119–142.

Knight, D. and Malone, S. 1993. Construction of Gravity Sewer between Newton and Wynhill Pumping Stations, Notts. Summary Report on Archaeological Investigations. Unpublished report, Trent & Peak Archaeological Unit, University Park, Nottingham.

Knight, D. and Malone, S. 1997. Evaluation of a Late Iron Age and Romano-British Settlement and Palaeochannels of the Trent at Chapel Farm, Shardlow & Great Wilne, Derbyshire. Unpublished report, Trent & Peak Archaeological Trust, University Park, Nottingham.

Knight, D. and Priest, V. 1998. Excavations of a Romano-British field system at Lamb's Close, Kelham, Nottinghamshire, *Trans. Thoroton Soc. Nottinghamshire* **102**, 27–37.

Knight, D. and Southgate, M. 2000. Rampton, Moor Pool Close, *Trans. Thoroton Soc. Nottinghamshire* **104**, 159–160.

Knight, D. and Southgate, M. 2001. Barrow-upon-Trent, Fleak Close, and Captain's Pingle, *Derbyshire Archaeol. J.* **121**, 201–202.

Knight, D., Hunt, C.O. and Malone, S. 1999. Auger Survey of Crown Estate Lands near Bingham, Nottinghamshire. Unpublished report, Trent & Peak Archaeological Unit, University Park, Nottingham.

Lambrick, G. 1992. The development of late prehistoric and Roman farming on the Thames gravels, in M. Fulford and E. Nichols (eds), *Developing Landscapes of Lowland Britain. The Archaeology of the British Gravels: a Review*, 78–105.

Lambrick, G. and Robinson, M. 1979. *Iron Age and Roman Riverside Settlements at Farmoor, Oxfordshire*. CBA Res. Rep. **32**. London: Oxfordshire Archaeological Unit and Council for British Archaeology.

Langley, R. and Drage, C. 2000. Roman occupation at Little Chester, Derby: salvage excavation and recording by the Trent & Peak Archaeological Trust 1986–1990, *Derbyshire Archaeol. J.* **120**, 123–287.

Leary, R.S. 1987. The pottery, in D. Garton, Dunston's Clump and the brickwork plan field systems at Babworth, Nottinghamshire: excavations 1981, 43–52.

Leary R.S. 1996a. Roman coarse pottery, in A.S. Esmonde Cleary and I.M. Ferris, *Excavations at the New Cemetery, Rocester, Staffordshire, 1985–1987*, 40–60.

Leary, R.S. 1996b. A Romano-British duck beaker from Red Hill, Ratcliffe-on-Soar, Nottinghamshire, *Trans. Thoroton Soc. Nottinghamshire* **100**, 164–167.

Leary, R.S. 2003. Sturton-le-Steeple: Fieldwalked Pottery. Unpublished report, Trent & Peak Archaeological Unit, University Park, Nottingham.

Liddle, P. 2001. An archaeological resource assessment. Roman Leicestershire and Rutland, *East Midlands Archaeological Research Framework*. http://www.le.ac.uk/archaeology/east_midlands_research_framework.htm

Lillie, M. 1998. Alluvium and warping in the Lower Trent Valley, in R. Van de Noort and S. Ellis (eds), *Wetland Heritage of the Ancholme and Lower Trent Valleys: An Archaeological Survey*, 103–122.

Limbrey, S. and Evans, J.G. (eds) 1978. *The Effect of Man on the Landscape: the Lowland Zone*. GBA Res. Rep. **21**.

Locker, A. 2000. Animal bone, in R. Bourn, J.R. Hunn and J. Symonds, Besthorpe Quarry, Collingham, Nottinghamshire. A multi-period occupation site, 114–115.

Long, A.J., Innes, J.B., Kirby, J.R., Lloyd, J.M., Rutherford, M.M., Shennan, I. and Tooley, M.J. 1998. Holocene sea-level change and coastal evolution in the Humber estuary, eastern England: an assessment of rapid coastal change, *The Holocene* **8**, 229–247.

Loughin, N. 1977. Dales Ware, a contribution to the study of Roman coarse pottery, in D.P.S. Peacock (ed), *Pottery and Early Commerce*, 85–146.

MacCormick, A.G., Dickson, J.H., Ransom, M. and Alvey, R.C. 1968. Three dug-out canoes and a wheel from Holme Pierrepont, Nottinghamshire, *Trans. Thoroton Soc. Nottinghamshire* **72**, 14–31.

Macklin, M.G. 1999. Holocene river environments in Prehistoric Britain: human interaction and impact, *Quat. Proc.* **7**, 521–530.

Macklin, M.G. and Lewin, J. 1993. Holocene river alluviation in Britain, in I. Douglas and J. Hagedorn (eds), *Geomorphology and Geoecology, Fluvial Geomorphology*, 109–122.

Mackreth, D. 1965. Nottingham, Broxtowe, *E. Midlands Archaeol. Bull.* **8**, 30.

Mauquoy, D. and Barber, K.E. 1999. A replicated 3000 yr proxy-climate record from Coom Rigg Moss and Felecia Moss, the Border Mires, northern England, *J. Quat. Sci.* **14**, 263–275.

May, J. 1994. Coinage and the settlements of the Corieltauvi in East Midland Britain, *Brit. Numis. J.* **64**, 1–21; Plate 1.

McElearney, G. 1991. Pollen Analysis from Scaftworth Roman Road Excavations, 1991. Unpublished report, University of Sheffield Archaeological Services.

McWhirr, A. 1970. The early military history of the Roman East Midlands, *Trans. Leicestershire Archaeol. Hist. Soc.* **45**, 1–19.

Miles, H. 1969. Excavations at Fisherwick, Staffs., 1968 – a Romano-British farmstead and a Neolithic occupation site, *Trans. S. Staffordshire Archaeol. Hist Soc* **10**, 1–22.

Millett, M. 1990. *The Romanization of Britain*. Cambridge University Press.

Millett, M. 1995. *Roman Britain*. London: Batsford/English Heritage.

Monckton, A. 2003. An archaeological resource assessment and research agenda for environmental archaeology in the East Midlands, *East Midlands Archaeological Research Framework*. http://www.le.ac.uk/archaeology/east_midlands_research_framework.htm

Morris, T. and Garton, D. 1998a. Romano-British ditch digging at East Carr, Mattersey, Lound Quarry, Nottinghamshire, *Tarmac Papers* **2**, 51–63.

Morris, T. and Garton, D. 1998b. East Carr, Mattersey, *Trans. Thoroton Soc. Nottinghamshire* **102**, 138–139.

Myers, A. 2001. An archaeological resource assessment of Roman Derbyshire, *East Midlands Archaeological Research Framework*. http://www.le.ac.uk/archaeology/east_midlands_research_framework.htm

O'Brien, C. 1978a. Land and settlement in Nottinghamshire and lowland Derbyshire, *E. Midlands Archaeol. Bull.* **12**, Supplement.

O'Brien, C. 1978b. Excavations at Holme Pierrepont Site 4. Unpublished summary report, Trent Valley Archaeological Research Committee, University Park, Nottingham.

O'Brien, C. 1979. Iron Age and Romano-British settlement in the Trent basin, in B.C. Burnham and H.B. Johnson (eds), *Invasion and Response. The Case of Roman Britain*, 299–313.

Oswald, A. 1937. *The Roman Pottery Kilns at Little London, Lincs.* Privately printed.

Oswald, A. 1949. A re-excavation of the Roman villa at Mansfield Woodhouse, Nottinghamshire, *Trans. Thoroton Soc. Nottinghamshire* **53**, 1–14.

Oswald, A. and Buxton, L.H.D. 1937. A Roman fortified villa at Norton Disney, Lincs., *Antiq. J.* **17**, 138–178.

Oswald, F. 1927. Margidunum, *Trans. Thoroton Soc. Nottinghamshire* **31**, 55–84.

Oswald, F. 1941. Margidunum, *J. Roman Stud.* **31**, 32–62.

Oswald, F. 1948. *The Commandant's House at Margidunum*. University College, Nottingham.

Oswald, F. 1952. *Excavation of a Traverse of Margidunum*. University of Nottingham.

Oswald, F. 1956. *The Last Days of Margidunum*. University of Nottingham.

Palfreyman, A. 2001. Report on the excavation of a Romano-British aisled building at Little Hay Grange Farm, Ockbrook, Derbyshire 1994–97, *Derbyshire Archaeol. J.* **121**, 70–161.

Palfreyman, A. and Ebbins, S. 2003. Redhill Iron Age and Romano-British site, Nottinghamshire: a new assessment, *Trans. Thoroton Soc. Nottinghamshire* **107**, 17–40.

Palmer-Brown, C. and Knight, D. 1993. Excavations of an Iron Age and Romano-British settlement at Aslockton, Nottinghamshire: interim report, *Trans. Thoroton Soc. Nottinghamshire* **97**, 146–147.

Peacock, D. P. S. (ed) 1977. *Pottery and Early Commerce*. London: Academic Press.

Phillips, C.W. 1934. The present state of knowledge of archaeology in Lincolnshire, *Archaeol. J.* **91**, 97–188.

Ponsford, M.W. 1992. A late Iron Age and Romano-British settlement at Rampton, Nottinghamshire, *Trans. Thoroton Soc. Nottinghamshire* **96**, 91–122.

Ponting, M. forthcoming. The coins from Glebe Farm, Brough, Nottinghamshire, in B. Vyner, *Archaeology on the A46 Fosse Way: Newark-Lincoln*.

Rackham, J. 2000. Soils and environmental background, in R. Bourn, J.R. Hunn and J. Symonds, Besthorpe Quarry, Collingham, Nottinghamshire. A multi-period occupation site, 115–116.

Radley, J. and Simms, C. 1967. Wind erosion in East Yorkshire, *Nature* **216**, 20–22.

Richmond, I.A. 1946. The four coloniae of Roman Britain, *Archaeol. J.* **103**, 57–84.

Riley, D. 1977. Roman defended sites at Kirmington, S. Humberside and Farnsfield, Notts, recently found from the air, *Britannia* **7**, 189–192.

Riley, D.N. 1980. *Early Landscape from the Air: Studies of Cropmarks in South Yorkshire and North Nottinghamshire*. Department of Prehistory and Archaeology, University of Sheffield.

Riley, D.N., Buckland, P.C. and Wade, J.S. 1995. Aerial reconnaissance and excavation at Littleborough-on-Trent, Notts., *Britannia* **26**, 253–284.

Rivet, A.L.F. (ed) 1969. *The Roman Villa in Britain*. London: Routledge and Kegan Paul.

Rivet, A.L.F. 1970. The British section of the Antonine Itinerary, *Britannia* **1**, 34–82.

Rivet, A.L.F. and Smith, C. 1979. *The Place-names of Roman Britain*. London: Batsford.

Robinson, M.A. and Lambrick, G.H. 1984. Holocene alluviation and hydrology in the Upper Thames Basin, *Nature* **308**, 809–814.

St Joseph, J.K. 1961. Air reconnaissance in Britain 1958–1960, *J. Roman Stud.* **51**, 112–135.

St Joseph, J.K. 1965. Air reconnaissance in Britain 1961–4, *J. Roman Stud.* **55**, 74–89.

St Joseph, J.K. 1977. Air reconnaissance in Roman Britain 1973–6, *J. Roman Stud.* **67**, 125–161.

Salisbury, C. 1995. An 8th century Mercian bridge over the Trent at Cromwell, Nottinghamshire, England, *Antiquity* **69**, 1015–1018.

Salisbury, C.R., Whitley, P.J, Litton, C.D. and Fox, J.L. 1984. Flandrian courses of the River Trent at Colwick, Nottingham, *Mercian Geologist* **9** (4), 189–207.

Samuels, J. and Buckland, P.C. 1978. A Romano-British settlement at Sandtoft, South Humberside, *Yorkshire Archaeol. J.* **50**, 65–75.

Scaife, R. 1999. Gonalston: Pollen Analysis of the Bronze Age and Romano-British Features. Unpublished report in Nottinghamshire SMR.

Shotton, F.W. 1978. Archaeological inferences from the study of alluvium in the lower Severn-Avon valleys, in S. Limbrey and J.G. Evans (eds), *The Effect of Man on the Landscape: the Lowland Zone*, 27–31.

Sitch, B. 1990. Faxfleet 'B', a Romano-British site near Broomfleet, in S. Ellis and D.R. Crowther (eds), *Humber Perspectives: A Region Through the Ages*, 158–171.

Smith, C.A. 1977. The valleys of the Tame and middle Trent – their populations and ecology during the late first millennium BC, in J.R. Collis (ed), *The Iron Age in Britain: a Review*, 51–61.

Smith, C.A. 1978. The landscape and natural history of Iron Age settlement on the Trent gravels, in B. Cunliffe and T. Rowley (eds), *Lowland Iron Age Communities in Europe,* 91–101.

Smith, D.J. 1969. The mosaic pavements, in A.L.F. Rivet, *The Roman Villa in Britain*, 71–127.

Smith, D.N., Roseff, R., Bevan, L., Brown, A.G., Butler, S., Hughes, G. and Monckton, A. submitted. Archaeological and environmental investigations of a Late Glacial and Holocene river valley sequence on the River Soar at Croft, Leicestershire, *The Holocene*.

Sparey-Green, C. 2002. Excavations on the south-eastern defences and extramural settlement of Little Chester, Derby 1971–2, *Derbyshire Archaeol. J.* **122**.

Stukeley, W. 1776. *Itinerarium Curiosum.* 2nd edition. London: printed for the author.

Sydes, R. and Symonds, J. 1985. *The Excavation of an Enclosure and Field System of Iron Age/Romano-British Date at Pickburn Leys.* First Report, February 1985. Sheffield: South Yorkshire County Council, Recreation, Culture and Health Department.

Taylor, J. 2001. An archaeological resource assessment and research agenda for the Roman period in the East Midlands, *East Midlands Archaeological Research Framework.* http://www.le.ac.uk/archaeology/east_midlands_research_framework.htm

Thompson, F.H. 1951. The Roman villa at Glebe Farm, Barton-in-Fabis, Notts.: excavations 1933–1949, *Trans. Thoroton Soc. Nottinghamshire* **55**, 3–20.

Thompson, F.H. 1958. A Romano-British pottery kiln at N. Hykeham, Lincolnshire, *Antiq. J.* **38**, 15–51.

Todd, M. 1967. An earthwork at Sawley, Derbyshire, *Derbyshire Archaeol. J.* **87**, 165–167.

Todd, M. 1968a. Trent Valley Ware: a Roman coarse ware of the middle and lower Trent valley, *Trans. Thoroton Soc. Nottinghamshire* **72**, 38–41.

Todd, M. 1968b. The commoner late Roman coarse wares of the East Midlands, *Antiq. J.* **48**, 192–209.

Todd, M. 1969. Margidunum: excavations 1966–8, *Trans. Thoroton Soc. Nottinghamshire* **73**, 7–104.

Todd, M. 1973. *The Coritani.* London: Duckworth.

Todd, M. 1991. *The Coritani.* Revised edition. Stroud: Alan Sutton.

Tomlin, R.S.O. 1983. Non Coritani sed Corieltauvi, *Antiq. J.* **63**, 353.

Turland, R.E. 1977. Towcester, Wood Burcote, *Northamptonshire Archaeol.* **12**, 218–223.

Van de Noort, R. and Davies, P. 1993. *Wetland Heritage. An archaeological assessment of the Humber Wetlands.* The Humber Wetlands Project, School of Geography and Earth Resources, University of Hull.

Van de Noort, R. and Ellis, S. (eds) 1998. *Wetland Heritage of the Ancholme and Lower Trent Valleys: An Archaeological Survey.* Humber Wetlands Project, University of Hull.

Van der Veen, M. and O'Connor, T. 1998. The expansion of agricultural production in late Iron Age and Roman Britain, in J. Bayley (ed), *Science in Archaeology*, 127–144.

Vyner, B. (ed) forthcoming. *Archaeology on the A46 Fosse Way: Newark-Lincoln.* CBA Res. Rep.

Wacher, J.S. 1964. Thorpe (Ad Pontem), *J. Roman Stud.* **54**, 159–162.

Wagner, P. 2001. Plant remains, in A. Palfreyman, Report on the excavation of a Romano-British aisled building at Little Hay Grange Farm, Ockbrook, Derbyshire 1994–97, 148–150.

Walker, J. 2001. Besthorpe Quarry, *Trans. Thoroton Soc.* **105**, 185.

Wardle, C. 2003. Roman Staffordshire: the Five Towns and beyond, *West Midlands Regional Research Framework for Archaeology*, Seminar 3. http://www.arch-ant.bham.ac.uk/wmrrfa/sem3.htm

Webster, G. 1973. *The Cornovii.* 1st edition. London: Duckworth.

Webster, G. 1991. *The Cornovii.* 2nd edition. London: Duckworth.

Wheeler, H. 1979. Excavation at Willington, Derbyshire, 1970–1972, *Derbyshire Archaeol. J.* **99**, 58–220.

Whimster, R.P. 1989. *The Emerging Past. Air Photography and the Buried Landscape.* London: RCHME.

Whimster, R.P. 1992. Aerial photography and the British gravels: an agenda for the 1990's, in M. Fulford and E. Nichols (eds), *Developing Landscapes of Lowland Britain. The Archaeology of the British Gravels: a Review*, 1–14.

Whitwell, J.B. 1970. *Roman Lincolnshire.* 1st edition. Lincoln: History of Lincolnshire Committee.

Whitwell, J.B. 1982. *The Coritani.* BAR Brit. Ser. **99**.

Whitwell, J.B. 1992. *Roman Lincolnshire.* 2nd edition. Lincoln: History of Lincolnshire Committee.

Willis, S. 1996. The Romanization of pottery assemblages in the east and north-east of England during the first century AD: a comparative analysis, *Britannia* **27**, 179–221.

Woodward, A. and Hill, J.D. (eds) 2002. *Prehistoric Britain. The Ceramic Basis.* Oxford: Oxbow Books.

Woolley, T.C.S. 1910. Crocolana, the Nottinghamshire Brough, *Trans. Thoroton Soc. Nottinghamshire* **10**, 63–72.

Zeepvat, R. (ed) 2000. *Three Iron Age and Romano-British Settlements on English Gravels. Excavations at Hatford (Oxfordshire), Besthorpe (Nottinghamshire) and Eardington (Shropshire) undertaken by Tempus Reparatum between 1991 and 1993.* BAR Brit. Ser. **312**.

7 THE MEDIEVAL LANDSCAPE

LEE ELLIOTT, HOWARD JONES and ANDY J. HOWARD

7.1 Introduction

This chapter considers the evidence for changes in the Valley environment from the end of the Roman occupation in the early fifth century to c.AD 1500, just prior to the dissolution of the monasteries. The earlier part of this period, up to AD 1066, encompasses the sub-Roman, Anglo-Saxon and Anglo-Scandinavian periods. These latter terms refer to cultural orientation, as implied by the archaeological and historical record, and unless stated should not be taken as indicative of geographical origin (Lucy 2000, 173, 174–86). With notable exceptions, evidence for the early Anglo-Saxon period remains predominantly funerary in character. Chronology is frequently imprecise, the early and frequently accidental character of many of the discoveries forcing a continuing reliance upon artefact-based dating for the period. With the exception of the Lower Trent Valley and neighbouring Lincolnshire, the separation of early and middle Anglo-Saxon ceramics remains problematic, posing particular difficulties for the identification of the earliest Anglo-Saxon settlement. The weight of evidence shifts towards settlements during the middle and later Anglo-Saxon periods, although there is an inherent bias towards higher status, ecclesiastical and proto-urban centres, dated by coins and pottery. During the later ninth century the Trent Valley passed into the Danelaw, although archaeological evidence of a Scandinavian presence remains limited (Graham-Campbell 2001; Hadley 2000, 1–41; Hadley 2001; Hall 2001).

The chronological framework for the later medieval period, from the Norman Conquest, is significantly reinforced by historical sources and the widespread survival of up-standing remains. Archaeological sites can be placed within this framework by the use of pottery and a variety of other diagnostic artefacts such as coins, buckles, strap-ends, seal matrices, pilgrim badges, leatherwork, floor tiles and roof furniture. Within most of the study area there is a continuous and well-understood ceramic sequence. This largely originates from urban centres in or immediately outside the Trent Valley, notably at Nottingham and in Lincolnshire at Torksey, Lincoln and Stamford, although key assemblages have yet to be published. Dating has been refined further by the application of dendrochronological and radiocarbon techniques, particularly for the dating of timber buildings and riverine structural remains (Arnold et al. 2002; Clay and Salisbury 1990), while archaeomagnetic dating has been applied to river sediments and structures such as kilns and clay floors (Barley 1981; Ellis and Brown 1998).

Discussion focuses primarily upon the floodplain, gravel terraces and Valley sides, with occasional reference where pertinent to sites lying within the immediate hinterland of the Trent. During this period, the sites along the Trent were linked culturally, economically and administratively to locations beyond the study area, the impact of which will be considered where appropriate. Reference has been made in discussions of earlier periods to the role of the Trent as a divide between upland and lowland zones of Britain, but during the later medieval period a significant east-west division may also be discerned. Influences on the Upper Trent in this later period lay to the south and west with such towns as Stafford and Tamworth, Staffordshire. For the Lower Trent and much of the Middle Trent, by contrast, ties lay to the east and Lincolnshire, perhaps fostered by navigable stretches of the Trent and former Danelaw affiliations. Until the fourteenth century economic ascendancy lay firmly with Lincolnshire, which possessed a substantially greater population and several of the country's wealthiest boroughs engaged in the cloth trade, including Lincoln and Boston (Beckett 1988, 52–53; Bennett and Bennett 1993, 42). Influences on the Valley landscape therefore varied considerably from west to east, with processes evident in one part often not applicable to the whole Valley.

Following O'Brien's 1978 synthesis, evidence for Anglo-Saxon settlement within the Trent Valley was reviewed by Losco-Bradley and Wheeler (1984) after excavations by the former at Catholme, Staffordshire (Losco-Bradley and Kinsley 2002). Since then, the study area has been considered as part of a number of regional overviews and county studies, notably by Stafford (1985), Brooks (1989) and Sawyer (1998). In addition, an important collection of papers has been produced which focuses on the neighbouring kingdom of Lindsey, bordering the Lower Trent Valley (Vince 1993). Previous syntheses of later medieval archaeological remains, specific to the Trent Valley, include those of Knight and Howard (1994) and Van de Noort and Ellis (1998), while more general coverage has been provided in such works as the Victoria County Histories. For the later medieval period, county based overviews and site specific reports exist for ecclesiastical architecture (Cox 1875–79; Cox 1912; Godfrey 1887; Leonard 1993; 1995; Pevsner 1993; 2001), vernacular buildings (Arnold et al. 2002; Meeson and Kirkham 1993; Summers 1988) and village earthworks (e.g. Challis and Bishop 1998). Additional to these syntheses are primary sources such as the Domesday Survey, charters, cartularies, deeds, borough accounts and cartographic evidence such as the Tudor Map of AD 1500–40 (Salisbury 1983), the Sherwood Forest Map of AD 1609 (Mastoris and Groves 1997) and the Inclesmoor Map of AD 1407 (Beresford 1986). Other valuable aids include a variety of illustrated antiquarian texts, notably by Thoroton (1677), Stukeley (1724), Deering (1751) and Dickinson (1801; 1805). Significant historical reviews of the region also exist, although a regional divide in the literature often leaves little consideration of the relationship between the East and West Midlands (Beckett 1988; Gelling 1992; Platts 1985; Rowlands 1987). Most recently, both periods have been assessed as part of the East and West Midlands Archaeological Research Framework Project thus reinforcing the artificial divide created by scholars between the upper and lower reaches of the Trent.

Research on the medieval period in the Trent Valley has benefited less than the later prehistoric and Roman periods from large-scale excavations as a result of aggregate extraction. Even so knowledge of this period has been enhanced by excavations at Anglo-Saxon settlements such as Girton (Kinsley 1998; Kinsley and Jones 1999), Nottinghamshire, and Catholme (Losco-Bradley and Kinsley 2002), and the shrunken medieval village at Church Wilne, Derbyshire (Knight and Howard 1994, 103–104), plus investigations of floodplain environments preserving medieval bridges and other riverine structures at Hemington, Leicestershire (Clay 1992; Cooper 1999; Cooper and Ripper 1994; Salisbury 1992) and Colwick, Nottinghamshire (Salisbury *et al.* 1984). Excavations of variable spatial extent have been undertaken within urban areas, including Burton-on-Trent and Stone, Staffordshire, Nottingham, Newark and Southwell, Nottinghamshire, and Torksey (Barley 1964; 1965; 1981; Elliott 2003a; 2003b; Hughes 1996; Kinsley 1993b; Meeson and Kirkham 1993; Todd 1977; Young 1983), and around the monastic sites at Lenton and Thurgarton, Nottinghamshire, Burton and Hulton Abbey, Staffordshire, and Breedon-on-the-Hill, Leicestershire (Beilby 1966; Gathercole and Wailes 1959; Kenyon 1950; Wise 1985). Many of these urban excavations have been on a small scale, and a substantial number of key sites, most notably in Nottingham, remains unpublished. Much significant recent excavation has centred upon prestigious sites, such as Nottingham and Newark Castles (Drage 1989; Elliott 1997; Malone 2000; Marshall and Samuels 1997; Taylor 1999; Young 2001), which can bias the excavation record towards particular classes of site and monument. The growing body of excavation data is enhanced by a substantial corpus of information obtained from aerial photographic and earthwork surveys, fieldwalking and the recording of standing buildings, which together provide evidence of an archaeologically rich landscape.

The following review has a strong archaeological and geoarchaeological focus, with only limited reference to place name, cartographic and documentary sources. Discussion is focused first upon the evidence for climatic fluctuations and the changing fluvial environment, followed by consideration of woodland clearance and management and the balance between pasture and arable cultivation. Later sections explore the impact of changing funerary practices and religious beliefs upon landscape development and the changing character of rural and urban settlement. Anglo-Saxon occupation focuses on the gravel terraces and coversands, where the influence of earlier landscape features on the location and development of cemeteries, settlements and later high-status religious and proto-urban centres provides a key theme linking much of the discussion of the Anglo-Saxon environment. Particular emphasis is also placed in the earlier part of this chapter upon the limited evidence for changes in settlement in the later Saxon period, which culminated in the medieval manorial landscape of nucleated village, church and open fields. Consideration of the processes affecting the later

medieval Valley landscape divides chronologically either side of the fourteenth century. Prior to this period (*c.*AD 1000 – 1300), the underlying theme is urban and rural population growth, accompanied by arable intensification, further woodland clearance and expansion into marginal lands, necessitating greater management of the landscape resources. This was followed by a phase of depopulation and reorganisation, attributable to expansion, agrarian crises, climatic instability and plague. This in turn resulted in settlement shrinkage and in many areas led to the abandonment of arable farming for a less labour intensive system of pasture.

7.2   Climatic change

In a recent review of evidence for climatic change in the first millennium AD, Petra Dark noted broad agreement in the general trends. A period of climatic deterioration extended from the end of the Roman period until the latter part of the millennium, when temperatures increased. This marked the onset of a warmer phase – the Medieval Warm Period – that was to last well into the later medieval period (Dark 2000, 19–33). This warm period extended from around AD 900 – 1300, but although generally warmer, changing convective patterns also affected the distribution and intensity of rainfall (Brown 1998). This phase of warmer weather, with mean annual air temperatures approximately 1°C higher than present across Europe, was possibly caused by the effects of increased solar output and higher sea surface temperatures (Brown 1998). Key evidence for periods of wetter and/or cooler climate during the earlier medieval period has been obtained from records of bog surface wetness, deduced from cores recovered from ombrotrophic mires in the uplands of northern Britain (*cf.* Barber *et al.* 1994; Barber *et al.* 2000). At Bolton Fell Moss, Cumbria, for example, Barber *et al.* (1994) identified a wetter shift around cal AD 950, while at Walton Moss approximately 5km to the south-east, Hughes *et al.* (2000) identified a wetter shift around cal AD 500 – the latter probably a continuation of the climatic deterioration identified during the later part of the Roman period. Farther north, at Coom Rigg Moss and Felecia Moss in the Scottish Borders, Mauquoy and Barber (1999) identified wet/cool shifts between cal AD 550–670 and cal AD 920–1060, whilst at Talla Moss Chambers *et al.* (1997) identified a wet shift around cal AD 881–1022. Rather closer to the Trent Valley, Chiverrell (2001) has identified wet shifts around cal AD 550–650 and cal AD 670–980 on the North Yorkshire Moors.

Within the Trent Valley, the onset of this deterioration may be manifested in the Roman period. Evidence of increased precipitation and flood frequency, resulting in alluviation, has been noted at a number of sites and may have been have been intensified by both an increase in arable production and technological developments (Chapter 6.3). Rising sea levels have also been noted as a contributory factor, resulting in reduced flow into the Humber and significant inland flooding (Dinnin and Buckland 1990; Eagles 1979, 192–3). It seems likely that this process extended into the early Anglo-Saxon period, although outside of the Lower

Trent Valley (Van de Noort and Ellis 1998) there is a dearth of published palaeoenviromental sequences spanning the Roman–Anglo-Saxon transition. Climatic deterioration is likely to have affected the character of post-Roman patterns of farming, although evidence for the balance of pastoral and arable regimes within the medieval landscape is limited by the paucity of pollen and faunal evidence from the region (Monckton 2001). At Mattersey, in Nottinghamshire, a peat deposit probably contemporary with the upper fill of a Romano-British field ditch was radiocarbon dated to 1460 ± 70 BP (Beta-84570, cal AD 430–690; Garton *et al.* 2000) and suggests increased waterlogging within the landscape.

In the early Anglo-Saxon period, climatic change, together with the collapse of the Roman infrastructure that supported agriculture in more marginal zones, may have resulted in a contraction to prime agricultural areas such as the river terraces. It has been suggested that in Nottinghamshire such a shift in the late Roman and early Anglo-Saxon period may underlie the historic contrast between the dense settlement of the Valley and more sparsely populated regions to the north and west (Bishop 1997; 2001). However, the model is speculative and relies heavily upon the much later evidence of the Domesday Survey. A small but growing number of metal detector finds from north Nottinghamshire also urges caution. Athough predominantly of later Anglo-Saxon date, several early objects have also been recovered, including at least six cruciform brooches dating to the sixth century (J. Sumpter, Bassetlaw Museum: pers. comm.).

From around AD 1300, increased climatic instability led to a general lowering of temperatures, accompanied by higher precipitation and storms (Lamb 1966). These changes are exemplified by records of bog surface wetness, which have identified cool/wet shifts at sites such as Coom Rigg Moss and Felecia Moss between cal AD 1110–1260 and cal AD 400–1470 (Mauquoy and Barber 1999) and on Talla Moss around cal AD 1400 (Chambers *et al.* 1997). Farther south, on the North Yorkshire Moors, Chiverrell (2001) has identified wet shifts around cal AD 1350–1450 and cal AD 1400–1620. Some of these later wet shifts fall outside the medieval period, and the changes are assumed to reflect deteriorating climate associated with the Little Ice Age of *c.*AD 1450–1850 (Grove 1988). Wetter conditions were particularly prevalent between AD 1315 and AD 1322, with harvest failures occurring in AD 1315, AD 1316 and AD 1321, while late rains prevented the ripening and harvesting of crops and resulted in famine in Europe between AD 1315 and AD 1317 (Platt 1978, 96).

Across the Valley floor, climatic changes in the later medieval period precipitated increased levels of river activity in the Middle Trent Valley, leading to lateral migration and flooding (Brown 1998; Brown *et al.* 2001). These changes, also associated with the effects of the Little Ice Age elsewhere, are recorded across other parts of Britain (Macklin 1999) and northern Europe (Rumsby and Macklin 1996). The effects of changing weather patterns are also indicated by increased storm surge activity around the British coastline, including the Humber Estuary (Long *et al.* 1998). This may be partly responsible for sea-level rise and inland flooding, particularly from the thirteenth century onwards (Eagles 1979, 192–3; Van de Noort *et al.* 1998), causing the loss of previously reclaimed coastal lands. Increased precipitation, in combination with woodland clearance, may also have increased significantly the volume of surface run-off entering the Trent, possibly leading to greater flooding of the floodplain. A reduction of meadowland may have occurred due to excessive wetness and waterlogging. In addition, examples may be found in the Trent Valley where settlement on marginal areas of the floodplain suffered decline, notably at Church Wilne (Knight and Howard 1994, 103–4). The less favourable climate may also have shortened the growing season, necessitating the use of more cold- and damp-tolerant crops, including maslin and dredge (Birrell 1979, 31) and possibly contributing to the abandonment of arable farming. Documentary sources indicate that peas and beans were used regionally as new crops (Beckett 1988, 51; Birrell 1979, 30–31), but unfortunately palaeobotanical evidence is sparse being limited to a handful of excavated sites such as Stone and Newark (Greig 1993; Moffett 1996). A possible indicator of increased dampness may be the growing use of corn-driers (Bigmore 1982, 169; Hurst 1971, 115), which may be demonstrated on a number of sites within the Valley and regionally (e.g. Newark and Southwell: Elliott 2003b; 2003c; Kinsley 1993b, 60). Elsewhere climatic change has been held responsible for evidence of innovation within the archaeological record, including the construction of house platforms and the use of cobbled surfaces in crewyards to offset the effects of excessively damp conditions (Hurst 1971, 121). Amongst the excavated settlements along the Valley, few features have been directly attributed to worsening climatic conditions. An exception is the deserted village of Waterton, Lincolnshire, where the cutting of more substantial drainage ditches for the disposal of excess water in the thirteenth and fourteenth centuries was considered a response to the wetter conditions (Van de Noort *et al.* 1998, 135–136).

7.3   Fluvial Geomorphology

The majority of the research concerning valley floor change along the Trent during the medieval period has been undertaken in the middle reaches of the river, from close to its confluence with the Rivers Dove and Derwent to around Colwick. It has been argued that this part of the Valley may be more sensitive to the effects of climatic change than other reaches, since these tributaries drain extensive areas of upland (Brown 1998). Recording and dating of archaeological structures and artefacts buried within sands and gravels between Hemington and Colwick, including fishweirs, revetments, bridges, a mill dam and anchor stones (Cooper and Ripper 1994; Losco-Bradley and Salisbury 1979; Salisbury 1981; 1992; Salisbury *et al.* 1984), together with analyses of cartographic (Salisbury 1983) and documentary records (Knight and Howard 1994, 32–3), have permitted the reconstruction of the floodplain in this part of the valley floor. Combined with the dating of natural sediments (Ellis and Brown 1998) and palaeohydrological and palaeoenvironmental datasets (Brown *et al.* 2001; Smith 2000), and detailed mapping of

Fig.7.1 *The Fleet, Collingham, Nottinghamshire: a medieval channel of the Trent (photograph: A.J. Howard)*

the palaeochannel resource (Baker 2003), this information provides a chronology of fluvial processes during the Anglo-Saxon and later medieval periods.

Between Hemington and Colwick, Brown *et al.* (2001) have demonstrated how the river was transformed from a single, meandering channel during the sixth century to an unstable, multi-channelled system during the tenth century. Between the tenth and fourteenth centuries, it was characterised by a stable, multi-channelled anastomosed planform, before resuming a stable, single channel during the fifteenth century that has remained largely unchanged to the present day (Fig.7.1). This change in channel planform may owe much to human manipulation of the channel. Brown (1998) has argued that, in spite of the Little Ice Age lasting until around AD 1850, the river resumed and maintained a single, stable channel from the fifteenth century due to the installation of 'training', 'flash' or 'kid' weirs to aid navigation (Brown *et al.* 2001).

Archaeological excavations and palaeoenvironmental information derived from insects have demonstrated that the substrate of the medieval river-bed in the Middle Trent comprised predominantly sands and gravels. This was a major factor leading to channel instability, although destabilisation of the valley floor arising from changing flood frequency and magnitude in response to variations in weather patterns was the primary reason for floodplain transformation (Brown *et al.* 2001; Smith 2000). The evidence for large floods from the eleventh century onwards is well recorded in both the documentary and archaeological records and the effects upon the natural and human environment were significant. In the Hemington reach, major floods were probably responsible for the destruction of a mill dam dated to *c.*AD 1140 and three bridges with wooden superstructures dated to around AD 1096, AD 1214 and AD 1240 (Brown 1998; Brown *et al.* 2001). Excavations around the pier bases of two of the three bridges provided evidence for significant scouring and rotation of the bases prior to collapse, while archaeological remains including wattle fencing and a timber frame appear to have been placed next to a couple of the pier bases in an attempt to prevent scouring (Cooper and Ripper 1994). Further erosion prevention measures implemented locally during Saxo-Norman times include the dumping upon the river bank and bank sides of large pieces of local Carboniferous and Triassic sandstone, together with quarry waste and recycled artefacts including millstones, querns,

reused building stone and part of a ninth century Anglo-Saxon cross (Salisbury 1992). Some of the smaller stones were used subsequently as anchor stones for fishing; the average weight was 19kg and the heaviest around 100kg (Salisbury 1992). At Colwick, Salisbury *et al.* (1984) estimated that lateral movement of the river had averaged up to *c.*0.3m per annum during the medieval period. However, there is evidence that channel migration during this period was also characterised by rapid avulsion during flood events (Brown *et al.* 2001). On a practical level, this led to problems in the area of land ownership. Documentary records provide plentiful evidence for land exchange subsequent to flooding, notably between the Manors of Sawley, Derbyshire, and Lockington, Leicestershire, after a flood during AD 1402 (Salisbury 1992).

Around Newark, analysis of a Tudor map dated stylistically to the period AD 1500–1540 indicates that the Trent and its tributaries formed a series of well defined channels providing power for water mills and sites for the construction of fishweirs (Salisbury 1983). The bifurcation of the channel past Kelham, Nottinghamshire, is argued to be an artificial course, created to supply the mills in that part of the valley, but no other evidence of fluvial environments is available (Salisbury 1983). In the Lower Trent, below Newark, Van de Noort *et al.* (1998) have noted how a number of shrunken and deserted medieval villages are situated well away from the present course of the river. Channel change, in some cases possibly reflecting rapid migration by avulsion, may have played a significant role in their decline. However, excavations at the deserted medieval village of Waterton revealed that flood deposits infilled the upper parts of ditches around the settlement, suggesting that the reasons for abandonment may have included climatic deterioration during the fifteenth and sixteenth centuries (Van de Noort *et al.* 1998, 135–136).

The intensification of agriculture during the later medieval period and the exploitation of more marginal lands must have created problems of soil erosion and colluviation, although the evidence for these processes within the geoarchaeological record is currently sparse. Evidence for overbank alluviation during this period is also limited. For the Anglo-Saxon period, Catholme provides the main published evidence for alluviation, which is strictly limited here to the lower terrace edge slope (Losco-Bradley and Kinsley 2002, 10–12). Possible evidence for later medieval alluviation was obtained from Adbolton, Nottinghamshire, where an accumulation of silt and clay was recorded above a gully containing eleventh or twelfth century pottery (Elliott 1996, 169). Since fine-grained alluviation was a key feature of the preceding Roman period, it is curious that this process is not identified more readily during the medieval period, especially with continued climatic deterioration (Dark 2000). However, a number of reasons may explain its scarcity. Firstly, the fluvial environment was characterised by high energy conditions and therefore finer grained sediments may have been flushed through the valley. Secondly, settlement and human activity appears to have been concentrated on the higher terraces well above the level of flooding, and therefore datable associations with flood deposits may prove more elusive. It has been suggested that frequent inundations at Church Wilne, which lay on marginal land at the floodplain edge, appear to have contributed to its shrinkage and long-term decline (Knight and Howard 1994, 103–4). Colluvial processes are even less well understood for the medieval period. The only demonstrable late or post-Saxon colluvial deposit has been recorded at Catholme, where colluvium in association with ridge and furrow was identified along the terrace edge sealing Romano-British and Anglo-Saxon deposits (Losco-Bradley and Kinsley 2002, 12). This highlights the potential of such deposits to preserve earlier remains, and identification of such accumulations should be a priority of future research within the valley.

In the Lower Trent Valley, the drainage and expansion of agriculture to the coastal lowlands during the warmer conditions associated with the Medieval Warm Period resulted in the shrinkage of peats. This exacerbated flooding in the fourteenth century, when Humber tides were reported to be four feet higher than before (Van de Noort et al. 1998). Also in this area, the expansion of arable farming up to the fourteenth century may have contributed to the accumulation of the aeolian sediments which blanket certain parts of the Valley floor. Reworking of blown sand deposits during the medieval period is known from the Vale of York (Matthews 1970). However, in the Trent Valley, evidence within the archaeological record comprises mainly the attraction of settlement to existing sand deposits, notably at Gainsborough and Torksey, Lincolnshire, and Girton. At Torksey, Barley (1981, 277) found kilns cut into the sand, which was used as filler within the pottery, although more recently possible structural remains have been identified sealed by a post-conquest blown sand layer (Albone and Field 2002, 56).

7.4   River resources and management

Over the last forty years, quarrying has resulted in the discovery of a number of nationally important archaeological structures and artefacts within the sands and gravels of the Valley floor, most notably at Colwick, Hemington and elsewhere within the Middle Trent Valley (Salisbury 1992; Salisbury et al. 1984). This has revealed traces of a diverse range of structures associated with fishing, milling and other river-based activities.

The role of the Trent in the development of Anglo-Saxon trade and commerce remains poorly defined, although it is likely to have played an important part in the movement of heavier and bulkier cargoes, particularly lead from the Peak District, and possibly in the transport of more fragile commodities such as pottery (Chapter 7.8.1). Symond's analysis of late Saxon pottery distributions in Lincolnshire (including parts of the Trent Valley) revealed a potential dichotomy between internal and inter-regional movement, which may have favoured road and river transport respectively (Symonds 2003, 128–35). Vince (2001), however, has urged caution in the assumption of a prominent early Anglo-Saxon role for the region's Roman roads, which is supported by the funerary use of the Fosse Way described below (Chapter 7.7.2). By the later Saxon period, the importance of road as well as river transport

is indicated by Domesday's notation for both Nottingham and Torksey (Morris 1977, 280a B6, B20). The increasing significance of road traffic may also be demonstrated by the construction of an eighth century bridge at Cromwell, Nottinghamshire, and three bridges at Hemington dated by dendrochronology to around AD 1096, AD 1214 and AD 1240 (Cooper et al. 1994; Salisbury 1995). All of the bridges at Hemington were destroyed by flooding (Brown et al. 2001) and excavation has shown the considerable efforts that were made to prevent destruction of these bridges (Fig.7.2). Such substantial investment was seen as an onerous duty by those responsible for the maintenance of bridges, leading to many disputes over obligations (Rye 1899a, 36–8; Knight and Howard 1994, 156–157). Opinion appears divided on the relative significance of the river and roads in medieval transport (cf. Edwards and Hindle 1991; 1993; Langdon 1993). Substantial bridges certainly spurred the development of the towns of Nottingham, Burton-on-Trent and Newark (Knight and Howard 1994, 154; Moxon et al. 1906; Rye 1903a), establishing them as key road crossings of the Trent into which passing trade was funnelled. Where bridges were not constructed, crossings were provided by fords or ferries, particularly in the lower reaches of the Trent (Van de Noort and Ellis 1998). Place-name evidence indicates the former presence of several ford sites, notably at Shelford, Wilford and Langford, Nottinghamshire (Gover et al. 1940, 205, 241, 251).

Assessment of the significance of the river as a transport route should also take account of the extent to which this may have been seasonally influenced, bearing in mind the likelihood of low summer water levels (recorded as being as little as 1ft 6in deep at Torksey before the nineteenth century) and the problem of winter floods (Beckwith 1967, 4). In addition, documentary evidence indicates that passage was often impeded by obstructions placed within the river, particularly fishweirs (Morris 1977, 280a B6, B20). The Domesday Survey records a fine of £8 for obstruction of the river, which was seen as a royal highway, and examples of disputes settled by royal commissions are described in detail by Losco-Bradley and Salisbury (1979) and Salisbury

Fig.7.2 *Thirteenth century bridge pier foundation, Hemington Quarry, Leicestershire (photograph: S. Ripper, ULAS, © Leicestershire County Council Heritage Services)*

(1983). Despite such difficulties, assessment of patterns of later medieval transportation in the region suggests that navigation of the Trent was possible as far as Repton in Derbyshire (Edwards and Hindle 1991). This may have been facilitated by the construction and maintenance of training, flash or kid weirs to prevent bank erosion, under the auspices of local landowners and other bodies such as the Borough of Nottingham (Brown *et al.* 2001; Salisbury 1981; Salisbury *et al.* 1984).

Apart from transport, the discovery of large numbers of fishweirs in the Middle Trent emphasises the importance of the river as a provider of food resources throughout the medieval period. These would have included a wide range of fish species, such as porpoise, salmon and sturgeon (Brown 1904, 30; Page 1907, 61), although detailed assessment of the contribution to the medieval diet is prevented by the paucity of significant bone data from excavated sites (particularly those located on the acidic terrace gravels). An Anglo-Saxon fishweir was discovered at Colwick in 1978 (Salisbury 1981); the structure comprised a double row of posts, and wattle fences, approximately 2.4m long (Fig.7.3). Two radiocarbon determinations yielded dates of 1260 ± 65 BP (Q-2030, cal AD 650–960) for a holly post and 1130 ± 30 BP (UB-2351, cal AD 780–990) for part of a holly hurdle. Previously at Colwick, Losco-Bradley and Salisbury (1979) had recorded a fishweir comprising a 'V-shaped' alignment of posts and wattle hurdles. Two radiocarbon dates on samples of an oak post and hawthorn and elder wattle yielded age estimates of 820 ± 70 BP (Har-552, cal AD 1030–1300) and 860 ± 60 BP

(Har-846, cal AD 1020–1290) respectively. Analysis of the Anglo-Saxon structure indicated the probable summer construction of the wattle panels in preparation for the autumn migration of eels (Salisbury 1981). This bears witness to the recommended list of summer tasks contained within estate memoranda of tenth and eleventh century date (Hooke 1998, 131). The wood used in the construction of the excavated fishweirs comprised a mixture of alder, ash, elder, hazel, hawthorn, oak, rowan and willow, and provides valuable insights into the region's woodland resources and management (Chapter 7.5). In addition, when destroyed and covered by layers of sediment, the fishweirs preserved alignments in the direction of former river flow. Plotting of their position and orientation in the quarries around Colwick and Hemington has provided detailed information on floodplain hydrology and channel change (Salisbury *et al.* 1984; Salisbury 1992).

The Colwick structures compare with a number of other examples from along the Trent which demonstrate methods of fishing employed between the seventh and twelfth centuries. In the Domesday Survey, the Nottinghamshire section alone lists 22 fisheries (Terrett 1962, 262–3). By the early 1990s, 18 post alignments dating from the ninth to eleventh centuries had been recorded at Hemington Quarry (Salisbury 1992), although those parallel to the flow were interpreted as revetments. Cooper (2003) provides a more up-to-date review of fishing-related archaeological finds at Hemington Quarry. In addition to other fishweir structures, the first artefactual evidence for fishing activities was recovered in 1999. This comprised

Fig.7.3 *Reconstruction of Anglo-Saxon fishweir at Colwick, Nottinghamshire (source: Salisbury 1981; drawing reproduced by permission of Dr C. Salisbury)*

an elliptical piece of wood with a central hole for the insertion of a handle, and was interpreted as a 'pulse stick' – a tool still used by fishermen in Germany to drive fish and eels into baskets and/or weirs (Cooper 2003, 35). A sheep metapodial was found adjacent to the 'pulse stick' and a piece of brushwood, and was interpreted as bait for eels. Other notable finds at Hemington include a large weir structure (HL 12), comprising two parallel lines of oak posts and wattle sheets forming a frame, infilled with large stone blocks and brushwood (Cooper 2003, 36). At the northern end of the structure, probably the riverward end, a V-shaped arrangement of posts was identified and interpreted as a sluice. Associated with this weir was a single, well preserved wicker fish basket interpreted as an eel trap. The function of structure HL 12, provisionally dated by dendrochronology to the mid-twelfth century, is unclear. The frame of parallel posts invites comparison with examples of mill base plates recorded at Bordesley Mill, Worcestershire, and Tamworth (Cooper 2003, 36), but Cooper (2003, 18) speculates whether the structure may in fact have formed part of a large 'fixed-engine' fishery, akin to those mentioned in medieval documents. Around Hemington Quarry, in addition to the discovery of structural remains, a number of grooved stones used to anchor fishing tackle have been found. By the early 1990s, 77 had been recorded and a withy band still attached to one anchor stone had been radiocarbon dated to 690 + 80 BP (OxA-2289, cal AD 1210–1420; Salisbury 1992).

As well as exploiting the Trent for food, the river was used as a valuable source of power for milling grain. Mills are likely to have been widespread on the Trent and its tributaries from Anglo-Saxon times. Domesday suggests as much, with mills focusing on the prime agricultural lands in the valleys of the Tame and Trent (Terrett 1962, 269 fig.71; Wheatley 1971, 205 fig.70, 206). In addition, excavations at the royal Mercian centre of Tamworth revealed the remains of a mill structure located on the River Tame, dated to the mid-ninth century (Rahtz and Meeson 1992). Structural remains of comparable date have yet to be recorded on the Trent, although at Hemington two parallel lines of oak posts and wattle panels forming a frame infilled with large stones and brushwood were interpreted as parts of a mill dam structure dating from the last quarter of the twelfth century (Clay 1992). The structure included part of a wheel breasting in which a vertical water wheel would have turned. This twelfth century structure overlay an earlier row of posts dated to between the ninth and twelfth centuries, which was interpreted as part of a fishweir incorporated within the mill structure (Fig.7.4). The early sixteenth century Tudor map of the Lower Trent and its tributaries around Newark shows six mills on the River Devon (Salisbury 1983), the abundance of mills possibly representing the culmination of riverine economic development and investment at the end of the medieval period.

The Trent also played a key role in the socio-political development of the region during both the Anglo-Saxon and later medieval periods. The Trent Valley appears as a chronological and perhaps cultural divide in the distribution of early Anglo-Saxon cemeteries of the fifth and sixth centuries (Chapter 7.7.2). The strategic importance of

Fig.7.4 *Timber frame of Norman mill dam recorded at Hemington Quarry, Leicestershire (source: Clay and Salisbury 1990; reproduced from Volume 147 of the Archaeological Journal by permission of the authors and the Royal Archaeological Institute)*

the Lower Trent, and in particular the Rossington Gap which provided access through the Humberhead marshes, is reflected in the location of the conflicts of the seventh century in the power struggle between Mercia and Northumbria. This culminated in AD 679 in the Battle of the Trent, which established Mercian supremacy, and the subsequent territorial arrangement was preserved as aspects of the later county boundaries (Brooks 1989, 161 fig.11.1; Stafford 1985, 96–7, 135). The political and religious core of the Mercian kingdom lay on the Middle Trent, with key centres at Lichfield, Staffordshire and Repton (Brooks 1989, 161–2). The Trent's linkage with the Humber and North Sea proved both economically advantageous and a strategic weakness, providing a routeway for penetration into Mercia. This is exemplified by the overwintering of the invading Danish army at Nottingham in AD 868–9, Torksey in AD 872 and Repton in AD 874, while as late as AD 1013 King Swein of Denmark was encamped at Gainsborough (Swanton 2000, 68–70, 72–3, 143).

7.5   Woodland clearance and management

The paucity of published pollen sequences from the Valley which span the first millennium AD necessitates a reliance on documentary evidence and place names for the extent of Anglo-Saxon woodland. The regeneration of woodland in the period has been viewed as a key indication of continuity or disruption to the managed landscape. Dark (2000) has reviewed the question at a regional and national level, and has shown that outside of northern England and southern Scotland few regions preserve significant evidence for prolonged woodland regeneration in the early Anglo-Saxon period. Although the Trent Valley included the medieval forest of Needwood in Staffordshire, the evidence of the Domesday Survey and the general absence of wood related place names suggests that the Middle Trent Valley had been largely cleared of extensive woodland by the eleventh century (Gelling 1992, 9, 10 fig.4; Sawyer 1998, 23 fig.2.6; Stafford 1985, 6–8 incl fig.1; Terrett 1962, 276; Wheatley 1971, 198).   The removal of large areas of woodland from forest law, particularly after AD 1230, saw increasing assarting and the use of brecks, notably in the Upper Trent (Birrell 1979, 6; Tomkinson 1985, 62) and the adjacent hinterlands of Sherwood and the Peak District (Beckett 1988, 49).   An idea of the woodland species present within the Valley may be gained from timbers surviving in waterlogged deposits. A ditch at Hoveringham, Nottinghamshire, which formed part of a possible later medieval water meadow complex, was lined with riven planks of willow (Woodhouse 1993), while posts used in fishweir construction at Hemington and Colwick included oak, alder and holly, with smaller numbers of ash, elder, hawthorn, purging blackthorn, rowan and willow (Losco-Bradley and Salisbury 1979; Salisbury 1981; 1992). The variety of wood at Colwick and Hemington was interpreted as evidence of opportunistic felling (Salisbury 1994, 156).

The value of the woodland resource in the Anglo-Saxon period and later is beyond doubt. Analysis of parish boundaries within the area of Needwood suggests

competing claims for timber and underwood in the Anglo-Saxon period (Hooke 1998, 219). Whilst the decline of the Roman period industries may have lessened demand, the transition to a timber-reliant architectural tradition would have placed its own demands on woodland. Wattle may have been used widely, as illustrated by finds of daub from Flixborough, Lincolnshire (Loveluck 1998, 152) and large quantities of fired daub with wattle impressions which were recovered from a Middle Saxon structure at Girton (Kinsley and Jones 1999). Early Anglo-Saxon laws were introduced to protect trees and emphasise the importance of woodland as a source of pannage (Hooke 1998, 142–3). The management of woodland and the use of coppiced timber is demonstrated in fishweirs dating from the eighth century at Colwick (Losco-Bradley and Salisbury 1979; Salisbury 1981) and from regular sized charcoal in fourteenth century oven deposits at Newark (Kinsley 1993b). In addition, upper branches and foliage may have been used for cattle fodder (Salisbury 1981). During the later medieval period, increased pressure was put on this diminishing asset by the intensification and expansion of arable farming into marginal land, as demonstrated at Laxton in the thirteenth century by the encroachment of arable into former woodland (Challis 2002, 68). Medieval documents indicate that timber for construction was often acquired from areas outside of the Valley (Laxton 1997, 74–75).

7.6   Pasture and arable

Throughout the Anglo-Saxon and later medieval period palaeobotanical evidence for the balance of pasture and arable and the range of cultivated crop species is sparse. At Chapel Farm, Shardlow, Derbyshire, for example, assessment of pollen preserved in the organic fill of a palaeochannel (A) dated by associated peat to 1350 ± 50 BP (Beta-099235, cal AD 600–780) indicated wetland grassland with arable agriculture on drier land nearby (Greig 1997). Although not radiometrically dated, a nearby palaeochannel (B1) at this site yielded cereal pollen including rye, possibly hemp and a single grain of flax, suggesting to the pollen analyst an occupied agricultural landscape in the vicinity which he noted would typically be of Saxon or later date – although further work would obviously be required to test this hypothesis (Greig 1997, 35). Significant assemblages of charred plant remains are limited to high status sites such as Flixborough, Lincolnshire, where cereal grains and pulses were recovered, and beyond the Valley at Eye Kettleby, Leicestershire, where bread wheat and hulled barley were retrieved (Loveluck 1998, 156; Monckton 2001, 22). The wider region has produced evidence for a variety of Anglo-Saxon crops, including barley, bread wheat and oats, and a possible change in wheat type, from the spelt of the Roman period to free-threshing wheat (Monckton 2001, 22). The acidity of soils on the terrace gravels inhibits the survival of bone, and hence limits analysis of patterns of animal husbandry and hunting to more general comments. The standard range of species such as sheep/goat, cattle, pig and horse are recorded, although the greater variety recorded at Flixborough (including deer, hare, geese, ducks, chickens, cranes, porpoise, dolphin and pilot whales) is consistent with its high status (*ibid.*). Loomweights and spindle whorls have been recovered from several settlement sites in the valley, suggesting textile processing (e.g. Brough, Nottinghamshire, Catholme, Girton and Willington), although raw materials could conceivably have been traded between settlements (Jones forthcoming; Kinsley and Jones 1999, 66; Carr and Losco-Bradley in Losco-Bradley and Kinsley 2002, 110–11; Wheeler 1979, 210–11).

Consideration of the distribution of ploughs recorded in the Domesday Survey suggests a strong arable component within the Valley by the later Anglo-Saxon period (Terrett 1962, 249 fig.63, 256; Wheatley 1971, 184–5 fig.62–3, 193). The expansion of arable farming using the open field system is likely to have placed pressure on grazing land and the provision of winter fodder (Hooke 1998, 116). This has been linked elsewhere to the conversion of floodplains to valuable meadow (Foard 2001, 23), an arrangement reflected in the Domesday records for the Valley (Terrett 1962, 261; Wheatley 1971, 201). Continued agricultural expansion is suggested by twelfth and thirteenth century pottery from manuring of medieval field systems, recovered by excavation and fieldwalking at South Muskham, Nottinghamshire, Hoveringham and Catholme (Elliott and Knight in prep.; Garton 2002; Losco-Bradley and Kinsley 2002).

There appears to have been a swing from arable towards pasture or meadow following the crises of the fourteenth century, which is reflected by surviving ridge and furrow earthworks and a general absence of fifteenth century pottery from field systems subject to investigation (*ibid.*). Significantly, this includes areas on the gravel terrace, which prior to AD 1300 had been almost exclusively the preserve of arable farming, with pasture and meadowland limited to the floodplain. The presence of sheep, cattle and horse grazing is recorded at several locations, particularly in the Upper Trent, including Alrewas, Burton-on-Trent, Hulton, Tutbury, Needwood and Yoxall, Staffordshire (Birrell 1979, 9–10; Rowlands 1987, 26; Tomkinson 1985, 61). Despite demand for wool and therefore pasture for

Fig.7.5 *Late medieval water meadow complex near Hoveringham, Nottinghamshire (© J. Pickering: photograph reference no. SF1163-26, 3-9-72, NMR no. SK 6846/11)*

sheep, it is suggested that river grazing along the Trent was more suitable for cattle, due to 'its wetness in winter and dryness in summer' (Lyth 1989, 20). Pollen assessment of the fill of a palaeochannel at Chapel Farm, Shardlow, radiocarbon dated from associated peat to 380 ± 50 BP (Beta-99238, cal AD 1430–1650), indicates the presence of Rat-Tail Plantain and daisy, which probably indicate heavily trampled, short-grazed grassland (Greig 1997: Palaeochannel AB). The presence of Great Burnet and Knapweed pollen hints of longer grassland or hay meadow nearby, whilst Stinking Mayweed indicates cornfields. Curiously, the pollen assemblage from channel V included 11% heather. It is unclear whether this was growing nearby or transported into the area, although it is worth noting that no macrofossils of heather were found in the sample (Greig 1997). Archaeological evidence for water management associated with the existence of possible water meadows has been identified at Hoveringham (Woodhouse 1993, 5; Fig.7.5), where excavations of a rectilinear complex of cropmarks, set adjacent to two water courses, revealed a ditch lined with riven willow planks dated by radiocarbon to 600 ± 110 BP (BM-2869, cal AD 1220–1490). However, other possible functions for the structure include warping and osier beds (*ibid.*). Due to a paucity of published faunal remains from both urban and rural sites, the animal husbandry regimes of the period remain poorly defined, leaving little evidence for the inter-relationships existing between urban and rural agricultural economies. What evidence there is originates mostly from urban excavation, where sheep/goat and cattle are noted as the most common species (Hughes 1996; Kinsley 1993b; Monckton 2001).

7. 7 Settlement and Population

7.7.1 The Late Roman – Early Anglo-Saxon Transition

The predominantly sixth century dating for the appearance of early Anglo-Saxon material within the Trent Valley (possibly later still in the upper reaches in Staffordshire) leaves a lengthy hiatus in the archaeological record. Within this section, consideration is given to current problems in tracing developments from the late fourth into the fifth century. The previous chapter outlined the evidence for the incorporation of large areas of the Valley within a highly organised pattern of land division. By the beginning of the fourth century, it appears that large swathes of the Valley had been cleared of major woodland and were densely settled, with clear evidence of a hierarchy of settlements integrated within the framework of a wider market economy. Major questions remain regarding the later history of these sites, and in particular their transition into the post-Roman period. No detailed review of fourth century evidence and, in particular, the late Roman ceramic sequence, has been attempted (R. Leary: pers. comm.), and the dearth of fine wares from the region and the conservative character of the local ceramic tradition hampers the establishment of more detailed chronologies for the later period (Taylor 2001, 6–7, 16).

Sites and finds attributable to the fifth century, whether of perceived British or Anglo-Saxon orientation, remain extremely sparse. The main exceptions occur on the eastern fringes of the Lower Trent Valley in Lincolnshire. Possible fifth century material includes a growing number of zoomorphic buckles from north Lincolnshire (Leahy 1993, 30), with more recent finds suggesting local production (Vince 2001, 9–10). To these can be added a recent metal detector find from the Middle Trent Valley at Scarrington, Nottinghamshire (L. Laing: pers. comm.). Burials and cemeteries of proven sub-Roman date remain elusive and are likely to remain so without the wider application of high precision radiocarbon dating, although occasional unfurnished burials from villas may indicate an early date (see below). A later fifth century date can be applied to occasional Anglo-Saxon stray finds (Alvey 1980, 83, fig.1 no.34; Laing forthcoming) and perhaps the earliest of the burials from the larger cremation cemeteries, such as Millgate, Newark (Kinsley 1989).

The extended stratigraphic sequences of urban sites offer enhanced opportunities for the identification of fifth century activity. In keeping with the wider pattern of evidence, early Anglo-Saxon material has been recovered from a number of the former Roman centres, including Little Chester (*Derventio*), Derbyshire, Littleborough (*Segelocum*), Brough (*Crococalana*), Castle Hill (*Margidunum*) and Thorpe (*Ad Pontem*), Nottinghamshire. However, the finds derive mostly from their periphery, and with the few exceptions noted above date to the sixth century or later (Alvey 1980; Jones 2002; Kinsley in Sparey-Green 2002, 84–121; Laing forthcoming; Riley *et al.* 1995, 283–4; Todd 1969, 78 and fig.34, 1–7). Whilst it is possible that these sites acted as foci within the emerging post-Roman landscape, detailed evidence for their role and the character of any activity within the former towns and small towns is generally lacking, and continuity cannot be demonstrated. Within the wider region, Lincoln (*Lindum*) provides the main exception, for analysis of the latest Roman layers has yielded convincing evidence for a stratified sequence of activity extending into the early fifth century (Steane and Vince 1993). This activity may have included a religious focus, for a Bishopric was established at Lincoln in the fourth century and evidence from St Paul-in-the-Bail may allow for a possible Christian presence in the sub-Roman period. However, both the dating and interpretation of the recorded sequence have been disputed (Steane 1991; Jones 1994; Sawyer 1998, Appendix 4). More limited evidence has also been recovered from Little Chester (*Derventio*), Derby, where drystone features and a group of post-pits succeeded the latest Roman layers and pre-date the early Anglo-Saxon cemetery (Sparey-Green 2002, 73–6).

A review of the unpublished excavation of a villa at Wood Meadow, Thurgarton, Nottinghamshire, has highlighted possible fifth century activity, including metalworking (L. Laing: pers. comm.). Examination of the pottery has indicated the presence of ceramic forms comparable to those identified in possible sub-Roman layers at Lincoln. Two unfurnished burials were also recorded, one covered by the collapse from an adjacent wall. Their dating is uncertain, particularly given the recurrent selection of former villa buildings and their immediate vicinity for early Anglo-Saxon burial (Williams 1997). However, the evidence for

fifth century activity, and the absence of grave goods, raises suspicions as to a sub-Roman identification.

The apparent hiatus between the conventional end of Roman administration and the widespread appearance of Anglo-Saxon material culture in the sixth century provides a substantial window for transitory social and economic patterns to be established. Dark (2000, 10–26) has summarised the changes in approach to this problem since the 1970's, and has argued for the continuity of independent provincial political organisation into the sixth century. However, whilst differing in their detail and chronology, the majority view is of cataclysmic late Roman and/or post-Roman decline and discontinuity. Emphasis is placed on collapse of the social and economic fabric, with an end to mass production and loss of technology. The result is a culture of low archaeological visibility with a prominent role for organic and perishable materials. In place of a hierarchical surplus-driven estate system, a new economy emerged based on subsistence agriculture and more localised patterns of exchange (Bassett 1989; Esmonde Cleary 1989; Faulkner 2000; Reece 1980; 2002). In contrast, attempts have been made to move away from notions of Roman – medieval continuity and discontinuity, replacing them with European concepts of 'Late Antiquity' and processes of transformation (Dark 1994; 2000; Webster and Brown 1997). An extended chronology for the circulation of coinage has been proposed, questioning the conventionally accepted dating for the end of production and the use of late Roman material culture. The continuation of developments in fashion and perhaps in eating, drinking and culinary practices, manifested as changes in assemblages of personal ornaments and in a contraction in the range of vessels in the late fourth century (Cool 2000), may also underlie current difficulties in the identification of a distinctive sub-Roman population (Dark 2000, 53–57, 135).

The limitations of the evidence from the Trent Valley are such that various models could be comfortably accommodated. By the late Roman period, the landscape appears to have been well populated and highly ordered, with enclosure extending to more marginal lands. Evidence from a number of sites suggests that flooding may have added to the pressures of economic and social change and led possibly to some relocation of settlement on the elevated and drier areas of the terraces (Chapter 6). More detailed studies in the Upper Thames Valley have indicated a similar sequence of expansion and retreat (Esmonde Cleary 1989, 105). As yet, however, the transition from the intensive landscape management suggested by the Roman evidence to the more elusive early medieval agricultural regime is poorly understood, and remains a key research priority. A number of sites, discussed in greater detail below, hint at a broad continuity of boundaries. At the very least, the current chronology for this change cautions that allowance must be made for an intervening social and economic system to have become established prior to the appearance of early Anglo-Saxon culture.

7.7.2 Early Funerary Landscapes

Despite an increase in the number of excavated settlements, the archaeological record of the early Anglo-Saxon period remains dominated by funerary evidence. Cemeteries and isolated burials occur throughout the valley and its fringes, with a clustering in the middle reaches (Fig. 7.16). The cemeteries at Wychnor and possibly Yoxall in Staffordshire represent the western limit of the Valley cemeteries, the isolated seventh century burial from Barlaston, Staffordshire, representing probably an outlier of the Peak District group. Consideration of the distribution of early Anglo-Saxon cemeteries of the later fifth and sixth centuries (Lucy 2000, 142 fig.5.10) suggests that the Trent Valley marks a chronological and possibly a cultural divide between areas south and east of the Trent, and upland zones to the north and west. In these latter areas, furnished burials are either absent or are dominated by the predominantly seventh century barrow burials of the White Peak (Ozanne 1963).

The cemeteries include inhumations, cremations and mixed rites (Bishop 1984; Heron 1889, 156–193; Kinsley 1989). Artefactual evidence indicates a floruit in the sixth century for the majority of the cemeteries (Meaney 1964; Stafford 1985, 83). In contrast to the evidence from neighbouring Lindsey (Leahy 1998), there is little reliable evidence for substantial numbers of fifth century burials in the Trent Valley. This may in part reflect the difficulty of achieving secure dates for poorly recorded cremation deposits, as few of the vessels were retained or adequately recorded. Fundamental flaws in Myres' (1977) proposed chronology of cremation urns have long been acknowledged (Arnold 1981; 1997, 16–17), and a detailed review of the dating of the Trent Valley cemeteries is well overdue. However, the more recently published cemetery at Millgate, Newark, includes both cremation urns and a limited number of artefacts (a barred zoomorphic comb and a glass vessel) attributable to the fifth century (Kinsley 1989, 19–20). Later centuries are also sparsely represented, although Broughton Lodge and perhaps Windmill Hill, Cotgrave in Nottinghamshire, and Wychnor may continue into the early seventh century (Bishop 1984; Kinsley 1993a; 2002, 23–7).

Accounts of early discoveries give little detail of the funerary rites. In contrast, more recent excavations at Windmill Hill, Cotgrave, and Holme Pierrepont, Nottinghamshire (Bishop 1984; Guilbert 2000; 2001; 2002), provide indications of funerary elaboration, including ring-ditches, burial mounds and prone or deviant burials suggestive of social outcasts or criminals (Fig.7.6). Female grave-goods in particular include artefacts traditionally equated with Anglian culture and dress fashion, such as annular and cruciform brooches and sleeve-clasps (Hines 1984; Lucy 2000, 134 fig.5.5; Owen-Crocker 1986). However, these and other artefact-based assumptions of identity have been shown to be overly simplistic (Dark 2000, 25–6; Lucy 2000, 174–81; Lucy and Reynolds 2002, 10).

Early medieval funerary studies are a relative newcomer to the landscape approaches favoured by scholars of prehistoric periods (Lucy and Reynolds 2002). A preliminary review suggests a significant role for landscape and earlier monuments in the placement of early Anglo-Saxon burials in the Valley, although assessment is hampered by the imprecision of recorded find spots. There is frequently a preference for locally elevated positions, placing emphasis on the continued visibility of the dead, as for example at Windmill Hill, Cotgrave, Borrowash, Derbyshire, and Stapenhill, Staffordshire (Bishop 1984; Briggs 1852; Heron 1889, 156–193). Others show proximity to river junctions, as at Wychnor and Millgate, Newark (Kinsley 1989; 2002). The association of prehistoric burial mounds with supernatural and/or fictional lineages during the early medieval period has been noted as providing a funerary context for the legitimisation of authority and ownership (Williams 1997). The re-use of prehistoric barrows at Borrowash and Swarkestone Lowes in Derbyshire is a trend that may be under-represented within the Trent Valley, since later graves are vulnerable to truncation by ploughing (Briggs 1852; Posnansky 1955). Satellite flat graves on the periphery of barrows have also been noted at Swarkestone and Hilton in Derbyshire (Challis and Kinsley 1995; Posnansky 1955). A number of cemeteries occur in association with Romano-British enclosures, as at Stapenhill, Wychnor, and Kings Newton, Derbyshire (Heron 1889, 156–193; Jewitt 1869; Kinsley 2002). Villas also attracted later burials, as perhaps at Southwell and Barton-in-Fabis, Nottinghamshire, possibly signalling a symbolic linkage with earlier centres of status and authority (Daniels 1966; L. Laing: pers. comm.). Re-use may also suggest a change in the perception of earlier landscape elements. At Cotgrave and Broughton Lodge, graves were cut into the Fosse Way, whilst burial mounds appear to have blocked the road near Saxondale and at Potter Hill, Nottinghamshire, perhaps suggesting an emphasis on its perception as a linear boundary rather than a route-way in the early Anglo-Saxon period (Bateman 1848; 1853; Kinsley 1993a; Stukeley 1776).

7.7.3 Shifting Funerary Traditions: the eighth to ninth centuries

There is little evidence for use of the Trent Valley cemeteries beyond the early seventh century, although the Cleatham cemetery in Lincolnshire did contain a number of later graves (K. Leahy: pers. comm.). In addition, the Sheffield's Hill and Roxby cemeteries in Lincolnshire provide clear examples of cemetery shift in the late sixth and early seventh centuries (Leahy and Williams 2001, 310–3). Recent excavations at Holme Pierrepont also provide grounds for speculation, the scarcity of grave goods allowing for a late sixth-seventh century or possibly later date (Guilbert 2000; 2001; 2002). This contrasts with earlier discoveries made nearby of furnished sixth century burials (Bateman 1848), which possibly implies an extended funerary sequence with a shifting focus. A small number of comparatively rich isolated burials can also be noted, as at Winthorpe and Oxton in Nottinghamshire (Rooke 1792; Samuels and Russell 1999). However, with these exceptions, there is a hiatus in the funerary record for the majority of the population, between the later seventh and ninth centuries. A linkage between this hiatus and the nominal conversion of Mercia by c. AD 700 is inconsistent with evidence for the weak relationship between the early church and burial location (Geake 1992, 89–90; Lucy and Reynolds 2002, 13; Morris 1983, 50). It is not until the tenth

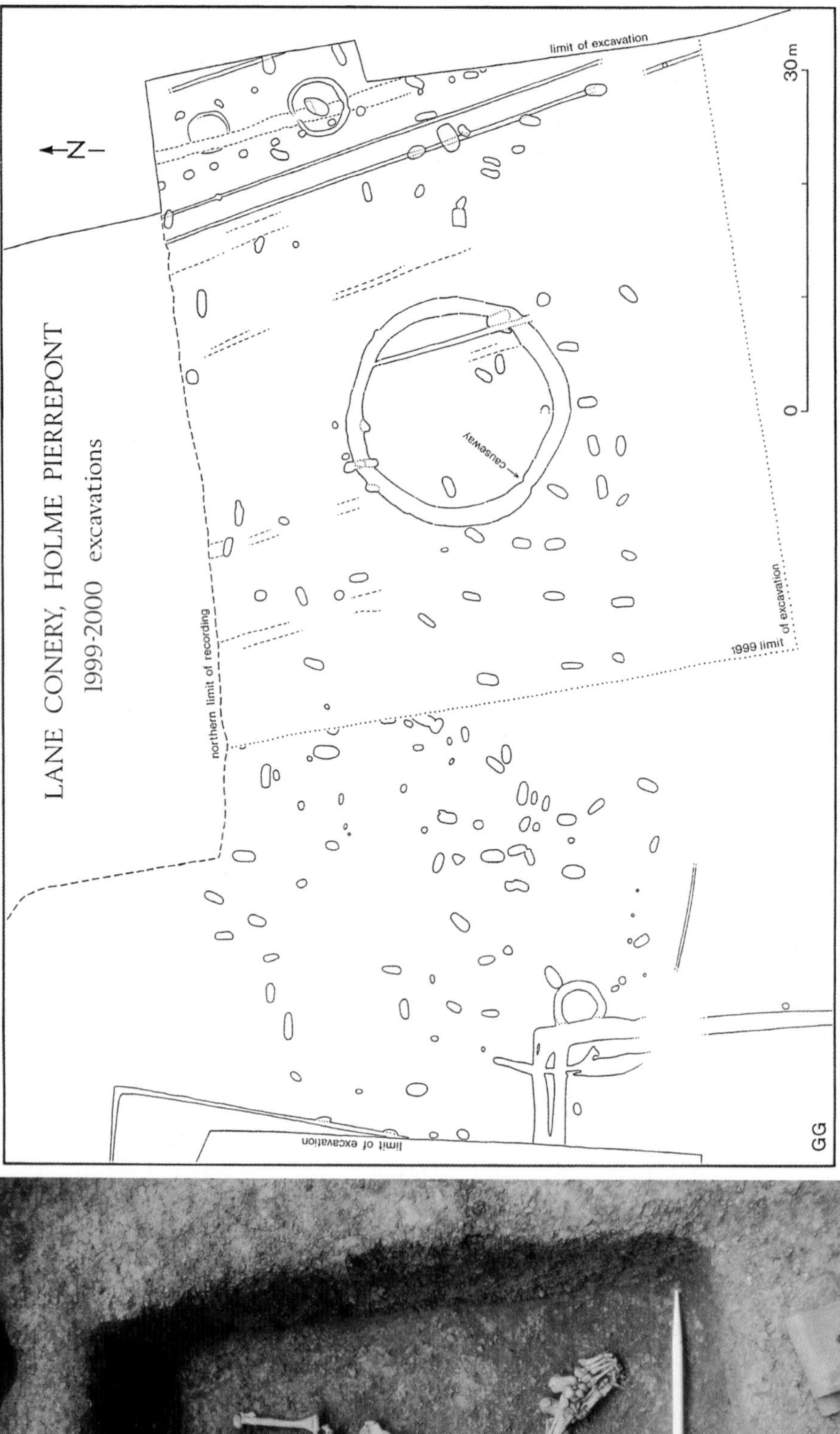

Fig.7.6 *An Anglo-Saxon burial with iron shield-boss and spearhead from Windmill Hill, Cotgrave, Nottinghamshire, and an Anglo-Saxon cemetery at Holme Pierrepont, Nottinghamshire (Photograph: M.W.Bishop, Nottinghamshire County Council, Environment Department. Plan: reproduced from Guilbert 2001 by permission of the author and the Thoroton Society of Nottinghamshire)*

century that unfurnished churchyard burial was established as the normative rite for the majority (Boddington 1990; Geake 1992; Hadley 2002, 210).

With the probable exception of Catholme (Losco-Bradley and Kinsley 2002, 40) and Oxton, burials of the eighth and ninth centuries are limited to probable religious communities and members of the ruling elite, as at Breedon-on-the-Hill and Repton, both of which retained intimate links with Mercian royalty (Biddle and Kjølbye-Biddle 2001; Dornier 1977; Kenyon 1950). At Repton, the linkage found monumental expression in the construction of the crypt and mausoleum (Biddle and Kjølbye-Biddle 2001, 50). Similarly, the church of St Alkmund, Derby, which is possibly an early royal foundation, contained an impressive stone sarcophagus – perhaps that of St Alkmund or Ealdorman Aethelwulf (Hadley 2000, 225–8; Radford 1976). At the high status site of Flixborough in the Lower Trent Valley, an extended sequence of activity from the seventh century to the post-conquest period includes a possible church and short-lived cemetery (Loveluck 1998).

A Scandinavian contribution to the developing funerary traditions of the region's elite can be discerned in monumental churchyard grave-covers. Examples dating to the later tenth and early eleventh centuries have been recovered from several locations in the Valley and its fringes, including Girton and East Bridgford in Nottinghamshire (Stocker and Everson 2001). The distribution of such monuments has been noted as indicating a shift in focus from churches of minster or 'senior' status to a more local ecclesiastical context (Hadley 2002, 228; Stocker and Everson 2001, 225–227). The evidence revealed by excavations at Repton and its vicinity includes the reuse of the Mercian royal mausoleum and the establishment of a barrow cemetery 4km away at Heath Wood, Ingleby, Derbyshire (Biddle and Kjølbye-Biddle 2001; Richards *et al.* 1995). The linkage with the over-wintering Great Danish Army of AD 873–4 is generally accepted, while the close association with an earlier funerary site has been interpreted as the highly symbolic appropriation of the Mercian royal ancestral mausoleum by the conquering Danish forces (Richards 2002, 165–70). Although exceptional, the evidence suggests the exploitation of well-established themes within the contemporary religious and funerary landscape, with the symbolic reuse of past monuments in key locations.

The landscape factors influencing earlier burial locations remained potent within this period of shifting religious beliefs. Repton's position on a bluff, overlooking the Trent, has been compared to that of the high status burial mounds at Taplow and Sutton Hoo (Stafford 1985, 106–7). Breedon's location is similarly striking, situated upon a prominent hill with impressive views in all directions. The positioning of the latter may have derived additional symbolism from its re-use of a former Iron Age hillfort (Kenyon 1950). The juxtaposition or superimposition of early churches and Roman sites may represent a further variation on this theme (Chapter 7.7.4).

7.7.4 Churches and the Parochial System

Examples of early churches preserving evidence of late Saxon construction or sculpture are scattered along the Trent Valley, including buildings at Marton, Lincolnshire, and in Derbyshire at Stanton-by-Bridge, Repton, Aston-on-Trent and Walton-on-Trent (Taylor and Taylor 1965a, 510–16, 568–69; 1965b, 412–415; Wardle 1994, 10–13). In addition, archaeological investigations of several churches within the region have revealed pre-Conquest foundations, notably at St Alkmunds, Derby, and in Nottinghamshire at St Peter's, Flawford, St Peter's, East Bridgford and All Saints, Cotgrave (Hill 1903; 1915; Elliott and Gilbert 1998; 1999; James 1994; Radford 1976). The locations of some of these early churches display interesting correlations with foci of Romano-British activity, as at the Nottinghamshire sites of Southwell, Flawford and Stanford-on-Soar, where evidence has been obtained for the superimposition and juxtaposition of church and Roman villa buildings (Daniels 1966; James 1994; Baker 1910). This recalls the possible appropriation of Roman structural remains as symbols of past authority, such as the Jewry Wall at Leicester, and perhaps the Mint Wall at Lincoln (Vince 2001, 15).

Analysis of documentary records and of the available archaeological and architectural evidence suggests that most churches in the Valley had been founded by the late twelfth century, by which period unfurnished churchyard burial was well established as the prevalent burial rite. Considerable movement in graveyard boundaries has been observed by excavation, notably at Southwell (Alvey 1975, 14; Elliott 2003a, 41–2 fig.1) and Newark (Abbott 1994), but the lack of published skeletal assemblages is insufficient for detailed discussion of the origins of churchyard burial in the region or the profile of the urban and rural populations.

Due to the local availability of only poor building stone, herring-bone masonry is a characteristic of many Saxo-Norman churches along the Middle and Lower Trent, including Averham, Flintham and Littleborough in Nottinghamshire, Sawley, Derbyshire, and Marton, Lincolnshire. Notable church construction is evident throughout the later medieval period along the Trent (Pevsner 1993; 2001). At Southwell, in the twelfth century, this may have included a workshop that proved influential in the construction of several parish churches within the Valley (Coffman and Thurlby 2000). Less studied are the chapels of ease, which were constructed in increasing numbers from the thirteenth century to serve those parishioners who lived some distance from the parish church (Wilkinson 1942, 67). A number of Bridge Chapels, for use by travellers, are recorded along the Trent at Swarkestone, Nottingham and Burton-on-Trent (Page 1907, 61; Rye 1903a, 8; Stevenson and Stapleton 1898). None of these examples remain, although St Mary's Bridge Chapel in Derby survives as a well-preserved example along the Lower Derwent (Currey 1931; Williamson 1931). Many of these chapels were maintained by monastic institutions (Page 1907, 61). From the late twelfth century the small two-celled church at Littleborough attached to Welbeck Abbey (Griffin 1909, 34) may have served a similar function at a ford crossing, possibly influencing its dedication to St Nicholas, the patron saint of seafarers.

The growth of churches is linked inextricably with the development of the parochial system, the origins of which, in common with neighbouring areas, may lie in the fragmentation of larger pre-conquest parochiae and estates. This process lacks the clarity of adjacent regions due to the dearth of Anglo-Saxon charters for much of the Trent Valley. The church at Flawford is of particular interest from the viewpoint of parish development, for this has been interpreted as possibly a 'superior church' with a large early administrative unit, or parochia (Hadley 2000, 233, 276). A similar model has been proposed for East Stoke, Nottinghamshire, where a large parochia may have fragmented in the later tenth and eleventh centuries, and Bishop (2001) has speculated that this may reflect an origin in a late Roman administrative area focused on the Roman small town at Thorpe (*Ad Pontem*). Recent discoveries of Anglo-Saxon metalwork, and the results of excavations outside the Roman small town at Brough (*Crococalana*), appear to confirm the influential role of former Roman centres in the location of early Anglo-Saxon activity, but it remains uncertain whether this is consistent with either a revived or continuing active role for earlier centres and their administrative territories. Whatever its origins, the parish system appears to have been well advanced by the Domesday Survey of AD 1086, although it continued to evolve and subdivide with the foundation of new churches and chapels (Wilkinson 1942, 67–68). A prevailing characteristic of the Middle and Lower Trent was the development of linear parishes stretching back perpendicular to the river (Fig.7.7). Similar linear organisation has been witnessed within the townships of the Lower Trent and elsewhere (Van de Noort *et al.* 1998, 131), providing each township with a share of meadow, arable, pasture, woodland and water (Rowley 1978, 15). Fluctuations in the course of the river have resulted in changes to parish boundaries, including the formation of extra-parochial lands (*Holmes*) as a result of river movement, notably around Lockington and Sawley (Salisbury 1992, 156).

7.7.5 Monastic and other Ecclesiastical Foundations

The fertile soils of the Trent Valley proved attractive to monastic foundations, the development of which had a significant impact on the landscape. The seventh century witnessed the establishment of monasteries, notably at Breedon-on-the-Hill and Repton, and the historical and archaeological evidence makes clear the interplay of royal and religious interests in their foundation (Biddle and Kjølbye-Biddle 2001; Dornier 1977). Later pre-Conquest foundations included the collegiate church at Southwell, dated to AD 956, and Burton Abbey, dated to AD 1002, while the many post-Conquest establishments included the Priories of Repton and Gresley in Derbyshire, Torksey, Fosse and Gokewell in Lincolnshire, Stone and Trentham in Staffordshire, Breedon-on-the-Hill in Leicestershire and Lenton, Shelford, and Thurgarton in Nottinghamshire (Cox 1907; 1910; Dickinson 1970a; 1970b; Hoskins and McKinley 1954; Page 1907). Orders seeking remote areas,

Fig.7.7 *Linear parishes either side of the Lower Trent Valley (drawing by J. Goddard)*

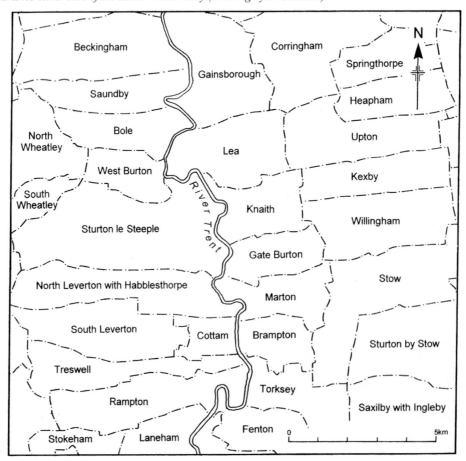

at the head of the Trent or within tributary rivers, included the Cistercians at Hulton Abbey and the Carthusians at Mattersey Priory (Cox 1910; Wise 1985) while later medieval cave hermitages at riverside and other locations are known from Lenton and Sneinton in Nottinghamshire and possibly Foremark in Derbyshire (White 1857; Young 2002). Although subject to various levels of fieldwork, none of the monastic sites in the Valley has been extensively excavated and published. A certain degree of speculation, therefore, remains regarding the ground plans of many sites and the location of ancillary structures.

Most monasteries held extensive agricultural estates managed from granges situated within and outside the Valley, and their presence impacted significantly upon the landscape and agricultural economy. The monastic estates possessed sizeable flocks of sheep, with Hulton, Shelford, Lenton and Mattersey all supplying wool to Italian and Flemish merchants (Lyth 1989, 17; Tomkinson 1985, 61–62). Many also held land in the towns; Burton Abbey and Stone Priory, in particular, were fundamental in the development of their adjacent boroughs. Burton Abbey, for example, which acted as a major landlord leasing out numerous tenements, was responsible for the town obtaining borough status, and the provision of a market, fair, grammar school and piped water supply (Tomkinson 2000, 23). The Abbey was also engaged in cloth production, owning a fulling-mill at Burton-on-Trent, as well as quarrying at Winshill, Staffordshire (Hannam and Greenslade 1970, 204). Further revenue was raised from the possession of church benefices. Repton Priory, which is a typical example, held a compact group of chapeleries and churches along the Trent comprising Repton, Newton, Bretby, Foremark, Ingleby, Ticknall and Willington in Derbyshire (Page 1907, 59). Several other monasteries also possessed fisheries and granary mills, while Repton Priory received meadowland in return for the maintenance of a chapel at Swarkestone Bridge (to which the prior was also appointed surveyor of tolls on the passage of goods: Page 1907, 61). Few of the fishponds and other ancillary features associated with monastic complexes have been studied, although industrial activity largely serving monastic consumption has been recorded; these include tile kilns at Lenton Priory and bronze-working furnaces at Thurgarton (Gathercole and Wailes 1959; Swinnerton *et al.* 1955). Monastic influence also extended to trade, with the annual fair at Lenton Priory assuming regional if not national importance. Lasting for eight days, it provided the yearly stock for many of Nottingham's traders (Barnes 1987; Grieg 1992).

Friaries, typically a later development, were founded in Nottingham and Newark. Catering for the urban poor, they lacked the entrepreneurial impact of rural monasteries. Friary possessions included tenements for lease within the towns and adjacent gardens and orchards (Cox 1910, 144–147). These have been the subject of only limited fieldwork, which is largely unpublished. Hospitals have also been recorded at several locations along the Trent, both extra- and intra-murally at Lenton, Nottingham, Newark, Southwell and Gonalston in Nottinghamshire and Castle Donington in Leicestershire (Cox 1910; McKinley 1954). Typologically, these can be divided into the four

established categories of 'leper houses, almshouses, hospices for poor wayfarers and pilgrims, and houses for the sick poor' (Gilchrist 1992, 102). Partial excavation of the associated cemetery at St Leonards in Newark suggests that it had served the general sick poor, with the skeletons exhibiting signs of a hard life and old age rather than infectious disease (Bishop 1983). In the absence of extensive excavation, ground plans for these establishments are largely speculative.

7.7.6 Rural Settlements

Anglo-Saxon Settlements

Despite the recent discovery and excavation of a small number of Anglo-Saxon settlements within the Valley and around its fringes, the picture is fragmented, and most sites remain divorced from their broader landscape context. Previous studies have supplemented the sparse settlement evidence with that of cemeteries and place names, thereby producing a coherent narrative (Losco-Bradley and Wheeler 1984; Stafford 1985). Catholme remains the most thoroughly excavated of the settlement sites, although even here the limits of occupation were not demonstrated by excavation (Losco-Bradley and Kinsley 2002, 3). Analysis of the morphology and chronological development of settlements is also hampered by the absence of stratigraphic sequences and the paucity of dating evidence. Detailed information on the economic basis of the settlements is also lacking, especially since the acid soils of the terraces provide hostile conditions for the preservation of bone and other organic material. Despite this, the evidence from Catholme, combined with more recent discoveries at sites such as Girton (Kinsley and Jones 1999; Kinsley 1998), permits preliminary observations on the processes linking the Romano-British landscape with the historical pattern of nucleated villages and open fields.

In addition to earlier excavations at Catholme and Willington, at least five rural settlements have been excavated within the Valley and its hinterland in more recent years. Evidence of settlement has been recovered at Girton, Brough, Langford and Holme Pierrepont in Nottinghamshire, although in the latter two instances evidence is limited to single structures (Jones 2002; Kinsley and Jones 1999; G. Guilbert: pers. comm.; Vyner forthcoming). Excavations near Castle Donington and beyond the study area at Eye Kettleby have also produced settlement evidence (Coward and Ripper 1998; Finn 1999). In addition, a number of stray finds which may imply occupation (in particular loomweights and pottery) are recorded in the Sites and Monuments Record as at Collingham (SMR 04316a), East Stoke (SMR 01548, 01644b, 03510b) and South Muskham (SMR 02995b), Nottinghamshire, and Curborough in Staffordshire (SMR 05115).

The impression is of a dispersed settlement pattern focusing upon the gravel terraces of the Middle Trent Valley and its fringes. However, intensive field walking around the Lower Trent is gradually revealing evidence of early Anglo-Saxon settlement in that area, including sites at Owston Ferry, Lincolnshire, and other locations on the

Triassic knolls of the Isle of Axholme (K. Leahy: pers. comm.). In addition to this somewhat later settlements are known at Flixborough (Loveluck 1998) and Belton in Lincolnshire, where *Grubenhäuser* were associated with middle Saxon material. Traces of Anglo-Saxon settlement in the Upper Trent Valley remain sparse. Sites in that area are predominantly late, and are limited to high status and ecclesiastical sites on the Valley fringe such as Lichfield and Tamworth (Rahtz and Meeson 1992; Webster and Cherry 1978, 177). In addition, the Sites and Monuments Record for Staffordshire lists a few stray finds, including pottery and metalwork from the Romano-British site at Curborough (SMR 05115). Settlement appears to have remained above the level of flooding, with the deposition of alluvium restricted to lower terrace edge slopes – as at Catholme and Willington (Losco-Bradley and Kinsley 2002, 10–12; Wheeler 1979, 58–60). River confluences attracted settlement, as at Catholme (Losco-Bradley and Kinsley 2002) and Willow Farm, Castle Donington (Coward and Ripper 1998), recalling a similar focus of funerary and ritual sites within confluence zones (Chapter 7.7.2). Comparison with the broader distribution pattern appears to confirm the valley focus, particularly for the earlier Anglo-Saxon period (Fig.7.16; Brooks 1989, 161, fig.11.1). However, the distribution of sites should be viewed with caution since four of the excavated settlements were discovered and excavated during aggregate prospection and extraction. Large scale field walking in North Lincolnshire has shown that early Anglo-Saxon settlement sites are not uncommon, but intensive work is needed in order to locate them (K. Leahy: pers. comm.).

The terraces adjoining the valley floor were the focus of substantial Romano-British occupation and cultivation, and there are indications that the boundaries of this earlier landscape provided a broad framework for the development of Anglo-Saxon settlement. At Catholme, Anglo-Saxon occupation centred on farmland belonging to a Romano-British settlement located *c.*700m to the south-west. The eastern limits to both settlements were defined by the terrace edge, marked by successive boundary features in the prehistoric and Roman periods, and re-cut as a ditch in the Anglo-Saxon period. A sequence of shifting settlement was proposed, although direct continuity was not demonstrated and the area containing the earliest phase of the Anglo-Saxon settlement remained unexcavated (Losco-Bradley and Kinsley 2002, 123). At Willington, a *Grubenhaus* cut a north-south boundary ditch, which had formed part of a Romano-British field system (Wheeler 1979, 127 fig.48, 129). Following the abandonment and infilling of the building, the boundary was re-established and influenced the alignment of subsequent medieval cultivation (Fig. 7.8). A similar picture has emerged at Brough, where the Anglo-Saxon ditched enclosures followed the east-west and north-south 'grain' of the Late Iron Age and Early Romano-British field system; this also appears to have influenced the orientation of medieval cultivation (Jones forthcoming). The Sheffield's Hill cemeteries were also located within the boundaries of an existing 'ladder' type field system (Leahy and Williams 2001, 310–3). The evidence is tentative, but may indicate that patterns of Romano-British land division survived the transition to the early Anglo-Saxon economy,

and in places may have continued to shape the developing medieval landscape.

Despite consideration of a Romano-British source for the building plans at Catholme (Losco-Bradley and Wheeler 1984), here and elsewhere in the Valley the forms and constructional techniques lie firmly within the architectural mainstream for Anglo-Saxon England (Fig.7.9). Although aspects of the settlement morphology at Catholme do appear to be unusual, with evidence for the grouping of buildings within ditched and/or fenced enclosures integrated with a system of trackways, these can be paralleled by the 'Butterwick' type settlement recognised in Lincolnshire and Yorkshire – for instance at Riby and Melton Ross in Lincolnshire and Butterwick in Yorkshire (Leahy 2003, 138–54; Steedman 1995; Stoertz 1997, 58–9, fig.30.1). The longevity of the Catholme enclosures, which is suggested by repeated recutting of boundaries, has prompted speculation regarding ancestral property units (Hamerow 2002, 123–129). Other Trent Valley settlements have provided little evidence for contemporary internal subdivisions. At Girton, buildings were scattered across the crest of a sand dune, an undated curving gully perhaps defining the south-eastern edge of the occupation focus (Kinsley and Jones 1999). More detailed evidence is forthcoming from the wider region. Later phases of a sixth to eighth century settlement at Quarrington, Lincolnshire, included enclosure ditches (Taylor 2003), while at Eye Kettleby a post-built fence line and a series of shallow discontinuous ditches which may have defined enclosures or fields were recorded (Finn 1999).

Within the Valley, there are continuing difficulties in establishing a chronology for key horizons of settlement shift and nucleation. Dating is complicated by the limited range of material culture from sites within the region, which consistently comprises mainly pottery, with few bone artefacts, metalwork or other datable small finds. The absence of significant quantities of diagnostic middle Saxon pot types is particularly problematic, as it has hindered the identification of later settlements in the Valley and neighbouring areas (Liddle 2001; Vince 2001). Scientific dating is available for Catholme and for Girton, and will be available in due course for Brough. Even where radiometric dating has been applied extensively, as at Catholme, the limited stratigraphic sequence hinders clarification of the processes of internal development (Hamerow 2002, 126; Losco-Bradley and Kinsley 2002, 115–123). Despite these problems, preliminary observations on key issues of settlement shift and the development of the later nucleated pattern are possible. Recent years have seen the recognition of a more variable sequence and chronology, leading to the formation of the nucleated village landscape, and its inextricable linkage with changes in landholding patterns and tenurial obligations in the later Saxon period (Foard 2001; Hadley 2000, 165–215; Hamerow 1991; Hayes and Lane 1992; Richards 2001). It is therefore encouraging that the emerging evidence from the Trent Valley and its fringes, although embryonic, is already suggestive of similar variation.

Processes of settlement drift and nucleation may be demonstrated at a number of excavated sites within the

Fig.7.8 *Plan showing the influence of Romano-British boundaries on the alignment of ridge and furrow at Willington, Derbyshire (modified from plan in Wheeler 1979)*

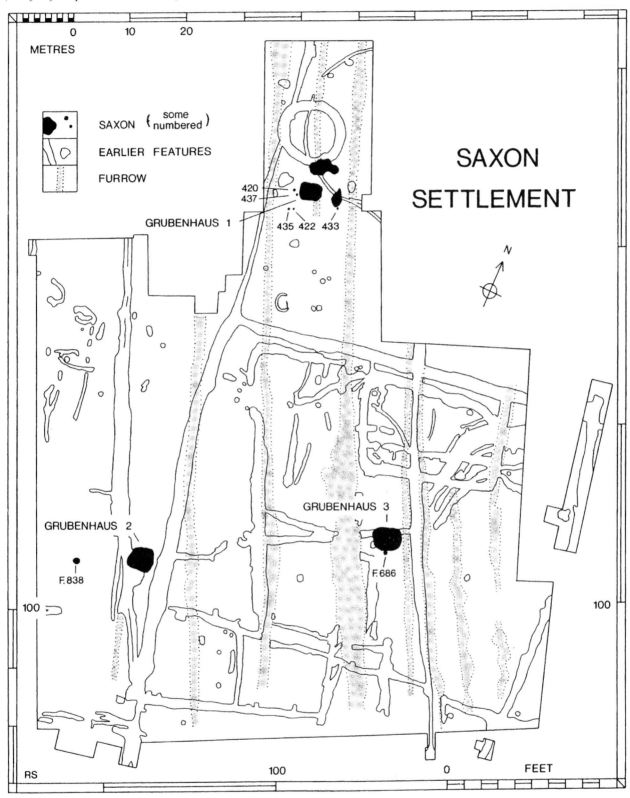

Trent Valley. At Catholme, radiocarbon dates allow for an extended sequence of occupation from at least the early seventh to late ninth century (Garton and Kinsley 2002, 120–3). Earlier origins are suggested by the proximity of the sixth century Wychnor cemetery to the unexcavated area of the settlement. The preferred sequence suggests relocation or settlement creep from the former Romano-British foci, possibly within the same estate or land unit.

The Anglo-Saxon settlement shows marked stability with long-lived and possibly ancestral property units extending into the later Saxon period (Fig.7.10). The absence of later radiocarbon dates and Saxo-Norman pottery may indicate abandonment by this date (*ibid.*, 123).

At Girton, settlement appears to have been located on the eastern edge of former Romano-British fields, although

Fig.7.9 *Anglo-Saxon post-pit building at Glebe Farm, Brough, Nottinghamshire (photograph: R.Holt)*

the date of its foundation or relocation are uncertain given the reliance on a single remnant magnetic date of cal AD 650–815 (Geoquest Associates, Durham) for a clay flooring (Kinsley and Jones 1999). A substantial scatter of pottery, dating from the late ninth to mid-eleventh centuries and probably derived from later cultivation, signals the abandonment of the settlement. Ridge and furrow also crossed the settlement area and, although not closely datable, appears to have respected a frequently re-cut ditched boundary that may have originated in the Saxo-Norman period (*ibid.*). A sequence of shifting settlement is suggested by the location of the historic village of Girton only 500m to the south of the Anglo-Saxon site; this includes a church with a monumental grave cover dating to between the mid-tenth and early eleventh century (Fig.7.11; Stocker and Everson 2001, 235 fig.12.6). Evidence from Eye Kettleby may suggest a similar process, since occupation dates from at least the sixth century and includes an area of possible middle Saxon date. The settlement was located immediately adjacent to a deserted medieval village, which included a building of tenth or eleventh century date (Finn 1999). Finally, the recovery of middle and late Saxon material from later medieval village centres, as at Laxton and Adbolton, hints at a chronological and spatial overlap in settlement location (Challis 1994a, 27–8; Elliott 1996).

The Trent Valley passed into the Danelaw during the later ninth century, but as in other areas there are few archaeological traces of a Scandinavian presence (Hadley 2000, 26–35). With the exception of the remarkable evidence associated with the over-wintering of the Great

Danish Army at Repton, noted above, archaeological evidence for Danish settlement remains elusive. At present, this stands in contrast to Lincolnshire where a large number of pieces of poor quality Scandinavian metalwork have been recorded (Leahy and Paterson 2001, 187–202). It is hoped that the appointment of a Portable Antiquities Scheme Finds Liaison Officer to cover Nottinghamshire and Derbyshire will address this problem and determine if the lack of Scandinavian material is real or apparent. Occupation at Catholme spanned the period of incorporation into the Danelaw, but showed no signs of the change in over-lordship (Hamerow 2002, 128). Scandinavian place name evidence, in particular the 'Grimston-hybrids' which combine a personal name with *tun*, is particularly prevalent in the Trent Valley, and has been linked with processes of estate fragmentation leading to smaller land units with closer individual associations (Hadley 2000, 138–9). The evidence has been seen as indicative of the role of Scandinavian landowners in the acceleration of existing late Saxon changes in land tenure, and the fragmentation of estates (Bishop 2001; Richards 2001, 275).

Later Medieval Rural Settlement

A characteristic of most rural settlement in the Valley between the late eleventh and fifteenth centuries was its location on the larger gravel islands and flanking terraces, leaving the floodplain for meadowland and other activities. Exceptions include the settlement of possibly marginal land at the confluence of the Trent with the Derwent at Ambaston and Church Wilne, Derbyshire (Knight and Howard 1994, 104) and the riverside sites of the Lower Trent which were

Fig.7.10 *Interpretative plan of principal features of the early medieval settlement at Catholme, Staffordshire (source: Losco-Bradley and Kinsley 2002; reproduced by courtesy of the authors and Trent & Peak Archaeological Unit)*

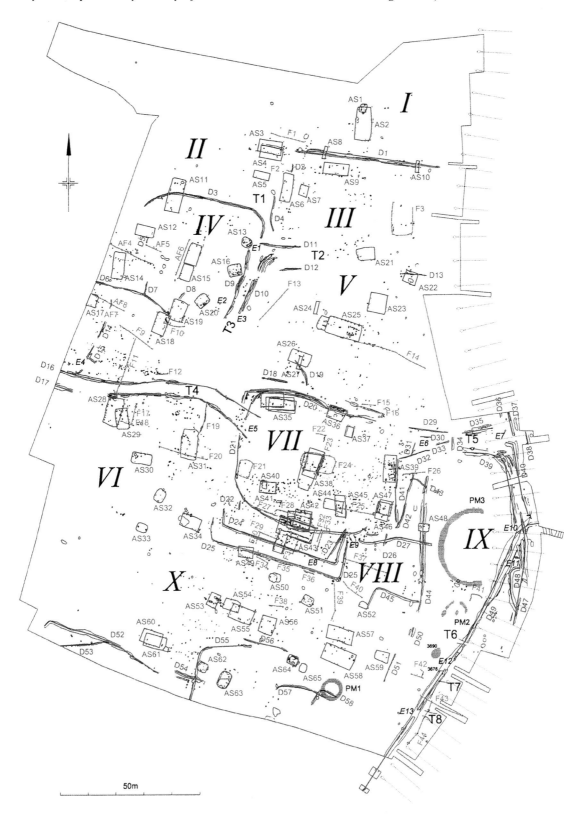

50m

situated on the raised leveés flanking the river (Fig.7.12; Van de Noort *et al.* 1998, 133).

Evidence for rural settlement patterns, in the absence of excavation, is in part largely dependent on historical map evidence and the appearance of current village and hamlet layouts, together with surveys of associated earthworks such as house platforms, hollow-ways and associated ridge and furrow. Many of these earthworks have been degraded by recent agricultural activity, while earthwork surveys in Nottinghamshire and Derbyshire indicate that many sites probably still await discovery (e.g.

Fig.7.11 *Model sequence of settlement migration and late Saxon nucleation at Girton, Nottinghamshire (photographs © Nottinghamshire County Council, with modifications by S.Baker)*

Iron Age and Romano-British settlement

Middle Saxon settlement, abandoned by the mid ninth century

Historic village core with church containing a mid tenth-eleventh century grave-cover

Challis and Bishop 1998). No large-scale archaeological investigations of village earthworks comparable to those conducted on neighbouring clayland sites such as Barton Blount in Derbyshire and Goltho in Lincolnshire have been carried out (Beresford 1975). More limited work has been undertaken at a scatter of sites along the Valley and in immediately adjacent areas, including Sinfin in Derbyshire, Sandon in Staffordshire, and Adbolton, Laxton, Keighton and Waterton in Nottinghamshire, although much of this remains unpublished (Challis 2002; Elliott 1996; Hurst 1971; Laing 2001; O' Brien 1974). From this evidence it is possible to discern the prevalence along the Lower and Middle Trent of nucleated settlement lying within open field systems. This seems to be the prevailing model for significant portions of the Upper Trent, although dispersed settlement was also widespread in parts, possibly reflecting

the organisation of the rural economy around woodland systems (Hunt and Klemperer 2003; Rowlands 1987, 18). Similar dispersed settlement is known within the adjacent woodland sites of the Peak District and Sherwood Forest (Beckett 1988). Its detection is difficult amongst the dominant nucleated pattern evident along most of the Valley, due to problems in identifying hamlets or farmsteads within the archaeological record. *Thorpe* sites and other outliers may indicate the development of dispersed settlements, possibly into former marginal lands, such as Easthorpe and Westhorpe at Southwell, both recorded in Domesday (Morris 1977, 283a 5,1).

The chronology of nucleation is poorly defined, although significant expansion is evident in many rural settlements up to around AD 1300. This may be linked to a general

Fig.7.12 *Riverside settlement on raised alluvial levées on the Lower Trent at Butterwick, Lincolnshire (© East Riding of Yorkshire Council)*

increase in prosperity, indicated for example by the rise in market charters (often initiated by landlords to increase revenue), and the population expansion of the twelfth and thirteenth centuries (Beckett 1988). Visible signs of this expansion include church construction, indicated by the presence of Romanesque and Early English work in the Valley churches (Pevsner 1993; 2001; Pevsner and Harris 2001). Limited evidence for new domestic building has also been recorded at several sites such as Adbolton, Church Wilne, Laxton and Waterton (Elliott 1996; Knight and Howard 1994, 103–4; Van de Noort *et al.* 1998, 136) comprising post-pits, foundation or drainage gullies and wattle and daub walling. This expansion may have taken the form of piecemeal 'organic' growth or may represent more deliberate planning. The latter is well illustrated at Laxton, where a single episode of planned growth associated with

the changing fortune of the landlord in the twelfth century may be postulated (Challis 2002, 68).

A protracted phase of village desertion and shrinkage commenced in the final centuries of the medieval period, following the climatic deterioration, agrarian crises and plague of the fourteenth century. This is indicated by the widespread survival of settlement and field-system earthworks such as Egginton and Church Wilne, Derbyshire, Marston in Staffordshire (Fig.7.13), and East Stoke and Thurgarton, and by excavations at Laxton, Keighton and Church Wilne (Challis 2002; Knight and Howard 1994; Laing 2001). Most of these represent nucleated sites, and little evidence is so far available for the effects of these processes on dispersed settlement. Desertion appears to have been a prolonged process, continuing at sites such as

Fig.7.13 *Deserted medieval village of Marston, Staffordshire (copyright reserved Cambridge University Collection of Air Photographs; photograph reference AQI 50)*

Adbolton and West Burton, Nottinghamshire, well into the post-medieval period (Holland 1967; Granby 1942).

The Manorial System

Central to the administration of rural settlement was the manorial system, which comprised a web of social, tenurial, agricultural and fiscal obligations and organisation, focused upon landowners and their places of residence and adminstration. This was firmly established by Domesday. Castle sites of the Motte and Bailey and Ringwork form, mostly constructed during the eleventh and twelfth centuries, are recorded at several rural settlements such as Owston and Laxton (Cathcart-King 1983). These have not been studied in detail, while few survive as earthworks (*ibid.*). Moated sites are present throughout the study area, with excavated examples at Burton Joyce and Stoke Bardolph, Nottinghamshire, Long Whatton, Leicestershire, Saxilby, Lincolnshire, and Bucknall and Burton-on-Trent, Staffordshire (Mein 1950; Neal 1989; Peverel Archaeological Group 1954; Stanyer and Brayford 1966; Tarver 1981; Whitwell 1969). These mostly comprise the limited investigation of the moat or internal areas, while little recording has been undertaken of associated features of the manorial complex, such as fishponds, gardens, orchards, mills, malt houses, barns and dovecotes, and their position within the landscape. Internal structures where exposed include stone and timber halls, with occupation usually originating in the twelfth or thirteenth centuries – thus suggesting a link with agrarian expansion, as alluded to elsewhere (Le Patourel and Roberts 1978, 48). Many moated sites occur as isolated features or on the periphery of settlements, while in the Lower Trent several occur on the floodplain (Van de Noort *et al.* 1998, 138–139). Rich artefactual evidence indicates their position within the administrative and economic hierarchy. Less well understood are non-moated manorial sites such as that at Epworth (Hayfield 1984). In the absence of moated earthworks, these sites can be difficult to locate, especially since many lie beneath or are incorporated within existing buildings, such as Ruddington Hermitage, Nottinghamshire (Pevsner 2001, 300) and Gainsborough Old Hall (Lindley 1991).

Fields and Field Systems

In contrast to earlier periods, no evidence for extensive Anglo-Saxon field systems has been identified by fieldwork within the Valley. This may be due partly to the typically shallow character of the few field ditches dated to this period – as recorded, for example, at Catholme and Brough and beyond the Valley at Eye Kettleby (Finn 1999; Jones forthcoming; Losco-Bradley and Kinsley 2002, 28–9). Explanations may also lie in models of continuity in core settlement areas (Hooke 1998, 116; Taylor 1981). Evidence has been noted above of the durable influence of earlier land-division through the Saxon period – notably at Willington (Fig.7.8), and Brough, where the orientation of fields and enclosures of Late Iron Age and Roman date appears to have influenced the arrangement of ridge and furrow (Jones forthcoming; Wheeler 1979, 127 fig.48, 129).

The origins of the medieval open field system remain unclear, but there are reasonable grounds to postulate its appearance in the Trent Valley in the later Saxon period. At Girton, for example, surface scatters of ninth to eleventh century pottery suggest the spreading of manure and hence arable cultivation of the former middle Saxon settlement (Kinsley and Jones 1999). In addition, at Catholme the stratigraphic and ceramic evidence suggested to the excavators a ninth to thirteenth century date range for the formation of ridge and furrow (Fig.7.14; Losco Bradley and Kinsley 2002, 12).

The Southwell Charter of AD 956 includes references to features suggestive of open field agriculture such as headlands and furlongs, whilst indications of Scandinavian influence in agricultural terminology hint at a ninth to tenth century development (Bishop 2001; Lyth 1989, 13). By the later medieval period, the predominance of arable farming using the open strip field system is illustrated by later enclosure maps and the widespread evidence for ridge and furrow from earthworks, cropmarks, fieldwalking and excavation, including such substantial palimpsests as are known at Egginton, Derbyshire. Few field systems have been the subject of any type of investigation. An exception is the surviving open field system at Laxton, operated on a three-field rotation, which provides a likely model for significant portions of the study area (Beckett 1989; Orwin 1954). Within marginal lands, the use of an infield-outfield system may have occurred, similar to that identified on former woodland sites in Nottinghamshire at Carburton on the Mansfield Plateau (Beresford and St. Joseph 1979, 45–4).

7.7.7 The Growth of Urban Settlement

The Development of Central Places

From at least the seventh century, a greater range of settlement types is apparent within the Valley and on its fringes, with the development of royal and ecclesiastical centres. This takes place against a historical backdrop of conflict, developing concepts of kingship, land tenure, and the polarisation of wealth (Brooks 1989; Scull 1993; Stafford 1985, 94-102). Sites draw upon various agencies to legitimise authority and status, including the re-use of locations with traditions of authority. Such processes underlie the emergence of defended centres of population, consumption and exchange, within a royal framework of fiscal and legal regulation.

A recent study considered evidence for early commercial foci revealed by metal detector finds within Lincolnshire (Ulmschneider 2000). These 'productive sites', distinguished by substantial quantities of eighth to ninth century coinage and a variety of metalwork, include Flixborough and possibly Torksey on the Lower Trent. Such sites demonstrate links with both inter-regional and international trade, as well as production. Excavation at Flixborough has indicated the presence of a high status

Fig.7.14 *Catholme, Staffordshire: ridge and furrow field system exposed by excavation, incorporating pottery up to the thirteenth century in date; colluvium (hatched) along eastern edge of site (source: Losco-Bradley and Kinsley 2002; reproduced by courtesy of the authors and Trent & Peak Archaeological Unit)*

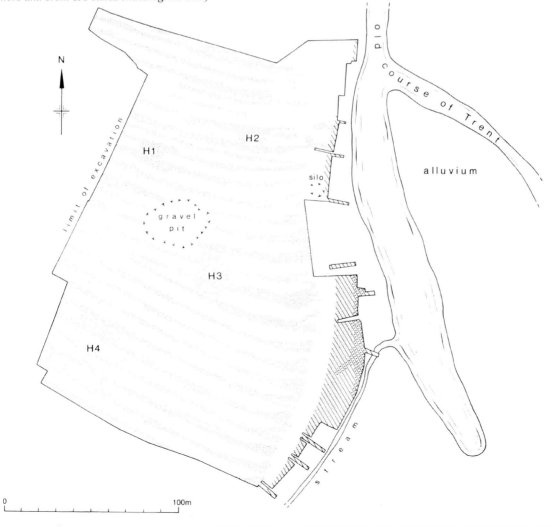

settlement with extensive trade contacts, represented by imported pottery, glass and lava querns, and evidence of on-site iron and lead working and carpentry (Loveluck 1998). At Melton Ross, it was possible to place a 'productive site' within a topographical, historical and administrative context (Leahy 2003).

There is general agreement that incorporation within the Danelaw acted to accelerate the economic development of emerging centres (Hadley 2000, 31–3; Stafford 1985, 49; Symonds 2003, 61; Vince 1994, 115). Both Nottingham and Derby have been noted as possible centres of large pre-Viking estates (Roffe 1986; 1997, 25-6). There is continuing uncertainty regarding the precise location of the pre-Norman centre at Derby relative to the Roman site at Little Chester. The latter provides evidence of re-use during the later Saxon period (Sparey-Green 2002, 64–83, 139–44), whilst there appears to have been a separate early ecclesiastical focus which attracted the burial of the Northumbrian King Ealhmund around AD 800 (Hall 1989; 2001, 145; Radford 1976). Interpretation of the archaeological evidence from Nottingham is frustrated by a shortage of published evidence. The earliest Anglo-Saxon material focuses on the east edge of the later Saxon borough (Young 1983, fig.5), and although the character of the occupation is unclear it may have included an enclosure of sixth to seventh century date. Subsequently, the focus of settlement shifted to the west, the defensive enclosure of the later Saxon borough being established by at least the second half of the ninth century (Young 1983). Historical evidence indicates a fluctuating pattern of Danish and English rule in the later ninth century and the first half of the tenth century, including the foundation of an additional burh on the south side of the Trent and the construction of a bridge in AD 920 (Roffe 1997, 28–9). In the later Saxon period, Nottingham became the pre-eminent borough in the Middle Trent and the centre of royal administration for a territory extending as far west as the River Dove (Roffe 1997, 29). The commercial character of the late Saxon borough is unclear, but a commercial function is clearly implied by its mint (*op.cit.*). In addition, the recent discovery of a large fragment of an Ipswich ware vessel hints at early access to inter-regional trade links (Vince 2001, 19).

Newark's nodal position relative to both road and river may have influenced its establishment as a defended centre in the late Saxon period. Although excavations have proved inconclusive (Kinsley 1993b), Roffe (1997, 30) has suggested fortification during the middle decades of the tenth century, enabling providing control of the lower reaches of the Trent. The allocation of a mint around this time would support its identification as an emerging centre of some importance. Torksey has also produced significant middle Saxon coin finds (Ulmschneider 2000, 65), and its kiln sites and the presence of dirham fragments and hack silver ingots are suggestive of urban status by the tenth century (Hall 2001, 150; Symonds 2003, 61).

Later Medieval Developments

Many of the post-Conquest towns along the Trent were of pre-Conquest foundation, often beginning with a military function, first as burghs and then as castle sites. This underlines the importance of their locations on key routes of communication. Central to this location for many was the proximity of a road crossing with notable bridges – as at Burton-on-Trent, Nottingham and Newark (Knight and Howard 1994, 150–158; Rye 1903). In addition, many of the towns of the Lower Trent, such as Torksey and Gainsborough, functioned as river ports, with smaller riverside centres at Walkerith, Owston Ferry and Burton upon Stather in Lincolnshire (Bennett and Bennett 1993, 56).

Although archaeological evidence for the development of many of these towns is piecemeal, it is possible to highlight broad trends. Post-Conquest signs of urban decline are indicated at a number of sites, notably at Torksey (Fig. 7.15) where burgesses fell from 213 to 102 (Morgan and Thorn 1986, T1-2). However, from the late eleventh to the fourteenth centuries, most towns exhibit growth under both lay and ecclesiastical direction. Excavations have revealed borough expansion and new house construction at Nottingham, Newark, Burton-on-Trent and Stone (Hughes 1996; Kinsley 1993b; Meeson and Kirkham 1993; Young 1983). Nottingham was substantially expanded by the addition of the Norman borough, castle and a large market place to the west of the Saxon borough. Both boroughs were initially enclosed together by a ditch and bank in the first half of the twelfth century and by a wall from the late thirteenth century (Barley 1965). Early evidence of growth in the town includes the construction of 23 houses on the infilled pre-conquest borough ditch by AD 1086 (Morris 1977, 280a, B17), while further new construction in the twelfth and thirteenth centuries has been recorded on sites at Drury Hill, Woolpack Lane, Fisher Gate, Boots Garage, Goose Gate and Halifax Place (Young 1983). Similar expansion is recorded for Newark under the Archbishop of York. In the twelfth century, the castle and church were rebuilt and the town was replanned around the market square. New construction has been revealed at Slaughter House Lane (Kinsley 1993b), accompanied in the thirteenth century by ribbon development in the Outer Borough (Barley 1966). At Burton-on-Trent, expansion occurred under the auspices of the Abbots of Burton, with development of the borough around AD 1187–1197; this was followed by the acquisition of a market charter and extension of the borough along the river toward Horninglow, Staffordshire (Meeson and Kirkham 1993, 21–22). Evidence of new construction is also recorded at Torksey and Stone (Albone and Field 2002; Barley 1964; 1981; Hughes 1996). The drive for urbanisation during this period is further indicated by the numerous applications for burgage and market charters (Beckett 1988, 59–64; Palliser 1972, 64–65; Palliser and Pinnock 1971, 50–51). Documentary sources suggest that the population at this time within the counties of Derbyshire, Leicestershire, Nottinghamshire and Lincolnshire rose dramatically from around 183,000 in AD 1086 to 558,000 in AD 1340 (Beckett 1988, 354).

The layout of towns along the Trent comprised several elements common to urban centres nationally. Due to their strategic location, castles were established in the eleventh century at Nottingham, Newark and possibly Burton-on-

Trent; the first two of these also possessed town defensive circuits (Barley 1965; Todd 1977). Motte and Bailey castles were constructed at several of the smaller centres between the eleventh and twelfth centuries, few of which survive (Cathcart-King 1983). Within Nottingham and Newark, town layout was influenced by the former presence of the pre-conquest boroughs, still fossilised within the existing street plans (Barley 1965; 1966). Both planned and more organic development is evident at several sites, including the area between the old and new boroughs of Newark (Barley 1966). Building plots of eleventh and twelfth century date, possibly lying side-on along street frontages, have been found at Drury Hill, Nottingham and Church Lane, Southwell (Elliott 2003a; Young 1983). These were superseded by the more commonly found long, narrow, end-on plots, with ancillary buildings and features lying to the rear, which are typically of twelfth century or later date. Industrial activities identified at the back of such plots include corn-driers/malting kilns, pottery kilns and horners' vats (Kinsley 1993b, 60; MacCormick 2001; Young 1983). The development of later extra-mural industry is evident at Nottingham, including pottery kilns in the area of the Victoria Centre and osier beds within the vicinity of the Broadmarsh. Central to the trade of individual towns was the market square, sizeable examples of which were built at Newark and Nottingham; these were also used for annual fairs, reflecting their importance as local and regional trading centres.

Fig.7.15 *View of shrunken borough of Torksey, Lincolnshire, showing the River Trent to the left and the Foss Dyke at the bottom (copyright reserved Cambridge University Collection of Air Photographs; photograph reference JE 37)*

Fig.7.16 *Distribution of the main Anglo-Saxon site types in the Trent Valley and neighbouring areas (based on a map compiled by G. Kinsley, with modifications by H. Jones and S.Baker)*

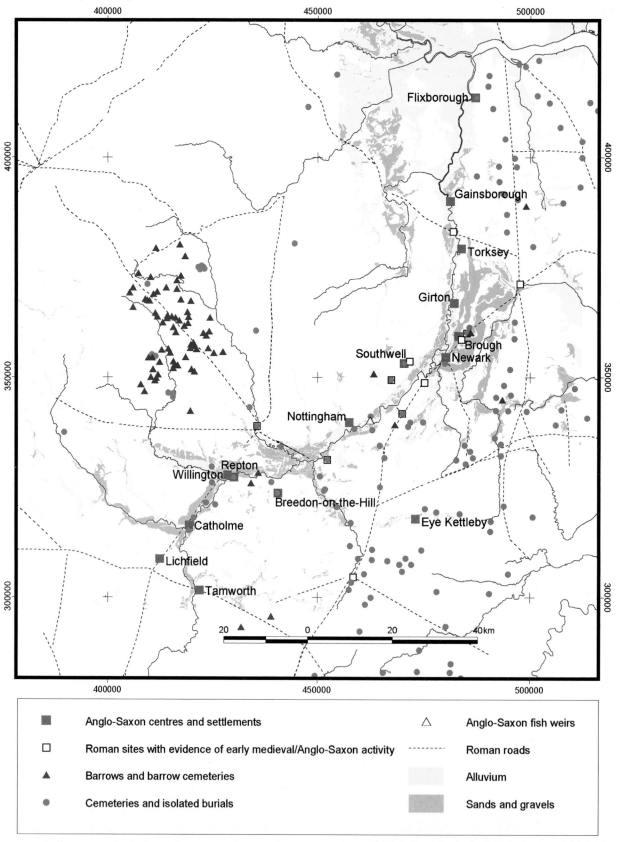

■	Anglo-Saxon centres and settlements	△	Anglo-Saxon fish weirs
□	Roman sites with evidence of early medieval/Anglo-Saxon activity	- - - -	Roman roads
▲	Barrows and barrow cemeteries		Alluvium
●	Cemeteries and isolated burials		Sands and gravels

Waterfront areas are common to many of the towns along the Trent. However, no excavations have yet occurred comparable to the Thames Valley sites, which have produced nationally important assemblages of pottery, leatherwork and evidence of timber-working techniques from waterlogged rubbish deposits used in reclamation (Miller *et al.* 1986; Milne 1992). Excavation of waterfront localities should be a future research priority in the Trent Valley. Quays are known at Gainsborough, Nottingham and Torksey (Beckwith 1967, 3; Cole 1906; Cox 1910, 144), while possible waterlogged former suburbs offer great environmental potential at Nottingham, Burton-on-Trent and Torksey. At Newark, limited excavation has revealed the deposition of rubbish over a natural river-cliff forming a rear boundary for plots with river frontages along Town Wharf, North Gate (Challis 1994b, 36). This material, dumped in part for land reclamation, dated from the twelfth to eighteenth centuries and sealed remains containing early to middle Saxon pottery – although no formal wharf structures were found (*ibid.*).

Building remains have been excavated to varying degrees at several urban sites, including Newark, Burton-on-Trent, Torksey, Southwell, Stone and Nottingham, but those from Nottingham, which represent the most substantial corpus, have yet to be fully published (Barley 1964; 1981; Elliott 2003a; Hughes 1996; Kinsley 1993b; Meeson and Kirkham 1993). Buildings were typically of timber construction, with stone less commonly used before the fourteenth century; even then, stone was used largely for dwarf stone walls associated with timber-framed structures. This follows national trends, although it may also reflect partly the poor quality of building stone available to many of the towns situated along the Valley. A possible consequence of this is the early use of brick on sites along the Middle and Lower Trent, as at Southwell (Elliott 2003a), Gainsborough Old Hall (Lindley 1991) and Holme Pierrepont (Pevsner 2001, 147–149). Timber construction remained important throughout the period, with several examples surviving or incorporated within standing buildings at Nottingham, Newark, Southwell and Burton-on-Trent (Arnold *et al.* 2002; Laxton *et al.* 1995; Meeson and Kirkham 1993; Samuels *et al.* 1996; Summers 1988). Timber used for construction was often sourced from beyond the Valley, including Sherwood Forest (Laxton 1997).

Urban decline has been noted in several towns from around AD 1300. In Nottingham, dereliction and abandonment of buildings occurred in virtually all those excavated areas showing reorganisation and expansion between AD 1100 and AD 1300. By the mid-fourteenth century, the majority of the former pre-conquest borough east of Stoney Street exhibited signs of abandonment, with the area near Woolpack Lane subjected to quarrying (Young 1983). Following the outbreak of plague in the fourteenth century, a substantial population decline is suggested for the East Midlands of between 30–50%. Lincolnshire was particularly affected, with its population falling from an estimated 400,000 to 200,000 – diminishing thereby its former ascendancy over the other East Midland counties (Beckett 1988, 354). Not all evidence, however, points to urban decline after AD 1300. Rather than complete decline, the picture is one of re-organisation. Substantial building is indicated, particularly for many urban churches, including the re-building of St Mary's, Nottingham, with additions to St Mary's, Newark. New religious foundations included friaries and hospitals, while secular construction is noted at the above-mentioned urban sites. Within Nottingham, the French Borough saw continued building at the churches of St Nicholas and St Peter, and the foundation of friaries on Beastmarket Hill and in the marshy suburbs of Broadmarsh, the latter representing marginal land liable to flooding up to the twentieth century. Certain industries appear to have relocated to extra-mural sites; these included pottery production, once evident within the eastern side of the town, which moved by AD 1250 and continued production until at least AD 1420 (Young 1983).

7.8 Regional Industries and Trade

7.8.1 The Anglo-Saxon Period

Studies of early Anglo-Saxon trade have attempted to track the embedded system of exchange through the most visible medium, namely imported items surviving within funerary contexts. These have provided models of high level gift exchange and itinerant traders (Huggett 1988). Finds within the cemeteries of the Trent Valley and its hinterlands of amber beads and ivory rings indicate its participation within such exchange patterns (Kinsley 1993, graves 1, 3, 46; Kinsley in Sparey-Green 2002, 101 fig.23). Ceramic studies within the region have provided an additional source of evidence for patterns of trade and exchange, some apparently focused upon riverine transport. The find spots of late Saxon Torksey ware suggest a prominent role for the Trent in its distribution, and it is probably significant that the production centre for Torksey Ware was positioned near the junction of the Foss Dyke and the Trent (Symonds 2003, 135). This argument is reinforced by petrological analyses of granodiorite-tempered pottery of early to middle Saxon date, assessment of which suggests a possible source at or close to the Mountsorrel granodiorite outcrop on the eastern fringe of Charnwood Forest, Leicestershire (Knight *et al.* 2003; Walker 1978; Williams and Vince 1997). Pots manufactured in this fabric were widely distributed, many possibly via the Trent, Soar and other tributaries, and provide important evidence for the early development of regional rather than local production (Williams and Vince 1997). The role of the Trent in the transportation of heavier cargoes such as lead also seems probable. Reference was made in the previous chapter to the transport to the Humber of Roman lead ingots from the White Peak (Chapter 6.4; Van de Noort and Davies 1993, 77), and it seems likely that a similar trade route was used in the Anglo-Saxon period – as suggested by discoveries at Flixborough and Riby (Loveluck 1998, 154, 157; Steedman 1995, 267–72).

The increased frequency of coin finds from Anglo-Saxon England during the seventh and eighth centuries suggests the re-establishment of a market economy. This was one element of a complex series of social and economic changes of this period, resulting in the establishment of permanent trading centres and the extension of royal fiscal controls on trade (Symonds 2003, 57–61; Vince 2001). Coin finds from the study area include eighth to ninth century examples from Breedon-on-the-Hill, Repton, Newark, Torksey and Flixborough (Early Medieval Corpus of Coin Finds), emphasising the link with specialised, high-status centres. The riverine focus of these sites, together with the emerging riverside boroughs, is suggestive of a prominent role for the Trent and associated rivers such as the Soar in the transportation of goods. However, the role of roads in the later Saxon and post-Conquest period should not be underestimated (Chapter 7.4).

7.8.2 Later Medieval Developments

Evidence for industrial activities along the Valley has been recovered mainly from excavations of urban sites in Nottingham and Newark, supplemented by documentary, street name and other sources. Old street names in Nottingham and Newark, for example, indicate the presence of many common former trades including Wheeler Gate, Fisher Gate, Fletcher Gate (flesh-hewers or butchers), Barker Gate (barkers or tanners), Carter Gate and Potter Gate (Gover *et al.* 1940, 14–17, 199–200). From a rental of Burton Abbey dated to *c.*AD 1319, 38 trades practised within the town of Burton-on-Trent can be deduced from the surnames present. Several of these represent activity reliant on water supply, such as the launderers who leased tenements adjacent to the river (Stuart 1994).

Significant industries of the Trent Valley included pottery production, cloth manufacture, leatherware, malting and alabaster-quarrying. Pottery production has been identified on a number of urban sites, including Torksey (Barley 1966; 1981), Nottingham (Young 1983) and Newark (Abbott 1994), and by the fourteenth century Nottingham had become a major centre of ceramic production distributing not only pottery but also floor tiles and roof furniture (Parker 1932) around the East Midlands (Young 1983). Later pottery production has also been demonstrated at rural sites such as Sneyd Green, Staffordshire, and Ticknall, the latter producing Cistercian and Midland Purple Wares (Brears 1971; Middleton 1984). Documentary sources indicate the importance of cloth production at urban sites throughout the period and later rural settlements (Beckett 1988). Little trace of this industry remains in the archaeological record, unfortunately, apart from the occasional street name such as Tenters Yard in Nottingham (Gover *et al.* 1940, 21). Evidence for leather working has been recovered from waterlogged deposits in Stone (Bevan 1996, 71), while Horners' vats have been found in Nottingham (Young 1983). Malting kilns or corn driers have been discovered at Newark and possibly Southwell (Elliott 2003b; Kinsley 1993b, 61), while in Nottingham at least 28 examples producing for both domestic and commercial markets have been identified (MacCormick 2001).

Few investigations have been made of the quarry workings which survive within the Valley (Lethbridge-Farmer 1916). Exploitation of alabaster was a significant industry for areas around Chellaston, Derbyshire, and Tutbury, while Nottingham carvers had an international reputation and supplied altar pieces and devotional objects to both foreign and local markets (Cheetam 1962). The poor quality of stone available within the Valley for construction and monumental sculpture necessitated use of outside sources from Lincolnshire, North Nottinghamshire and Derbyshire (Alexander 1995; Butler 1964), although localised outcrops of Skerry and Lias were used for some wall fabrics and foundations, as at All Saints Church, Cotgrave (Elliott and Gilbert 1999). Medieval iron production has been recorded in regions adjacent to the Valley, including the thirteenth century smelting site situated on the Coal Measures at Stanley Grange, Derbyshire, utilising local resources of iron ore and timber for fuel (Challis and Southgate 1999).

Along with coal and lead from the Peak District, iron was traded to urban centres by road and river, boats travelling downstream to Lincolnshire returning with corn (Beckett 1992, 23). Trade was facilitated by the developing network of local and regionally significant markets and fairs, linked by road and river transport. Despite the sea links of the river ports on the Lower Trent, the impact of international trade is unclear in the archaeological record. Limited evidence for continental imports is provided by finds such as fine glassware, Saintonge pottery from south-west France, and fruit stones such as figs and grapes; these are currently represented by small quantities of material, thus preventing accurate assessment of the extent of such trade (Hughes 1996; Hurst 1991; Webster and Cherry 1972).

7.9 Conclusion

Changes in the Valley environment during the Anglo-Saxon period bear the imprint of climatic deterioration, but were driven largely by anthropogenic factors. The Roman period may represent a high water mark in the expansion of settlement, with the extension of agriculture into more marginal zones (Chapter 6). In contrast, the sub-Roman and early Anglo-Saxon period may have witnessed a contraction and refocusing of activities on the elevated gravel terraces and coversand deposits. This represents a re-entrenchment of core areas of settlement, favouring sites above the level of seasonal flooding. The early Anglo-Saxon landscape of the Valley remained predominantly funerary, and a comprehensive review is long overdue. More recent discoveries at Cotgrave and Holme Pierrepont have revealed a complexity and potential chronological depth lacking in accounts of earlier discoveries. As elsewhere, the funerary landscape embraces distinctive topographic locations and earlier monuments in a symbolic linkage of communities with the landscape and its perceived history and mythology. Evidence of settlement is sparse but increasing, and suggests a significant role for the boundaries of the inherited Romano-British landscape as a framework for early development. Problems remain in identifying the processes by which the dispersed settlement pattern of the early period transformed into the historic nucleated landscape. However, recent discoveries provide embryonic models of development, and have highlighted locations such as Girton where the total landscape approaches applied so successfully elsewhere in the East Midlands might be employed to great effect. It is encouraging that the limited evidence is already broadly consistent with the trends emerging from areas such Northamptonshire and central southern England, which see the linked development of nucleated settlement and open field systems in the ninth and tenth centuries (Foard 2001; Hooke 1998, 120). At the same time, the Trent Valley presents its own distinctive character. In contrast to the discontinuity of the Northamptonshire sequence, where furlongs show no relationship to the layout of the underlying early-middle Anglo-Saxon settlements (Foard 2001), the picture is one of broad continuity. Medieval ridge and furrow at Willington and Brough shows respect for the grain of the landscape established by earlier field systems. The development of more specialised and high status centres from the seventh century reveals similar themes, distinctive topographic

Fig.7.17 *Medieval sites referred to in the text, compiled by S. Baker*

(1.Adbolton; 2.Alrewas; 3.Ambaston; 4.Aston-on-Trent; 5.Averham; 6.Barlaston; 7.Barton Blount; 8.Barton-in-Fabis; 9.Belton; 10.Borrowash; 11.Boston; 12.Breedon-on-the-Hill; 13.Bretby; 14.Brough; 15.Broughton Lodge; 16.Bucknall; 17.Burton Joyce; 18.Burton-on-Trent; 19.Burton-upon-Stather;20. Carburton; 21.Castle Donington; 22.Catholme; 23.Chellaston; 24.Church Wilne;, 25.Cleatham; 26.Collingham; 27.Colwick; 28.Cotgrave; 29.Cromwell; 30.Curborough; 31.Derby; 32.East Bridgford; 33.East Stoke; 34.Egginton; 35.Eye Kettleby 36.Flawford; 37.Flintham; 38.Flixborough; 39.Foremark; 40.Gainsborough; 41.Girton; 42.Gokewell; 43.Gonalston; 44.Gresley; 45.Hemington; 46.Holme Pierrepont; 47.Horninglow; 48.Hoveringham; 49.Hilton; 50.Hulton; 51.Ingleby; 52.Keighton;53.Kelham; 54.Kings Newton; 55.Langford; 56.Laxton; 57.Lenton; 58.Lichfield; 59.Lincoln; 60.Littleborough; 61.Little Chester; 62.Lockington; 63.Long Whatton; 64. Margidunum [East Bridgford]; 65.Marston; 66.Marton; 67.Mattersey; 68.Melton Ross; 69.Mountsorrel; 70.Needwood; 71.Newark; 72.Newton; 73.Nottingham; 74.Owston Ferry;75.Oxton; 76.Potter Hill; 77.Quarrington; 78.Repton; 79.Riby; 80.Ruddington; 81.Sandon; 82.Saxilby; 83.Saxondale; 84.Sawley; 85.Scarrington; 86.Shardlow; 87.Sheffield's Hill (Roxby); 88.Shelford; 89.Sinfin; 90.Sneinton; 91.Sneyd Green; 92.Southwell; 93.South Muskham; 94.Stafford; 95.Stamford; 96.Stanford-on-Soar; 97.Stanley Grange; 98.Stanton-by-Bridge; 99.Stapenhill; 100.Stoke Bardolph; 101.Stone; 102.Swarkestone Lowes; 103.Tamworth; 104.Thorpe; 105.Thurgarton; 106.Ticknall; 107. Torksey; 108.Trentham; 109.Tutbury; 110.Walkerith; 111.Walton-on-Trent; 112.Waterton; 113.West Burton; 114.Wilford; 115.Willington; 116.Winshill; 117.Winthorpe; 118.Wychnor;119.Yoxall.

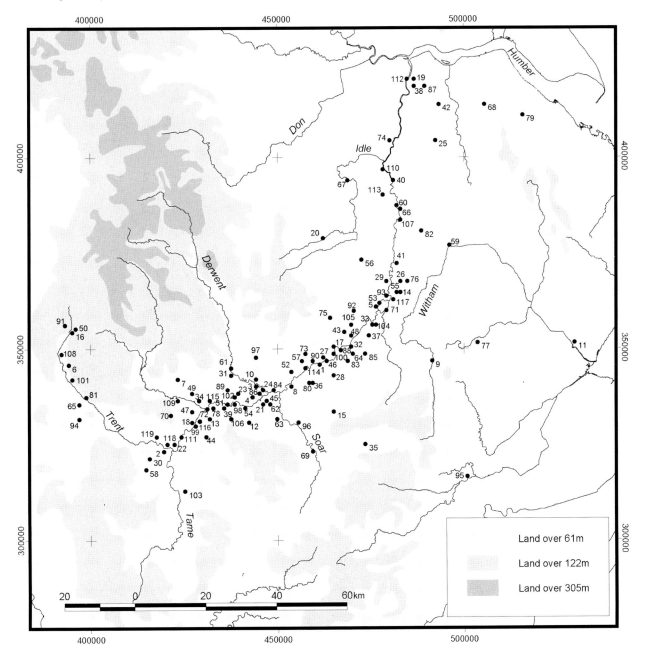

locations and earlier centres of authority and administration proving influential factors in shaping the new religious and commercial landscapes.

Significant differences have been noted in this chapter between the upper, middle and lower reaches of the Valley during the post-Conquest period, but although due allowance must be made for intra-regional variability a number of broad trends may be discerned which suggest parallels with developments nationally. Between approximately AD 1100 and AD 1300, population growth and expansion may be demonstrated at urban and rural sites along the Trent, with a marked trend in rural areas towards nucleation. These changes were accompanied by the intensification of arable open field farming, woodland clearance, increased exploitation of the river, the development of urban industry and a growing network of local and regional markets and fairs linked by road and river. The end result of these developments was a complex and highly managed landscape, closely directed by lay and ecclesiastical landlords. The fourteenth century, which suffered a combination of climatic deterioration, agrarian crises and plague, witnessed depopulation and the reorganisation of settlement and agriculture, including a shift in emphasis from arable to pasture. Relations between the Trent Valley and neighbouring areas also changed significantly during this latter period with the economic decline of Lincolnshire.

The river played a key role in the development of the human landscape and the regional economy throughout the medieval period, influencing in particular the location of towns at major bridge crossings, the development of river ports, the character of local trades and industries, the agricultural economy and even the layout of parish boundaries. In addition, much important structural and artefactual evidence has been obtained from archaeological investigations of the floodplain and river terraces – most spectacularly at Hemington, where the dynamic fluvial environment has contributed to the preservation of riverine structures of national significance. Significantly less emphasis has been placed by comparison with earlier periods upon palaeoenvironmental analyses of organic deposits contained in abandoned river channels or other wetland environments or upon waterlogged sites such as urban waterfronts, while many questions remain on the subjects of alluviation and colluviation. It is recommended therefore that greater priority be placed in archaeological research upon the analysis of organic and alluvial or colluvial deposits with the aim of shedding further light upon developments in the medieval landscape of this major Midlands river valley.

REFERENCES

Aberg, F.A. (ed) 1978. *Medieval Moated Sites*. CBA Res. Rep. **17**. London: Council for British Archaeology.

Abbott, C. 1994. Results of an Archaeological Watching Brief conducted at the Co-Operative Store, Kirkgate, Newark. Unpublished report, Trent & Peak Archaeological Unit, University Park, Nottingham.

Albone, J. and Field, N. (eds) 2002. Torksey, Castle Farm, *Lincolnshire Hist. Archaeol.* **37**, 56.

Alexander, J.S. 1995. Building stone from the East Midlands quarries: sources, transportation and usage, *Medieval Archaeol.* **39**, 107–135.

Alvey, R.C. 1975. The site of the Southwell Minster Grammar School extension, 1971, *Trans. Thoroton Soc. Nottinghamshire* **79**, 14.

Alvey, R.C. 1980. Some recent Anglo-Saxon finds from Nottinghamshire and Lincolnshire, *Trans. Thoroton Soc. Nottinghamshire* **84**, 82–85.

Arnold, A.J., Howard, R.E., Laxton, R.R. and Litton, C.D. 2002. *The Urban Development of Newark-on-Trent: A Dendrochronological Approach*. English Heritage Centre for Archaeology Report 95/2002.

Arnold, C.J. 1981. Early Anglo-Saxon pottery: production and distribution, in H. Howard and E.L. Morris (eds), *Production and Distribution: a Ceramic Viewpoint*, 243–255.

Arnold, C.J. 1997. *An Archaeology of the Early Anglo-Saxon Kingdoms*, 2nd edition. London: Routledge.

Baker, C.L.V. 1910. St John the Baptist, Stanford on Soar, *Trans. Thoroton Soc. Nottinghamshire* **14**, 2–9.

Baker, S. 2003. The Trent Valley: Palaeochannel Mapping from Aerial Photographs, Trent Valley 2002: Advancing the Agenda in Archaeology and Alluvium (Component 2a). Trent & Peak Archaeological Unit, University Park, Nottingham. http://www.tvg.org.uk/palaeochannels.pdf

Barber, K.E., Chambers, F.M., Maddy, D., Stoneman, R. and Brew, J.S. 1994. A sensitive high-resolution record of late Holocene climatic change from a raised bog in northern England, *The Holocene* **4**, 198–205.

Barber, K.E., Maddy, D., Rose, N., Stevenson, A.C., Stoneman, R. and Thompson, R. 2000. Replicated proxy-climate signals over the last 2000 yr from two distant UK peat bogs: new evidence for regional palaeoclimatic teleconnections, *Quat. Sci. Rev.* **19**, 481–487.

Barley, M.W. 1964. The medieval borough of Torksey: excavations 1960–2, *Antiq. J.* **44** (2), 165–187.

Barley, M.W. 1965. Medieval Town Wall, Park Row excavations 1964, *Trans. Thoroton Soc. Nottinghamshire* **69**, 50–65.

Barley, M.W. 1966. Evolution of settlement: medieval period, in K.C. Edwards (ed), *Nottingham and its Region*, 204–214.

Barley, M.W. 1981. The medieval borough of Torksey: excavations 1963–68, *Antiq. J.* **61**, 264–291.

Barnes, F.A. 1987. Lenton Priory after the Dissolution: its buildings and fair grounds, *Trans. Thoroton Soc. Nottinghamshire* **91**, 79–95.

Bassett, S. (ed) 1989. *The Origins of Anglo-Saxon Kingdoms*. Leicester University Press.

Bassett, S. (ed) 1992. *Death in Towns*. London: Leicester University Press.

Bateman, T. 1848. Discoveries of Romano-British and Saxon remains in Nottinghamshire, *J. Brit. Archaeol. Assoc.* **3**, 297–300.

Bateman, T. 1853. On early burial-places discovered in the county of Nottingham, *J. Brit. Archaeol. Assoc.* **8**, 183–192.

Beckett, J.V. 1988. *The East Midlands from AD 1000*. London: Longman.

Beckett, J.V. 1989. *A History of Laxton: England's Last Open-Field Village*. Oxford: Basil Blackwell.

Beckett, J.V. 1992. Lincolnshire and the East Midlands: a historian's perspective, *Lincolnshire Hist. Archaeol.* **27**, 23–26.

Beckett, J. (ed) 1997. *A Centenary History of Nottingham.* Manchester University Press.

Beckwith, I.S. 1967. The river trade of Gainsborough 1500–1850, *Lincolnshire Hist. Archaeol.* **2**, 3–20.

Beckwith, I. 1988. *The Book of Gainsborough.* Buckingham: Barracuda Books Ltd.

Beilby, B.W. 1996. Excavations at the Cluniac Priory of the Holy Trinity, Lenton, 1962–64, *Trans. Thoroton Soc. Nottinghamshire* **70**, 55–62.

Benito, G., Baker, V.R. and Gregory, K.J. (eds) 1998. *Palaeohydrology and Environmental Change.* Chichester: Wiley.

Bennett, S. and Bennett, N. (eds) 1993. *An Historical Atlas of Lincolnshire.* University of Hull Press.

Beresford, G. 1975. *The Medieval Clayland Village: Excavations at Goltho and Barton Blount.* London: Society for Medieval Archaeology.

Beresford, M.W. 1986. Inclesmoor, West Riding of Yorkshire, in R.A. Skelton and P.D.A. Harvey (eds), *Local Maps and Plans from Medieval England,* 147–161.

Beresford, M.W. and Hurst, J.G. 1971. *Deserted Medieval Villages.* Guildford: Lutterworth Press.

Beresford, M.W. and St. Joseph, J.K.S. 1979. *Medieval England: an Aerial Survey.* Cambridge University Press.

Bevan, L. 1996. Leather, in G. Hughes, Excavations within a medieval and post-medieval tenement at Stone 1993.

Biddle, M. and Kjølbye-Biddle, B. 2001. Repton and the 'great heathen army' 873–4, in J. Graham-Campbell, R. Hall, J. Jesch and D. N. Parsons (eds), *Vikings and the Danelaw,* 45–96.

Bigmore, P. 1982. Villages and towns, in L. Cantor (ed), *The English Medieval Landscape,* 154–192.

Birrell, J.R. 1979. Medieval agriculture, in M.W. Greenslade and D.A. Johnson (eds), *A History of the County of Stafford,* vol.6, 1–48.

Bishop, M.W. 1983. Burials from the cemetery of the Hospital of St Leonard, Newark, Nottinghamshire, *Trans. Thoroton Soc. Nottinghamshire* **87**, 23–35.

Bishop, M.W. 1984. An Anglian cemetery at Cotgrave, Nottinghamshire, *Trans. Thoroton Soc. Nottinghamshire* **88**, 106.

Bishop, M.W. 1997. Landscape history, in *Nottinghamshire Countryside Appraisal,* Chapter 8 – Trent Washlands, 7–14. Nottingham: Nottinghamshire County Council.

Bishop, M.W. 2001. An archaeological resource assessment of Anglo-Saxon Nottinghamshire, *East Midlands Archaeological Research Framework.* http://www.le.ac.uk/archaeology/east_midlands_research_framework.htm

Bishop, M. and Challis, K. 1998. Village earthwork survey in Nottinghamshire, *Medieval Settlement Research Group Ann. Rep.* **13**, 26–32.

Boddington, A. 1990. Models of burial, settlement and worship: the final phase reviewed, in E. Southworth (ed), *Anglo-Saxon Cemeteries: a Reappraisal,* 177–199.

Branson, J., Brown, A.G. and Gregory, K.J. (eds), 1996. *Global Continental Changes: the Context of Palaeohydrology.* Geol. Soc. Spec. Pub. **115**. London: Geological Society.

Brears, P. 1971. *The English Country Pottery: its History and Techniques.* Newton Abbott: David and Charles.

Briggs, J. 1852. In Proceedings of the congress held at Derby, *J. British Archaeol. Assoc.* **7**, 362–363.

Brooks, N. 1989. The formation of the Mercian Kingdom, in S. Bassett (ed), *The Origins of Anglo-Saxon Kingdoms,* 159–170.

Brown, A.G. 1998. Fluvial evidence of the Medieval Warm Period and the late medieval climatic deterioration in Europe, in G. Benito, V.R. Baker and K.J. Gregory (eds), *Palaeohydrology and Environmental Change,* 43–52.

Brown, A.G., Salisbury, C.R. and Smith, D.N. 2001. Late Holocene channel changes of the Middle Trent: channel response to a thousand year flood record, *Geomorphology* **39**, 69–82.

Brown, C. 1904. *A History of Newark-on-Trent: being the Life Story of an Ancient Town.* Vol. 1. Newark: S. Whiles.

Brown, T. 2002. Floodplain landscapes and archaeology: fluvial events and human agency, *J. Wetland Archaeol.* **2**, 89–104.

Butler, L.A.S. 1964. Minor monumental sculpture in the East Midlands, *Archaeol. J.* **121**, 111–153.

Cantor, L. (ed) 1982. *The English Medieval Landscape.* London: Croom Helm.

Carver, M. (ed) 1992. *The Age of Sutton Hoo.* Woodbridge, Suffolk: Boydell Press.

Cathcart-King, D.J.C. 1983. *Castellarium Anglicanum.* Millwood, New York: Kraus International.

Challis, K. 1994a. Trial excavation at Top Lane, Laxton, Nottinghamshire, *Trans. Thoroton Soc. Nottinghamshire* **98**, 24–31.

Challis, K. 1994b. Trial excavations at Town Wharf, Newark-on-Trent, Nottinghamshire, *Trans. Thoroton Soc. Nottinghamshire* **98**, 32–37.

Challis, K. 1995. Recent excavations at Laxton, Nottinghamshire, *Medieval Settlement Research Group Ann. Rep.* **10**, 20–23.

Challis, K. 2002. Settlement morphology and medieval village planning: a case study at Laxton, Nottinghamshire, *Trans. Thoroton Soc. Nottinghamshire* **106**, 61–70.

Challis, K. and Bishop, M. 1998. Village Earthwork Survey in Nottinghamshire 1994–96, *Trans. Thoroton Soc. Nottinghamshire* **102**, 69–78.

Challis, K. and Kinsley, G. 1995. Early Anglo-Saxon Derbyshire: interim report on the first two seasons of DAAC funded research. Unpublished report, Trent & Peak Archaeological Trust, University Park, Nottingham.

Challis, K. and Southgate, M. 1999. Stanley Grange, *Derbyshire Archaeol. J.* **119**, 292–294.

Chambers, F.M., Barber, K.E., Maddy, D. and Brew, J. 1997. A 5500-year proxy-climate and vegetation record from Blanket mire at Talla Moss, Borders, Scotland, *The Holocene* 7 (4), 391–399.

Chandler, J.H. (ed) 1993. *John Leland's Itinerary: Travels in Tudor England.* Stroud: A. Sutton.

Cheetham, F.W. 1962. *Medieval English Alabaster Carvings in the Castle Museum, Nottingham.* Nottingham: City of Nottingham Art Galleries and Museums Committee.

Chiverrell, R.C. 2001. A proxy record of late Holocene climate change from May Moss, northeast England, *J. Quat. Sci.* **16**, 9–29.

City of Lincoln Archaeology Unit. 1990. *Lincoln Archaeology 1989–90.* Lincoln: City of Lincoln Archaeology Unit.

City of Lincoln Archaeology Unit. 1991. *Lincoln Archaeology 1990–1991.* Lincoln: City of Lincoln Archaeology Unit.

Clay, P. 1992. A Norman mill dam at Hemington Fields, Castle Donington, Leicestershire, in S. Needham and M.G. Macklin (eds), *Alluvial Archaeology in Britain*, 163–168.

Clay, P. and Salisbury, C.R. 1990. A Norman mill dam and other sites at Hemington Fields, Castle Donington, Leicestershire, *Archaeol. J.* **147**, 276–307.

Coffman, P. and Thurlby, M. 2000. The influence of Southwell Minster on Romanesque churches in Nottinghamshire, *Trans. Thoroton Soc. Nottinghamshire* **104**, 37–46.

Cole, R.E.G. 1906. The Royal Burgh of Torksey, its Churches, Monasteries and Castle, *The Architectural & Archaeological Society of the Counties of Lincoln & Nottingham* **28** (2), 451–530.

Cool, H.E.M. 2000. The parts left over: material culture into the fifth century, in T. Wilmott and P. Wilson (eds), *The Late Roman Transition in the North: Papers from the Roman Archaeology Conference, Durham 1997*, 47–65.

Cooper, L. 1999. Castle Donington/Lockington-Hemington, Hemington Quarry, *Trans. Leicestershire Archaeol. Hist. Soc.* **73**, 91–97.

Cooper, L.P. 2003. Hemington Quarry, Castle Donington, Leicestershire, UK: a decade beneath the alluvium in the confluence zone, in A.J. Howard, M.G. Macklin and D.G. Passmore (eds), *Alluvial Archaeology in Europe*, 27–41.

Cooper, L. and Ripper, S. 1994. The medieval Trent bridges at Hemington Fields, Castle Donington, *Trans. Leicestershire Archaeol. Hist. Soc.* **68**, 153–161.

Cooper, L., Ripper, S. and Clay, P. 1994. The Hemington bridges, *Curr. Archaeol.* **140**, 316–321.

Coward, J. and Ripper, S. 1998. Castle Donington, Willow Farm, *Trans. Leicestershire Archaeol. Hist. Soc.* **73**, 86–91.

Cox, J.C. 1875–9. *Notes on the Churches of Derbyshire*, vols 1–4. Chesterfield: Palmer and Edmunds; London: Bemrose and Sons.

Cox, J.C. 1907. The religious houses of Derbyshire, in W. Page (ed), *The Victoria History of the County of Derbyshire*, vol. 2, 41–92.

Cox, J.C. 1910. The religious houses of Nottinghamshire, in W. Page (ed), *The Victoria History of the County of Nottinghamshire*, vol. 2, 79–179.

Cox, J.C. 1912. *County Churches: Nottinghamshire.* London: George Allen.

Currey, P.H. 1931. Bridge and chapel of St. Mary at Derby, *J. Derbyshire Archaeol. Nat. Hist. Soc.* **52**, 57–74.

Daniels, C.M. 1966. Excavation on the site of the Roman villa at Southwell, 1959, *Trans. Thoroton Soc. Nottinghamshire* **70**, 13–54.

Darby, H.C. and Maxwell, I.S. (eds) 1962. *The Domesday Geography of Northern England.* Cambridge University Press.

Darby, H.C. and Terrett, I.B. (eds) 1971. *The Domesday Geography of Midland England.* Cambridge University Press.

Dark, K.R. 1994. *Civitas to Kingdom: British Political Continuity 300–800.* Leicester University Press.

Dark, K. 2000. *Britain and the End of the Roman Empire.* Stroud: Tempus.

Dark, P. 2000. *The Environment of Britain in the First Millennium A.D.* London: Duckworth.

Darlington, J. 1994. *Stafford Past: A Guide to the Archaeological and Historical Sites of the Stafford Area.* Stafford: Stafford Borough Council.

Deering, C. 1751. *The History of Nottingham.* Reprint 1970 of *Nottinghamia vetus et nova, or An historical account of the ancient and present state of the town of Nottingham.* Wakefield: SR Publishers

Dickinson, J.C. 1970a. Stone Priory, in M.W. Greenslade (ed), *The History of the County of Stafford. Victoria History of the County of Staffordshire*, vol. 3, 240–247.

Dickinson, J.C. 1970b. Trentham Priory, in M.W. Greenslade (ed), *The History of the County of Stafford. Victoria History of the County of Staffordshire*, vol. 3, 255–260.

Dickinson, W. 1801, 1805. *Antiquities Historical, Architectural, Chorographical, and Itinerary, in Nottinghamshire and the Adjacent Counties: comprising the Histories of Southwell (the Ad Pontem) and of Newark (the Sidnacester, of the Romans), interspersed with Biographical Sketches, and Profusely Embellished with Engravings, in Four Parts.* Vol. 1 (parts 1 & 2) Newark: Holt and Hague for Cadell and Davies, London; vol. 2 (parts 3 & 4) Newark: M. Hague.

Dinnin, M. and Buckland, P.C. 1990. A note on the environmental evidence from the St Mark's Goodsyard Site, Lincoln, in City of Lincoln Archaeology Unit, *Lincoln Archaeology 1989–90*, 30–31.

Dornier, A. 1977. The Anglo-Saxon monastery at Breedon-on-the-Hill, Leicestershire, in A. Dornier (ed), *Mercian Studies*, 155–168.

Dornier, A. (ed) 1977. *Mercian Studies.* Leicester University Press.

Doubleday, W.E. and others. 1941–51.
Articles on Nottinghamshire villages, mostly from the *Nottinghamshire Guardian 1941–1951*. Volume of newspaper cuttings, East Midlands Collection, University of Nottingham.

Drage, C. 1989.
Nottingham Castle, a place full royal. *Trans. Thoroton Soc. Nottinghamshire* **93**.

Drinkall G. and Foreman, M. 1998.
The Anglo-Saxon Cemetery at Castledyke South, Barton-on-Humber. Sheffield Excavation Rep. **6**. Sheffield: Sheffield Academic Press.

Eagles, B.N. 1979.
The Anglo-Saxon Settlement of Humberside. BAR Brit. Ser. **68**.

Early Medieval Corpus of Coin Finds. 2003.
www-cm.fitzmuseum.cam.ac.uk/Coins

Edwards, J.F. and Hindle, B.P. 1991.
The transportation system of medieval England and Wales, *J. Hist. Geogr.* **17** (2), 123–134.

Edwards, J.F. and Hindle, B.P. 1993.
Comment: inland water transportation in medieval England, *J. Hist. Geogr.* **19** (1), 12–14.

Edwards, K.C. (ed) 1966.
Nottingham and its Region. Nottingham: British Association for the Advancement of Science.

Elliott, L. 1996.
A 'porcupine' Sceat from Adbolton deserted medieval village, Nottinghamshire, *Trans. Thoroton Soc.* **100**, 169–170.

Elliott, L. 1997.
Standard Hill, Nottingham, *Trans. Thoroton Soc. Nottinghamshire* **101**, 24–25.

Elliott, L. 2003a.
Excavations at the Minster Chambers, Southwell, Nottinghamshire, *Trans. Thoroton Soc. Nottinghamshire* **107**, 41–64.

Elliott, L. 2003b.
Southwell, Sacrista Prebend, *Trans. Thoroton Soc. Nottinghamshire* **107**, 207–208.

Elliott, L. 2003c.
Markham Moor, *Trans. Thoroton Soc. Nottinghamshire* **107**, 202–203.

Elliott, L. and Gilbert, D. 1998.
All Saints Church, Cotgrave, *Trans. Thoroton Soc. Nottinghamshire* **102**, 137–138.

Elliott, L. and Gilbert, D. 1999.
All Saints Church, Cotgrave, Nottinghamshire. A Report on the Archaeological Recordings. Unpublished report, Trent & Peak Archaeological Unit, University Park, Nottingham.

Ellis, C. and Brown, A.G. 1998.
Archaeomagnetic dating and palaeochannel sediments: data from the medieval channel fills at Hemington, Leicestershire, *J. Archaeol. Sci.* **25**, 149–163.

Esmonde Cleary, S. 1989.
The Ending of Roman Britain. London: Batsford.

Faulkner, N. 2000.
The Decline and Fall of Roman Britain. Stroud: Tempus.

Faull, M. (ed) 1984.
Studies in Late Anglo-Saxon Settlement. Oxford University Department for External Studies.

Finn, N. (ed) 1999.
Eye Kettleby, Leicestershire: Revised Assessment and Updated Project Design. Unpublished report 99/35, University of Leicester Archaeological Services.

Foard, G. 2001.
An archaeological resource assessment of Anglo-Saxon Northamptonshire (400–1066), *East Midlands Archaeological Research Framework*. http://www.le.ac.uk/archaeology/east_midlands_research_framework.htm

Ford, D.A. 1995.
Medieval Pottery in Staffordshire, AD 800–1600: A Review. Staffordshire Archaeological Studies **7**. Stoke-on-Trent City Museum & Art Gallery.

Garton, D. 2002.
Walking fields in South Muskham and its implications for Romano-British cropmark landscapes in Nottinghamshire, *Trans. Thoroton Soc. Nottinghamshire* **106**, 17–40.

Garton, D. and Kinsley, G. 2002.
Absolute chronology, radiocarbon dates, in S. Losco-Bradley and G. Kinsley, *Catholme. An Anglo-Saxon Settlement on the Trent Gravels in Staffordshire*, 120–123.

Garton, D., Arnold, A. and Elliott, L. 2000.
Mattersey, East Carr, *Trans. Thoroton Soc. Nottinghamshire* **104, 156**.

Gathercole, P.W. and Wailes, B. 1959.
Excavations on Castle Hill, Thurgarton, Nottinghamshire 1954–5, *Trans. Thoroton Soc. Nottinghamshire* **63**, 24–56.

Geake, H. 1992.
Burial practice in seventh and eighth century England, in M. Carver (ed), *The Age of Sutton Hoo*, 83–94.

Gelling, M. 1992.
The West Midlands in the Early Middle Ages. Leicester University Press.

Gibson, A. (ed) 2003.
Prehistoric Pottery, People, Pattern and Purpose. Prehist. Ceramics Res. Group Occas. Publ. **4**; BAR Int. Ser. **1156**.

Gilchrist, R. 1992.
Christian bodies and souls: the archaeology of life and death in later medieval hospitals, in S. Bassett (ed), *Death in Towns*, 101–118.

Godfrey, J.T. 1887.
Notes on the Churches of Nottinghamshire, Hundred of Rushcliffe. London: Bemrose.

Good, G.L., Jones, R.H. and Ponsford, M.W. (eds) 1991.
Waterfront Archaeology. CBA Res. Rep. **74**.

Gover, J.E.B., Mawer, A. and Stenton, F.M. 1940.
The Place-names of Nottinghamshire. Cambridge University Press.

Graham-Campbell, J. 2001.
Pagan Scandinavian burial in the central and southern Danelaw, in J. Graham-Campbell, R. Hall, J. Jesch and D.N. Parsons (eds), *Vikings and the Danelaw (Selected Papers from the Proceedings of the Thirteenth Viking Congress)*, 105–123.

Graham-Campbell, J., Hall, R., Jesch, J. and Parsons, D.N. (eds) 2001.
Vikings and the Danelaw (Selected Papers from the Proceedings of the Thirteenth Viking Congress). Oxford: Oxbow Books.

Granby, J. 1942.
Our Notts. Villages. Many ups and downs in record of Adbolton, *Nottinghamshire Guardian*, January 31st 1942.

Greenslade, M.W. (ed) 1970.
A History of the County of Stafford. Victoria History of the County of Stafford, vol. 3. Oxford University Press for Institute of Historical Research.

Greenslade, M.W. and Johnson, D.A. (eds) 1979.
A History of the County of Stafford. Victoria History of the County of Stafford, vol. 6. Oxford University Press for Institute of Historical Research.

Grieg, J. 1993.
Environmental samples analysis, in G. Kinsley, Excavations on the Saxo-Norman town defences at Slaughter House Lane, Newark on Trent, Nottinghamshire, 54–55.

Greig, J. 1997. Pollen and plant macrofossils, in D. Knight and S. Malone, Evaluation of a Late Iron Age and Romano-British Settlement and Palaeochannels of the Trent at Chapel Farm, Shardlow & Great Wilne, Derbyshire (SK 455305), 24, 34–35, Appendices 5 and 6.

Greig, P. 1992. The layout of Lenton Fairground, 1516, *Trans. Thoroton Soc. Nottinghamshire* **96**, 130–134.

Griffin, H.J. 1909. Littleborough Church, *Trans. Thoroton Soc. Nottinghamshire* **13**, 33–36.

Grove, J.M. 1988. *The Little Ice Age*. London: Routledge.

Guilbert, G. 2000. Holme Pierrepont, Lane Conery, *Trans. Thoroton Soc. Nottinghamshire* **104**, 153–4.

Guilbert, G. 2001. Holme Pierrepont, Lane Conery, *Trans. Thoroton Soc. Nottinghamshire* **105**, 189–194.

Guilbert, G. 2002. Holme Pierrepont Quarry, *Trans. Thoroton Soc. Nottinghamshire* **106**, 149–154.

Hadley, D. 2000. *The Northern Danelaw: its Social Structure, 800–1100*. Leicester University Press.

Hadley, D. 2001. In search of the Vikings: the problems and the possibilities of interdisciplinary approaches, in J. Graham-Campbell, R. Hall, J. Jesch and D.N. Parsons (eds), *Vikings and the Danelaw (Selected Papers from the Proceedings of the Thirteenth Viking Congress)*, 13–30.

Hadley, D. 2002. Burial practices in Northern England in the later Anglo-Saxon period, in S. Lucy and A. Reynolds (eds), *Burial in Early Medieval England and Wales*, 209–228.

Hall, R.A. 1974. The pre-conquest burgh of Derby, *Derbyshire Archaeol. J.* **94**, 16–23.

Hall, R.A. 1989. The Five Boroughs of the Danelaw: a review of present knowledge, *Anglo-Saxon Engl.* **18**, 149–206.

Hall, R. 2001. Anglo-Scandinavian urban development in the East Midlands, in J. Graham-Campbell, R. Hall, J. Jesch and D.N. Parsons (eds), *Vikings and the Danelaw (Selected Papers from the Proceedings of the Thirteenth Viking Congress)*, 143–155.

Hamerow, H. 1991. Settlement mobility and the 'middle Saxon shift': rural settlement patterns in Anglo-Saxon England, *Anglo-Saxon Engl.* **20**, 1–18.

Hamerow, H. 2002. Catholme: the development and context of the settlement, in S. Losco-Bradley and G. Kinsley, *Catholme. An Anglo-Saxon settlement on the Trent Gravels in Staffordshire*, 123–129.

Hannam, U.C. and Greenslade, M.W. 1970. Burton Abbey, in M.W. Greenslade (ed), *A History of the County of Stafford. Victoria History of the County of Stafford*, vol. 3, 199–121.

Hayes, P.P. and Lane, T.W. 1992. *The Fenland Project, Number 5: Lincolnshire Survey, the South-West Fens*. East Anglian Archaeology Report **55**. Sleaford: Heritage Trust of Lincolnshire.

Hayfield, C. 1984. Excavations on the site of the Mowbray Manor House at the Vinegarth, Epworth, Lincolnshire, 1975–76, *Lincolnshire Hist. Archaeol.* **19**, 5–28.

Heron, J. 1889. Report on the Stapenhill explorations, *Trans. Burton-on-Trent Nat. Hist. Archaeol. Soc.* **1**, 156–193.

Hill, A. du Boulay. 1903. St. Peter's Church, East Bridgford, *Trans. Thoroton Soc. Nottinghamshire* **7**, 99–118.

Hill, A. du Boulay. 1915. East Bridgford Church, *Trans. Thoroton Soc. Nottinghamshire* **19**, 47–55.

Hines, J. 1984. *The Scandinavian Character of Anglian England in the pre-Viking Period*. BAR Brit. Ser. **124**.

Holland, D. 1967. A note on the deserted village of West Burton, *Trans. Thoroton Soc. Nottinghamshire* **71**, 70–71.

Hooke, D. 1998. *The Landscape of Anglo-Saxon England*. Leicester University Press.

Hoskins, W.G. and McKinley, R.A. (eds) 1954. *Victoria History of the County of Leicester*, vol. 2. London: Oxford University Press for University of London Institute of Historical Research.

Howard, A.J., Macklin, M.G. and Passmore, D.G. (eds) 2003. *Alluvial Archaeology in Europe*. The Netherlands: Swets & Zeitlinger.

Howard, H. and Morris, E.L. (eds) 1981. *Production and Distribution: a Ceramic Viewpoint*. BAR Brit. Ser. **120**.

Huggett, J.W. 1988. Imported grave goods and the early Anglo-Saxon economy, *Medieval Archaeol.* **32**, 63–96.

Hughes, G. 1996. Excavations within a medieval and post-medieval tenement at Stone 1993, *S. Staffordshire Archaeol. Hist. Soc. Trans.* **37**, 58–102.

Hughes, P.D.M., Mauquoy, D., Barber, K.E. and Langdon, P.G. 2000. Mire-development pathways and palaeoclimatic records from a full Holocene peat archive at Walton Moss, Cumbria, England, *The Holocene* **10**, 465–479.

Hunt, J. and Klemperer W. 2003. The archaeology of Medieval Staffordshire: an overview, *West Midlands Research Frameworks, Seminar 5*. http://www.arch-ant.bham.ac.uk/wmrrfa/sem5.htm

Hurst, J.G. 1971. A review of archaeological research to 1968, in M. Beresford and J.G. Hurst (eds), *Deserted Medieval Villages*, 76–144.

Hurst, J.G. 1991. Medieval and post-medieval pottery imported in Lincolnshire, in D. Tyszka, K. Miller and G.F. Bryant (eds), *Land, People and Landscapes*, 49–65.

James, H.M. 1994. Excavations on the site of Flawford Church, Ruddington, Nottinghamshire, *Trans. Thoroton Soc. Nottinghamshire* **98**, 134–136.

Jewitt, L. 1869. On the discovery of an Anglo-Saxon cemetery at King's Newton, in the county of Derbyshire, *Reliquary* **9**, 2–8.

Jones, H. 2002. Brough, Glebe Farm, *Trans. Thoroton Soc. Nottinghamshire* **106**, 147–148.

Jones, H. forthcoming. Anglo-Saxon settlement at Glebe Farm, Brough, Notts, in B. Vyner (ed), *Archaeology on the A46 Fosse Way: Newark-Lincoln*.

Jones, M.J. 1994. St Paul-in-the-Bail, Lincoln; Britain in Europe?, in K. Palmer (ed), *Churches Built in Ancient Times: Recent Studies in Early Christian Archaeology*, 325–347.

Keevill, G., Aston, M. and Hall, T. (eds) 2001. *Monastic Archaeology*. Oxford: Oxbow Books.

Kenyon, K.M. 1950. Excavations at Breedon-on-the-Hill, Leicestershire, 1946, *Trans. Leicestershire Archaeol. Hist. Soc.* **26**, 17–82.

Kinsley, A.G. 1989. *The Anglo-Saxon cemetery at Millgate, Newark-on-Trent, Nottinghamshire*. Nottingham Archaeol. Monogr. **2**. Department of Classical and Archaeological Studies, University of Nottingham.

Kinsley, A.G. 1993a. *Broughton Lodge, Excavations on the Romano-British Settlement and Anglo-Saxon Cemetery at Broughton Lodge, Willoughby-on-the-Wolds, Nottinghamshire 1964–8*. Nottingham Archaeol. Monogr. **4**. Department of Classical and Archaeological Studies, University of Nottingham.

Kinsley, A.G. 1993b. Excavations on the Saxo-Norman town defences at Slaughter House Lane, Newark-on-Trent, Nottinghamshire, *Trans. Thoroton Soc. Nottinghamshire* **97**, 14–63.

Kinsley, A.G. 1995. Excavation of medieval and post medieval buildings at Nottingham Shire Hall 1994, *Trans. Thoroton Soc. Nottinghamshire* **99**, 55–64.

Kinsley, G. 1998. Interim report on archaeological watching briefs and excavations at Girton Quarry Extension, Newark, 1997–98, *Tarmac Papers* **2**, 41–49.

Kinsley, A.G. 2002. The Wychnor cemetery, in S. Losco-Bradley and G. Kinsley, *Catholme. An Anglo-Saxon settlement on the Trent Gravels in Staffordshire*, 23–27.

Kinsley, G. and Jones, H. 1999. Summary report on archaeological watching briefs and excavations at Girton Quarry Extension, Newark, 1997–9, *Tarmac Papers* **3**, 57–68.

Klemperer, W. 2001. The Hulton Abbey Project: research archaeology and public accountability, in G. Keevill, M. Aston and T. Hall (eds), *Monastic Archaeology*, 183–191.

Knight, D. and Howard, A.J. 1994. *Archaeology and Alluvium in the Trent Valley. An Archaeological Assessment of the Floodplain and Gravel Terraces*. Trent & Peak Archaeological Unit, University Park, Nottingham.

Knight, D. and Malone, S. 1997. Evaluation of a Late Iron Age and Romano-British Settlement and Palaeochannels of the Trent at Chapel Farm, Shardlow & Great Wilne, Derbyshire (SK 455305). Unpublished report, Trent & Peak Archaeological Unit, University Park, Nottingham.

Knight, D., Marsden, P. and Carney, J. 2003. Local or non-local? Prehistoric granodiorite-tempered pottery in the East Midlands, in A. Gibson (ed), *Prehistoric Pottery, People, Pattern and Purpose*, 111–125.

Laing, L. 2001. Excavations on the deserted Medieval settlement of Keighton, Nottinghamshire, 2000–01, *Trans. Thoroton Soc. Nottinghamshire* **105**, 37–56.

Laing, L. forthcoming. Some Anglo-Saxon artefacts from Nottinghamshire, *Anglo-Saxon Stud. Archaeol. Hist.* **13**.

Lamb, H.H. 1966. *The Changing Climate*. London: Methuen.

Langdon, J. 1993. Inland water transport in medieval England, *J. Hist. Geogr.* **19** (1), 1–11.

Laxton, R. 1997. A 13th century crisis in the Royal Forest of Sherwood in Nottinghamshire, *Trans. Thoroton Soc. Nottinghamshire* **101**, 73–98.

Laxton, R., Litton, C.D. and Howard, R.E. 1995. Nottinghamshire houses dated by dendrochronology, *Trans. Thoroton Soc. Nottinghamshire* **99**, 45–51.

Le Patourel, H.E.J. and Roberts, B.K. 1978. The significance of moated sites, in F.A. Aberg (ed), *Medieval Moated Sites*, 46–55.

Leahy, K. 1993. The Anglo-Saxon settlement of Lindsey, in A. Vince (ed), *Pre-Viking Lindsey*, 29–44.

Leahy, K. 1998. The early Saxon context, in G. Drinkall and M. Foreman, *The Anglo-Saxon Cemetery at Castledyke South, Barton-on-Humber*, 6–17.

Leahy, K.A. 2003. Middle Saxon Lincolnshire: an emerging picture, in T. Pestell and K. Ulmschneilder (eds), *Markets in Early Medieval Europe: Trading and Productive Sites, 650–850*, 138–154.

Leahy, K.A. and Paterson, C. 2001. New light on the Viking presence in Lincolnshire: the artifactual evidence, in J. Graham-Campbell, R. Hall, J. Jesch and D. Parsons (eds), *Vikings and the Danelaw, Selected Papers from the Proceedings of the Thirteenth Viking Congress*, 187–202.

Leahy, K.A. and Williams, D.J. 2001. Sheffield's Hill, two Anglo-Saxon cemeteries, *Curr. Archaeol.* **175**, 300–303.

Leonard, J. 1993. *Derbyshire Parish Churches*. Derby: Breedon Books.

Leonard, J. 1995. *Staffordshire Parish Churches*. Derby: Breedon Books.

Lethbridge-Farmer, R. 1916. Chellaston Alabaster, *J. Derbyshire Archaeol. Nat. Hist. Soc.* **38**, 135–146.

Liddle, P. 2001. An archaeological resource assessment of Anglo-Saxon Leicestershire and Rutland, *East Midlands Archaeological Research Framework*. http://www.le.ac.uk/archaeology/east_midlands_research_framework.htm

Lindley, P. (ed) 1991. *Gainsborough Old Hall*. Occ. Pap. Lincolnshire History and Archaeology **8**. Lincoln: Society of Lincolnshire History and Archaeology.

Long, A.J., Innes, J.B., Kirby, J.R., Lloyd, J.M., Rutherford, M.M., Shennan, I. and Tooley, M.J. 1998. Holocene sea-level change and coastal evolution in the Humber estuary, eastern England: an assessment of rapid coastal change, *The Holocene* **8**, 229–247.

Losco-Bradley, P.M. and Salisbury, C.R. 1979. A medieval fish weir at Colwick, Nottinghamshire, *Trans. Thoroton Soc. Nottinghamshire* **83**, 15–22.

Losco-Bradley, S. and Kinsley, G. 2002. *Catholme. An Anglo-Saxon Settlement on the Trent Gravels in Staffordshire*. Nottingham Studies in Archaeology **3**. Department of Archaeology, University of Nottingham.

Losco-Bradley, S. and Wheeler, H. 1984. Anglo-Saxon settlement in the Trent Valley: some aspects, in M. Faull (ed), *Studies in Late Anglo-Saxon Settlement*, 101–114.

Loveluck, C.P. 1998. A high-status Anglo-Saxon settlement at Flixborough, Lincolnshire, *Antiquity* **72**, 146–161.

Lucy, S. 2000. *The Anglo-Saxon Way of Death*. Stroud: Sutton Publishing Ltd.

Lucy, S. and Reynolds, A. (eds) 2002. *Burial in Early Medieval England and Wales*. Soc. Medieval Archaeol. Monogr. **17**. London: Society for Medieval Archaeology.

Lyth, P. 1989. *A History of Nottinghamshire Farming*. Newark: Cromwell Press.

MacCormick, A. 2001. Nottingham's underground maltings and other medieval caves: architecture and dating, *Trans. Thoroton Soc. Nottinghamshire* **105**, 73–100.

McKinley, R.A. 1954 — Religious Houses, in W.G. Hoskins and R.A. McKinley (eds), *Victoria History of the County of Leicester*, vol. 2, 1–54.

Macklin, M.G. 1999. — Holocene river environments in Prehistoric Britain: human interaction and impact, *Quat. Proc.* **7**, 521–530.

Malone, S. 2000. — Newark, the Castle, *Trans. Thoroton Soc. Nottinghamshire* **104**, 156.

Marshall, P. and Samuels, J. 1997. — *Guardian of the Trent: The Story of Newark Castle*. Nottingham: Nottinghamshire County Council Leisure Services.

Mastoris, S. and Groves, S. (eds) 1997. — *Sherwood Forest in 1609*. Thoroton Society Record Series **40**. Nottingham: Thoroton Society.

Matthews, B. 1970. — Age and origin of Aeolian sand in the Vale of York, *Nature* **227**, 1234–1236.

Mauquoy, D. and Barber, K.E. 1999. — A replicated 3000 yr proxy-climate record from Coom Rigg Moss and Felecia Moss, the Border Mires, northern England, *J. Quat. Sci.* **14**, 263–275.

Meaney, A. 1964. — *A Gazetteer of Early Anglo-Saxon Burial Sites*. London: Allen and Unwin.

Meeson, R.A. and Kirkham, A. 1993. — Two medieval buildings in Horninglow Street, Burton-upon-Trent, *S. Staffordshire Archaeol. Hist. Soc. Trans.* **34**, 21–34.

Mein, A.G. 1950. — Excavations at Burton Lodge Farm, Burton Joyce, Notts., 1950: Preliminary Report. Unpublished report, Peverel Research Group Annual Report, 25–28.

Middleton, S. 1984. — The Sneyd Green medieval kilns: a review, *Staffordshire Archaeological Studies* **1**, 41–47.

Miller, L., Schofield, J. and Rhodes, M. 1986. — *The Roman Quay at St Magnus House, London*. London Middlesex Archaeol. Soc. Special Pap. **8**. London: London and Middlesex Archaeological Society.

Milne, G. 1992. — *Timber Building Techniques in London AD 900–1400*. London Middlesex Archaeol. Soc. Special Pap. **15**. London: London and Middlesex Archaeological Society.

Moffett, C. 1996. — The plant remains, in G. Hughes, Excavations within a medieval and post medieval tenement at Stone 1993, 79–85.

Monckton, A. 1995. — Environmental archaeology in Leicestershire, *Leicestershire Archaeol. Hist. Soc. Trans.* **69**, 32–41.

Monckton, A. 2001. — An archaeological resource assessment and research agenda for environmental archaeology in the East Midlands, *East Midlands Archaeological Research Framework*. http://www.le.ac.uk/archaeology/east_midlands_research_framework.htm

Morgan, P. and Thorn, C. (eds) 1986. — *Domesday Book: Lincolnshire*. Chichester: Phillimore.

Morris, J. (ed) 1977. — *Domesday Book. 28, Nottinghamshire*. Chichester: Phillimore

Morris, R. 1983. — *The Church in British Archaeology*. CBA Res. Rep. **47**.

Moxon, R., Lott, F.E., Oswell, B.L. and Day, L.J. 1906. — Notes on excavations of the foundations of the old Burton Bridge, *Trans. Burton-on-Trent Nat. Hist. Archaeol. Soc* **5** (2), 192–195.

Myres, J.N.L. 1977. — *A Corpus of Anglo-Saxon Pottery of the Pagan Period*. 2 vols. Cambridge University Press.

Neal, M. 1989. — A medieval moat at Sinai Park, Burton upon Trent, *Staffordshire Archaeol. Hist. Soc. Trans.* **30**, 26–29.

Needham, S. and Macklin, M.G. (eds) 1992. — *Alluvial Archaeology in Britain*. Oxford: Oxbow Books.

Nicholson, R.A. and O'Connor, T.P. (eds) 2000. — *People as an Agent of Environmental Change*. Symposia of the Association for Environmental Archaeology **16**. Oxford: Oxbow Books.

Nixon, M. 1966. — The River Trent, in K.C. Edwards (ed), *Nottingham and its Region*, 144–156.

O'Brien, C.F. 1974. — Sinfin, Derbyshire – a Field Survey. Unpublished report, Trent Valley Archaeological Research Committee Rep. **8**, 41–43.

O'Brien, C. 1978. — Land and settlement in Nottinghamshire and lowland Derbyshire, *E. Midlands Archaeol. Bull.* **12**, Supp.

Orwin, C.S. and C.S. 1954. — *The Open Fields*. 2nd edition. Oxford: Clarendon Press.

Owen-Crocker, G. 1986. — *Dress in Anglo-Saxon England*. Manchester University Press.

Ozanne, A. 1963. — The Peak dwellers, *Medieval Archaeol.* **6–7**, 15–52.

Page, W. (ed) 1906. — *Victoria History of the County of Lincolnshire*, vol. 2. London: Constable. Reprinted 1988 for University of London Institute of Historical Research, Folkestone: Dawson and Sons Ltd.

Page, W. (ed) 1907. — The *Victoria History of the County of Derbyshire*, vol. 2. London: Constable and Company Ltd. Reprinted 1970 for University of London Institute of Historical Research, London and Folkestone: Dawsons of Pall Mall.

Page, W. (ed) 1910. — *The Victoria History of the County of Nottinghamshire*, vol. 2. London: Constable and Company Ltd. Reprinted 1970 for University of London Institute of Historical Research, Folkestone: Dawsons of Pall Mall.

Palliser, D.M. 1972. — The Boroughs of medieval Staffordshire, *N. Staffordshire J. Field Stud.* **12**, 63–73.

Palliser, D.M. and Pinnock, A.C. 1971. — The markets of medieval Staffordshire, *N. Staffordshire J. Field Stud.* **11**, 49–63.

Parker, A. 1932. — Nottingham pottery, *Trans. Thoroton Soc. Nottinghamshire* **36**, 79–124.

Pestell, T. and Ulmschneilder, K. (eds) 2003. — *Markets in Early Medieval Europe: Trading and Productive Sites, 650–850*. Macclesfield: Windgather Press.

Peverel Archaeological Group. 1954. — Stoke Bardolph 1954. Peverel Archaeological Group Annual Report, 29–33.

Pevsner, N. 1993. — *The Buildings of England:Derbyshire*. Revised by E.Williamson. Harmondsworth: Penguin.

Pevsner, N. 2001. — *The Buildings of England:Nottinghamshire*. Revised by E.Willamson. Harmondsworth: Penguin.

Pevsner, N. and Harris, J. 2001. — *The Buildings of England:Lincolnshire*. Revised by N. Antram. Harmondsworth: Penguin.

Platt, C. 1978. *Medieval England. A Social History and Archaeology from the Conquest to AD 1600.* London: Routledge & Kegan Paul.

Platts, G. 1985. *Land and People in Medieval Lincolnshire.* Lincoln: History of Lincolnshire Committee for Society of Lincolnshire History and Archaeology.

Posnansky, M. 1955. The Bronze Age round barrow at Swarkeston, *Derbyshire Archaeol. J.* **75**, 123–139.

Rackham, J. (ed) 1994. *Environment and Economy in Anglo-Saxon England.* CBA Res. Rep. **89**.

Radford, C.A.R. 1976. The church of St Alkmund, Derby, *Derbyshire Archaeol. J.* **96**, 26–61.

Rahtz, P. and Meeson, R. 1992. *An Anglo-Saxon Watermill at Tamworth.* CBA Res. Rep. **83**.

Reece, R. 1980. Town and country: the end of Roman Britain, *World Archaeol.* **12** (1), 77–92.

Reece, R. 2002. Britons and Saxons in Gloucestershire: forward from the Romans, *Glevensis* **33**, 3–4.

Richards, J.D. 2001. Finding the Vikings: the search for Anglo-Scandinavian rural settlement in the northern Danelaw, in J. Graham-Campbell, R. Hall, J. Jesch and D.N. Parsons (eds), *Vikings and the Danelaw (Selected Papers from the Proceedings of the Thirteenth Viking Congress)*, 269–277.

Richards, J.D. 2002. The case of the missing Vikings: Scandinavian burial in the Danelaw, in S. Lucy and A. Reynolds (eds), *Burial in Early Medieval England and Wales*, 156–170.

Richards, J.D., Jecock, M., Richmond, L. and Tuck, C. 1995. The Viking barrow cemetery at Heath Wood, *Medieval Archaeol.* **39**, 51–70.

Riley, D.N., Buckland, P.C. and Wade, J.S. 1995. Aerial reconnaissance and excavation at Littleborough-on-Trent, Notts., *Britannia* **26**, 253–284.

Roffe, D. 1986. *The Derbyshire Domesday.* Darley Dale: Derbyshire Museum Service.

Roffe, D. 1997. The Anglo-Saxon town and the Norman conquest, in J. Beckett (ed), *A Centenary History of Nottingham*, 24–42.

Rooke, H. 1792. Roman remains in Sherwood Forest, discovered by Hayman Rooke, Esq., F.A.S., and communicated by him in a letter to the Right Hon. Sir George Yonge, Bart., *Archaeologia* **10**, 381–384.

Rowlands, M.B. 1987. *The West Midlands from AD 1000.* London: Longman.

Rowley, T. 1978. *Villages in the Landscape.* London: Orion.

Rowley, T. (ed) 1981. *The Origins of Open Field Agriculture.* London: Croom Helm.

Rumsby, B.T. and Macklin, M.G. 1996. River response to the last Neoglacial cyle (the 'Little Ice Age') in northern, western and central Europe, in J. Branson, A.G. Brown and K.J. Gregory (eds), *Global Continental Changes: the Context of Palaeohydrology*, 217–233.

Rye, H.A. 1899a. The origin and history of the Monk's Bridge, *Trans. Burton-on-Trent Nat. Hist. Archaeol. Soc.* **4** (1), 32–47.

Rye, H.A. 1899b. Burton Abbey Dissolution inventories, *Trans. Burton-on-Trent Nat. Hist. Archaeol. Soc.* **4** (1), 65–74.

Rye, H.A. 1903a. The Great Bridge of Burton on Trent, *Trans. Burton-on-Trent Nat. Hist. Archaeol. Soc.* **5** (1), 4–21.

Rye, H.A. 1903b. Some further notes on Burton Abbey plan, *Trans. Burton-on-Trent Nat. Hist. Archaeol. Soc.* **5** (1), 35–44.

Salisbury, C.R. 1981. An Anglo-Saxon fish-weir at Colwick, Nottinghamshire, *Trans. Thoroton Soc. Nottinghamshire* **85**, 26–36.

Salisbury, C.R. 1983. An early Tudor map of the River Trent in Nottinghamshire, *Trans. Thoroton Soc. Nottinghamshire* **87**, 54–59.

Salisbury, C.R. 1991. Primitive British fishweirs, in G.L. Good, R.H. Jones and M.W. Ponsford (eds), *Waterfront Archaeology*, 76–87.

Salibury, C.R. 1992. The archaeological evidence for palaeochannels in the Trent Valley, in S. Needham and M.G. Macklin (eds), *Alluvial Archaeology in Britain*, 155–162.

Salisbury, C.R. 1994. Hemington Fields, Castle Donington, *Trans. Leicestershire Archaeol. Hist. Soc.* **68**, 179–182.

Salisbury, C.R. 1995. A bridge too old – a Mercian bridge over the Trent at Cromwell, Nottinghamshire, *Trans. Thoroton Soc. Nottinghamshire* **99**, 121–123.

Salisbury, C.R., Whitley, P.J., Litton, C.D. and Fox, J.L. 1984. Flandrian courses of the River Trent at Colwick, Nottingham, *Mercian Geologist* **9** (4), 189–207.

Samuels, J. and Russell, A. 1999. An Anglo-Saxon burial near Winthorpe Road, Newark, Nottinghamshire, *Trans. Thoroton Soc. Nottinghamshire* **103**, 57–83.

Samuels, J., Charles, F.W.B, Henstock, A. and Siddal, P. 1996. A very old and crasey howse: the Old White Hart Inn, Newark, Nottinghamshire, *Trans. Thoroton Soc. Nottinghamshire* **100**, 19–54.

Sawyer, P. 1998. *Anglo-Saxon Lincolnshire.* History of Lincolnshire **3**. Lincoln: History of Lincolnshire Committee.

Scull, C.J. 1993. Archaeology, early Anglo-Saxon society and the origins of kingdoms, *Anglo-Saxon Stud. Archaeol. Hist.* **6**, 65–82.

Skelton, R.A. and Harvey, P.D.A. (eds) 1986. *Local Maps and Plans from Medieval England.* Oxford: Clarendon.

Smith, D.N. 2000. Disappearance of Elmid 'Riffle Beetles' from lowland river systems in Britain – the impact of alluviation, in R.A. Nicholson and T.P. O'Connor (eds), *People as an Agent of Environmental Change*, 75–80.

Southworth, E. (ed) 1990. *Anglo-Saxon Cemeteries: a Reappraisal.* Stroud: A. Sutton.

Sparey-Green, C. 2002. Excavations on the south-eastern defences and extramural settlement of Little Chester, Derby 1971–2, *Derbyshire Archaeol. J.* **122**.

Stafford, P. 1985. *The East Midlands in the Early Middle Ages.* Leicester University Press.

Stanyer, S.C. and Brayford, S.E. 1966. Preliminary excavation of Lawn Farm moated site, Bucknall, Stoke-on-Trent, *City of Stoke-on-Trent Museum Archaeol. Soc. Rep.* **2**, 7–10.

Stapleton, A. 1907. *The Churches and Monasteries of Old and New Nottingham*. Nottingham: Walter H. Haubitz.

Steane, K. 1991. St Paul in the Bail: a dated sequence, in City of Lincoln Archaeology Unit, *Lincoln Archaeology 1990–1991*, 28–31.

Steane, K. and Vince, A. 1993. Post-Roman Lincoln: archaeological evidence for activity in Lincoln in the 5th–9th centuries, in A. Vince (ed), *Pre-Viking Lindsey*, 71–79.

Steedman, K. 1995. Excavation of a Saxon site at Riby Cross Roads, Lincolnshire, *Archaeol. J.* **151**, 212–306.

Stevenson, W. and Stapleton, A. 1898. *Some Account of the Religious Institutions of Old Nottingham*. 2nd series. Nottingham: Thomas Forman and Sons.

Stocker, D. and Everson, P. 2001. Five towns funerals: decoding diversity in Danelaw stone sculpture, in J. Graham-Campbell, R. Hall, J. Jesch and D.N. Parsons (eds), *Vikings and the Danelaw (Selected Papers from the Proceedings of the Thirteenth Viking Congress)*, 223–243.

Stoertz, C. 1997. *Ancient Landscapes of the Yorkshire Wolds: Aerial Photographic Transcription and Analysis*. Swindon: RCHME.

Stuart, D.G. 1994. A rental of the Borough of Burton, 1319, in *Collections for a History of Staffordshire*, Staffordshire Record Society, Fourth Series **16**, 1–52.

Stukeley, W. 1724. *Itinerarium Curiosum, or, An Account of the Antiquitys and Remarkable Curiositys in Nature or Art, Observed in Travels thro' Great Brittan*. London: printed for the author.

Stukeley, W. 1776. *Itinerarium Curiosum*, 2nd edition. London: Baker and Leigh.

Summers, N. 1988. *A Prospect of Southwell*. Revised edition. Southwell: Kelham House.

Swanton, M. (ed) 2000. *The Anglo-Saxon Chronicles*. London: Phoenix Press.

Swinnerton, H.H., Chalmers, W.R. and Posnansky, M. 1955. The medieval tile works of Lenton Priory, *Trans. Thoroton Soc. Nottinghamshire* **59**, 84–97.

Symonds, L.A. 2003. *Landscape and Social Practice: the Production and Consumption of Pottery in 10th Century Lincolnshire*. BAR Brit. Ser. **345**.

Tarver, A. 1981. Interim report on the medieval moated site, Long Whatton 1981. Bull. Loughborough & District Archaeol. Soc. **2** (5), 31–46.

Taylor, C.C. 1981. Archaeology and the origins of open-field agriculture, in T. Rowley (ed), *The Origins of Open Field Agriculture*, 13–21.

Taylor, G. 1999. Newark Castle, *Trans. Thoroton Soc. Nottinghamshire* **103**, 95–96.

Taylor, G. 2003. An Early to Middle Saxon settlement at Quarrington, Lincolnshire, *Antiq. J.* **83**, 231–280.

Taylor, H.M. and Taylor, J. 1965a. *Anglo-Saxon Architecture*. vol.1. Cambridge University Press.

Taylor, H.M. and Taylor, J. 1965b. *Anglo-Saxon Architecture*. vol.2. Cambridge University Press.

Taylor, J. 2001. An archaeological resource assessment and research agenda for the Roman period in the East Midlands, *East Midlands Archaeological Research Framework*. http://www.le.ac.uk/archaeology/east_midlands_research_framework.htm

Terrett, I.B. 1962. Nottinghamshire, in H.C. Darby and I.S. Maxwell (eds), *The Domesday Geography of Northern England*, 233–277.

Thoroton, R. 1677. *The Antiquities of Nottinghamshire*. London: Robert White for Henry Mortlock.

Todd, M. 1969. The Roman settlement at Margidunum: the excavation of 1966–8, *Trans. Thoroton Soc. Nottinghamshire* **73**, 6–104.

Todd, M. 1977. Excavations on the medieval defences of Newark, 1976. *Trans. Thoroton Soc. Nottinghamshire* **81**, 41–54.

Todd, M. (ed) 1978. *Studies in the Romano-British Villa*. Leicester University Press.

Tomkinson, J.L. 1985. The history of Hulton Abbey, in P.J. Wise (ed), *Hulton Abbey: a Century of Excavation*, 57–74.

Tomkinson, J.L. 2000. *Monastic Staffordshire: Religious Houses in Medieval Staffordshire and its Borderlands*. Leek: Churnett Valley Books.

Tyszka, D., Miller, K. and Bryant, G.F. (eds) 1991. *Land, People and Landscapes*. Lincoln: Lincolnshire Books for Lincolnshire County Council Recreational Services.

Ulmschneider, K. 2000. Settlement, economy and the "productive" site, *Medieval Archaeol.* **44**, 53–80.

Van de Noort, R. and Davies, P. 1993. *Wetland Heritage: an Archaeological Assessment of the Humber Wetlands*. Humber Wetlands Project, University of Hull.

Van de Noort, R. and Ellis, S. (eds) 1998. *Wetland Heritage of the Ancholme and Lower Trent Valleys: an Archaeological Survey*. Humber Wetlands Project, University of Hull.

Van de Noort, R., Fenwick, H., Head, R., Miller, K. and Steedman, K. 1998. Introduction to the archaeological survey, in R. Van de Noort and S. Ellis (eds), *Wetland Heritage of the Ancholme and Lower Trent Valleys. An Archaeological Survey*, 123–140.

Vince, A. (ed) 1993. *Pre-Viking Lindsey*. Lincoln Archaeol. Stud. **1**. City of Lincoln Archaeology Unit.

Vince, A. 1994. Saxon urban economies: an archaeological perspective, in J. Rackham (ed), *Environment and Economy in Anglo-Saxon England*, 108–119.

Vince, A. 2001. An archaeological resource assessment and research agenda for the early and middle Anglo-Saxon period (c. 400–850) in the East Midlands, *East Midlands Archaeological Research Framework*. http://www.le.ac.uk/archaeology/east_midlands_research_framework.htm

Vyner, B. 2002. Langford, Fosse Way, *Trans. Thoroton Soc.* **106**, 154–155.

Vyner, B. (ed) forthcoming. *Archaeology on the A46 Fosse Way: Newark-Lincoln*. CBA Res. Rep.

Walker, J. 1978. Anglo-Saxon traded pottery, in M. Todd (ed), *Studies in the Romano-British Villa*, 224–228.

Wardle, C. 1994. Evidence for the Anglo-Saxon date of the church of St. Laurence, Walton on Trent, *Derbyshire Archaeol. J.* **114**, 10–13.

Webster, L. and Brown, M. 1997. *The Transformation of the Roman World*, AD 400–900. London: British Museum Press.

Webster, L.E. and Cherry, J. (eds) 1972. Medieval Britain in 1971, *Medieval Archaeol.* **16**, 189.

Webster, L.E. and Cherry, J. 1978. Medieval Britain in 1977, *Medieval Archaeol.* **22**, 142–188.

Wheatley, P. 1971. Staffordshire, in H.C. Darby and I.B. Terrett (eds), *The Domesday Geography of Midland England*, 163–216.

Wheeler, H. 1979. Excavation at Willington, Derbyshire, 1970–1972, *Derbyshire Archaeol. J.* **99**, 58–221.

White, F. 1857. *History, Gazetteer and Directory of the County of Derby*. Sheffield: Francis White & Co.

Whitwell, J.B. 1969. Excavations of the site of a moated medieval manor house in the parish of Saxilby, Lincolnshire, *J. British Archaeol. Assoc.* **32**, 135–142.

Wilkinson, R.F. 1942. The ruined and lost churches of Nottinghamshire, *Trans. Thoroton Soc. Nottinghamshire* **46**, 66–72.

Williams, D.F. and Vince, A. 1997. The characterisation and interpretation of early to middle Saxon granitic tempered pottery in England, *Medieval Archaeol.* **61**, 214–220.

Williams, H. 1997. Ancient landscapes and the dead: the reuse of prehistoric and Roman monuments as early Anglo-Saxon burial sites, *Medieval Archaeol.* **41**, 1–32.

Williamson, F. 1931. Additional notes on the Bridge Chapel, *J. Derbyshire Archaeol. Nat. Hist. Soc.* **52**, 75–79.

Wilmott, T. and Wilson, P. (eds) 2000. *The Late Roman Transition in the North: Papers from the Roman Archaeology Conference, Durham 1997*. BAR Brit. Ser. **299**.

Wise, P.J. (ed) 1985. *Hulton Abbey: a Century of Excavation*. Staffordshire Archaeological Studies: Museum Archaeological Society Report (New Series) **2**.

Woodhouse, G. 1993. Tarmac Hoveringham: Archive Report. Unpublished report, Trent & Peak Archaeological Unit, University Park, Nottingham.

Young, C.S.B. 1983. *Discovering Rescue Archaeology in Nottingham*. Nottingham City Council Museums.

Young, G.A.B. 2001. Nottingham Castle, *Trans. Thoroton Soc. Nottinghamshire* **105**, 195.

Young, G.A.B. 2002. Castle Boulevard, Lenton Hermitage, *Trans. Thoroton Soc. Nottinghamshire* **106**, 145.

Index

Note: Bold type indicates Figure number